ACTS OF CONSCIENCE

COLUMBIA STUDIES IN CONTEMPORARY AMERICAN HISTORY

ACTS OF CONSCIENCE

*Christian Nonviolence
and Modern American Democracy*

Joseph Kip Kosek

Columbia University Press   New York

Columbia University Press
Publishers Since 1893
New York   Chichester, West Sussex

Library of Congress Cataloging-in-Publication Data
Kosek, Joseph Kip.
    Acts of conscience : Christian nonviolence and
modern American democracy / Joseph Kip Kosek.
       p. cm. — (Columbia studies in contemporary
American history)
    Includes bibliographical references and index.
    ISBN 978-0-231-14418-6 (cloth : alk. paper)—
    ISBN 978-0-231-14419-3 (pbk. : alk. paper)—
    ISBN 978-0-231-51305-0 (electronic)
    1. Nonviolence—Religious aspects—Christianity. 2.
Civil disobedience—Religious aspects—
Christianity. 3. Christianity and politics—United States.
4. United States—Church history.
I. Title. II. Series.
BR517.K67   2009
261.80973—dc22   2008013775

Columbia University Press books are printed
on permanent and durable acid-free paper.
This book was printed on paper with recycled content.
Printed in the United States of America
c 10 9 8 7 6 5 4
p 10 9 8 7 6 5 4 3 2 1

Chapter 3 originally published in a slightly different
form in "Richard Gregg, Mohandas Gandhi, and the
Strategy of Nonviolence," *Journal of American History* 91
(March 2005): 1318–1348; Copyright © Organization
of American Historians. All rights reserved. Used with
permission.

For Anne

I have heard
That guilty creatures sitting at a play
Have by the very cunning of the scene
Been strook so to the soul, that presently
They have proclaim'd their malefactions.
. . .
The play's the thing
Wherein I'll catch the conscience of the King.
—Shakespeare, *Hamlet* (Act II, Scene ii)

I am a soldier of Christ, I cannot fight.
—Martin of Tours (A.D. 356)

Contents

Illustrations

Abbreviations

CORE	Congress of Racial Equality
CPS	Civilian Public Service
FOR	Fellowship of Reconciliation
IWW	Industrial Workers of the World
MIA	Montgomery Improvement Association
MOWM	March on Washington Movement
NWLB	National War Labor Board
SDS	Students for a Democratic Society

ACTS OF CONSCIENCE

Introduction

This book traces the history of a radical religious vanguard. The guiding principle of this group, which I call "Christian nonviolence," has long been dismissed as marginal, eccentric, or impossibly saintly, but I take a more sophisticated approach. For these rebels, the example of Jesus showed the immorality and futility of organized violence in any circumstance and for any cause. Yet Christian nonviolence, for them, was not a matter of fixed dogma, but rather an active process of interpreting religion in the modern world. They believed that their uniquely gruesome era required new political formations and new ways of thinking. The Christian nonviolent tradition, by putting the problem of violence at the center of its theory and practice, offers an alternative model of political action and an alternative history of the twentieth century.

"I . . . believe," the radical Christian pacifist A. J. Muste wrote during World War II, ". . . that in the degree that anybody is any good it is because he has both Don Quixote and Sancho Panza in himself and somehow effects a creative synthesis of them."[1] Muste's acute awareness of the relationship between high ideals and practical tactics suggests the multidimensional qualities of Christian nonviolent "acts of conscience," which ranged from sit-ins to conscientious objection to, sometimes, mere interracial socializing. At one level, these were extreme existential "acts"

that broke sharply with the law, social convention, and even the practitioner's own instinct for self-preservation. In another way, though, no instance of nonviolent action was a solely individual affair. These acts also
contained a ritual dimension that fostered camaraderie and discipline in
realms removed from ordinary life. This was never more true than during
the Montgomery bus boycott of 1955–1956, when boycotters assembled
in the sacred space of black churches to attend training workshops that
simulated the experience of boarding integrated buses. Here, as they pre-
tended to be peaceful riders or angry white supremacists, they rehearsed
both their individual courage and their vision of a racially harmonious
world. Those training sessions spoke as well to a third connotation of the
word *acts*. Unlike antimodern pacifists such as the Amish, Muste and his
associates turned nonviolence into a theatrical "act," a calculated performance attuned to the sympathies of audiences, especially those created
by new forms of mass media. Christian nonviolent "acts of conscience,"
then, were not expressions of pure sainthood, nor were they shallow publicity stunts that cynically used faith as a cover for more important things.
The existential, ritual, and spectacular dimensions of nonviolence all operated simultaneously. Acts of conscience were at once individual and social, at once sincerely spiritual and self-consciously spectacular, at once
Don Quixote and Sancho Panza.

The virtuosos of Christian nonviolence in this story first coalesced during World War I in an antiwar organization called the Fellowship of Reconciliation (FOR). The Fellowship attracted talent out of all proportion to
its small size. The roster of people who were, at one time or another, leaders in the FOR reveals a hidden history of American political dissent.[2] At
the head of the list stands Muste, dubbed "the No. 1 U.S. pacifist" by *Time*
magazine in 1939. He helped guide opposition to every major American
military campaign from World War I to Vietnam, while also building industrial unionism well before the 1930s and promoting racial justice well
before the 1960s. Norman Thomas, the head of the Socialist Party in the
United States for decades, spent pivotal early years in the FOR, as did
Reinhold Niebuhr, who later became the most important American theologian of the twentieth century and a severe critic of pacifism. Nowhere
was the Fellowship's effect more crucial, though, than in the civil rights
movement. March on Washington organizer Bayard Rustin, Congress of
Racial Equality (CORE) director James Farmer, and James Lawson, whose
leadership of the 1960 Nashville sit-ins helped spark the formation of the

Student Nonviolent Coordinating Committee, were all products of this effervescent Christian nonviolent culture.

Some of the Fellowship's less prominent names became important at crucial moments in history. Gordon Hirabayashi joined the group as a college student in 1940. Two years later, he refused to register for the Japanese American internment program, eventually challenging the constitutionality of internment before the Supreme Court. Richard Gregg, a Harvard-trained lawyer, abandoned his career to go to India and learn from Mohandas Gandhi; he later became the most important early theorist of militant nonviolence in the United States. After the Montgomery bus boycott, Martin Luther King Jr. cited Gregg's *The Power of Non-Violence* as one of his most important influences. George Houser, a theological student who went to jail rather than register for the World War II draft, helped start CORE and later led the American Committee on Africa, the most vigorous American anticolonial organization of the 1950s and 1960s. Surprisingly, the American right can also find Christian nonviolence in its political DNA. J. B. Matthews, a virulent anticommunist and adviser to Joseph McCarthy in the 1950s, was the executive secretary of the FOR back in the 1930s, before his drastic political rebirth as a Red hunter. Socialism, liberalism, the labor movement, anticolonialism, civil liberties, civil rights, and even conservatism: Fellowship leaders, or former leaders, influenced the major political traditions and social movements of modern American democracy. Some of these figures eventually repudiated their pacifist inclinations entirely, yet all were shaped by their encounters with Christian nonviolence. This tradition, far from a mere affectation of the 1960s, is essential to any serious attempt to understand the nation's history and politics.[3]

These radicals also developed a robust global outlook that reached beyond the borders of the United States. Violence, after all, was a transnational scourge. This book begins with some American war relief workers in England during the First World War and ends with A. J. Muste's 1967 visit to Hanoi at the age of eighty-two. In between, radical Christian pacifists journeyed to Nicaragua to protest American imperialism and antiimperialist guerrilla warfare, to the Soviet Union to investigate the progress of the Communist experiment, and, most importantly, to India to evaluate the growing independence movement and its most remarkable leader, Gandhi. Certainly the Fellowship leaders paid special attention to American military action, American class conflict, and American racial terror. However, their condemnation of all organized violence and their relentless search for alternatives to it necessitated a persistent attention to the whole world, an attention far removed from the usual stereotypes of pacifism as insular and retiring. The American FOR itself was part of a global organization with branches in many countries and was connected as well to a somewhat autonomous International Fellowship of Reconciliation. These radicals tried to imagine a transnational spiritual "fellowship" that would override the more parochial demands of nation, race, and class.[4]

The Fellowship of Reconciliation was distinctive in combining religion, absolute pacifism, and a broad field of social action. Parallel peace organizations that emerged out of the Great War, such as the War Resisters League and the Women's International League for Peace and Freedom, had more secular orientations and focused more specifically on the problem of international war, at least in their early years. Other groups, such as the American Friends Service Committee and the Methodist Federation for Social Service, were affiliated with specific Christian denominations. The Socialist Party, whose membership overlapped extensively with that of the FOR, never put nonviolence at the center of its program. The post–World War II peace organizations, such as the Committee for a Sane Nuclear Policy, were all latecomers, as was the nonviolent civil rights movement and the New Left. Dorothy Day's Catholic Worker had little influence before the 1940s. The Fellowship encouraged many of these more recent efforts, but it was the original American proponent of modern Christian nonviolence.

Despite pacifism's historical importance, it appears in political discourse today primarily as an epithet. Few conservatives, liberals, or radicals categorically oppose the use of violence to achieve justice or security, however much they might object to a specific war, revolution, or coup d'état. Most ethical thinking about organized violence follows some version of "just war" theory, which holds that armed force is morally legitimate under certain conditions and in accord with certain rules of conduct. This approach can hardly comprehend Muste's sweeping statement at a 1940 Quaker meeting: "If I can't love Hitler, I can't love at all." The pragmatist philosopher Sidney Hook, for one, thought that such a declaration made "a mockery of sane discourse."[5] No wonder, then, that some political analysts have recently suggested that the threat of radical Islam demands a revival of Reinhold Niebuhr's tough-minded Cold War liberalism, with its reliance on the judicious use of armed force in the service of democracy. Violence is regrettable, these new "realists" explain, but surely it's better than a quixotic love for the terrorists.[6]

The "fighting faith" of Niebuhr and Arthur Schlesinger Jr. had its strengths, and any awareness of history would be valuable in counteracting our nation's current political myopia. However, the "tough" liberals of the mid-twentieth century and their more recent apologists ignore the Christian nonviolent tradition's most profound insight. The problem of the twentieth century, the pacifists contended, was the problem of violence. It was not, as such, Fascism, Communism, economic inequality, or the color line, though all of those were deeply implicated. It was, above all, the fact of human beings killing one another with extraordinary ferocity and effectiveness. Muste, whether or not he did in some sense "love Hitler," offered a chillingly sane autobiographical perspective on the slaughter. "People in my age group," he noted in 1951, "have moved, since their graduation from college in pre–World War I days, out of what many regarded as the dawn of the era of permanent peace into what may, with considerable accuracy, be described as an era of permanent war." Muste wrote those words in the discouraging days of the early Cold War, but in a broader sense the "era of permanent war" remains an apt description of the intervening decades, not least the reign of the "war on terror." Richard Cheney unwittingly echoed Muste when he said, shortly after the September 11, 2001, attacks, that this latest war "may never end."[7]

Pacifists certainly failed to solve the problem of "permanent war," but the uncomfortable truth is that everyone else failed, too, even the liberal realists. Recent estimates put the total number of people killed by organized violence in the twentieth century between 167 million and 188 million, which works out to some five thousand lives unnaturally ended every single day for a hundred years. Of course, the deaths came not at regular intervals, but rather in concentrated spasms unprecedented in their destructive power. More men and women lost their lives in World War II— the "good war"—than in any other disaster thus far produced by human beings. We should take radical Christian pacifists seriously not because they were always right, but because they force us, as they forced their contemporaries, to confront these terrible truths. They insisted more emphatically, more sanely, than Niebuhr and the realists that the elimination of violence was not mere tilting at windmills but the most urgent modern project. Whether pacifist or not, we neglect that project at our peril.[8]

The Fellowship of Reconciliation's leaders warned that the problem of violence was far more extensive than the specific phenomenon of armed conflict between nations. I have retained the term *pacifist*, with its more limited antiwar connotations, largely because no single word exists for "proponent of nonviolence." However, "nonviolence" better expresses the broad approach of these dissenters. The Fellowship of Reconciliation's unwieldy name, containing neither the words *war* nor *peace*, hints at this capacious outlook. These radicals opposed the two world wars, but they also denounced the brutality of imperialism in India, Nicaragua, and the Philippines. At the same time, they worked to stop the industrial and racial conflict that, in many cases, threatened the citizens of the United States even more directly than did international warfare.[9]

This expansive vision, encompassing not only war but all organized violence, showed a sophistication and prescience that belie pacifism's reputation for simple-mindedness. Fellowship leaders were well aware that the millions of violent deaths in the twentieth century were the result of political purges and ethnic cleansing as well as rival armies in conflict. Furthermore, their interpretations looked forward to the post–Cold War world, where the model of industrial interstate warfare is becoming increasingly obsolete. That model, exemplified in the two world wars, had long obscured a shadow history of guerrilla warfare that included such disparate phenomena as the French Resistance, the Chinese civil war, the Algerian war of independence, and the Vietnam War. Now more nebulous forms of organized violence, characterized by their nonstate actors, their improvised weapons, and their merging of battlefront and home front, have become the norm. The new mode of "war" (we have no other word) was exemplified in the multinational intervention in Bosnia in the 1990s, the terrorist attacks of September 11, 2001, and the U.S.-led invasions of Afghanistan and Iraq. As policymakers and protesters alike try to comprehend this new landscape, the radical Christian pacifists offer historical precedents for thinking about the uses of violence and nonviolence in ways that go beyond the classic paradigm of opposing armies fighting on battlefields for their respective nation-states.[10]

Alongside unprecedented bloodshed, the avatars of Christian nonviolence witnessed the rise of modern forms of representation and communication. Theirs was an "age of publicity," the eminent pacifist minister John Haynes Holmes observed, "when nothing is hid from the pencil of the reporter any more than from the eye of God." Acts of conscience, then, were a response to both modern violence and modern media. These innovators slowly realized that, in a world of mass spectatorship, actual killing was inextricably linked to representations of killing. In telling their

story, this book supplies a historical context for the convergence of violence and spectacle that now dominates our public life. From Abu Ghraib
and Daniel Pearl to Rodney King and Columbine, recent debates about
violence are also debates about words and images, about videos and web-
sites and blogs. The Christian nonviolent avant-garde comprehended
very early the revolutionary effects of this mass-mediated world. They realized that nonviolence, like violence, might have a symbolic effect that
operated somewhat independently of its social reality. Radical pacifist
acts of conscience gained a unique power by combining religious themes
of suffering and redemption with novel uses of mass media and mass
spectatorship.[11]

What, though, was so unique about *Christian* nonviolence? On the subject
of religion, this book has upsetting things to say to skeptics and believers
alike. First, I assert that, in the ostensibly secular twentieth century, many
of the most principled American opponents of violence grounded their
convictions in Christian faith. I see no logical reason why Muste's assertion that "pacifism must be, is, religious" should be true, but in actual
historical terms it is surprisingly accurate. Certainly, some absolute pacifists, such as Roger Baldwin and Scott Nearing, took their stand against
violence on purely secular grounds. However, the crucial developments
in modern American nonviolence sprung from the Christian culture of
the Fellowship of Reconciliation. The decline of the Fellowship's strain of
radical Christianity has not led to enlightened secularism, but rather to
an impoverishment of political discourse about violence.[12]

The precise boundaries of the Fellowship's Christian theology are impossible to delineate. After all, many of the organization's leaders came to
the group as a way of escaping the confining dogmas of ordinary church
life. Some of them, such as Kirby Page and Sherwood Eddy, retained
fairly conventional liberal Protestant theologies, even though their politics
stood to the left of the mainline denominations. Others rejected orthodox
Christianity. John Haynes Holmes stepped outside even the minimal re-
straints of Unitarianism when he renamed his Church of the Messiah in
New York City the "Community Church" and welcomed Jews and Hindus along with the Christians. Then, too, all of the Fellowship leaders
came to believe that Gandhi was, in one way or another, their spiritual
ally, despite his Hindu identity. Even a few stray secularists, such as the
Socialist Party leader Devere Allen, participated actively in the FOR, their
numbers growing by the 1940s and 1950s.

Though the edges of the Fellowship's Christian culture were permeable, the center was firm. The example of Jesus provided the model for Christian nonviolence and distinguished it from a wide range of other approaches to achieving peace and justice. Even Allen, who rejected the "supernatural attributes or episodes" of Jesus's story, admitted to "revering him as a person in many ways unique among mankind." Gandhi's fulsome praise of Jesus, despite his rejection of Christianity, eased the Indian leader's acceptance by his American admirers. These radicals took their inspiration from the cross, where the suffering of Jesus had ended in apparent defeat but had somehow redeemed the world. The Fellowship leaders did not share the evangelical faith that Christ's blood had been a literal sacrifice to save sinful humanity from eternal damnation at the hands of a wrathful God, a notion that Kirby Page considered "repugnant to ethical minds to-day." Rather, they thought that the cross was a symbolic explanation of an ongoing paradox: love triumphed precisely when it appeared to lose. True power proceeded not from the barrel of a gun but from the more subtle effects of moral courage.[13]

This theological approach was hardly unique to pacifists, but the Fellowship leaders accented the themes of violence and nonviolence in the crucifixion story. Jesus had voluntarily chosen not to impose the kingdom of God by force, while his enemies had erroneously assumed that violence was synonymous with power. While admitting that the death of Jesus was not precisely analogous to the ordeals of a conscientious objector or a bus boycotter, radical Christian pacifists argued that the drama of redemptive suffering described in the gospels was still happening in the twentieth century. To outsiders, voluntary suffering could look like nothing more than humiliating masochism, an embarrassing failure to accept the modern view that pain is a problem to be fixed, not a source of power or a sign of virtue. Other skeptics echoed Nietzsche's theory of *ressentiment*, accusing the pacifists of self-righteously reveling in their suffering to prove their moral superiority. Within the Fellowship, though, the threats, beatings, and imprisonments endured by practitioners of acts of conscience had a transcendent dimension that looked toward a higher truth.[14]

Based on this theology of the cross, the politics of Christian nonviolence stood worlds apart from that of the conservative evangelicalism now so prominent in American public life. The Fellowship's commitments to pacifism, the labor movement, racial equality, and socialism placed them squarely on the left, providing a historical context for the "religious left" that so many recent commentators have proposed as an antidote to the "religious right." Indeed, this book shows that progressive religion in the United States was not confined to the speeches of Martin Luther King Jr., but had a robust presence throughout the twentieth century.[15]

The Fellowship's radicals, however, were not simply the praying wing of the American left, adding a pious sheen to essentially secular causes. Christian pacifists often went their own way. They infuriated many liberals by opposing American intervention in two world wars, they earned the contempt of many radicals for their staunch anticommunism, and some other potential allies just wished they would stop talking about Jesus so much. Because of a loyalty to absolute values that transcended political expediency, Christian nonviolent politics never fit entirely comfortably in the constellation of American radicalism. This book uncovers both an overlooked strain of American radical action and a potent critique of American politics, including the politics of both liberalism and radicalism.

The Fellowship's religious dissent struck at the core of liberal democratic theory. The development of classical liberalism occurred in the shadow of the brutal seventeenth-century European wars of religion. Enlightenment thinkers as diverse as Hobbes, Locke, Hume, and Montesquieu agreed that extreme religious commitment (though not necessarily religion itself) posed a dangerous threat to social order. An analogous reaction against absolute values occurred in the wake of the American Civil War, when John Dewey, Oliver Wendell Holmes, and other political thinkers shrank from the devastation that resulted, in their view, from the runaway extremism of two opposing moral crusades. Pragmatism, with its tendencies toward contingency, compromise, and experimentation, was one result of what was arguably the first modern war. Epitomized by the political philosophy of Dewey and then by the politics of Franklin Roosevelt, pragmatism, broadly defined, dominated liberal American social thought and political culture during most of the period under consideration in this book.[16]

The radical Christian pacifists found the pragmatist view incomplete, despite their alliances with Dewey and other pragmatists on specific issues. They held that the method of weighing relative moral goods and reserving absolute commitment provided a shaky foundation during crises, namely crises of violence. In those moments, the thumb of deadly force always seemed to tip the moral scales, turning even the most ethical pragmatists into apologists for killing. In 1948, for instance, Muste charged that "Reinhold Niebuhr, the radical," and John Foster Dulles, the Cold Warrior, had become "virtually a team." Niebuhr's high-minded defense of just wars, so compelling in theory, served in practice as a moral veneer for sordid power politics.[17] Disappointed with pragmatist capitulations, the Fellowship's religious radicals developed a powerful indictment of the use of physical force by liberal democratic societies, even in such apparently unimpeachable causes as the struggle against Nazism in the 1940s and against Soviet Communism in the 1950s. This vanguard also demonstrated how the pragmatist outlook allowed some forms of violence, such as racial terror in the American South, to continue unabated. Indeed, proponents of nonviolence such as Muste and Rustin, not secular pragmatists, provided the moral and strategic foundations of the civil rights movement. Whether in Hiroshima or Alabama, the Fellowship leaders believed that a lack of firm mooring in ethical absolutes allowed Americans to tolerate unconscionable brutality.

On the other hand, these dissenters were not mere utopians, as their critics so often charged. They imbibed the modern spirit of political experimentalism. When they looked at Gandhi, they saw not (or not only) a transcendent Eastern mystic, but a strategist who described his work as "experiments with truth," a phrase that Dewey could well have coined. The alchemy of truth and experiment reached its American apogee in Martin Luther King Jr., who led a moral crusade that was simultaneously a stunning display of creative political strategy. Such juxtapositions raised difficult questions. Was strategic nonviolence merely "war without violence," as the title of a 1939 book had it, and if so, could a pacifist conscientiously support such a "war"? Could the religious ethos itself become a spectacle, a strategy to be used when advantageous or discarded when unnecessary? Far from the unsullied realm of saints and prophets, the FOR leaders worked amid the messy ambiguities of earthbound politics.

Christian nonviolence mounted a radical assault on the American liberal tradition, but it also upset some common assumptions about radicalism itself. The Fellowship's major competitor on the left was Communism, which never had a large U.S. membership but garnered a significant penumbra of sympathizers. For the followers of Karl Marx, whether orthodox Communists or splinter groups such as the Trotskyists, the Fellowship leaders developed a strong antipathy, though they absorbed many of those followers' crucial insights concerning power and social conflict. Marxism proved to be the most powerful left-wing ideology in the twentieth century, achieving impressive victories in Russia, China, and the postcolonial

Third World, but the FOR held that it was an illusory alternative to the status quo. From the perspective of Christian nonviolence, the differences in outlook between Marxists and liberal pragmatists were unimportant compared to the willingness of both groups to countenance bloodshed if it served their purposes. The Fellowship leaders claimed that revolutionary violence marked the failure of radicalism, not its fulfillment. As contemporary critics search for viable traditions of dissent in the wake of Marxism's ethical and political exhaustion, the Fellowship's insights look increasingly pertinent. For all its eccentricities, the humane core of Christian nonviolence still poses a stark challenge to liberals and radicals alike.

Christian nonviolence did not begin in the Fellowship of Reconciliation. The Christian religion's strictures against force go back all the way to its founder, who notoriously enjoined his disciples to turn the other cheek to violent attackers, a practice distinct from either fighting or fleeing. Still, for all the Fellowship leaders' claims to have revitalized the original gospel, their faith had precursors in more recent historical developments as well. The idea of Christian pacifism gained new life in the Radical Reformation of the sixteenth century. Radical Reformers criticized the Catholic Church, but they also disparaged Martin Luther, John Calvin, and other leaders of the more prominent Magisterial Reformation, which gained the favor of secular rulers and eventually created new religious justifications for the legitimacy of secular power. To the Radical Reformers, no Protestant was more notorious than Henry VIII, who kept most of the trappings of Catholicism but cynically placed himself, rather than the Pope, at the head of the new Church of England. In this context, some dissenters expanded their critique of the Catholic Church to include a denunciation of all worldly authority. The participants in this movement, including the English Nonconformists (Christians outside the official Anglican Church) and the Anabaptists on the Continent, had little in common other than their belief that the new Protestants were like the old Catholics in their refusal to take the Bible and the example of Jesus seriously. Not all Radical Reformers were pacifists, but many of them were, and all of them championed the superiority of the believer's conscience over the dictates of earthly power. In the face of intense persecution, many of their followers found their way to the New World. On the eve of World War I, when my story begins, religious pacifism in the United States was primarily the purview of the Quakers, Mennonites, Brethren, and an array of smaller Protestant sects that had emerged out of the Radical Reformation.[18]

The Fellowship's radicals respected these older traditions, but found them too religiously conservative and too politically irrelevant. During World War I, conscientious objectors of the FOR variety looked askance at the biblical literalism of the sectarians they met in prison. Later, when the "peace churches" sought an alternative service system for World War II objectors, many Fellowship leaders condemned the plan as an odious acquiescence to the state that created a haven for religious dissenters but failed to challenge the war system as such. Even the Quakers, the most liberal and politically active of the sectarian groups, came in for occasional censure. They were "timid," one World War I conscientious objector wrote, with "a fatal lack of . . . revolutionary or even religious fervor for innovation."[19] Such criticism was unfair, but it showed the growing sense of a break between the older traditions and the "innovation" that emerged in the first half of the twentieth century. Many FOR members were Quakers, but most of the influential leaders did not have strong ties to that tradition. They were looking for something new, a "fellowship" at once wholly religious, wholly modern, and wholly radical.

If the peace churches were inadequate, so, too, was the modern peace movement. On the eve of World War I, most peace advocates had adopted the pragmatist approach of moderate incremental reform through established channels. Organizations such as the Carnegie Endowment for International Peace, formed in 1910, held that peace was a project for an enlightened elite and a boon to the continued expansion of global capitalism. Few peace organizations professed absolute pacifism, so they supported American intervention in the Great War or offered only muted criticism. The most prominent exception to this cautious outlook was the Universal Peace Union, formed after the Civil War by former abolitionists. Prefiguring the Fellowship of Reconciliation's attempt to fuse peace and justice, the small membership of the Universal Peace Union tied its religious pacifism to the suffrage movement, Native American religious autonomy, black equality, and the rights of labor. By World War I, though, the Universal Peace Union was fizzling out.[20]

The Fellowship leaders usually turned first to radical abolitionism as the precedent for their own project. They were the spiritual, and sometimes literal, descendants of antislavery radicals. Many grew up in environments suffused with the memory of the successful crusade against the "peculiar institution." John Haynes Holmes considered the abolitionist Theodore Parker a "proud possession" in his family; Parker had even performed the wedding of Holmes's grandparents. Other pacifists sought less to claim their legacies than to overcome them. Kirby Page, one of the Fellowship's most outspoken antiracists, was the grandson of steadfast Confederates.[21]

Pacifism, the leaders of the FOR believed, was the new abolitionism. "Concerning war," Sherwood Eddy declared, "like William Lloyd Garrison on the great moral issue of slavery, I count myself an abolitionist."[22] Garrison's legacy offered several advantages. It gave pacifism a broader compass by rhetorically linking the violence of war to the violence of racism. Garrison, originally an ardent pacifist, had in fact made such a link himself. His New England Non-Resistance Society was the peace organization that most clearly foreshadowed the FOR in its capaciousness, its radicalism, and its religious fervor. Certainly, the predominantly white male Fellowship tended to think of Garrison and Parker far more often than they remembered Frederick Douglass or Sojourner Truth. Nonetheless, their defiant invocation of antislavery identified them unequivocally with the legacy of native American radicalism.

The audacity of the Garrisonians captivated the Christian pacifists. Holmes recalled Theodore Parker's defiance of the Fugitive Slave Law and asserted that "in war, even more emphatically than in slavery, we have an institution that is an open betrayal of humanity and Christianity, and we can therefore have nothing to do with it." Such statements implied that, against the gradualist policies of the more recent progressives, neo-abolitionists might have to go to extremes, even breaking the law if necessary. Abolitionism showed that public commitment by a few to absolute religious values, without compromise, could spark a revolution. The success of that revolution was not the least of its charms. War looked like an ineradicable part of human societies, but had not slavery been the common sense of an earlier era? The pacifists' selective genealogy associated them with a social movement that worked, while distancing them from the more ambiguous legacy of pacifism itself.[23]

The Christian nonviolence of the Fellowship of Reconciliation was not simply abolitionism in a new key, though. It arose at a very different historical moment. These figures were raised in, or found their way to, a liberal Protestantism profoundly altered by the influence of the Social Gospel. As elaborated by Washington Gladden, Walter Rauschenbusch, and others in the late nineteenth and early twentieth centuries, the Social Gospel declared that Christians had a religious obligation to change un-Christian social structures, not simply to work for the salvation of individuals. Though this new trend in religious reform had much in common with antebellum efforts, it took a more systematic view of social change, eschewing Garrison's anarchist call to "repudiate all human politics." After initial resistance, the Social Gospel became assimilated into the American Protestant mainline by the time of the Great War.[24] Still, a key question remained: what was the uniquely Christian outlook on political and social questions, the "independent Christian ethic," as Niebuhr once put it? Secular socialists had championed economic redistribution. Secular progressives sought to bolster the democratic process and end corruption in government. Secular experts of various kinds worked to counter the worst problems in modern cities and modern factories. Religious people had provided the impetus for many of these activities, but faith did not seem necessary for any of them to continue.[25]

In the wake of the First World War, the condemnation of violence became the signature attribute of social Christianity. Even Niebuhr, despite his strenuous opposition to pacifism, recognized its religious power. The problem of violence had been less central in the earlier Social Gospel, but beginning with the Great War, secular ideologies faltered repeatedly when confronted with the choice to participate in organized bloodshed. Wilsonian Progressivism, Communism, and Rooseveltian liberalism all countenanced deadly force at one time or another, though all agreed, in the abstract, that killing was a hideous affair. Under these conditions of intellectual and political dissonance, radical pacifism provided new life for religious dissent in America.

The first chapter of my story considers the Great War as a spiritual crisis that led a group of liberal Protestant ministers, students, and reformers to commit themselves to nonviolence as the purest expression of Christianity. Chapter 2 traces their attempts to create a new kind of modern Christian pacifism in the 1920s. The next two chapters address the upheavals of the Depression decade, when the Fellowship gained new strength from its discovery of Mohandas Gandhi, but also faced threats from jingoists on the right and Marxists on the left. World War II, the subject of chapter 5, was a time of wrenching contradictions for the pacifists, decimating their ranks at the same time that it provided conditions for their postwar success and forged a new generation of radicals who would bring it about. The sixth chapter shows how Fellowship leaders helped define an "age of conscience" in the decade after the war through antinuclear protests, anticolonialism, and early civil rights campaigns. Finally, the conclusion offers reflections on the ferment of nonviolence in the 1960s and beyond.

In the end, this book describes less the "creative synthesis" that Muste imagined than an ongoing creative tension. The Fellowship circle sought to transform the modern world by going back to the two-thousand-year-old example of Jesus. The group failed miserably at its central purpose—eliminating war between nations—but made nonviolent direct action a powerful new method of achieving social change. Committed to authentic religious truth, these radicals were pioneers in the creation of carefully orchestrated media performances. Neither saints nor fools, they tried to understand the promise and catastrophe of modernity in the twentieth century. Their efforts might help us work toward a goal at once modest and quixotic: that this century could be less violent than the last.

CREON *(to* ANTIGONE*): You—tell me not at length but in a word.*
   You knew the order not to do this thing?
ANTIGONE: *I knew, of course I knew. The word was plain.*
CREON: *And still you dared to overstep the law?*
ANTIGONE: *For me it was not Zeus who made that order.*
   Nor did that Justice who lives with the gods below
   mark out such laws to hold among mankind.
   Nor did I think your orders were so strong
   that you, a mortal man, could over-run
   the gods' unwritten and unfailing laws.   —Sophocles, Antigone

I   Love and War

Evan Thomas and Harold Gray sailed across the Atlantic in the fall of 1917, as the United States was deepening its commitment to the war in Europe. Like thousands of their compatriots, the two young Americans worried about their fate as they prepared for a struggle against a hostile nation. However, Thomas and Gray sailed west, and the hostile nation they feared was their own. The two had been doing relief work for the Young Men's Christian Association in England, where they had become absolute pacifists, believing that war was inherently contrary to the example set by Jesus Christ. Their stance had led them to question their efforts for the YMCA, which provided important support for the Allied campaign. Furthermore, Thomas and Gray believed that, as Y secretaries, they would receive exemptions from military service, thereby allowing them to avoid combat without publicly disclosing their unpopular pacifist positions.[1] For Gray, it felt "too much like the middle ground of the coward" to finesse his antiwar stance by remaining with the YMCA. "We knew," he concluded sadly, "we had been false to our Master."[2] The two resigned their positions and returned to the United States to register for the draft. Upon being conscripted, they were granted conscientious objector status, but then repeatedly challenged the official rules governing their conduct. By the time the war ended, Thomas and Gray had been sentenced to life in prison for refusing to obey military orders.

The kind of dramatic reversals that sent an idealistic Y worker to Alcatraz, where Gray eventually spent a few months before being pardoned, produced a new politics of dissent during the Great War and its immediate aftermath. The liberal Protestants who held to absolute pacifism in these years were, for the most part, reluctant radicals. Before the war, they had been respectable leaders of churches, YMCAs, and reform organizations. Influenced by the Social Gospel, they had sought to make America into a more virtuous society through the regulation of industry, the assimilation of immigrants, and the improvement of urban life. Some were active in taking the Christian message to unconverted peoples in foreign lands. They believed that their reforming religion was more or less in accord with the enlightened outlook of progressive political leaders such as Woodrow Wilson, and they assumed that, although their nation had its problems, Christianity and American civilization generally reinforced each other. These religious idealists had thought little about war, for they were sure that such a self-destructive method of settling disputes would wither away in the modern world. The Great War transformed their lives. Initially, liberal Protestants seemed united in their disdain for the conflict, but by 1917 opinion had turned vehemently in favor of the war. As a result, Christian pacifists lost their positions as ministers and reformers, losing their moral authority as well. In a few cases, they even went to prison.

The small group that defended Christian nonviolence in these years faced a spiritual crisis as well as a political one. The result was not the disillusionment of the more famous "Lost Generation," immortalized in Ernest Hemingway's *The Sun Also Rises*. Instead, Christian pacifists took the calamity in Europe as a call to reinvent their faith, not abandon it. They came to believe that their Christianity had been too sanguine about the inevitability of moral progress and too comfortable in its proximity to political power. The life of Jesus, they now discovered, was radical, and it was most radical in its total commitment to nonviolence. Along with John Haynes Holmes, Kirby Page, A. J. Muste, and other dissenters, Thomas and Gray would work out a daring new kind of modern spiritual politics.

The YMCA hardly seemed like fertile ground for religious radicalism. Formed in the mid-nineteenth century to guard young men against the perils of urban life, the Y had become one of most vibrant mainline Protestant organizations by the time of the Great War. Targeting the growing urban middle class, the organization appealed to businessmen for support and promoted an optimistic version of Christian life that stressed individual morality, physical health, and civic virtue. In general, the YMCA's focus on optimism, hard work, moral earnestness, and the conversion of the entire world to Christianity offered little serious challenge to American business, American education, or American imperialism.[3]

In the late nineteenth century, university students formed a new collegiate wing of the YMCA. Just as the parent organization had sought to moralize the secular city, so the Christian students responded to the increasing secularization of the American university. By 1900, one quarter of all college-age men claimed membership in the student Y. Some of these collegians looked abroad as well, with a small group of students establishing the Student Volunteer Movement for Foreign Missions, a recruiting organization that sought overseas missionaries to hasten "the evangelization of the world in this generation," as the group's motto put it. [4]

Despite the dominant conservatism of the YMCA, the dynamic student-missionary network that attracted Thomas and Gray did more than valorize the status quo. John R. Mott, the Methodist layman who presided over that network, played a major role in rousing young people to action. Mott's aggressive approach to foreign missions was chauvinistic, to be sure, but it also piqued the interest of his audiences in other nations and other cultures.[5] In this way, the student YMCA had more in common with the Peace Corps of the 1960s than with the Moral Majority of the 1980s. Joseph B. Matthews, later a prominent Christian pacifist, reflected on the power of this internationalist appeal. "John R. Mott," he wrote, "was the man who stirred our imaginations, who lifted our horizons beyond America." Though Matthews admitted that Mott's vision had been in reality "a species of religious imperialism," he also recognized that it had given countless young people a more cosmopolitan view of the world. By contrast, Matthews recalled that the influence of Woodrow Wilson's New Freedom upon him in 1912 was "slight."[6] Many of the nation's most ambitious young people first engaged modern international politics and culture through the YMCA's idealistic, moralistic religion.

In some cases, Mott's idealism and moralism pointed toward political activism and social reform. The YMCA's main goal was always the expansion of the Christian religion, but the student-missionary wing also became a kind of clearinghouse for the progressive ideas that were gaining influence in the first decades of the twentieth century. Mott himself was not particularly doctrinaire in his religious beliefs, remaining aloof from the fundamentalist controversy that wracked American Protestantism in these years, nor was he especially conservative politically. In keeping with his irenic disposition, he helped to popularize a moderate version of the Social Gospel outlook that held political and economic reform to be a religious duty.[7] In April 1914, for instance, he held a "Conference on Social Needs" at Garden City, New York, that included Walter Rauschenbusch, Harry F. Ward, and other leading exponents of social Christianity. Soon after, he presided over an interracial student conference at Clark University in Atlanta that featured Booker T. Washington and Willis D. Weatherford, a Southern white promoter of interracial initiatives.[8]

This new emphasis on the earthly implications of Christianity hardly radicalized the YMCA. Y members may have pondered the evils of segregation at an occasional interracial event, but their local chapters were still all-white or all-black. Indeed, much of the Social Gospel itself was fairly benign, working for the gradual improvement of dilapidated tenements, corrupt local governments, and other conspicuous scourges of city life. However, due to Mott's efforts, students who joined the YMCA learned about the ethical dilemmas of modern industry, entered into religious communion with students from other races, regions, and nations, and immersed themselves in foreign cultures as missionaries. These young people participated in a religion that spoke directly to the contemporary world.

Despite its wide-ranging work, the American YMCA was hardly prepared for a war that would tear apart Western Christendom. Before 1914, domestic reform and non-Western missions seemed more urgent than anything going on in Europe. In 1912 and 1913, Mott visited cities across India and China on an extensive evangelistic campaign, taking with him Sherwood Eddy, the YMCA Traveling Secretary for Asia. Eddy had been a tireless globe-trotter since his first voyage to India in 1896, when he was twenty-five years old. He combined confident Christianity with genuine attention to cultural difference. In his early years as a missionary, he diligently learned Tamil, a language widely spoken in southern India, and even briefly became a vegetarian in order to gain sympathy with his Hindu audiences. His boundless zeal had carried him to the highest ranks of the Protestant missionary enterprise.

With their transnational sensibilities and energetic demeanors, Mott and Eddy were well suited to undertake war work in Europe when events finally turned their attentions there. Soon after the conflict began in August 1914, Mott went abroad to set up YMCA programs for soldiers and prisoners of war in England, France, and Germany (personal letters from President Wilson smoothed his path across borders). In 1916, Eddy plunged into the new project. He had ministered to soldiers before, when he spoke to occupying American troops in the Philippines on one of his many Asian tours, but now a much bigger opportunity awaited him. Sailing to England on the *New Amsterdam* in July, he envisioned "a mighty spiritual revival" among the soldiers. "Surely when such an unspeakable price is being paid in blood," he wrote, "there ought to be an adequate spiritual result."[9]

Traveling on the *New Amsterdam* with Eddy was a group of bright, adventurous YMCA workers. Kirby Page, Eddy's personal secretary, was a particularly good example of the opportunities that the organization offered for precocious young men. Born in Texas in 1890, Page was a true child of the South; one of his grandfathers was a slave owner and the other died fighting for the Confederacy. He had overcome numerous obstacles to achieve his position as Eddy's assistant. His alcoholic father had abandoned him, along with his mother and two brothers, when he was nine. The family moved often and suffered frequent financial hardship, but Page, a gifted writer, speaker, and athlete, managed to attend college at Drake University, where he studied to become a minister.

At Drake, Page broadened his social and religious horizons. During his youth, the Page family belonged to the Church of Christ, a conservative sect so strict that congregants sang hymns without organs or pianos, for they saw musical instruments as sinful corruptions of the original New Testament style of worship. "I was taught," he remembered, "that we were the true church and only our members would be saved. All other church members and non-members would be damned eternally in a literal hell of fire." In college, though, he encountered the works of Francis Peabody, Washington Gladden, Walter Rauschenbusch, and other early exponents of the Social Gospel, while also becoming the president of the campus YMCA. The YMCA and his college courses allowed Page to move gradually away from his conservative religious and social upbringing. It was possibly at a YMCA event that he first shared a meal with an African American, an experience he remembered for many years afterward. Also, like many in the college YMCA, he learned of the wider world outside his own country and strongly considered becoming a foreign missionary.

Page did not learn pacifism in college, however. "I have no recollection," he later wrote with regard to his Drake years, "of even a single serious conversation about the duty of a Christian to refuse to engage in any war." The Church of Christ had sometimes condemned war as part of its rejection of the sinful world, but Page seems not to have encountered this strain of pacifism in his youth. At any rate, when the Great War came, the Page children took highly divergent paths. One of Page's brothers joined the American military, while the other, a devotee of end-time speculation, interpreted the conflict as a sign of the impending Apocalypse. Page chose a third route, sailing to Europe to win the Allied soldiers for Christ.[10]

Page's voyage allowed him to meet other educated young Christians. His cabin mate was Harold Gray, a Harvard student and the son of a Ford Motor Company attorney, and the two soon established a rapport. Page also got to know Max Yergan, a black YMCA secretary from Shaw University who was headed to Africa to support the war effort there (he would have a long career as a missionary in South Africa and, later, as a prominent pan-Africanist and socialist). Yergan, Page wrote home, "is making a profound impression on me. I admire him tremendously and feel that he is as fine a fellow as one could desire for a real friend. Truly Jesus Christ does transcend all racial and color lines." The two new friends would arise before breakfast to go for early morning runs on the deck of the ship. Once again, the YMCA pushed, however tentatively, the boundaries of American social convention.[11]

The "fine fellows" sailing to Europe on the *New Amsterdam* embodied the modern vision of Christian masculinity. Indeed, the friendship of Page, Gray, and Yergan arose amid the "muscular Christianity" that defined so much of male Protestant experience in the early twentieth century. The YMCA was a leading proponent of the idea that religion needed strong men to carry forward the work of God on earth, so the early morning runs that Page and Yergan undertook were more than mere exercise. They symbolized a religious commitment, extending even across racial lines, to building the vigorous male bodies necessary to serve Jesus Christ in a war zone.[12]

When they landed in England, Eddy and Page began their adventure in strenuous religion. The YMCA offered a variety of services for soldiers, focusing on evangelism, entertainment, and recreation. Eddy took the military conflict as a spiritual metaphor, signing up soldiers on his "War Roll" as they pledged "by God's help to fight His battles, and bring Victory to His Kingdom." In one of his favorite sermons, he preached that "The Greatest Battle of the War" was in fact "the inner fight for character," thereby suggesting that Christianity was itself war, a real battle for real men. In 1918, Eddy would pen *The Right to Fight*, a defense of the

Allied cause. His new secretary also assumed at first that the Allies were justified in the war against Germany.[13]

Yet even as Kirby Page received the dictation of Eddy's tracts and signed up soldiers on the War Roll, he began to have doubts about the morality of war. So did Harold Gray. In October 1916, Gray wrote his family that he and Page were "trying to thrash out the problem of whether a man is ever justified in using force to the extent of taking life, particularly in the light of Jesus' life and teachings." A month later Gray announced: "I am a pacifist from the word go."[14] Soon Evan Thomas joined these deliberations. Thomas was an American YMCA secretary who had been studying theology in Edinburgh until he, like Gray, left to work in German prisoner-of-war camps. He had considered the pacifist position earlier than the others, writing to his brother Norman in late 1915 that he was "ready to take the out and out non-resistant basis so far as war is concerned."[15]

Hoping to promote the kingdom of God, these men had landed in something like hell. Eddy invoked the metaphor fairly specifically, comparing the front lines to "an inferno" and describing how "a burning farmhouse or exploding ammunition dump illuminates the sky as from some vast subterranean furnace flung open upon the heavens."[16] Working closely with soldiers and POWs, the YMCA adventurers witnessed the horrifying results of the Great War's unprecedented slaughter, results that their acquaintances back in the United States encountered only secondhand. In Europe, they had to preach their vision of Christian manhood to soldiers with missing arms and legs, as well as those suffering from pneumonia and trench foot. They undoubtedly met men debilitated by "shell shock," which robbed victims of any kind of martial virtue. "Men become like weak children," wrote one contemporary observer of the condition, "crying and waving their arms madly, clinging to the nearest man and praying not to be left alone." Here were unlikely candidates for the War Roll.[17]

Alongside this physical and mental devastation lurked a moral crisis. The YMCA's main goals were to provide religion and recreation behind the lines, so the organization's workers produced comparatively little writing about the atrocities of the front, significant as these no doubt were to them. They more often detailed the effects of the war on individual moral character, a tendency that would continue among radical Christian pacifists in decades to come. "Many men who have been able to keep straight in peace time," Eddy observed, "have not been able to resist the temptations which have come upon them as a flood in war time." Despite his support of the Allied cause at this point, he published controversial writings detailing the prevalence of venereal disease in the British, and later American, soldiers' camps. In a similar vein, Thomas wrote that the war "gives free reign [sic] to men's baser passions . . . wine & women play a big part with the soldiers here." The "curse of drink," he argued hyperbolically at one point, was "worse than the war." Their observation of the deterioration of individual morality in wartime became critical to the YMCA secretaries' embrace of absolute pacifism.[18]

For Page in particular, the moral nihilism of the war produced a crisis of religious language. In these years, the YMCA was well known for its blithely confident mode of public discourse. One historian has even suggested that the organization's distinctive "optimism at Armageddon" defined American conceptions of World War I and helped to shape a uniquely American modernity. When he first arrived in England in 1916, Page was a typical mouthpiece for the language of the YMCA. "The evangelistic meetings are going on with increased power," he gushed in one report letter. "It is wonderful how God is using these meetings to stir men up and get them to thinking of the higher things in life."[19]

After Page adopted his pacifist views, the YMCA narrative began to fail him. In the summer of 1917, on his second visit to England, he found himself conversing with a prostitute in London's Piccadilly Circus. "She was bitter and rebellious," Page explained in a report letter, "and said that she no longer believed there was a good God, and when I asked her what she thought of Jesus Christ, with a sneer she replied: 'I'll tell you what I think of Jesus Christ, He was only a d— fool!'" Despite the young minister's pleading, he could not change her mind, for she "said that she loved her life of sin and shame and that she did not care to listen to a sermon." Page offered no resolution to this story, but left the prostitute's blasphemous language to stand without rebuttal. In another letter that same summer, Page related a conversation with a skeptical soldier who explained that the "Bible says to love your enemies, . . . but down in the camp or out at the front it can't be done." Page commented dryly: "One cannot but wonder how many others there are with a like difficulty." Here again, the critic of religion got the last word. For Page, "optimism at Armageddon" was no longer possible.[20]

The turn to pacifism by Page and the others was not a purely instinctual revulsion against the horrors of war. After all, Eddy supported the

Allied campaign for the duration, and few other YMCA men ended up in prison with Thomas and Gray. For the dissenting minority, the pacifist position was as much a result of careful rethinking as it was of disgusted recoil. During their time abroad, Page, Thomas, and Gray held monthly seminars, where they discussed readings and presented papers on social and religious questions. In 1917, the three put enormous effort into writing and distributing individual statements of their pacifist principles.[21] Other intellectual experiences contributed to the group's new outlook. In one prison camp, Gray found among the Germans "several university men . . . who spoke English fluently and who certainly did not correspond to the current idea of savage Huns." The group also came into contact with the English peace movement, talking with William Orchard, a famous Anglican preacher, and Henry Hodgkin, a prominent English Quaker. The young Americans respected the ideas of educated people, whether English pacifists or German soldiers.[22]

The YMCA secretaries' nascent pacifism sprung from their liberal Protestant outlook, but also went beyond it. Page's essay "The Sword or the Cross," a product of the YMCA secretaries' seminars, revealed the ways that moralism, individualism, and strenuous Christian living could lead to unexpected conclusions. Eschewing the conservative faith of his Texas boyhood, Page noted that his opposition to war was "not based on proof-texts or a literalistic interpretation of the Sermon on the Mount, but rather upon the conviction that Jesus' own life, when observed in its completeness, must be the interpretation of His teaching." The view that the life of Jesus, rather than Biblical dogma, was the surest guide for Christians came through in a number of important liberal Protestant books in this period, including Charles Sheldon's *In His Steps* (1897) and Harry Emerson Fosdick's *The Manhood of the Master* (1913). The lesson Page drew from that life was unambiguous: "Jesus faced the concrete problem of war and refused to adopt it." Such refusal was the only choice for those who shared the YMCA attitude that all life, personal and social, should be under Christ's sway. "War," Page argued, "is the direct antithesis of the spirit of Jesus, and participation in it by the Christian involves the forsaking of the way of the cross and the following the way of the world." This was an absolute moral imperative to be obeyed regardless of consequences, for "it is never necessary for a Christian to compromise." Page's manifesto pushed familiar YMCA themes—of following Christ's example, of total commitment to the virtuous life—to surprising new ends.[23]

ASSOCIATION
YMCA
MEN
JULY 1918   PRICE 15 cts.

That Liberty Perish Not

FIGURE I.I
July 1918 issue of the
YMCA journal *As-
sociation Men*, depicting
a cross and the Statue
of Liberty towering
over a group of soldiers
and a Y building. By
the time that this im-
age appeared, a small
contingent of YMCA
workers had rejected the
idea that the war would
promote Christianity
and democracy. (Kautz
Family YMCA Archives,
University of Minnesota.)

Page and his friends soon became estranged from the organization that
employed them, accusing the Y of subordinating Christian ideals to military and nationalist demands. Harold Gray worried that "the Y.M.C.A. and
the Red Cross appear little more than parts of the army, efficiency departments," while Thomas feared that his religious views had become "too
radical" to allow him to stay with the organization after the war. Another
disenchanted secretary accused the YMCA and the churches of "shifting
their basis from a Christian to a purely patriotic one."[24] The Christian
student network had given these ambitious young men opportunities
for overseas adventure, spiritual community, and humanitarian service.
However, by taking the religious morality of the YMCA to what was, in
their view, its logical conclusion, they moved beyond the world that Mott

and Eddy had forged. When in 1918 Page sought to return to England a third time, Eddy explained that a new YMCA regulation barred pacifists from service in the relief effort.[25]

A different kind of agonizing over the war was going on across the ocean. On April 2, 1917, Woodrow Wilson asked Congress for a declaration of war to make the world "safe for democracy." Then, on May 18, the Selective Service Act became law. The concept of a historical "generation" is notoriously imprecise, but the draft immediately created an age-based distinction that would determine the trajectory of the YMCA workers in Europe. Anyone from twenty-one to thirty years old on June 5, 1917, gained a new identity as a potential soldier. Sherwood Eddy was forty-six. As an ordained Disciples of Christ minister, Kirby Page was exempt. But in the fall of 1917, Evan Thomas and Harold Gray sailed back across the Atlantic, to an America very different from the one they had left the year before.

Soon after the Great War began, even before Page, Thomas, and Gray left for Europe, some liberal Christians in the United States had organized to express their opposition to the conflict. The irrepressible John Mott took the lead. In the summer of 1915, he brought Henry Hodgkin, the English Quaker, to America to promote the Fellowship of Reconciliation, a new Christian pacifist organization. Hodgkin had first talked about forming an international Christian pacifist organization with Friedrich Siegmund-Schultze, a chaplain to Kaiser Wilhelm II, as the war began in August 1914. Both men had ties to the international network of YMCAs and student Christian groups that Mott directed. Four months after his meeting with Siegmund-Schultze, Hodgkin organized the Fellowship of Reconciliation at Cambridge University.[26] The group sought to establish "a world-order based on Love," as demonstrated through the life of Jesus. In keeping with this mission, FOR members declared that, "as Christians," they were "forbidden to wage war," thereby expressing the hope that transnational religious loyalties might prove more powerful than the demands of national allegiance.[27]

Hodgkin was initially skeptical about extending his new venture across the ocean. In the United States, he noted, joining such an organization would be "comparatively easy" and members might lack the devotion that they displayed in England, which was actually at war. Nonetheless, he overcame his reservations, and on November 11–12, 1915, Mott convened another conference at Garden City, where he had held the "Conference on Social Needs" the year before. About seventy-five men and women attended, and out of that core a new American peace organization emerged.[28] Mott's timing, as usual, was uncanny. Only a week before the conference, President Wilson had for the first time given public support to the campaign for preparedness by announcing the expansion of the regular army and the creation of a large reserve force. The war had begun to come home, if only in a limited way.

Initially, the Fellowship featured the same combination of Christian parochialism and expansive sentiment that marked Mott's YMCA. The FOR, like its English counterpart, was explicitly Christian, its members exclusively Protestant. They were primarily educated white men and women from New York City and the Quaker strongholds around Philadelphia, though local Fellowship groups soon formed throughout the Northeast and in a few other urban centers.[29] In keeping with the Quaker influence, the Fellowship maintained a commitment to individual spiritual autonomy, as expressed in an early statement: "It is intended that members shall work out personally and in their own way, what is involved in their membership. There is no program or theory of social reconstruction to which all are committed. The chief method is a life lived in loyalty to Christ, expressing itself in every activity and relation of life."[30]

The 1915 Garden City conference bore certain similarities to the "Conference on Social Needs" that Mott had organized there the year before. The new peace group's members clearly saw pacifism in terms of American domestic reform, particularly the reform of industry. One member felt that the Statement of Principles should add a passage committing the group "to the abolition of the competitive system," though this was voted down. The members also discussed whether the antiwar stance in the group's principles ("as Christians, we are forbidden to wage war") should be omitted "or that some test from commercial life be substituted for it." The creation of a peace organization that did not even declare its opposition to war was probably not what Henry Hodgkin had in mind, but the conflagration across the ocean still seemed a less urgent target for Christian reformers than did the "social question," even with the new threat of the preparedness movement.[31]

Soon after the Garden City conference, Edward Evans, the executive secretary of the new Christian pacifist group, sent a packet of FOR literature to Norman Thomas, a Presbyterian minister and the older brother of Evan.[32] Thomas ran a mission in Italian Harlem called the American Parish, and his career had progressed under the influence of the Social

Gospel. Educated at Woodrow Wilson's Princeton University and Union Theological Seminary, he learned the tenets of religious and political liberalism and joined the networks of social workers in New York City. His employer at the American Parish was William Adams Brown, a Union professor and prominent liberal theologian. Thomas's decision to work in Harlem accorded with the priorities of many urban white reformers, who believed in the central importance of assimilating immigrants and ameliorating their harsh living and working conditions. By the time he joined the FOR, Thomas had become one of the leading experts on New York City's polyglot religious landscape.[33]

John Haynes Holmes, another future leader of the Fellowship, liked to preach an annual sermon on international peace, but in general he, too, was more interested in the "social question." Holmes was the Harvard-educated minister at the Unitarian Church of the Messiah on Park Avenue in Manhattan. A founder of the National Association for the Advancement of Colored People in 1909, he imagined himself a kind of neo-abolitionist, not least because his grandparents had been strong supporters of the famous antislavery Unitarian cleric Theodore Parker. Holmes came to espouse the Social Gospel after his reading of Henry George and especially Walter Rauschenbusch, with whom he maintained a personal acquaintance until the latter's death in 1918.[34] Holmes contributed to the Social Gospel bookshelf himself with his 1912 volume *The Revolutionary Function of the Modern Church,* wherein he called for "an indefinite extension of the field of religious activity" that would involve the church in the elimination of disease, poverty, and crime. Jesus, Holmes insisted, "was not only a prophet of religious truth, but an instigator of social reform."[35]

Like Theodore Parker, Holmes had a wide-ranging appetite for moral crusades, and like Parker, he was a religious celebrity. Since his arrival at the Church of the Messiah, he had become one of those "princes of the pulpit" whose opinions and activities frequently received attention in the mainstream press. But he was an unorthodox prince. In 1915, for example, the *New York Times* covered a meeting of unemployed workers at the Church of the Messiah that featured a speech by a member of the Industrial Workers of the World (IWW) and a tirade by another man who announced that being out of work had made him "hate God, and hate you people and hate the churches and hate the Government." At one point, according to the *Times,* the proceedings had "threatened to break up in a row." Mediating between fashionable Park Avenue parishioners and social malcontents became Holmes's particular specialty.[36]

FIGURE I.2
John Haynes Holmes at the
grave of the Unitarian minister
and abolitionist Theodore Parker
in Florence, Italy. (John Haynes
Holmes Papers, Library of Congress.)

Despite such dramatic incidents, Thomas and Holmes fit fairly comfortably within the Social Gospel wing of Progressivism. Their concerns
about labor, immigrants, poverty, and urban government were quite common among their peers in New York and elsewhere. Their elite, educated
status was also typical, as was the hint of noblesse oblige that sometimes
colored their work. Finally, perhaps even more than other Progressives,
Thomas and Holmes stressed a version of social reform that was inseparable from individual morality. Thomas sought political change to improve the plight of immigrants in Harlem, but he also denounced crap
games, the shooting of firecrackers, and "moving picture houses . . . admitting children unaccompanied by parent or guardian."[37] Soon after the
United States entered the war, he would refuse to lend the FOR mailing
list to Max Eastman for use by the *Masses*, apparently because Eastman's
publication was too libertine to be associated with the Christian pacifists.[38] Similarly, Holmes interspersed his sermons on socialism, labor,

and war with denunciations of "free love" as "everlastingly wrong."[39] This concern for individual virtue, along with a suspicion of play and pleasure, betrayed an ascetic impulse that would remain at the heart of Christian nonviolence.

As Thomas and Holmes grew more interested in the Great War and its repercussions, they decided to participate in an antiwar group of reformers and social workers who met at Lillian Wald's Henry Street settlement house. This assemblage, which also included Jane Addams, Florence Kelley, and Paul U. Kellogg, formally organized itself around the same time as the Fellowship of Reconciliation and eventually became known as the American Union Against Militarism. Led by Crystal Eastman, Max's sister, the American Union was the most important liberal antiwar group from 1914 to 1917, establishing branches in every major American city.[40] Like the Fellowship, its opposition to war initially looked fairly respectable. Members of the American Union Against Militarism saw the work for peace as one more social reform effort, just as Mott viewed the Fellowship of Reconciliation as one more vehicle to hasten a Christian world. Wilson welcomed representatives of the American Union to the White House and listened sympathetically to their arguments.[41]

Before 1917, the president carried the hopes of social reformers like Thomas and Holmes. As a Christian and an intellectual, he seemed to be one of them. Wilson was also sympathetic to a progressive agenda, conferring with leading liberals and even socialists on policy questions. His first Secretary of State was William Jennings Bryan, who, though embarrassingly unsophisticated by the standards of Ivy League graduates such as Thomas and Holmes (and Wilson), was a Christian pacifist of a sort and a determined foe of big business. In 1916, the president provided compelling evidence that he shared the values of the American Union with respect to both war and domestic reform. The Wilson campaign stressed the president's success in keeping the country out of war, but equally important were a flurry of domestic moves that he made in the months before the election, placing two prominent liberal judges, Louis Brandeis and John Hessin Clarke, on the Supreme Court and signing progressive laws regulating farm loans, child labor, and workers' compensation. For all of these reasons, Norman Thomas voted Democratic in 1916, just as he had four years earlier. His brother Evan was "delighted over Wilson's re-election."[42]

The tide turned soon after Wilson won a second term. On January 31, 1917, Germany announced that it would resume unrestricted submarine warfare, leading the United States to break off diplomatic relations. A month later, Wilson released the Zimmerman note, a German communication encouraging Mexico to reclaim the southwestern United States through a military assault. On April 2, Wilson asked Congress to declare a very particular kind of war. The nation would fight for "no conquest, no dominion" and would "seek no indemnities for ourselves, no material compensation for the sacrifices we shall freely make." Nonetheless, violence would be necessary to safeguard the "rights of mankind."[43] The moral ground of Thomas, Holmes, and other Christian pacifists had shifted beneath them. They had always opposed the rabid militarism of jingoists and reactionaries, but that was easy. The defenders of nonviolence would fight their most heartbreaking battles against people like Wilson, high-minded supporters of war who championed armed force as an instrument for securing justice and human rights.

In the face of German aggression and Wilson's elevated rhetoric, progressive sentiment soon turned to favor American intervention. The philosopher John Dewey was the most prominent left-leaning intellectual who defended Wilson's about-face. Dewey's career had begun within a liberal Protestant ethos. He had been active in the Student Christian Association when he was in Ann Arbor in the 1880s, and in his early career had sought to harmonize Christianity with modern epistemology. He had long since left that line of inquiry behind, though, when he came to New York in 1904. For Dewey, religion required a belief in absolutes that had no place in modern philosophy or politics.[44]

The debate between the pacifists and the war's defenders raised a question that would linger long after the war was over: what was the place of absolute moral standards in complex modern societies? In his defense of the war effort, Dewey framed pacifism as irresponsible and reckless idealism, an extreme position that was irrelevant to modern life and not so different from militarism, which he considered its mirror image. In holding to their rigid definitions of righteousness, "the seekers for retributive justice" as well as "the 'stop the war' at any cost pacifist group" failed to adopt a historical perspective. "Both are so overwhelmed by the present, the amiable pacifists by its woes and the vengeful punishers by the wrongs done by those who brought it on, that they cannot see those long stretches of the future which in making war worth while also determine its just aims." Pacifism, he explained, was one form of the "passion" that was so dangerous in human affairs.[45]

William Adams Brown offered a liberal Protestant version of this argument. From his post at Union Theological Seminary, Brown had become one of the leading promoters of the "new theology" that stressed the contingent nature of God's revelation and the importance of Christianity's adaptation to modern culture. In his 1916 book *Is Christianity Practicable?*, Brown sharply denounced the war in terms of the Social Gospel; it had come as the result of a "social system" that was "largely selfish and unchristian." Yet Brown was unwilling to embrace pacifism. Though he had "the greatest respect" for those who opposed all war, he found that they were trying to "apply an absolute ideal to a progressive society." Unfortunately, war was not "a simple choice between right and wrong," as the pacifists saw it. For Brown, pacifism was a kind of fundamentalism.[46]

These charges stung some of the pacifists. Jane Addams, a member of a small FOR group in Chicago, remembered that war's opponents "were always afraid of fanaticism, . . . of a failure to meet life in the temper of a practical person." Wilson, Dewey, Brown, Mott, and Addams, all born between 1856 and 1865, had carried on long personal struggles against their inherited religious and political certainties, and in doing so helped to create modernism in religion, pragmatism in philosophy, and Progressivism in politics. "Every student of our time had become more or less a disciple of pragmatism," Addams explained. Any recourse to absolute values reminded this generation of the obscurantist biblical orthodoxy and cruel laissez-faire economics that they despised. Addams feared that by embracing pacifism she may have come full circle, back to a new version of the rigid Calvinism of her youth. "We slowly became aware that our affirmation [of pacifism] was regarded as pure dogma," she recalled.[47]

Some Christian pacifists, younger than Addams, accepted the absolutist label more willingly. The day before Wilson asked Congress for a declaration of war, Holmes preached a sermon, covered on the front page of the *New York Times*, that laid out his personal opposition to American intervention. Never particularly modest, he quoted statements of conscience from Martin Luther, Patrick Henry, and Theodore Parker. "Mistaken, foolish, fanatical, I may be; I will not deny the charge," he exclaimed. "If war is right, then Christianity is wrong, false, a lie. If Christianity is right, then war is wrong, false, a lie." Brown's conception of pacifism as passionate absolutism could hardly have found more apt expression. The stunned trustees at the Church of the Messiah held a meeting to discuss removing Holmes from his pulpit, but concluded that, although they disagreed with the views of their maverick minister, they would not ask him to resign. Nevertheless, the national debate over the war was growing increasingly contentious.[48]

The prewar network of progressive social reformers fractured under the pressure. Even the opponents of U.S. intervention split up, with the American Union Against Militarism fizzling out in late 1917.[49] Meanwhile, rifts grew between pacifists and prowar liberals. Norman Thomas discovered this when William Adams Brown became a leader in the war work of the Federal Council of Churches. The Federal Council, drawing representatives from the mainline denominations of American Protestantism, sought to coordinate religious and recreational work among soldiers, with particular focus on providing chaplains. Some of the most powerful figures in American religious life signed up to help, including Robert Speer, Harry Emerson Fosdick, and Shailer Mathews. Along with Brown, they promoted a Wilsonian outlook that sought to navigate between extremes of pacifism and militarism. In this context, Norman Thomas's opposition to the war was bound to create conflict. Brown tolerated his outspoken mission worker for a while, but when Thomas began to promote socialism along with pacifism, Brown reluctantly asked him to leave the American Parish, a move that Thomas already seemed to have been considering.[50]

Fault lines emerged among the founders of the Fellowship of Reconciliation. Most significantly, John Mott quietly withdrew soon after his crucial role in founding the organization. After the declaration of war, he offered Wilson the full support of the YMCA, quickly convening a "Conference on Army Work" at Garden City, where in 1915 the opponents of war had gathered to form the Fellowship of Reconciliation. Later, Mott joined the Root Commission, which went to Russia in part to keep that country in the war on the side of the Allies. Henry Hodgkin, the founder of the original FOR in England, was alarmed to learn that his ostensibly pacifist friend had made speeches encouraging the Russians to carry on the conflict. The "trust placed in you by men & women of all nations," he wrote to Mott, was a "priceless treasure." By supporting the war, Mott had used this trust "in the interests of a conflict which divides the constituency that has trusted you." Such action, Hodgkin maintained, "is not worthy of you or of the high office which you hold." As Hodgkin surmised, national loyalties had trumped the global Christian consciousness that the FOR had hoped to bring into being.[51]

The rifts between Thomas and Brown, and between Hodgkin and Mott, were painful, but within the bounds of civil disagreement. Indeed, if prowar sentiment had been restricted to Wilson's speeches and the pages of the New Republic, dissenters would have had little reason to feel alienated. However, the domestic war effort did not proceed according to liberal tenets of respect and forbearance, as even John Dewey would eventually acknowledge. Unprecedented legal repression and vigilante attacks shocked and debilitated the antiwar movement, demonstrating to Christian pacifists that the appalling violence of the Great War was not confined to Europe.[52]

Wilson maintained that the nation would enter the war with the professorial disinterestedness that he himself exuded. He expressed confidence that Americans would do battle "without passion" and "observe with proud punctilio the principles of right and fair play we profess to be fighting for." Instead, waves of violent repression swept across the home front. Wilson had proclaimed the conflict a "People's War," but throughout the United States the people warred with each other. German Americans endured brutal attacks by fellow citizens, while jingoists tried to scrub the nation clean of German literature and music, and Theodore Roosevelt backed a campaign to stop the teaching of the German language in American schools. Labor radicals and socialists suffered as well. On July 1, 1917, in a scene reenacted throughout the country, a mob attacked a parade organized by various radical groups in Boston, beating the marchers and forcing them to kiss the American flag. Nor was such intimidation practiced solely by vigilantes. The Wilson administration itself aggressively silenced dissenters, especially through enforcement of the Espionage and Sedition Acts, which had the effect of making any opposition to the war a potentially criminal offense. Most famously, Eugene V. Debs was arrested and sentenced to prison after giving a fiery antiwar speech in Canton, Ohio. Debs, who had garnered nearly a million votes as the Socialist presidential candidate in 1912, ended up a victim of Wilson's highly selective "principles of right and fair play." The Christian pacifists who were coalescing in the FOR were astonished to discover that, like these immigrants and radicals, they, too, had become threats to national security.[53]

An incident in Los Angeles revealed the shrinking space for any kind of dissent. Three ministers planned an antiwar conference to begin on October 1, 1917. The meeting, one organizer wrote to FOR headquarters back east, could "swell the ranks and increase the strength of the Fellowship of Reconciliation out here on the Coast."[54] His optimism was misplaced. The "Christian Pacifists," as they became known, were denied the use of a municipal hall in Long Beach, and on the afternoon of the first day of the conference, they found their alternative site surrounded by police. After moving to yet another location, the conference began, but police soon interrupted it and arrested the organizers on charges of holding an unlawful assembly. When the participants tried to continue the meeting in private homes, vigilantes broke it up and chased them out of town.[55]

The opponents of the Christian Pacifists insisted that they were part of a revolutionary socialist conspiracy. At the trial of the organizers, a key piece of evidence was a copy of the *Masses*, the influential radical journal, that had been found in a desk at the conference. The *Los Angeles Times* insisted that the event was a cover for the People's Council for Democracy and Peace, a secular socialist antiwar organization. That was not all. Attendees at the conference, the newspaper noted ominously, included "negroes and Mexicans, bootblacks and disciples of Yogi." The *Times* also printed a condemnation from the fire-breathing evangelist Billy Sunday, in town for a massive preaching campaign, who implied that the Christian Pacifists ought to be treated like Frank Little, an organizer for the IWW who had recently been lynched in Montana. In court, the ministers who organized the conference were all sentenced to prison.[56]

Though imprisonment of antiwar clergy was rare, many ministers learned that opposing the national crusade put their exalted religious status in jeopardy. John Haynes Holmes, who kept his job despite his outspoken denunciation of American military action, was exceptional. Few of his colleagues fared so well, and a small but steady stream of rebellious clerics made their way to the FOR when their churches refused to accept their pacifism. Episcopal church authorities forced the resignation of Paul Jones, a bishop in Utah, after he spoke at the Christian Pacifist conference in California. In 1919 he became the executive secretary of the FOR, a position he would hold for a decade. John Nevin Sayre, an Episcopal minister in Suffern, New York, tried to become a military chaplain or a YMCA secretary when the United States entered the war, but John Mott warned him that his pacifist convictions would make this nearly impossible. He, too, soon left his church and joined the Fellowship, where he served as either chair or co–executive secretary of the organization every year from 1924 to 1946. At the Greenwich Presbyterian Church in New York City, congregants forced the exit of pastors William Fincke and Edmund Chaffee after the two made public comments opposing the war. Both would spearhead the involvement of the FOR in the labor movement. For these dissenters, the Fellowship of Reconciliation functioned as an alternative pastorate, allowing them to pursue religious work without the ideological constraints imposed by a local congregation.[57]

This changing membership moved the Fellowship of Reconciliation further from the American religious and political mainstream. The charter members of the Fellowship had initially assumed that their cause enjoyed widespread support. They believed that the efforts of committed Christians in positions of authority could lead society toward a more humane social order. Now the nation's religious leaders had turned to support the war or, by maintaining their opposition, had lost much of their public influence. Disappointed by both church and state, the Fellowship turned more radical. Though never disconnected from sources of political and religious influence, it came to view such influence far more suspiciously.

The Christian pacifists' fraught new relationship to power became more clear in a controversy over the *World Tomorrow*. Begun in 1918 (with the title the *New World*), this journal emerged as the most important forum for the ideas of Christian nonviolence. Though it was never formally affiliated with the Fellowship of Reconciliation, Fellowship leaders edited it and wrote many of its articles. The Espionage Act had given Postmaster General Albert Burleson the authority to ban from the mails any material judged to impede the war effort, so on these grounds Burleson suspended the September 1918 edition of the *World Tomorrow*, apparently because of an article by Norman Thomas opposing U.S. intervention in Russia. Thomas went with John Nevin Sayre to visit Burleson, who refused to relent. So Sayre, whose brother Francis had married Wilson's daughter, arranged a meeting with the president. Wilson agreed to release the paper, one of only two incidents where he overruled Burleson. Other dissenting papers received harsher treatment; when Max Eastman appealed to Wilson to overrule Burleson's suspension of the *Masses*, the president refused. Yet the *World Tomorrow* controversy also showed a new distance between the opponents of war and the president that they had supported.[58]

As this incident suggests, the FOR was developing an unexpected new focus. "Disarmament . . . ," Holmes later recalled, "was a lost cause" after America declared war, but "there came suddenly to the fore in our nation's life the new issue of civil liberties."[59] Given that so many of its members had lost the moral influence they had exercised through pulpits, journals, and settlement houses, "the new issue" was a natural point of interest that marked a larger turning point in the politics of American liberalism and radicalism. Progressive reformers had paid little attention to freedoms of speech, assembly, and conscience before World War I. After all, the whole thrust of the Progressive movement was away from individual rights, with their connotations of economic laissez-faire and social anarchy. For liberal Protestants, free speech had uncomfortable associations with the sex radicals who defied the Comstock Act or the incendiary anarcho-syndicalists of the IWW. The Espionage and Sedition Acts changed the political landscape, for they made even the most respectable pacifist vulnerable to arrest and imprisonment.[60]

The emergence of the issue of civil liberties, particularly the case of conscientious objectors, further confused and fragmented old political alliances. "I have been interested to note," wrote Norman Thomas, "that apparently one cannot judge a man's position in the matter of conscientious objectors from his general theological or social views. In other words liberals and conservatists form new lines on this question."[61] Thomas, Holmes, and other liberal Christians played formative roles in the National Civil Liberties Bureau, an offshoot of the American Union Against Militarism that would become the American Civil Liberties Union. There they found themselves in league with an eclectic mix of secular reformers such as Roger Baldwin. Indeed, civil liberties served as a powerful rallying point precisely because the issue was amenable to two different accents—an agnostic interpretation that sought to protect a free marketplace of ideas and a Christian emphasis on the freedom of the Christian conscience to follow God wherever he might direct. The second interpretation dominated the thinking of two YMCA workers returned from Europe in the fall of 1917: Harold Gray and Norman Thomas's brother, Evan.

When asked to report for military service, Thomas and Gray claimed conscientious objector status. Theirs was a highly unusual choice that revealed the differences between absolute pacifism and the more diffuse opposition to the war that pervaded many segments of American society. Most draftees accepted their fate, thereby swelling the nation's military to over three million men during the war. Of those who did not wish to become soldiers, the vast majority simply refused to show up for induction or left their army camps. Over three hundred thousand of these "slackers" and "deserters" plagued recruiting efforts, compared to just under four thousand men who officially registered as conscientious objectors. Indeed, more Americans evaded the draft during World War I than during the Vietnam War. These outlaws were disproportionately immigrants, African Americans, and rural dwellers, a far cry from the elite pedigrees of Thomas and Gray. While pacifist conscientious objectors were uncommon, this unorganized resistance showed a broader dissatisfaction with the nation's first modern attempt at conscription.[62]

Provision for conscientious objection in the Selective Service Act was sketchy, extending to members of any "well-recognized religious sect" that was historically pacifist. The category was a bureaucratic oversimplification, for in reality many members of "peace churches" served in the military, while, conversely, antiwar sentiment appeared across the religious spectrum. Then, too, local draft boards had great latitude in bestowing conscientious objector status. The FOR debated whether to consider its own members exempt under the Selective Service provision, but, in typically lenient fashion, decided to allow "each individual to determine whether he should claim exemption on this ground."[63] Evidently, most individuals chose not to do so.

The most likely candidates to be conscientious objectors were members of groups such as the Mennonites, a predominantly German American sect concentrated in the mid-Atlantic and midwestern countryside. Mennonites had little tolerance for the cosmopolitan, activist Protestantism of the YMCA. Their peace witness was rooted in a strict interpretation of the Bible and a deep suspicion of secular politics that discouraged running for public office and even voting in elections. Mennonites and other conservative sectarians accounted for about three-quarters of all conscientious objectors.[64]

Though they generally got along well with other types of objectors, Thomas and Gray distinguished their own pacifism from that of the Mennonites and other antimodern groups. At Fort Riley, Kansas, and the other military camps where they lived, they found that their own religion was far more sophisticated than that of their fellow conscientious objectors. The faith of the pacifist sects resembled "slavery," Thomas complained, and Harold Gray agreed, noting with disdain that the sectarians interpreted their Bibles with "painful literalness." For the former YMCA secretaries, some kinds of pacifism were better than others.[65]

Military officials displayed little interest in the finer points of Protestant theology, nor did they always observe the distinction between principled conscientious objectors and ordinary "slackers." Indeed, the fears among the conscientious objectors of the regimented, totalizing authority of the state took on an ironic twist in the day-to-day life of the camps, where their treatment was arbitrary and ad hoc. For instance, when Thomas, Gray, and other so-called absolutists refused noncombatant service, camp authorities were at a loss. The two sides engaged in endless debates con-

FIGURE 1.3   Conscientious objectors at Fort Riley, Kansas, 1918. Front row (l-r): William A. Dunham, Howard W. Moore, Henry Monsky, Sam Solnitski. Back row (l-r): Evan Thomas, Harold Gray, Roderick Seidenburg. (Norman Thomas Papers, Manuscripts and Archives Division, The New York Public Library, Astor, Lenox, and Tilden Foundations.)

cerning the boundaries of military jurisdiction. Could the conscientious objectors be ordered to rake the leaves around the camp? Did they have to salute military officers?

In the summer of 1918, Thomas, Gray, and two other objectors, frustrated by their ambiguous status, began a hunger strike in the military camp at Fort Riley. They argued that they were prisoners, not soldiers, and as such the government should prepare their food and otherwise provide for them. Gray explained to his family that "the government had taken my body, which it would no longer permit me to use as I liked, and . . . it should therefore take care of it." All of the objectors eventually resumed eating after a few weeks, though not before some were force-fed through tubes thrust down their throats.[66]

In undertaking the hunger strike and other forms of resistance, Thomas and Gray occasionally recognized that their noncooperation was a complex drama with its own rules and logic, not simply an ethical response to an immoral demand by a political authority. The machinations in the camps were part of a moral struggle, but they also contained a symbolic significance. Nonresistance, wrote Gray, was "a game in which patience is the biggest factor," while Thomas admitted: "There is an element of fight & also give & take in this that makes life interesting." The two were, however, uncomfortable with this dimension of their actions. Thomas acknowledged that the hunger strike had "a ridiculous side . . . which I see as well as the next man," while Gray concluded that the maneuvering of the objectors often made for "rather a queer performance." Indeed, Gray stopped his hunger strike after realizing that it might be interpreted as a suicide attempt, and he soon regretted such "mad behavior." These dissenters were pioneering a strategic, pragmatic, and self-conscious form of nonviolence, but they did not yet have a language to discuss and defend it.[67]

Outside the camps, conscientious objectors sparked further debate over the meaning of moral absolutism. In the *New Republic*, John Dewey urged leniency for them, but argued that their agonizing about the evils of war revealed the obsolescence of traditional moral education. He acknowledged the widespread appeal of antiwar feeling before 1914: "In our colleges the Y.M.C.A.'s were even more ardent promoters of peace sentiments than were intercollegiate socialist clubs." Yet such "moral training," he wrote, "emphasizes the emotions rather than intelligence, ideals rather than specific purposes, the nurture of personal motives rather than the creation of social agencies and environments." It had produced a conscience that sought only "to maintain itself unspotted from within" and to search for "a fixed antecedent rule of justification." In the modern world, conscience needed to link with "the moving force of events" in order to "have compulsive power instead of being forever the martyred and the coerced." Thomas and Gray had scoffed at the sectarian conscientious objectors, but Dewey argued that the former YMCA men were themselves the champions of a simple-minded antimodernism.[68]

The conscientious objector issue, though, allowed the Christian pacifists to argue that the supporters of war were in fact the absolutists. Norman Thomas charged that "in war we adopt a large measure of the Prussian ideal," meaning that the state becomes "a metaphysical entity, a sort of god, to whom the individual should cheerfully offer his life." "Conscription of the conscientious objector . . . ," he maintained, "is worse than chattel slavery, for the slave may still be in heart and conscience free." Here again the abolitionist legacy defined the Fellowship leaders' view of war.[69]

Norman Thomas and John Nevin Sayre tried to intervene on behalf of the conscientious objectors, but their attempts revealed the attenuation of the progressive networks that they had counted on before the war. Once again, Wilson and Mott disappointed them. Sayre had pleaded with the

president to apply draft exemptions to individuals rather than denominations, appealing to Wilson's own Protestant principles: "Conscience is always an individual and personal thing, and in the Protestant view at least,
the creed or principles of a religious organization cannot be substituted
for it." Wilson replied that such a plan was impossible "because it would
open the door to so much that was unconscientious." Other than ameliorating the worst abuses of the conscientious objectors, Wilson provided
little assistance until after the war was over. Norman Thomas expressed
his feelings of betrayal in a letter to Mott, charging that "though you do
not now agree with these Conscientious Objectors, in the case of some
of them it was your own addresses that gave them part of their spiritual
background for their present stand." Apparently, Mott made no reply. By
the time the war ended, Evan Thomas and Harold Gray had been sentenced to prison, Thomas for refusing to eat during his hunger strike and
Gray for not obeying an officer's order to help maintain the grounds at his
military camp.[70]

Despite such abuse, some pacifists in the FOR still clung to the last rem-
nants of the faith in Wilsonian Progressivism that they had possessed in
1916. The president had insisted that the war, however unpleasant, was
a necessary step on the road to a just and durable peace. His attempts to
secure that peace resonated with the ideas of the Fellowship of Reconciliation's leaders. Wilson's proposal for a League of Nations drew heavily
on the programs of socialist, labor, and peace movements in the United
States and England, while his insistence on national self-determination
gave traction to critiques of imperialism in colonized nations as well as in
the West. A postwar "Wilsonian moment," felt around the world, held out
the prospect of a new kind of international order.[71]

The FOR circle simply could not resist incorporating Wilsonian ideals
into its own antiwar rhetoric. Perhaps thinking of his divided congregation, Holmes called for "true Pacifists" to unite with "true Militarists,"
those prowar liberals who fought for noble goals of peace and security,
"on the high plane of spiritual idealism which is common to us both."
Holmes insisted that Wilson's vision, while not convincing him personally to support the war, had accurately laid out America's moral responsibility. In another sermon, Holmes insisted that pacifists, ironically, had
"best comprehended the President's position, and given it support." They
had not compromised their stand, "but the war having come, they rejoice
that it is to be fought with an unselfish and not a selfish purpose." As

peace negotiations began in Paris, Holmes warned that the statesmen involved were hardly idealists, but he had "faith that Mr. Wilson has read
aright the signs of the times; and has resolved to secure an agreement
among the nations which shall safeguard democracy as surely as it estab-
lishes enduring peace."[72]

The Paris Peace Conference crushed the faith of Holmes and his fellow
pacifists. Wilson's vision of an international summit of equals was scut-
tled as the victorious Allies dictated the terms of settlement, mandating
reparations and territorial concessions from the Central Powers. The British and French insisted on keeping their colonies, while Japan's proposal
to have the conference endorse racial equality failed to gain approval. The
delegates did eventually agree to join together in a League of Nations, but
to the FOR circle the modifications of Wilson's original vision were fatal
flaws. The World Tomorrow, like many liberal journals, initially supported
the president's plan for an international organization, but by the fall of
1919 had come to oppose the peace settlement. The agreement was a triumph of the prewar style of diplomacy, these pacifists argued, and had
created an "imperialistic alliance" of the Allied nations that would bring
"not peace but new wars" to Europe. "It seems incredible," Holmes admitted in a critique of the Versailles Treaty, "that President Wilson has
given his assent to this wretched business." By the time that Congress
nixed American entry into the League of Nations, the pacifists' tenuous
support for the president had evaporated.[73]

Wilson's failure crystallized a central tenet of the emerging Christian pacifist worldview: violence, no matter how apparently justified, destroyed the open communication necessary for democracy. Wilson's own
conception of the League of Nations had suggested as much. The League,
he had argued, would be "the organized moral force of men throughout
the world," shining the "searching light of conscience" on warmongers.
"Just a little exposure will settle most questions," the president promised.
Given this focus on the moral power of world opinion, both pacifist and
nonpacifist progressives reacted with outrage when the delegates in Paris
barred the press from their deliberations. Wilson did protest the secrecy
at Versailles, but he had acquiesced in the draconian restriction of speech
in his own country during the war. The antiwar progressives who fell
victim to the government's aggressive actions in 1917 and 1918 turned
against the president just at the time that he needed articulate champions
of his League of Nations, and they did not fail to note this tragic reversal.
"If Mr. Wilson had not deliberately approved the legalized tyranny of the

Espionage Act, and the autocratic and reckless administration of that Act by the Post Office Department and the Department of Justice," argued the *World Tomorrow,* he would have found the support he needed in the "League fight" with Congress. For the pacifists, the violence of the war in Europe and its repercussions on the home front had overwhelmed its progressive internationalist justification.[74]

The events of 1919 and 1920 ultimately produced a kind of vindication for the FOR circle. Even Dewey conceded that the "consistent pacifist" was now "entitled to his flourish of private triumphings" in light of the postwar failures of Wilsonian ideals. The government began to back off from its harsh punishment of opponents of war. A higher court overturned the conviction of the Christian Pacifists in California, while the conscientious objectors, including Thomas and Gray, were one by one discharged or pardoned.[75] Still, the continued official persecution of labor radicals and Communists, alongside a rash of domestic social upheavals, confirmed the pacifists' belief that the war had unleashed forces of hatred impossible to control. Violence involving African Americans in East St. Louis and Chicago led the *World Tomorrow* to proclaim a "race war" in the United States. Though "we were told that military training and the experiences of war would discipline America," ran one editorial, the recent brutality directed against black citizens "would seem to prove that the opposite is the case." Robert Whitaker, one of the California Christian Pacifists, wrote that recent animus toward Japanese immigrants was "a part of the general increase of the suspicions and antipathies begotten by the Great War. . . . California's Germany just now is Japan."[76]

The most ominous conflict was the new "industrial warfare." Between 1915 and 1920, the labor movement sustained a level of activity and influence unprecedented in American history, as union membership nearly doubled and many industries were organized for the first time. The strength of the newly unionized workers in a wartime economy, along with the rapid expansion of large corporations, led to an explosion of strikes, many of them resulting in bloodshed. Foreign soldiers did not occupy American territory during the Great War, but federal troops did enforce labor peace across the nation.[77] Observing this militarization of American capitalism, Norman Thomas argued that the moral justification of armed force in Europe made it impossible for the war's supporters to condemn violence by dissenters at home. John Haynes Holmes concurred, arguing that "we can't give medals of honor to the men who use violence against their enemies, and prison sentences to men who refuse to use violence against their enemies, and expect that the lesson thus learned in time of war will not be rigidly applied in time of peace." Thomas and Holmes begged a crucial question: was the radical labor movement violent or nonviolent?[78]

The Janus face presented by the IWW shows how difficult that question became. In some ways, the IWW was one of the most obvious precursors to the militant Christian nonviolence that would emerge out of the FOR circle. The Wobblies, as IWW members were known, were resolutely antiwar, refusing membership to any worker who voluntarily enlisted in the military. Drawing on an eclectic mix of anarchist, syndicalist, and Marxist ideologies, the group practiced early forms of nonviolent direct action by refusing to work, defying laws they believed to be unjust, and courting physical attacks by police. In addition, the prewar "free speech fights" over the Wobblies' right to make public addresses looked forward to the concerns of conscientious objectors and the ACLU.

The Wobblies were not in the habit of killing people to achieve their aims, yet many Americans regarded them as dangerous threats. Violence as a cultural concept never meant mere physical conflict but was instead part of a broader symbolic world. IWW leader Elizabeth Gurley Flynn recognized this fact when she said of violent action that "it's especially dramatic when you talk about it and don't resort to it." Indeed, the Wobblies frequently deployed the language of class war and violent revolution. The subtleties of Gurley Flynn's position were lost on most observers, particularly the IWW's powerful enemies in business and government, while even within the organization, nonviolence was regarded as a strategy to achieve a new economic order, not as a guiding ethical principle.[79]

Radical labor groups such as the IWW, then, were seldom physically violent, but they were spectacularly contentious in ways that repulsed many Christian pacifists. Though the FOR forthrightly condemned the use of force by employers, its members formed two opposing sides with regard to labor activity. The division centered on the meaning of the strike. One side saw it as a continuation of war by other means, a method of involuntary coercion. Edward Evans, a Pennsylvania Quaker, found strikes "exceedingly difficult to square with a complete Christian ideal." Though he admitted the hypothetical possibility of "a Christian strike," he did not think that one had ever occurred. "I cannot believe that the best way to Christianize the world is to encourage the spirit and practice of the strike," he admitted. Evans noted that, while some people argued that the strike was the only option for workers, "so have many people said that war is the only method, when dealing with certain situations, such as that presented by Germany in 1914."[80] John Haynes Holmes also came down against the strike, particularly in its most recent incarnations. Though it had initially been "an act of martyrdom," it had become "an act of war" based upon the "principle of coercion." Holmes, generally sympathetic to labor, believed in political action and the formation of a "co-operative industrial state" as more ethical methods of social change.[81]

The FOR members who supported strikes also made analogies with the Great War. Norman Thomas contended that "the difference is enormous" between "a concerted effort to kill" and "a concerted laying down of tools," while Robert Whitaker turned the tables on strike opponents by claiming that the "present system of industry *is war*, continuous, relentless, and calamitous." Those who participated in that system were complicit in its inherent violence. A. J. Muste suggested that a striker was a kind of conscientious objector, and Evan Thomas allowed that his absolutist stance during the war "amounted to a strike." These pacifists were rethinking the prewar Social Gospel, which had focused mainly on the domestic reform of industry and government, in the light of the problem of war that now commanded their attention.[82]

Muste would forge the Fellowship's most durable connection to labor. His family had emigrated from Holland when he was a boy, settling in a tightly knit immigrant community in Michigan where, he remembered, "the church . . . was the center of social life and culture, as well as of worship and religious training." While preparing for the ministry, he absorbed the liberal Protestant outlook at Union Theological Seminary, where he also met Norman Thomas. Like other early members of the Fellowship, Muste had not seriously considered the antiwar position. "I had never been given an inkling," he later explained, "that there might be such a thing as a pacifist interpretation of the Gospel."

Soon after the Great War broke out, Muste accepted a pulpit at Central Church in Newtonville, Massachusetts. For a while he vacillated on the question of the war, but by the end of 1916 he had joined the Fellowship of Reconciliation and adopted a pacifist stance. His congregation initially supported him, but when soldiers from the church began to be killed and wounded, Muste's relationship with his parishioners cooled. He found that "the parents and their friends felt that, holding the views I did, I could not adequately comfort them. To tell the truth, I did not feel that I could either." He resigned his position and began a period of drifting through various kinds of pacifist organizations. He did volunteer work helping conscientious objectors for the National Civil Liberties Bureau and joined a Quaker meeting in Providence, Rhode Island. Then he headed a group in Boston called "The Comradeship," a dedicated collective of pacifist radicals who practiced an intense, semicommunal spiritual discipline. Muste described the assemblage as "in one sense a left wing of the Fellowship of Reconciliation." The members of the Comradeship actively sought an outlet for their spiritual energies. "We had . . . a feeling," Muste recollected, "that nonviolence had to prove itself in actual struggle; otherwise it was a mere abstraction or illusion." He felt "the sting of the charge that during the war, while others risked their lives, we had stood on the sidelines and 'had it easy.'" A textile strike in Lawrence, Massachusetts, provided the opportunity that Muste had been awaiting.[83]

Muste and his friends in the Comradeship may have been especially attracted to Lawrence because of its fame as the site of a famous 1912 strike led by the IWW. More immediately, the Christian pacifists filled a leadership gap. The American Federation of Labor opposed the new strike of unorganized workers, and wartime repression had decimated the Wobblies, so unaffiliated ethnic leaders such as Anthony Capraro did much of the organizing for the walkout. Muste became executive secretary of the strike committee, probably because of his facility with the English language, his respected status as a minister, and his connections to outside resources. Two other ministers from the Comradeship, Cedric Long and Harold Rotzel, also joined the committee.

The ministers, Muste later recalled, "were tossed into a raging ocean." On the first day of the strike, "police . . . waded into the [picket] lines, clubbing right and left." On another day of picketing, mounted officers forced Muste and Long down a side street, away from the rest of the marchers. They beat the two men, knocking Long unconscious, and took them to jail, where a police captain "spoke scathingly" to Muste "of the disgrace of a minister of the Gospel behaving in such a way that he 'had to be thrown in jail.'" Police also set up machine guns on major streets in the city.

The ministers won some victories, however. Facing workers infuriated by the appearance of the machine guns, Muste insisted "that cheerfulness was better for morale than bitterness and that therefore we would smile as we passed the machine guns and the police." Despite the efforts of an agent provocateur, this approach prevailed and bloodshed was averted. As with Thomas and Gray in prison, Muste's assessment assumed that nonviolence could be both a deeply held philosophy and a psychological strategy that had a logic of its own. None of the pacifists, however, had worked out the implications of this double meaning at the time. Muste was primarily trying to settle a strike, and after more than three months he did. Just as the workers were about to cave in, the owners of the textile mills agreed to most of their demands. The strike was over and a new opportunity for pacifist action had opened up.[84]

Out of the strike arose a new union, the Amalgamated Textile Workers Association. Muste served as its general secretary, with Long, Rotzel, and the indefatigable Evan Thomas obtaining other key positions. The association became a key player in the "new unionism" that sought to organize ethnic workers along industrial lines via a centralized, well-staffed organization, thus prefiguring the strategy of the Congress of Industrial Organizations in the 1930s. Throughout 1919, a series of actions led by the association in Passaic and Paterson, New Jersey, as well as Lawrence, seemed to foreshadow a new labor movement, one especially amenable to Christian nonviolence.[85]

Ultimately, though, the Christian pacifist experiment failed in the Amalgamated Textile Workers Association. After its initial successes, the union locals, weakened by official repression, factional division, and economic downturn, faded away by 1921. In actuality, ethnic leaders had been at least as important as the Christian outsiders in maintaining the union, while on the ground the textile workers found the pacifist philosophy of nonviolence rather abstract, accepting it in only the most limited and instrumental way.[86] At the same time, union politics proved to be an assault on the moral consistency of the pacifists. Evan Thomas, particularly disillusioned by the experience, quit both the labor movement and, until World War II, the peace movement. He became a doctor and developed pioneering treatments for syphilis, perhaps remembering the suffering he encountered in English hospitals during the war. Long and Rotzel, too, found that their ideals could not bend to accommodate the realities of unions and strikes. On the other hand, A. J. Muste distinguished himself as the most important Christian pacifist in the labor movement during the next fifteen years. The correct application of pacifism to the "industrial warfare" was perplexing to many in the FOR circle. "While there is no question in our minds," Paul Jones explained, "that war and the method of Jesus are always incompatible, we have not been able to express with the same definiteness our attitude toward that other war which goes by the name of competitive business."[87]

The war years left the Fellowship both confident of its convictions and uncertain of the future. The results of the Great War had fulfilled the direst predictions of the Christian pacifists. Many supporters of American intervention, including Sherwood Eddy, changed their minds and embraced strong antiwar positions by the early 1920s. Yet the war had brought the pacifists into uncharted political and religious territory. They had pushed the ideals of John Mott and Woodrow Wilson to their logical extremes, extremes that Mott and Wilson themselves were unwilling to accept. Moreover, some of the ideals themselves had proven inadequate in the face of the Great War and the new, more aggressive labor movement. As the leaders of the FOR lost their moral and cultural authority, they turned increasingly skeptical of the systems of power that governed politics, industry, religion, and society. They came to believe that those systems were often achieved and maintained by brute force. Opposing war was not enough. In the 1920s, the radical Christian pacifists took on all kinds of violence, at home and abroad.

We expect to prevail through the foolishness of preaching—striving to commend ourselves unto every man's conscience, in the sight of God.
—William Lloyd Garrison, "Declaration of Sentiments, 1838"

2   Social Evangelism

In 1923, a sociology professor named Clarence Marsh Case published the first extensive scholarly analysis of nonviolence to appear in America. The book, *Non-Violent Coercion: A Study in the Methods of Social Pressure,* was a revision of Case's 1915 doctoral dissertation, completed at the University of Wisconsin under the renowned sociologist Edward A. Ross. Case began with a historical survey covering major religious traditions, along with smaller Christian sects such as the Quakers and Mennonites. Then he turned to more recent developments: strikes, boycotts, conscientious objection to the Great War, and the peculiar career of a rising political leader in India named Mohandas Gandhi.

As in many dissertation projects, Case hewed closely to his sources and offered little general analysis. It was left to Edward Ross to suggest the profound implications of "non-violent coercion" in a short preface to his student's book. Ross, like Case, was unaffiliated with the Fellowship of Reconciliation, but he took nonviolence very seriously. The technology of killing, he explained, had become so effective that both international war and domestic uprisings were now little more than exercises in mass suicide. Under such conditions, "the old-fashioned method of passive resistance, practised for ages on a small scale by petty groups, is coming into favor." However, that "old-fashioned method" had begun to transform itself through the use of new forms of mass media and new concepts of spectatorship. Nonviolent resisters triumphed, Ross argued, by "exciting the sympathy of disinterested onlookers" and gaining their support. "The spectacle of men suffering for a principle *and not hitting back* is a moving one," he observed. Such a spectacle could shift the locus of power "from the will of the stronger to the court of public opinion, perhaps of world opinion." This kind of political dynamic was a uniquely modern phenomenon, for only in recent times had so many spectators been so easy to reach. Writing well before the age of television began, Ross noted that mass media technologies ("wireless and print and radio") had exponentially increased the number of listeners and readers in the world, so that "every intelligent member of the human race" could follow a conflict occurring anywhere. By making a "spectacle" of a "principle," he mused, "the method of *non-violent coercion* . . . may have a future no man yet dreams of."[1]

In the decade following the Great War, the leaders of the Fellowship of Reconciliation began to imagine the future that Ross evoked. The 1920s have long been seen as the first decade of a recognizably "modern" America, and at this time radical Christian pacifists began to work out their own forward-looking style of political dissent. At first glance, their advances do not seem as strikingly innovative as jazz, *The Great Gatsby,* or the sound film. Certainly, the Fellowship did not achieve mass appeal, numbering a mere 2,000 members in 1920, 3,000 in 1924, and 6,000 in 1928.[2] Then, too, the modernism of Christian nonviolence often appeared in the guise of tradition. The FOR held up the example of Jesus as the basis for individual conduct and the institution of the family as the model for human community. Yet, as Edward Ross suggested, twentieth-century developments had given new significance to apparently "old-fashioned" modes of thought and action. If pacifists clung stubbornly to moral absolutes, they increasingly did so with the knowledge that, in Ross's formulation, a "principle" might well become a "spectacle." As they challenged capitalism, imperialism, racism, and war, these innovators made Christian nonviolence a complex strategy as well as a religious conviction. In their increasing self-consciousness, their use of new communication technologies, and their transnational outlook, they shared in the "modern temper" that defined the twenties.

The avant-garde vision of these radicals began with a new conception of human communication. As Ross had observed, they were living through the emergence of mass media, a process that did much to make the 1920s seem uniquely "modern." Mass-circulation magazines, feature-length motion pictures, phonographs, radio, and middlebrow books brought about a revolution as dramatic as the later transformations wrought by television and the Internet. The pacifists could imagine a universal nonviolent fellowship not only because they believed all human beings to be created in the image of God, but also because they saw new systems of communication bringing those human beings into more immediate contact with each other than ever before. In these early years, the Fellowship leaders could not quite conceive of the visually arresting performances that would distinguish nonviolence in the 1960s. They still thought of communication primarily in terms of words, transmitted orally or in print. However, their growing sense that nonviolence depended not only on physical actions but on strategic representations brought them closer to Edward Ross's notion of making a "spectacle" out of a "principle."[3]

The experience of the war, though, tempered any utopian dreams about the beneficent power of mass communication. The men and women in the FOR had experienced the conflict as a dramatic silencing of speech. Accustomed to large audiences of listeners and readers, they found themselves removed from their pulpits and reform organizations and their writings banned from the mails. Then, at the broadest level, the Great War itself seemed in retrospect to have been a case of colossal misunderstanding. Absent a polarizing ideological issue such as slavery or, later, Fascism, the conflict looked like a wholly unnecessary slaughter occasioned by a lack of dialogue among the participants. Woodrow Wilson had made just this claim in his bid for a League of Nations. "If the Central Powers had dared to discuss the purposes of this war for a single fortnight," Wilson supposed, "it never would have happened, and if, as should be, they were forced to discuss it for a year, war would have been inconceivable." Based on their individual experiences as well as their interpretation of the war as a whole, the pacifists came to assume that authentic communication and violence were diametrically opposed. "No war," Kirby Page explained, "can be waged on a basis of absolute truth." The victory of "absolute truth" depended on the creation and protection of the right kind of public speech.[4]

The dark twin of true speech was propaganda. To stir support for American mobilization at home and abroad, the U.S. government had formed the Committee on Public Information. Led by former muckraker George Creel, this agency deployed all the technology of modern media, publishing pamphlets, placing patriotic ads in magazines, making films, and employing "Four Minute Men," speakers who traveled around the country giving short speeches promoting the war. Creel was ecstatic over the success of the Committee on Public Information in energizing the nation to support intervention in Europe. The Great War, he thought, had been unprecedented in its "recognition of Public Opinion as a major force." He saw his campaign, "the world's greatest adventure in advertising," as a liberal alternative to the drastic state censorship that prevailed in European countries.[5]

Many liberals and radicals, whether pacifist or not, looked askance at Creel's enthusiasm. As they grew increasingly disenchanted with the legacy of the war, they blamed wartime propaganda for leading Americans to support a military venture that now appeared misguided and fruitless. Walter Lippmann, a disappointed Wilsonian, took this explanation a step further, arguing that modern communication technologies were eroding democratic citizenship itself. In his 1922 book *Public Opinion* he claimed that "what each man does is based not on direct and certain knowledge, but on pictures made by himself or given to him." Political debate was not the reasoned deliberation of principled interlocutors, but a crude battle of prepackaged "stereotypes" (Lippmann was the first to use the term, originally a name for a printing process, in its modern sense). Citizens in a democracy could no longer accumulate the expertise necessary to assess the complex problems of the modern world, so the only alternative, in this pessimistic view, was the cultivation of a class of experts who could decipher and solve those problems in a rational way.[6]

The pacifists shared Lippmann's disenchantment with modern misuses of language. "Throughout the war," Kirby Page lamented, "the peoples of the earth were fed upon lies, half-truths and misrepresentations." Visiting Germany in the early 1920s, Sherwood Eddy found that the people there "believe the propaganda they have been reading in their papers . . . as implicitly as the Allies believe theirs. Each has been reading almost exclusively of the sins, hypocrisy and atrocities of the enemy."[7] Page, Eddy, and their colleagues viewed disingenuous communication as inextricably linked to mass slaughter. Unlike Lippmann, though, the pacifists maintained their faith in democracy, arguing that although American and European citizens had been horribly deceived, they were not fundamentally irrational. Rather than calling for Lippmann's class of experts, the pacifists attempted to create spheres of honest communication, accurate information, and open debate, for they still believed that ordinary people could discover political and moral truth.

The New York City Labor Temple, under the leadership of Edmund Chaffee, was one important site of authentic speech for the radical Christian pacifists. Chaffee grew up in Michigan and began law school there, then decided to become a minister. After attending Hartford Theological Seminary and Union Theological Seminary, he served as an assistant pastor under William Fincke at Greenwich Presbyterian Church in New York City.[8] Influenced by the preaching of John Haynes Holmes, he was a pacifist by 1917, claiming that "munitions manufacturers" and "great commercial interests" were behind the push for American involvement in Europe. He also condemned the Espionage Act and censorship, seeing the war as an unwelcome intrusion of state power into individual lives. "What bothers me most and gives me the deepest concern," he wrote, "is that our liberties seem to be going one by one." Like Holmes, he was a defiant absolutist, acknowledging that he took "a very extreme position," but insisting that "it is the only Christian position and I must hold to it no matter what comes." Their steadfastness soon cost Chaffee and Fincke their ministerial positions. Soon after losing his job, Chaffee ended up working for the American Red Cross in Palestine.[9]

Like so many of the pacifists, Chaffee formed his social views based in part on experience outside his home country. During his time with the Red Cross, he managed an orphanage in Jerusalem, which he found to be a cosmopolitan center containing "practically all races, all sorts and conditions of men." One day a Russian Jewish colleague took Chaffee to a dinner party, where the latter was astounded to find that "at the table there were seven different languages continuously spoken. . . . I think it was the most interesting table at which I ever sat."[10] Until his sudden death in 1936 Chaffee would attempt to recreate the table in Jerusalem, where diverse people met on a plane of equality and mutual respect. Perhaps no other experience could have prepared him so well for the linguistic and human diversity of New York's Lower East Side.

Back in America, Chaffee dedicated himself to promoting dialogue as the director of Labor Temple, a Social Gospel project of the Presbyterian Church. Charles Stelzle, a machinist-turned-evangelist, had founded Labor Temple as a way to bring together church people and representatives of the labor movement. In its early years, Labor Temple provided poor relief, religious services, and entertainment for the residents in its

FIGURE 2.1
Edmund Chaffee, director
of the New York City Labor
Temple, 1920s. (Edmund
B. Chaffee Papers, Special
Collections Research Center,
Syracuse University Library.)

working-class neighborhood. The institution also gave more direct assistance to the labor movement; in 1919 it had provided housing for workers' children during the tense days of the Lawrence textile strike.

Dialogue, though, was perhaps the most important purpose of Labor Temple. Open forums and adult education programs brought together people of various beliefs and backgrounds, and Stelzle welcomed all kinds of social and political radicals. In the winter of 1914–15, he held a "free-for-all discussion" with the Industrial Workers of the World to debate their practice of invading churches during the week to use for shelter. Even before Chaffee's tenure, pacifism was one of the diverse political positions that found support at Labor Temple. A 1915 antiwar speech there by Jessie Wallace Hughan led to the formation of the Anti-Enlistment League, a short-lived group that opposed conscription. Stelzle, and Chaffee after him, sought to prove that Christian people could engage in honest discussion of controversial issues, that religion was more than a cover for class interests.[11]

From the time he became director in 1921, Chaffee defended the idea of free and open debate against critics right and left. "Free speech is valuable," he insisted, "because it does away with much violence."[12] Still, his Presbyterian sponsors often questioned the appearance of radical speakers on Labor Temple programs. Henry Sloane Coffin, a Labor Temple founder, leading Presbyterian minister, and later president of Union Theological Seminary, generally supported Chaffee's work, but even he had his limits. In one incident, he complained about an appearance by V. F. Calverton, the editor of the radical journal *Modern Quarterly*. Calverton promoted a wide range of political and cultural nonconformity, but his unconventional ideas about sex irritated Coffin the most. "We do not want anyone who is not sound on so fundamental a principle as monogamy giving public lectures under the auspices of the Church," he fumed. On another occasion, Coffin objected to a speech by John Haynes Holmes at a Labor Temple dinner: "Holmes is not a man who commends himself to the good judgement of any of us. I do not think that we have any occasion to provide him with an extra opportunity to speak." Coffin posited that any ministers appearing under the auspices of Labor Temple should represent "evangelical Christianity," so Holmes's position on the left wing of Unitarianism made him suspect. Chaffee's responses are apparently not preserved, but religious and secular radicals continued to appear at his forums.[13]

Conservatives were also part of the spectrum of Labor Temple debate. In 1925, Chaffee fielded a complaint from Blanche Watson, a pacifist and early American promoter of Gandhi's ideas, regarding a Labor Temple speech by the notorious Lothrop Stoddard. Stoddard had gained fame as a racial theorist with the publication of his 1920 work *The Rising Tide of Color against White World Supremacy*. As its title suggests, the book described with alarm the prospect of a global conflagration that would obliterate the "white race." In his response to Watson, Chaffee maintained that "while I, like you, disagree fundamentally with Mr. Stoddard, yet I think we are obligated to give him a hearing. A platform which is open only to Radicals and Liberals," he argued, "is not really a free platform, it must be open to Conservatives and Reactionaries also." Chaffee went on to list the many antiracist speakers that he had invited. If free speech was going to prevent violence, one could not rig the game.[14]

Nonetheless, Chaffee did countenance some restrictions. Free expression was, for him, an act of putting forth one's views on political and social issues, not a license to pursue unconventional aesthetic or cultural paths. This distinction came through in his complaints about a restaurant that opened next door to Labor Temple. Some of his issues were practical—an awning blocked part of the Labor Temple entrance, for instance. Yet Chaffee also balked at the dancing and drinking that went on at the establishment, as well as the pictures inside and out. These were, "unless you are a futurist, rather objectionable. In one case at least they border on the immoral," he grumbled. He was willing to turn Labor Temple into a kind of bazaar of diverse ideas, no matter how far outside the mainstream, but he remained deeply suspicious of the popular culture and modernist aesthetics of the Jazz Age.[15]

Furthermore, while Labor Temple offered a vibrant space for open debate and intellectual exchange, it did not really solve the problem of propaganda. The attitude of Chaffee and the FOR leaders toward that problem had a double edge. They were horrified by the distortion and manipulation of language during the war, but they were also impressed by the power of the technique. Propaganda had prompted millions of people to support a war that was, in the pacifists' view, neither morally defensible by its participants nor materially beneficial to them. Surely mass persuasion could also be a tremendous force for good. At Labor Temple, Chaffee worked as an arbiter, a referee enforcing the rules of intellectual engagement. But because the pacifists also wanted to act, their developing approach to human communication took on another dimension.

Speech became not only the antidote to violence, but also a substitute for armed combat, a benign way of exercising power in the world. Chaffee himself encouraged this more active role in a talk entitled "Ethics and Propaganda." Could propaganda, he asked, ever be justified? He condemned outright lies and deceptions, as well as truthful propaganda by persons "merely interested in their own advantage" or by those who "bull doze, or overawe or violate the personality of another." Yet propaganda was acceptable, he concluded, if it was "motivated by honest desire to help one's fellows and . . . conducted with scrupulous regard for the truth and in the spirit of respect for others." That use of language, Chaffee argued, was in fact a "positive duty" and had produced "many of the greatest advances in the welfare of men." Labor Temple itself, Chaffee wrote later, was "a propagandist institution." This was true "not in the sense of trying to make Presbyterians or even Christians in the theological meaning of the word." Rather, Labor Temple sought to convince individuals to emulate Jesus and worked to "change our social order into the Kingdom of God." The committed pacifist, then, could be more than a referee.[16]

The idea that words could stand in for weapons occasionally came through quite explicitly. In 1922, FOR leader John Nevin Sayre published in the *World Tomorrow,* the Fellowship's unofficial journal, a hypothetical program of nonviolent resistance to foreign invasion. Citing the tremendous influence of war propaganda, he suggested that a conquered nation could effectively employ "an unarmed propaganda of truth." Sounding rather like George Creel, Sayre described "a great publicity campaign" by the occupied country, complete with "newspapers, magazines, pamphlets, parades and demonstrations by pickets"—in short, "all the resources of logic, psychology, advertisement and the dramatic art." The battle could even be carried to the enemy, using airplanes to drop messages on the homes of the hostile invader. However fantastic, the "propaganda of truth" was an early attempt to envision the kind of nonviolent spectacles that had so intrigued Edward Ross.[17]

Sherwood Eddy and Kirby Page came the closest to enacting Sayre's vision of a "propaganda of truth" in this early period. They were not citizens of a conquered nation (which probably worked to their advantage), but they did want to effect a political and social transformation. Many called their work "social evangelism," a combination of religious apologetics and worldly critique, primarily concerning war, capitalism, and racism. Page had considered joining relief efforts after the war, but decided that he needed to do the more "fundamental work" of building support for a new social and international order.[18] Eddy came to similar conclusions. Even before he embraced absolute pacifism in the early 1920s, he felt a call to promote "the social principles of Jesus applied to our American life." Eddy's new project angered conservatives in the Young Men's Christian Association and led Elbert Gary, head of the United States Steel Corporation, to threaten a boycott of the organization by business leaders. However, John Mott, never a radical but always broad-minded, defended Eddy and urged him to stay in the Y. He did, and became a force on the organization's left wing. Together, Eddy and Page spread a Christian nonviolent gospel that was distinctive less for its intellectual or theological content than for its novel uses of mass communication.[19]

Public speaking was still one of the most important forms of mass communication in the 1920s. Page's oratorical gifts had been clear as early as his college days at Drake, when he was chosen Junior Class

speaker. After the war, he maintained a relentless schedule of engagements, once boasting to his wife that he had given seventy-five addresses
in thirty days, "an all-time record for me." Page's strenuous speechmak-
ing recalled nothing so much as his earlier devotion to vigorous Christian
athleticism during the war.[20]

Eddy, too, possessed an uncommon talent and energy. He already
had a long career as an orator, stretching back to his missionary years in
Asia, but now he turned his attention increasingly to American college
students. Though he was in his fifties, his grueling tours made him a minor campus celebrity. His meetings went on for days, with attendance at
a single hours-long session frequently exceeding one thousand students.
An American Legion official who wanted to prevent an Eddy campaign
in Fayetteville, North Carolina, explained that pressure had to be applied
quietly. "It is best not to attempt to put over any public propaganda against
Mr. Eddy," he observed, "for there is nothing better in the world to in-
sure a packed house."[21] The period between the Great War and the Great
Depression supposedly saw the consolidation of a hegemonic consumer
culture that exalted hedonism, material goods, and instant gratification,
particularly among young people, but Eddy's college work revealed a persistent interest in religion, morality, and social reform.[22] He wrote after a
meeting at Northwestern University that students' opposition to war was
"gaining headway as truly as the Abolitionist Movement against slavery
did a generation ago in these same colleges."[23]

Eddy's programs blended religious and social issues, as shown by his
report of a meeting at Southern Methodist University. He found, as did
most of his associates in the North, that the South was "very backward in
both social and theological problems and unbelievably prejudiced on the
race problem." He decided that he needed to do some "plain speaking,"
so he "opened the lectures with a two hours battering at the solar plexus"
by asking his audience a series of questions; here again language became
a surrogate for violence. The subject matter of Eddy's queries ranged
from the existence of God and the authority of the Bible to "the 'open
shop' drive" and the Ku Klux Klan. "The college," he recounted, "was boil-
ing with interest." One day he talked for almost seven hours. At the final
session, almost every student present "publicly accepted Christ," while
Eddy also noted with pride that groups had been organized "for the study
of industry, the negro problem, and the Bible."[24]

Such a list seems jarring in its juxtaposition of evangelical Christianity
and left-leaning social concerns, but the Christian pacifists did not sepa-

FIGURE 2.2
Sherwood Eddy, ca. 1934.
(George Sherwood Eddy
Papers, Special Collections,
Yale Divinity School Library.)

rate personal religious commitment from liberal and even radical politics. In a meeting at the University of Missouri, Eddy gave a talk to two
thousand students on "campus problems—cribbing, cheating . . . , lying,
betting, gambling, drinking, indifference, and impurity in all its forms."
Then, later, he denounced the city of Columbia, where the university was
located, for a recent lynching (this turned the atmosphere "very tense," he
noted).[25] Eddy called his message the "whole gospel," an appellation intended to encompass both the "individual gospel" and the "social gospel."
He took on lying and lynching with the same relentless determination.

The explosion of radio into American lives offered new opportunities
to extend the pacifists' "social evangelism." Before the consolidation of
the medium in the 1930s, small, specialized stations offered ready forums. Chaffee, Holmes, Page, and their colleagues often appeared on
the progressive New York station WEVD (the call letters were a tribute
to Eugene Victor Debs) and occasionally on more mainstream stations

FIGURE 2.3
Kirby Page. (Disciples of
Christ Historical Society,
Nashville, Tennessee.)

as well. Chaffee read from Walter Rauschenbusch's book of Social Gospel prayers on the air, while Page participated in debates on Gandhi and disarmament.[26]

The Christian pacifist vanguard also tried to create a "propaganda of truth" in written form. Here they participated in another media revolution: the vast expansion of bookselling, book reading, and book reviewing during the interwar period. Publishers and public-minded intellectuals sought to create a "middlebrow culture" that would democratize knowledge by bringing it to a broad audience, a phenomenon exemplified by the founding of the Book-of-the-Month Club in 1926. The Fellowship of Reconciliation circle was deeply enmeshed in this new print culture. Will Durant, whose bestselling *The Story of Philosophy* became the paradigmatic middlebrow text, taught at Labor Temple School from 1913 to 1921, then worked as the school's director until 1927, when his book sales allowed him to become a full-time author. *The Story of Philosophy* was based partly on Durant's Labor Temple lectures, revealing the richness of the intellectual life that Chaffee created there.[27]

Eddy and Page benefited from the growth of specifically religious publishing. In the 1920s major commercial presses established religion departments for the first time. In 1927 a Religious Book Club was founded on the model of the Book-of-the-Month Club, and it frequently chose books by prominent Christian pacifists. Fellowship authors appealed to publishers because they tended to downplay arcane theological disputes, providing instead accessible accounts of Christianity's relationship to pressing social, economic, and political questions. Eddy and Page wrote with a broad audience in mind. For instance, Page thought that the readers of his 1922 "discussion group text-book" *Christianity and Economic Problems* would be "primarily . . . college students and church members of the so-called middle class." Between the wars, he and Eddy wrote or coauthored about thirty books and numerous pamphlets dealing with religion, international affairs, economic reform, and racial justice.[28]

Through their writing, Eddy and Page sought to create new communities of readers and reformers. The authors assumed that their works would be discussed and argued over by groups of engaged citizens, not simply pondered in isolation. So, like other middlebrow texts, books by Eddy and Page contained outlines, bibliographies, and study questions for book clubs. Furthermore, the FOR was organized into local "Fellowship groups" that were conducive to such interactions. Against the specter of propaganda, and against Lippmann's despair over the possibilities of democratic citizenship, the pacifists put forth their books as tools that might enable thoughtful deliberation and practical action.[29]

The Fellowship circle remained suspicious of the literary marketplace, though, for the war had shown the fickleness of public taste. Page had tried in 1917 to publish an antiwar manuscript called "The Sword or the Cross," an expanded version of the essay he had shared with his YMCA colleagues. Publishers rejected it because, as one put it, "times are not normal, and we fear the general statement would be misunderstood." When he had finally raised money to have the book printed in 1921, it had sold miserably.[30] So two years later he took a more aggressive role after the publication of *War: Its Causes, Consequences, and Cure* (written "primarily for middle class intellectuals"). He obtained from some wealthy members of the FOR a fund of several thousand dollars to send the book out to ministers, YMCA and YWCA secretaries, libraries, teachers, and editors. He also sent two thousand copies to James Maurer, the head of the Pennsylvania Federation of Labor who worked closely with A. J. Muste at Brookwood Labor College. Of the first edition of one hundred thousand copies of *War,* Page estimated that between "ten and fifteen thousand copies have actually been sold," the rest having been distributed free of charge. In the back of a later pamphlet edition, Page invited readers to "cooperate by sending copies to your friends—by the dozen or by the thousand." Through Page's alternative distribution system, his books and pamphlets flooded the nation's churches, colleges, union halls, and reform organizations.[31]

Just as Page doubted the effectiveness of the marketplace, he also showed a fundamental distrust of the deceptive possibilities of language. His books were heavily derivative of other, more specialized writing, often employing lengthy direct quotation, as if trying to present facts unvarnished by interpretation. One reader described Page, not unsympathetically, as less a writer than a "creative editor," while another noted his "splendid massing of facts." Page defended his method: acknowledging the "irritating effects of endless quotations," he thought that "first-hand testimonies" and "the conclusions of specialists" would be more convincing than "my personal opinions." He considered his books not as bold intellectual statements but as manuals for practical use. The endless streams of data and quotes were there because the average teacher or minister "does not have easy access to relevant sources, or lacks time to make the required research," a consideration easy to forget in the era of the Google search.[32] Page's books did, in fact, become useful reference sources for at least some readers. *Moral Man and Immoral Society,* Reinhold Niebuhr's incisive 1932 critique of pacifism, used several quotations from politicians and intellectuals that Niebuhr found in Page's book *National Defense.* The intellectual ferment within the FOR in the 1930s relied on the print culture that Eddy and Page created.[33]

Furthermore, Page and Eddy were effective in their own time, at least in pacifist circles. A 1927 survey of FOR members showed that Page's books had influenced them more than any others. Page beat out his mentor Sherwood Eddy, who finished third in the poll; the Bible came in second. Page's audiences at least occasionally saw him both as a producer of middlebrow literature and as part of a tradition of popular political writing. Discussing *National Defense,* one reader wrote that he had done "a 'Will Durant' with a very dry subject," while another suggested that "the book might have much the same relation to world peace, That 'Unkle [*sic*]

FIGURE 2.4   Cartoon by Winsor McCay, *New York American*, June 5, 1931. In this critique of religious politics, Uncle Sam admonishes "Clerical Pacifists" to stop undermining "National Defense" and get back to church. (General Research Division, The New York Public Library, Astor, Lenox, and Tilden Foundations.)

Tom's Cabin' did to the abolition of slavery."[34] Page and Eddy moved their radical Christian critique into the mainstream of American political discourse. Page had been unable to recall a single discussion of religious pacifism during his college years, but now it was increasingly unlikely that any politically engaged collegian could have avoided the subject. The pacifist position never won over more than a small minority of college students, though during the 1920s hundreds did pledge to oppose all wars at conferences of Christian groups such as the Student Volunteer Movement.[35] In the wider culture, though Christian nonviolence did not garner anything like a mass following, it gained a legitimate place in the ecology of American dissent.

Some observers thought that the "propaganda of truth" was more propaganda than truth. Sherwood Eddy's brother Brewer, a prominent liberal Protestant, was one of his most persistent critics. In part, Brewer's arguments reflected the fact that he was simply more conservative than Sherwood, particularly on economic questions. If Jesus preached today, Brewer contended, his message would not "be subversive to law, nor would [it] necessarily break with the earnest minded employers and leaders of our communities." More fundamentally, Brewer's criticisms suggested that the Christian gospel was simply untranslatable into the language of any political project. He charged that by preaching absolute pacifism and far-reaching economic reform Sherwood had become "a committed champion to a minority cult rather than a broad and balanced Christian, seeing wrongs and rights on both sides."[36] Page received similar chiding from his old YMCA friends. Wasn't it true, one asked, "since you have been giving so much time to social, economic and political questions, that you have fallen back into a less vital ministry than you have once known?" The suspicion that political activism was only a poor substitute for the true religious life haunted the pacifists. Page's friend Henry P. Van Dusen suggested that perhaps he was "tending to look at the people you are with in a more impersonal and objective way," losing "that intense personal interest in each man and woman . . . which you *must* have had when you were doing such powerful personal evangelism." A 1931 cartoon in a New York newspaper promoted a similar idea by its depiction of Uncle Sam admonishing a "Clerical Pacifist" to stop meddling in politics and get back to church.[37]

From a different quarter, other critics wondered why Page and Eddy needed Christian faith at all. In a 1929 book entitled *The Twilight of Christianity,* the pacifist historian Harry Elmer Barnes lauded the Christian radicals' attention to social and economic problems, but expressed frustration with their continuing allegiance to Jesus. Kirby Page, Barnes complained, insisted upon tying his peace program to "scanty and perhaps non-authentic passages from the hypothetical teachings of an obscure Palestinian peasant who had never witnessed or read of a first-class war," when in fact "Mr. Page himself is an infinitely better informed and more trustworthy guide to religious reconstruction than Jesus and all the Old Testament prophets combined." Sherwood Eddy was also an experienced and knowledgeable reformer, so "his own views on modern social and economic conditions," Barnes thought, "should command infinitely more respect than those of Jesus, who lived a very restrained and provincial existence in a distinctly backward economy." Their religious and secular critics raised essential questions for the pacifists: was there any such thing as a Christian politics? If so, what would it look like?[38]

For the Fellowship circle, a Christian social order began with virtuous individuals. While the example of Jesus taught pacifism, antiracism, and economic redistribution, it also modeled a strict code of personal integrity. A few secular pacifists in the FOR, such as Devere Allen, apparently got away with mere tolerance of the Christian religion, but even they tended to conform to this culture of moral uprightness.[39] The alcohol taboo, though not observed by all members, was particularly striking. John Haynes Holmes, a stalwart Prohibitionist, boasted that he would "never under any circumstances allow a drop of alcohol to pass my lips," while A. J. Muste noted late in life that he had "never been drunk." This unyielding moral seriousness extended to every aspect of the pacifists' personal lives, for they believed that only individual virtue could produce a Christian society. "No social system," Edmund Chaffee declared, "can dispense with the ordinary virtues of honesty, fair-dealing, persistent work and good will. They are not as frequently said, 'bourgeois virtues.'"[40] That contention separated Christian nonviolence from two other positions on the left. The first was the cultural radicalism associated with Greenwich Village, which denounced the stuffy "bourgeois virtues" as obstacles to modern fulfillment.[41] The second, sometimes overlapping position was Marxism, which saw emphasis on individual rectitude as an ideological cover for class power.

Christian nonviolence departed from bohemians and Marxists, too, in its valorization of the family. If the individual was the building block of the moral revolution, the family was its most important structure, representing in miniature the ideal human community. "The religion of Jesus," Kirby Page believed, "can best be described in terms of the home: God is Father, men are brothers, all life is a domestic affair." Reinhold Niebuhr, a pacifist during the twenties, thought that "the family relation" was "the most ethical relation men know."[42] Unlike some other American radicals at this time, the pacifists refused to label the family an inherently reactionary or oppressive institution. "The family virtues ought *never* to be abandoned," Page warned. Those virtues included "sympathy, kindliness, love, forbearance, patience, forgiveness and sacrifice."[43]

The family served the FOR rhetorically as the site of actually existing nonviolence. The pacifists described the domestic sphere as the leading edge of an unprecedented modern transformation in social relations. Here, Holmes declared, "pacifism has won its victory." He noted the increasing unpopularity of corporal punishment by parents; it was merely "a resort of desperation on the part of those who know no better way." He claimed, furthermore, that the history of marriage showed a decreasing reliance on the physical prowess of the male and an increasing role for the "compulsion of love," making the successful modern marriage "a purely pacifist institution." The common view among the leaders of the Fellowship was that the problems of gender inequality had been solved, or soon would be.[44]

Beyond the home, the experience of women in the public sphere held keys to the larger triumph of pacifism. "Woman," John Nevin Sayre pointed out, "has attained to her present status of comparative freedom and equality, through something entirely other than the resort to armed force." Similarly, Norman Thomas, writing in 1921, thought that the recent suffrage victory had revealed a new "contribution to political technic." Because "war between the sexes would be unthinkable," suffragists in England and America had used picketing, hunger strikes, and other nonviolent means to dramatize their convictions. "Public sentiment . . . did not enjoy the spectacle of women in jail for no greater offense than advertising their sentiments on banners," Thomas noted. To a remarkable degree, the men who led the FOR sought alternatives to war in the experiences of women. One writer to the *World Tomorrow* perceived these gendered implications of pacifist doctrine. "Your magazine," he scoffed, "belongs in the class with Lydia Pinkham's Vegetable Compound—for women and girls only."[45]

The appreciation of feminine power, however, occurred in a setting largely devoid of public female authority. Leading women pacifists, such as Jane Addams and Dorothy Detzer, were members of the Fellowship, but they gave most of their energies to the Women's International League for Peace and Freedom, another organization born in the crucible of the Great War that focused specifically on national lobbying efforts.[46] The FOR leadership remained almost exclusively male, and surviving evidence suggests that Grace Hutchins, the sole woman to ascend to the top position of Executive Secretary during the organization's first forty years, may have found its clerical culture at least occasionally inhospitable. A few years before leaving the Fellowship for the Communist Party, she observed in a *World Tomorrow* article that "some of the most radical men who accept woman's equality as a fundamental principle are yet the most dominating in relation to women in daily life." To be sure, wives of FOR leaders often endured lives of financial difficulty, frequent moves, and de facto single parenthood, even as some of them made crucial contributions to the pacifist project behind the scenes. While Fellowship secretary Howard Kester traveled around the South promoting pacifism and racial equality, his wife, Alice, did "all of the organizational stuff . . . all of the writing, the planning and so forth," the couple's daughter Nancy remembered. For a time, Alice even earned money for the household by working at Gimbels department store in New York City. Holmes, looking back on his life in 1959, was "appalled" by his lack of attention to his family. He had retained "antiquated notions" about the place of women, allowing his wife to bear unfair domestic burdens while he furthered his public career. The promotion of the ideal family, then, may have allayed personal feelings of guilt about actual wives and children.[47]

At a broader level, the pacifists' interpretive history of gender relations depended upon some strategic omissions. If the rise of companionate marriage was a "victory" for nonviolence, as Holmes claimed, it was also a victory for the secular sex radicals who had championed that domestic model far more assiduously than had Christian pacifists. The FOR leaders were male feminists by the standards of the time. When Holmes's Community Church and Chaffee's Labor Temple opened their doors to the famous birth control advocates Abraham and Hannah Stone in the early 1930s, those institutions put themselves at the leading edge of progressive religious thinking about gender and sexuality. However, the pacifists had no taste for the radical critique of marriage that animated Emma Goldman or the young Margaret Sanger. "The free lover . . . ," Holmes once preached, "becomes a moral anarchist." The FOR circle echoed the feminist demands for women's equality and independence, but rejected the more fundamental challenges to Christianity and the "family virtues" that those demands encompassed.[48]

This subterranean cultural conservatism also shaped the pacifists' attempts at bridging racial divides, as shown in the treatment of two African American staff members at the World Tomorrow, Egbert Ethelred Brown and Wallace Thurman. In 1926, the editors proudly proclaimed that theirs "was the first journal published by white people to come out fairly and squarely on equal opportunity for Negroes in all relationships of life," an assertion that revealed both the World Tomorrow's place in the political vanguard and the racial makeup of its leadership. Some African Americans did in fact work for the publication. The periodical office was a familylike "office coöperative" that "refused to accept office conventions peculiar to the present social order." As part of this new bureaucratic model, the World Tomorrow "mingled Negro and white on an equal basis."[49]

The journal, while never wealthy, occasionally hired assorted reformers and radicals even more desperate for cash. Ethelred Brown fit this category, working for the journal from 1929 until it folded in 1934. He was an immigrant from Jamaica and one of the first black Unitarian leaders in America, founding the Harlem Community Church in 1920. The institution was named after John Haynes Holmes's Community Church, and Holmes became one of Brown's most important supporters in the otherwise ambivalent Unitarian establishment. Though details are scarce, Brown's stay at the *World Tomorrow* seems to have been agreeable to all sides. "I almost forgot that I was a Negro living in America," he wrote upon his departure, "so cordial was the treatment I received."[50] His tenure suggested to the pacifists that the cooperative ethic of a homogeneous family could also apply to more diverse groups.

Wallace Thurman, one of Brown's predecessors, had found less success. Thurman, most famous for his play *Harlem* and his novel *The Blacker the Berry*, was part of the cohort of young Harlem Renaissance artists that included Zora Neale Hurston and Langston Hughes. He worked on the *World Tomorrow* office staff until 1927, when chief editors Devere Allen and Kirby Page fired him. Thurman frequently came late to work, Allen explained to Grace Hutchins, and spent "literally *hours*" during the day editing *Fire!!*, a short-lived black avant-garde journal (*Fire!!* would later be considered a seminal cultural production of the Harlem Renaissance). The staff, Allen went on, had gone to extremes to help him, even lending him money. In response, the supposedly destitute Thurman "gave a somewhat costly party to a bunch of friends up in Harlem, in the grand Greenwich Village–Harlem style." As Allen saw it, his disorganization and irresponsibility ended his career at the *World Tomorrow*.[51]

Given Thurman's general reputation for hard drinking and decadent living, Allen's account of the debacle sounds credible. Yet the editor's frustrations also reveal the Fellowship's pervasive suspicion of modernist culture in the "grand Greenwich Village–Harlem style." Thurman himself recognized this aspect of his predicament, telling Langston Hughes shortly before his dismissal that "electric sparks are in the air." Kirby Page, he wrote, was "certain that I am a lewd young thing given to lewd thoughts." A *World Tomorrow* secretary had told Page that Thurman "was carrying all the girls in the office out to Harlem cabaret parties and up to my room."[52] Though the revelry may have been exaggerated, Wallace Thurman clearly posed some challenges to the "family virtues," so the pacifists kept their distance despite their commitment to racial equality. In the cases of Brown and Thurman, the white pacifists in the FOR were willing to cross the boundary of race, but only if they did not also have to transgress their cultural and religious norms.

The Christian pacifists became less surefooted as they moved outward to larger spheres of human organization. They were convinced of the primacy of individual virtue and confident of the cosmic righteousness of the family unit. The creation of "fellowship" in complex economic and political structures proved more difficult. FOR leaders agreed that current systems of business and government depended upon violence, but from that point of departure they took different paths. The rough consensus that characterized pacifist thinking about individuals and families fragmented into a kaleidoscope of approaches to the problems of capitalism and war. All agreed, though, that nonviolence was a wholly modern response to modern political and economic problems, not an escape from those problems.[53]

The twenties was not an ideal time to begin a moral revolution in economic life. For the first time in American history, the dominance of corporate capitalism looked unassailable, and dissenters were in retreat. The Red Scare of 1919 decimated American radicalism, setting a pattern for the rest of the decade. The Socialist Party never again matched its impressive showing in the 1912 presidential election, while the Communist Party was still minuscule in numbers and influence. Throughout the 1920s, dubbed "the lean years" by one labor historian, unions lost significant ground, victimized by employers' repression of organizing efforts and technological changes that decreased workers' control over the conditions of their labor. The labor movement also struggled with racial and ethnic divisions as new black and immigrant workers confounded established union leadership.[54] The FOR condemned antilabor practices from the beginning. One of Kirby Page's first major published articles, in 1922, was a critical analysis of the policies of the United States Steel Corporation.[55] Judge Gary was an easy target, given his avowed conservatism and antipathy to unions. The pacifists were less sure about the ethical alternatives to corporate capitalism. What kind of economic community would uphold Christian values?

One answer was to rely on the goodwill of business owners themselves. The Fellowship's favorite capitalist was Harold Hatch, owner of the Dutchess Bleachery in Wappinger Falls, New York. Hatch, a devoted FOR member, was one of a few unconventional employers in the 1920s who attempted a top-down democratization of industry, beginning with their own companies. Like William Hapgood's Columbia Conserve Company, John J. Eagan's American Cast Iron Pipe Company, and Arthur "Golden Rule" Nash's Cincinnati textile factory, Hatch's bleachery was an experiment with a different kind of labor-management relationship. Unlike most "welfare capitalist" schemes of the 1920s, the Dutchess Bleachery offered real authority to the unskilled workers, many of them immigrants, who made up the majority of its labor force. Under the "Partnership Plan," as Hatch's system was called, employees gained significant power to determine company policy, establishing insurance and disability funds, profit sharing, vacations, a playground, and evening classes. Hatch had apparently solved the problem of the new industrial workplace by privileging cooperation over conflict; the Dutchess Bleachery looked like nothing less than a business of "family virtues."[56]

Hatch was a crucial figure in the Fellowship of Reconciliation for two reasons. First, he was an essential source of funds in an organization that had chronic trouble with finances. Kirby Page depended on his largess to send out all those free copies of *War: Its Causes, Consequences, and Cure.*[57] Second, Hatch filled an important position in the pacifists' social matrix. He was the virtuous capitalist, his presence affirming the group's aspirations to universality. With Hatch, the FOR was a true *fellowship* that transcended class division, incorporating capitalists and workers into one harmonious whole.

His example proved difficult to emulate, though. Representatives at a 1925 conference of the Fellowship for a Christian Social Order (a group closely tied to the FOR) voiced their skepticism, admitting the success of "experiments" like Hatch's as "local ventures" but worrying that they were "merely idealistic oases without power to spread."[58] Most pacifists, while supportive of Hatch's cooperative capitalism, placed more of their energies into the labor movement. The two were not always at odds. Hatch did not oppose unions and was in fact a financial supporter of A. J. Muste's Brookwood Labor College, one of the Fellowship's most successful projects.

At Brookwood, Muste pinned his hopes on the agency of workers rather than on that of capitalists. Brookwood had begun after the war as a progressive community school near Katonah in upstate New York, with Edmund Chaffee's old copastor William Fincke and his wife, Helen, serving as directors. In 1921, the leaders of the school changed it into a residential labor college that would educate adult workers and train them for union leadership, turning to Muste to lead the new venture. Brookwood was part of a new adult education movement that produced experiments ranging from New York City's liberal New School for Social Research in 1919 to the Carnegie-funded American Association for Adult Education in 1926. Well to the political left of those institutions, Muste's college became one of the most important sites of cooperation between organized labor, pacifism, and progressive intellectuals during the 1920s.[59]

Brookwood Labor College tried to set a pattern for a new kind of labor movement that was at once a new kind of human community. Students at the college interacted on the model of the ideal family, performing cooperative labor, eating meals in the common dining room, and sharing in leisure activities. The school aspired to gender and racial equity, advertising "an absolute equality of opportunity and responsibility as between the sexes" and admitting African Americans along with immigrants from Europe, Asia, and Latin America. The school also embraced ideological diversity, welcoming Communists and Socialists alongside a wide array of other labor radicals. At one May Day celebration, students hoisted pictures of American Federation of Labor leader Samuel Gompers, Eugene Debs, Karl Marx, and Vladimir Lenin. "The composition of the student body being what it was," Muste recalled, "some of them were as irked by having Gompers' picture on the wall as others were by Lenin's," but the "catholicity" of Brookwood's culture required a full range of labor heroes to be represented. Muste's inclusiveness looked forward to the strategies of the Congress of Industrial Organizations, where several Brookwood graduates eventually landed.[60]

"Save for the fact that it stands for a new and better order, motivated by social values rather than pecuniary ones, Brookwood is not a propagandist institution," the college's brochure read. "It seeks the truth, free from dogma and doctrinaire teaching." At the same time that Sayre, Chaffee, Eddy, and Page were forging their own "propaganda of truth," Muste's college, too, combined open dialogue with political purpose. Brookwood challenged conventional educational institutions by providing classes on the history and politics of the working class, taught by teachers with experience in the labor movement. At the same time, the college sought to transcend the exclusiveness and factionalism that had crippled so many organizing efforts. In a period when unions frequently excluded black workers, Muste convened a 1927 "Symposium on the Negro in Industry" that featured E. Franklin Frazier, A. Philip Randolph, and other black and white intellectuals and labor leaders.[61]

Brookwood also tried to connect worker and antiwar causes, though its primary focus was always the former. Peace conferences at the college brought famous speakers ranging from the civil libertarian Roger Baldwin to the pluralist philosopher Horace Kallen to the Catholic reformer

John A. Ryan. At Labor Temple and other venues, the Brookwood traveling theater troupe performed antiwar plays such as "Peace Is No Job of
Ours," an indictment of the munitions industry. Here, on a very small
scale, was a deliberate attempt to make a performative "spectacle" of nonviolent "principle."[62]

The capaciousness of Brookwood was in part a product of Muste's own
personality. Len De Caux, a student at the college in the 1920s, remembered him as "essentially the moderate." Displaying the radical Christian pacifist preference for dialogue over dogma, he "always looked for
the center with his 'On the one hand. . . . But on the other hand. . . .'"
Muste was not a "moderate" in the conventional political sense of being
halfway between conservatism and liberalism. Rather, he sought common ground on the left where diverse kinds of radicals could unite. In his
Brookwood years, Muste was less committed to organized Christianity
than were most other Fellowship leaders, and his secular orientation may
have helped his mediation efforts. Nonetheless, more explicitly religious
pacifists could support Brookwood's inclusive outlook as both a sign of
human unity and a shrewd political tactic.[63]

Not everyone was convinced. For all its diversity, Brookwood was in
the end dedicated to promoting the labor movement, sharing with other
Christian pacifist projects a suspicion of beauty and pleasure for their
own sakes. Sarah Cleghorn, a pacifist poet who taught literature and composition, reluctantly resigned from Brookwood when she found her teaching philosophy at odds with the prevailing ideological climate there. The
workers at the school, she remembered, were "Labor Puritans" seeking
a teacher "who in writing would help them turn out better editorials, appeals, résumés of Labor history, controversial writings; who could assist
them to contrive Labor dramatics, turn out humor and perhaps fiction,
but all with the one end." For her, the "propaganda of truth" could seem
little different from the usual variety.[64]

Another challenge to Muste's agenda came from his old colleague in
the Lawrence strike, Cedric Long. Long had abandoned union organizing and become a leader of the Cooperative League of America, where
he worked until his death in 1931. While Brookwood promoted the possibilities of a militant radical labor movement, Long preached the gospel of consumers' cooperation. The two alternatives clashed in the pages
of the *World Tomorrow*, where Long published "Can Capital and Labor
Get Together?" in September 1929. He feared that the "New Unionism"
preached by Muste and others would lead to a rapprochement between

employers and workers, as labor agreed to play by the rules of the profit system. "How define labor unionism?" Long asked. "Is not its beginning and in large part its very existence dependent upon capitalism itself?" The cooperative movement, by contrast, stood "strictly outside the capitalist economic order." Inspired by the famous Rochdale cooperative in nineteenth-century England, cooperatives allowed consumers to own the businesses that they patronized, creating an alternative economic system that was "harmless and mild-mannered" but that would gradually undermine the existing order.

Muste wrote back the next month, taking Long to task for overstating the significance of the cooperative movement. In his irenic way, he asserted that unions and cooperatives would stand or fall together. Still, Long highlighted a conundrum that had dogged the Christian pacifists since their radicalization during World War I. The labor movement became a test case for thinking about the complexities of violence and coercion in a modern, interdependent society. For some Fellowship leaders, such as Muste, participation in the movement was a kind of nonviolent action that sought to counteract the brutality of capitalism, but others saw labor as complicit in that brutality through rough-and-tumble union politics and through acquiescence in the "profit system." Those skeptics looked for other alternatives, such as Long's cooperatives. In the end, though, the approaches of Hatch, Muste, and Long, divergent as they were, relied on a common assumption: nonviolence had profound consequences for economic, not just political, life.[65]

Muste's efforts at Brookwood had real influence on the course of American industrial unionism. Ironically, the Fellowship leaders had far less effect on international relations in this period. Two ineffectual peace efforts bracket the 1920s: on one end, the Versailles Treaty and the formation of the League of Nations, and on the other the 1928 Kellogg-Briand pact, an agreement in which the United States and the major powers of Europe foreswore armed conflict. The pacifists in the Fellowship backed a variety of internationalist programs during this period. John Haynes Holmes promoted a legalist approach that would outlaw war and create a World Court to adjudicate disputes. Kirby Page and John Nevin Sayre, while acknowledging the weaknesses of the League of Nations, insisted that the United States should join it.[66]

The pacifists were ambivalent about these political measures, which may explain why they made few original contributions to them. The peace plans that they supported had usually been developed by politicians and lawyers who were primarily interested in international order, whether enforced by armies or not. Then, too, the FOR circle found many anti-war measures altogether too superficial. After the signing of the Kellogg-Briand treaty, Page complained that "the chief weakness of the peace forces is that they tend to concentrate too exclusively upon the attainment of current political measures, and usually fail to support a thoroughgoing process of education." The pacifists often fell into a double bind, unwilling to support merely formal antiwar statutes, but also unsure of how to enforce peace without resorting to armed coercion.[67]

Informed by their experiences during the Great War, these dissenters put more faith in the extreme actions of dedicated individuals than in the evolution of legal and political institutions. That was the model laid out by the founder of Christianity, they thought. Page noted that "Jesus lived in a turbulent world" defined by war and imperialism, yet he forsook violence and urged his followers to do the same. His way, Page insisted, "may lead to persecution and suffering and seeming defeat, but it alone leads to rec-onciliation and redemption and life." Even the more secular members of the Fellowship stressed the primacy of bold individual action in securing peace. Devere Allen, who saw Jesus more as an exemplary human than as the Son of God, contrasted proposals for international institutions with his own notion of war resistance. A critical mass of conscientious objec-tors, Allen thought, could produce something like the syndicalist general strike and render military action impossible. He juxtaposed the World Court to the more potent "court of conscience," and the outlawry of war to "those who have already risen to say in no uncertain tones, 'As for us, we have already outlawed war from this time on.'" Against Walter Lipp-mann's faith in experts, the Fellowship circle believed that the scourge of war would yield to the democratic actions of principled dissenters.[68]

To this end, the radical Christian pacifists tried to change Americans into conscientious objectors by molding the institutions of American cul-ture. John Nevin Sayre led a coalition of pacifist groups to form the Com-mittee on Militarism in Education in 1925. Its main project was protest-ing Reserve Officer Training Corps programs in American colleges, an effort that would become much more widespread in the 1960s. Emerging out of the preparedness movement that preceded American intervention in World War I, ROTC programs spread to over one hundred institutions of higher learning by 1919. At many schools military classes and training were compulsory, thereby bearing a disquieting resemblance to wartime conscription and leading Niebuhr to accuse ROTC of instilling in students the "conviction that war is natural and inevitable." Sayre, Niebuhr, and others urged students and university officials to oppose this militarization of civilian life because they thought that rebellious citizens had to act in accord with their individual consciences to prevent the next Great War in Europe.[69]

Many accounts of Christian nonviolence focus on that next European war, finding the pacifists ineffectual for not preventing it, naïve for believing it could be prevented, or, in a different vein, worthy of uncritical adoration for holding to their moral ideals in the face of national opprobrium. Such conclusions truncate the complexity of nonviolence into a narrow debate over World War II strategy. While the two world wars had overwhelming significance, European politics did not limit the FOR leaders' thinking about war. Notably, they linked military violence to racism in their own country and imperialism abroad. As the European-centered devastation of the two world wars becomes increasingly distant from contemporary circumstances, the non-Western aspects of the Christian nonviolent vision seem increasingly relevant.

The transnational perspective of the pacifists meant that they tended to see race in global rather than national terms. "The racial problem in the United States," wrote Sherwood Eddy and Kirby Page, "is two-fold in character: internal and external." The persecution of African Americans and immigrants from Europe and Japan, they thought, went together with "the increasing tension between the Orient and the Occident," a tension born of war and imperialism. Other commentators would expand the East-West dichotomy to include Africa and Latin America. Race became a central category in the radical Christian pacifists' political analysis because war and racial hatred so often went together. Even the Great War in Europe, with its ostensibly "white" combatants, had led Americans to racialize the German enemy as the savage Hun. Furthermore, racism thwarted the domestic model of religion that envisioned the whole world as a harmonious family. Jesus "treated men of every colour and tongue as sons of a common Father," Page explained, "and therefore brothers beloved."[70]

The "racial problem," for the Fellowship circle, was contiguous with the problem of violence. To help explain the scourge of "internal" racial violence, the radical Christian pacifists made one of their most audacious links between war and race. Despite their admiration for the antislavery cause, they maintained that the Civil War had been a tragic error. This position was somewhat disingenuous, requiring a careful selection of abolitionist heroes (favorites were William Lloyd Garrison, who never clearly supported the war, and Theodore Parker, who died the year before it began). The point, however, was that violence, once unleashed, would escape the control of even the most exemplary cause. The Civil War, ostensibly justified because it eliminated slavery, had led to the horror of the Jim Crow South. "The harm done by that war," explained Allen, "was to go on poisoning the life of the American people, black and white alike, for generations." The condemnation of the Civil War was a minor theme among the pacifists, and they could not always maintain clarity on the subject, indebted as their generation was to the myths of the heroic Union. Furthermore, the pacifist position was a form of self-defense, for nonpacifist liberals brought up the example over and over. "If the method which you propose . . . to use against war had been used against slavery," the sociologist Charles Ellwood complained to Kirby Page, "I fear that we would never have gotten rid of it."[71]

The renunciation of the Civil War was more than simply defensive, though. It also provided an impetus for the radical Christian pacifist crusade against racial violence and discrimination. Throughout the 1920s, the FOR condemned lynching, the resurgent Ku Klux Klan, and racial segregation with a vigor that few white reform organizations could match. Lynching was "the great American atrocity," John Haynes Holmes declared, perhaps implying a parallel with the German "atrocities" that had so incensed the nation several years earlier. For some African Americans, the antiracist aspect of the Fellowship's program proved more attractive than the group's pacifist stance. The black minister and educator Howard Thurman recalled that, when he joined the FOR as an undergraduate at Morehouse College in the early 1920s, he "had no particular interest in the peace movement per se." Rather, he felt that membership gave him "a sense of immunity to the assaults of the white world of Atlanta, Georgia." Thurman, who became one of the few prominent black leaders in the early FOR, looked toward the later work of James Farmer and Bayard Rustin with his emphasis on racial violence rather than international war.[72]

Turning to the "external" arena of racial conflict, radical Christian pacifists condemned the violence of Western imperialism. Here they were uniquely situated to take a global view, rather than a merely Euro-American one. Despite their disillusionment with John Mott and the YMCA, the pacifists still had strong connections to the transnational Protestant missionary network, a network concentrated outside Europe. FOR leaders received regular correspondence from missionaries around the world, particularly in India and China, while many pacifists worked in the foreign field themselves. Harold Gray went to China after his World War I ordeal. Edmund Chaffee's wife, Florence, had worked as a missionary in Syria, and the couple considered undertaking foreign mission work for years after Chaffee accepted his job at Labor Temple. The modern religion of these adventurers opened up diverse transnational vistas.[73]

The missionaries did more than provide firsthand interpretations of far-off lands, though that service was important. They also brought the Fellowship into another debate over the relationship of religion and violence. Before the Great War, the missionary enterprise carried on relatively untroubled by concerns about imperialism, but during the 1920s numerous critics came to interpret the conflict as a struggle for foreign colonies, sending Protestant missions into a period of intense self-criticism. "A missionary enterprise may be a kind of sublimated imperialism," Reinhold Niebuhr admitted in 1927. Furthermore, the missionary in past times had been "quite willing to permit the physical force, which the Christian nations had raised to an obsession, to offer him special protection." The pacifists in the Fellowship continued to believe in the value of missionary work; they did not see the propagation of Christianity, at least in its enlightened liberal form, as inherently imperialist. Still, they viewed military and economic domination as a violation of the all-important family ethic. "The races and groups of mankind are obviously not living as a family," Niebuhr noted, "but they ought to."[74] During this time the FOR consistently opposed armed intervention by the United States in Asia and urged the U.S. government to grant independence to the Philippines. Nonviolence, in the pacifists' view, had to be global in its reach.[75]

The Fellowship's most elaborate effort to fight American imperialism came in Nicaragua. The years misleadingly labeled the "interwar" period saw a substantial number of American military interventions, particularly in Central and South America. United States Marines maintained a presence in Nicaragua almost continuously from 1912 to 1933 as the United States tried to ensure political stability and protect its economic investments. After brokering a settlement that ended the nation's 1926–1927 civil war, the American government stepped up its military occupation, while also creating a native army, the Nicaraguan National Guard (Guardia Nacional de Nicaragua), to help maintain order. A maverick general named Augusto Sandino dissented from this settlement, inducing his followers (the original "Sandinistas" who would inspire the revolutionaries of 1979) to undertake guerrilla attacks on American troops and business interests.[76]

Predictably, the FOR denounced the 1927 U.S. occupation of Nicaragua. The organization sent letters to thousands of ministers asking them to oppose the campaign, while the FOR conference that year took "Imperialism" as its theme and brought a Nicaraguan representative to speak. This event led to an invitation from the Nicaraguan Federation of Labor to send a delegation south to the affected country itself. Late in 1927, Sayre, supported by Idaho Senator William Borah, decided to lead an "adventure for peace" to resolve the crisis. He took with him Elbert Russell, a Quaker professor of religion at Duke University; Carolena Wood, a representative of the American Friends Service Committee; and Robert Jones, a graduate student from Cuba. The trip would turn into something of a fiasco, but it marked an early attempt by radical pacifists to create a "propaganda of truth" by making a "principle" into a "spectacle."[77]

Sandino had become an important symbol for Communists and other groups on the left, but the Christian pacifists refused to make him into an anti-imperialist hero. After all, the general was hardly an exemplar of nonviolence. Nonetheless, the Sandinista uprising had shown the urgency of the anti-imperialist project. The effort to end international violence, Sayre insisted after the trip to Nicaragua, had to "do more than offer Europe outlawry of war treaties. Good as I believe they are, the crucial test is whether we can help the world get away from its present practise of exploitive imperialism." For Sayre, American relations with Latin America, as well as with Asia, held the seeds of future wars but also offered possibilities for "a new and constructive practise of friendship, cooperation, security and freedom." He left for Central America to offer the radical Christian pacifist gospel as an antidote to both imperialism and its violent opposition.[78]

The four members of the peace team wound their way with difficulty through Guatemala, El Salvador, Honduras, and, at last, Nicaragua. In El Salvador, Sayre and Wood had to be rescued after their boat hit an obstacle and began to sink. In Nicaragua, the group's automobile became stuck in a rut and had to be pulled free by a team of oxen. Then, on Christmas Day, a different car broke an axle, forcing the adventurers to hitch a ride fifteen miles to the nearest town. Alongside these temporary setbacks were more intractable limitations. Jones, the only member of the delegation who spoke Spanish, was not a member of the FOR and had been "exceedingly hesitant," he later recalled, to join the peace team. On the trip,

FIGURE 2.5   John Nevin Sayre (r) and Robert Cuba Jones in Jinotega, Nicaragua, December 1927. (DG 117, Box 7, John Nevin Sayre Papers, Swarthmore College Peace Collection.)

tensions developed between him and Sayre. An entry from Sayre's journal betrays impatience with his translator: "Waited & waited & waited & waited for Robert to get statements for new[s]papers typed." Jones, for his part, thought that the goal of the mission was foolish. Anticipating a fact-finding operation, he soon discovered that "activist Sayre was determined to try to interview Sandino and personally make a peace effort," against the advice of virtually every person that the group encountered. Jones later blamed the trip for disrupting his academic schedule enough to prevent him from completing his doctorate.[79]

Indeed, the quest for Sandino degenerated into a wild goose chase. The delegation first met with the American chargé d'affaires at Managua, who refused to cooperate. "I suggested," the official recounted, "that with their ignorance of Latin American conditions and psychology and their inability to speak Spanish the delegation could hardly hope to succeed." The rebuff disappointed Sayre, but then the group received long-awaited letters of introduction from Sócrates Sandino, the general's half-brother, whom Sayre had met in Brooklyn. The letters were addressed to Augusto Sandino and to his father, Gregorio. Brandishing these documents, the peace group visited Gregorio, who put them in touch with Sandino's wife, Blanca. She agreed to relay a letter from the peace team to her husband.

In the letter, Sayre and the others stressed their opposition to the U.S. invasion of Nicaragua, but asked Sandino to consider that "further fighting is not the right or effective way to accomplish any good for Nicaragua." Sandino sent a letter back insisting that the Marines leave before he would disarm, but Sayre apparently never received the message, probably because the Americans had launched a full-scale offensive against the guerrillas at the same time. The exhausting journey ended in anticlimax and defeat.[80]

Still, the trip demonstrated the pacifists' new awareness of the relationship between violence and mass media. Jones was surely right about the failure of the peace mission as high diplomacy, but he missed the importance of it as symbolic political performance. The Sandino rebellion itself had revealed the close connection between actual killing and media representations of violence. As early as the summer of 1927, Sandino had become a minor international celebrity, approached repeatedly, though unsuccessfully, by filmmakers interested in putting his story onscreen. Meanwhile, his letters and manifestos appeared in the Latin American and world press, and in 1928 he sat for a series of interviews, later published in the *Nation*, with the American journalist Carleton Beals. The American invasion, too, captured the imagination of the mass media. Cecil B. DeMille sent a representative to the State Department to ask about filming the Marines in action in Nicaragua. He was refused, but Frank Capra did fictionalize the conflict in his 1929 film *Flight*, which portrayed Sandino as the "bandit Lobo." Several other films followed in the same vein, depicting Nicaragua as a jungle populated with primitive, dangerous, and exotic characters.[81]

Sayre was attempting, however haphazardly, to make nonviolence relevant in this mass-mediated world. The peace team's letter to Sandino said fairly little about the religious basis of pacifism, trying instead to convince the general that violence made for bad publicity. "No matter how bravely you might die in a final fight with the U.S. marines," the Americans warned, "the story of what you might do would be inevitably colored by the propaganda of war." Because Sandino's enemies had power over "the telegraphs, radios and other machinery for news dissemination," Sayre reasoned, "you would be photographed to the world as your enemies picture you"—that is, as "a common bandit." Sayre argued that if Sandino stopped fighting, "military censorship is lifted and there is much more chance for truth to be known." The American official who had earlier snubbed the delegation had a similar awareness of media strategy. The pacifists could not be allowed to visit Sandino, he insisted, because "if they were killed the sensational publicity which would result would be most unfortunate."[82]

Getting to Sandino was, arguably, not even the point. Several years before the Central American trip, Sayre had imagined a nonviolent "propaganda of truth" that shared many attributes with his Central American adventure. The important parts of the effort came before and after the rejection in Nicaragua. During their journey, the pacifists issued press releases, gave interviews, held mass meetings, and spoke on the radio. Elbert Russell thought the team received "good press" in most of the Central American capitals; an exception was San Jose, Costa Rica, where, Russell explained, "New Year's celebrations and the coming of [Charles] Lindbergh crowded us out of print."[83] Back in the United States, Sayre recounted his adventure to various audiences: at Brookwood Labor College, on a monthlong speaking tour through the Midwest, and in print in the *World Tomorrow*. The *New York Times* included a brief account of the peace mission in the middle of its front-page coverage of the Marines' January assault. The bizarre machinations that so infuriated Robert Jones actually made a good story, by turns suspenseful, amusing, exotic, and inspiring. The Nicaragua trip was certainly not a flawless performance, nor did it gain media coverage on the scale that Babe Ruth or Lindbergh attained. Nevertheless, the peace mission's intentional creation of a public moral confrontation was an early step in the use of nonviolence as a political strategy, not simply a personal philosophy. During a speech in Nicaragua at the University of León, Sayre had discussed an anticolonial leader who, more than anyone else, exemplified this shift: Mohandas Gandhi.[84]

Gandhi was the most potent symbol of the FOR's emerging opposition to imperialism, but he had larger significance as well. The figure of the Mahatma has become at once so venerated and so eccentric as to elude rigorous analysis. The "strange little brown man," as the title of an early biography had it, can look a bit quaint beside more fashionable anticolonial heroes such as Frantz Fanon.[85] Nonetheless, decades before Fanon wrote *The Wretched of the Earth*, Gandhi carried the hopes of independence movements in Asia and Africa, antiracist movements in the United States, and peace movements around the world. The Mahatma first gained widespread global fame during his first noncooperation campaign in 1920. So, just as pacifists were emerging from the tumult of the Great War to seek nonviolent alternatives, they began to read about Gandhi's work. It was a propitious historical convergence.

82   SOCIAL EVANGELISM

The FOR leaders embraced Gandhi with an enthusiasm that bordered on worship, quickly appropriating him for their own moral revolution. The *World Tomorrow* first published an essay by Gandhi in September 1920, then dedicated an entire issue to him in December 1924. The Indian émigré Haridas Muzumdar, whose book *Gandhi the Apostle* was the first biography to be published in the United States, spoke on the Mahatma at the 1923 Fellowship conference. The exchange went the other way, too. Gandhi once reprinted a pamphlet by Kirby Page in his journal *Young India*.[86] Gandhi's most tireless American advocate in these early years, though, was John Haynes Holmes. Holmes first preached on Gandhi in the 1921 sermon "Who Is the Greatest Man in the World Today?," which had the Indian leader beating out Vladimir Lenin and the French pacifist Romain Rolland for that honor. Other sermons, speeches, and articles followed, as Holmes made his Community Church into a center for Gandhian inquiry. One of his congregants, Blanche Watson, traveled to India in the early 1920s and wrote some of the first American eyewitness accounts of the noncooperation movement. Muzumdar also received support from the Community Church. In a long dedication that opened *Gandhi the Apostle,* Muzumdar called Holmes "my teacher, my spiritual mentor." For his part, Holmes pronounced the biography "indispensable" and displayed it on his church's literature table.[87]

For the Fellowship, this Indian Hindu was an expression of true Christian ideals, a genuine follower of the example of Jesus. He was "one of the greatest Christians of all time," Edmund Chaffee proclaimed, while Holmes called him "the Christ of our age." The radical Christian pacifists tended to downplay Gandhi's Hindu identity, to say the least. E. Stanley Jones, an American missionary in India who later joined the FOR, explained that although "Gandhi is a Hindu it does not mean that he could not be Christian in the very springs of his character and draw a great part of his spiritual sustenance from Christ. Such is indeed the case."[88] In fact, Gandhi's career suggested that the vast Protestant missionary enterprise had not been in vain. Although it had failed to produce Christian nations in the East and now seemed tarnished by the brutality of imperialism, the introduction of Christianity to Asia had nevertheless produced results. Obviously, the Mahatma did not adhere to Christian creeds, but the Fellowship leaders had always downplayed creeds and insisted instead on the primacy of the example of Jesus, whom Gandhi openly and fervently admired. A British historian has recently argued that many British Christians thought of India in terms of "fulfilment theology," a faith that non-

FIGURE 2.6
Special issue of
the *World Tomorrow*
devoted to Mohandas
Gandhi, December
1924. (Seeley G. Mudd
Library, Yale University.)

Christian religions, and Hinduism in particular, would gradually evolve into Christianity. Many Americans, inside and outside the Fellowship, saw Gandhi in this teleological framework.[89]

Some radical Christian pacifists, though, gave the Mahatma's career even more sweeping religious import. To them, Gandhi seemed to mark the emergence of a new religion, beyond Hinduism *and* traditional Christianity. John Haynes Holmes considered him to be a "religious leader" of "universal significance," working for the "spiritual liberation of mankind." When Holmes called Gandhi "the Christ of our age," he was placing the Indian in a Christian tradition, but also positioning him in a broader lineage of revolutionary spiritual innovators that included "Lao-tse, Buddha, Zoroaster and Mohammed." Holmes, to be sure, was one of the most theologically radical members of the Fellowship. In 1919, he had removed the Unitarian label from his congregation's name and begun calling it the Community Church as an expression of his search for a religion that would supersede orthodox Christianity. Though few of the Fellowship leaders went this far, their devotion to the Mahatma was often an indirect criticism of the parochialism and prejudice that they disliked in their fellow American Protestants. The encounter with Gandhi helped fuel a profound shift in the radical Christian pacifist view of the spiritual world. As Protestants, they had seen their religion as a competitor with Catholicism, Judaism, Hinduism, and all other faiths, but now they began to understand true religion, in all its varieties, as the last hope against the onslaught of a vicious, heartless secularism.[90]

Alongside this spiritual innovation, Gandhi represented a new kind of practical pacifism. For the Fellowship, he showed that nonviolence could work as a method of social and political change. Holmes pointed out that radical pacifism had formerly relied on "men of transcendent personality and influence," such as Thoreau and Tolstoy, while manifesting a tendency toward "a remote or other-worldly type of life." The Fellowship of Reconciliation in the twenties devised various methods to surmount these limitations: a new print culture, open forums, labor education, and even an arduous visit to Nicaragua. Nothing held more promise for pacifism's future effectiveness, though, than the events in India. "If the Mahatma succe[e]ds in his great venture," Holmes predicted, "non-resistance will be made for the first time in history a universal principle of life." At the very least, Christian nonviolence in the United States might get a fighting chance.[91]

Thinking back to the personalities who dominated world news at the time, the one who stood out most from all the others in terms of his visual image was without a doubt Gandhi. Although he was one of the people who was most caricatured and about whom huge numbers of anecdotes circulated, his image managed to instil the idea that in him there was something serious and true, though very remote from us. —Italo Calvino, "The Duce's Portraits"

EDITOR: *Machinery is the chief symbol of modern civilization; it represents a great sin....*
READER: *Is it a good point or a bad one that all you are saying will be printed through machinery?* —*Mohandas Gandhi*, Hind Swaraj

3   The Gandhian Moment

In 1930, Mohandas Gandhi reached one of the high points of his long career. He had gained some international attention during his first noncooperation campaign, which lasted from 1920 to 1922, but he was imprisoned at the end of it, and in the years after his release in 1924, writing and domestic reforms consumed his attention. Then, in the spring of 1930, he strode back onto the world stage with the famous "March to the Sea," a protest against the British salt tax. Walking for twenty-four days with a band of devoted *satyagrahis* at his side and a huge crowd behind him, Gandhi arrived at the seashore on April 6 and grasped a handful of salt in symbolic defiance of the colonial monopoly. The event, Gandhi's American biographer Louis Fischer would later write, had "required . . . the sense of showmanship of a great artist." Inspired by the march, Indians all along the coast began to produce their own salt illegally, confounding British authorities.

On May 21, a few thousand of Gandhi's followers, their leader by this time in jail once again, advanced on the British-owned Dharasana Salt Works. In this primal scene of modern nonviolence, Indian police beat the demonstrators senseless with lathis, long wooden clubs clad in iron. Readers around the world marveled at the United Press wire report describing the "sickening whack of the clubs on unprotected skulls" as "not one of the marchers even raised an arm to fend off the blows." In the wake of the salt protests and their brutal repression, the diminutive Mahatma seemed to grow in stature as the moral authority of British colonialism shriveled. The next year, Gandhi traveled to London for highly publicized negotiations concerning India's future, becoming a source of fascination to both allies and enemies in England and securing the prominent role in global politics that he would hold until his assassination in 1948.[1]

The "salt *satyagraha*" and the Round Table Conferences produced a Gandhian moment in the United States. During the first half of the 1930s, American newspapers, along with liberal journals such as the *Nation, New Republic,* and *Crisis,* reported regularly on the Indian independence movement. The African American press in particular carried extensive news about the struggle against British rule and interpreted Gandhi's actions in terms of broader anticolonial and antiracist efforts. In Congress, Senator John J. Blaine sponsored a proindependence resolution that compared the struggle in India to the American Revolution, while the Indian émigré Haridas Muzumdar announced during a rally at Philadelphia's Independence Hall that the salt *satyagraha* was India's Boston Tea Party. Most dramatically, Americans heard Gandhi address them over their radios for the first time on September 13, 1931, calling on "the conscience of the world" to come to his country's aid. The Mahatma's singular persona crept into the lexicon of popular culture as well. In Cole Porter's hit song "You're the Top," featured in the 1934 musical *Anything Goes,* the name of the teetotaling ascetic provided an awkward rhyme for "Napoleon Brandy."[2]

Gandhi continued to attract the Christian pacifists in the Fellowship of Reconciliation as if by a magic spell. Sherwood Eddy and Kirby Page visited his Sabarmati ashram in 1929, and John Haynes Holmes met him in London two years later. They all came to believe that the Mahatma was developing the method of political action that they had sought since the end of the Great War. During the 1920s, the pacifists had strenuously promoted peace and justice, yet their efforts at "social evangelism" remained disturbingly amorphous. They wrote books and pamphlets, gave speeches, and lobbied government officials, but their work lacked the passion and drama of the war years. Gandhi, on the other hand, had achieved astonishing results. He solved a religious conundrum as well, namely that the Fellowship's activities had done little to distinguish radical Christian pacifism from other strains of American reform. Indeed, the most successful ventures that the Fellowship supported were the American

Civil Liberties Union and Brookwood Labor College. While the FOR read-
ily cooperated with secular reformers, these organizations seemed not to
depend at all upon a specifically religious outlook, however much they
gained from the participation of religious people. Gandhi, on the other
hand, had made spiritual values an indispensable part of the quest for
peace, justice, and liberty. In combining efficacy and spirituality, he became the answer to the pacifists' prayers.

The Fellowship leaders did more than benefit from America's Gandhian moment; they helped to create it. For example, John Haynes Holmes played a crucial role in the first American publication of Gandhi's
autobiography. In 1926, Holmes had received an issue of Gandhi's journal *Young India* that contained the first installments of the Indian leader's
life story. The American minister was ecstatic and immediately sought
permission to use the pieces in his own religious periodical, *Unity*. "May
I say," Holmes wrote to Gandhi, "that I am proposing to do everything in
my power to advertise your story so that it may reach the farthest possible
public."[3] The autobiography appeared serially in *Unity* over the next few
years, another attempt at the Christian nonviolent "propaganda of truth."
During that time, Holmes, Gandhi, and Charles Andrews, an Anglican
minister and one of Gandhi's closest English associates, negotiated with
Macmillan to publish Gandhi's writings in book form. The upshot was a
sprawling three-volume project, with Andrews abridging the text of Gandhi's major works and Holmes providing an introduction to one of the
volumes. Andrews's haphazard modifications sapped some of the power
of the texts, but the Macmillan edition of the autobiography (the second of
the three volumes) was the only one published in the United States until
after Gandhi's death. Readers who wished to peruse the Indian's life story
in its original form (or rather, in its original English translation from the
Gujarati) had no choice but to obtain a copy from overseas or cobble it
together from back issues of *Unity*. In short, Holmes, with his network of
pacifists and Indian expatriates, had become a vital source of information
during Gandhi's rise to global prominence.[4]

The FOR leaders also tried to serve as Gandhi's American advisers. He
had initially considered a trip to the United States following his voyage
to England in 1931, but Holmes, Eddy, Page and several other prominent
U.S. clergymen discouraged him from coming. The "press in America,"
Page explained, "is so unethical and sensational that it would exploit
you if you come to this country, and grossly misrepresent your cause."[5]
Holmes agreed, discussing the matter with Gandhi in London and later

recalling that he "shrank from the mere possibility of Gandhi's presence, like his pictures in the movies, being greeted by rude laughter." The Indian leader took this advice and never did travel to the United States. He stated in a front-page *New York Times* story: "Holmes, in whose opinion I place the greatest reliance, tells me my visit would be misunderstood, that I would be exploited, ridiculed and misinterpreted." Gandhi mentioned the 1921 U.S. visit of Albert Einstein, lamenting that "most Americans regarded him only as a spectacle."[6]

This was, perhaps, not the whole story. Gandhi had officially been invited by an eclectic group of distinguished Americans that included *New York Times* publisher Adolph S. Ochs, General Motors president Alfred P. Sloan, and the philosopher John Dewey. Pacifists, in other words, would not be calling the shots, a state of affairs that Holmes may have had in mind when he wrote to Gandhi that he should "come not in response to any single invitation from any individual or group but should come on your own initiative and as your own master." Regardless of these turf wars, the controversy over Gandhi's American visit shows how attuned pacifists had become to the power of mass media. Their specific strategy of keeping Gandhi away seems questionable in retrospect, but their focus on strategy itself heralded a new era for Christian nonviolence.[7]

The man who, during the Gandhian moment, worked out the implications of nonviolent strategy more completely than anyone else was a Harvard-trained lawyer named Richard Gregg. Holmes, Eddy, and Page were forceful preachers and promoters, but they produced relatively little analysis of the content of Gandhi's philosophy. Gregg took up that challenge. He had not been much interested in the Fellowship during the Great War, but became one of its most important leaders by the end of the 1930s. He explained how the ideas of a "half-naked fakir" (in Winston Churchill's infamous phrase) could revolutionize democracy in the modern world.

Richard Bartlett Gregg was America's first major theorist of nonviolent action, and like many innovators he is difficult to categorize. Born in Colorado Springs in 1885, he later lived in Massachusetts, New York, Vermont, Pennsylvania, Wisconsin, Illinois, and, most importantly, India, before spending his last years in a retirement home in Eugene, Oregon. The son of a Congregational minister, Gregg held to a deep religious faith that underlay all his work. He nevertheless remained suspicious of organized Christianity and, unlike most early Fellowship leaders, was never ordained himself. Some thought that he must be a Quaker (and this mistake persists in a few recent accounts), but Gregg felt no inclination to join even this most inclusive and broad-minded of Christian traditions. "I do not belong to any church," he once explained to John Nevin Sayre. "I'd rather work from the outside."[8] His interests were diverse: he became most widely known for his writings on pacifism and nonviolence, but also published works on religion, science, economics, sexual ethics, and organic farming. Finally, though his theories highlighted the performative dimensions of politics, Richard Gregg was no performer. He "was a quiet and very humble man," one admirer remembered, "painstaking in his speech and writing." Another explained that he was "one of the quietest radicals in history."[9]

Gregg's radicalism was not immediately apparent. Like his father and three brothers, he attended Harvard College, where he studied mathematics and science and initially planned to be an electrical engineer. He compiled a good record at Harvard, serving as class treasurer and graduating cum laude in 1907. "Though a quiet fellow," a class publication noted, "he is one of the most popular men in his class." Gregg eventually chose not to pursue engineering, instead returning to Harvard to obtain a law degree. Then his education took a very different turn.[10]

The events that would eventually lead Gregg to India began with intense industrial conflict, not with the peace movement. After practicing law for a few years, he opened an office in 1915 with Robert G. Valentine and Ordway Tead, two experts in the emerging fields of personnel management and industrial psychology. The men were, he remembered, "employed sometimes by employers, sometimes by labor unions, sometimes by joint associations of employers and unions."[11] No doubt they kept busy in these years of intense conflict between corporations and workers, conflict that sometimes led to bloodshed. Gregg may have first become aware of such battles during his youth in Colorado, where the mining industry produced some of the most brutal strikes in the nation, later culminating in the Ludlow Massacre of 1914.[12]

In the midst of these clashes, the United States entered the war in Europe. Gregg later recalled that he "did not receive any church training against war" as a youth. On the contrary, his father "was all for fighting the Germans," and two of Gregg's siblings did medical work among the soldiers. Gregg, however, was developing an absolute opposition to war; he later stated, in typically oblique fashion, that he "had given myself religious training in this matter" (he was also slightly too old to be

drafted). Yet he seems not to have become involved in the peace movement either, playing no major role in the first years of the Fellowship of
Reconciliation.[13]

The labor war in the United States, not the Great War in Europe, remained Gregg's top priority. He went to work for the National War Labor
Board (NWLB), where he glimpsed the promise of industrial democracy
but learned the limits of government mediation as a means of achieving
it. Woodrow Wilson created the NWLB in the spring of 1918 to manage
labor relations during the war. Containing equal numbers of employers'
and employees' representatives, the NWLB worked to settle industrial disputes before they could become serious enough to disrupt war mobilization. The leaders of the NWLB, William Howard Taft and Frank Walsh,
were legal professionals like Gregg, with Taft representing employers' interests and Walsh advocating for labor. The NWLB unexpectedly became
a leading supporter of workers' rights, offering employees an officially
sanctioned venue outside the workplace to seek resolution of their disputes. Looking back, Gregg thought that it had "accomplished much real
service to American industry," particularly by breaking down resistance
to unions.[14]

This progressive moment was short-lived, though. Joining the NWLB
shortly before the armistice in Europe, Gregg became the administrative
examiner for a case at the Bethlehem Steel Company. After much negotiation, the government had in July 1918 ordered a settlement favorable to
the Bethlehem workers, but when the war ended the company president
refused to abide by the ruling. The NWLB had only advisory power, and all
through the winter Gregg tried unsuccessfully to enforce the settlement,
finally brokering a compromise agreement in March 1919. Soon after, the
agency itself was dismantled, a harbinger of employers' retrenchment in
the twenties. The legalist solution to labor disputes had proven precarious
at best.[15]

After leaving his government job, Gregg began doing statistical, legal,
and public relations tasks for the Railway Employees' Department, an
amalgam of unions representing the workers who built and maintained
the nation's trains.[16] Having enjoyed unprecedented prosperity during
the wartime nationalization of the railroads, the Railway Employees' Department had become the kind of centralized modern labor organization
that required the professional expertise of people such as Gregg. Within
a few years, however, the railway shopmen found themselves pinched by
a slumping economy, harassed by antiunion railroad owners, and aban-

FIGURE 3.1
Richard Bartlett Gregg,
1932. (Harvard University
Archives, call number
HUD 307.505, Box 811.)

doned by Warren Harding's probusiness policies. On July 1, 1922, after a
series of layoffs and a wage cut, four hundred thousand of them went out
on strike.

The railway shopmen's strike of 1922 probably did more to shape Richard Gregg's ideas about violence than did all the military slaughter of the
Great War. A total of 1.6 million workers walked off their jobs that year,
not only railway shopmen but also miners, textile workers, and many
others.[17] The ensuing labor battles posed a far more immediate threat
to American security than Europe's battles over territory ever had. Soldiers marched through the streets of many industrial communities in
the United States during the summer of 1922, while local marshals and
company guards patrolled major railroad shops in Chicago, where Gregg
worked, and in cities across the nation. Guards occasionally fired on striking railway workers, who fought back by kidnapping and assaulting replacement workers, sabotaging trains, and dynamiting tracks. In this cli-

mate, the Harding administration became increasingly intent on ending the conflict, and in September a federal judge issued an injunction that condemned the strike as a conspiracy in violation of the Sherman Antitrust Act. Over the next few months, the shopmen reached separate agreements with the railway companies and returned to work. Federal law had given the railroad owners almost total victory.[18]

Sometime during the railway strike, "when feeling was most bitter," Gregg had seen a glimmer of hope in a Chicago bookstore, where he had come across "an article about Gandhi which gave some quotations from him." He was profoundly interested and, he later remembered, "got hold of everything about him and by him that I could find." To this minister's son, the peculiar Indian Hindu "seemed more like Christ than anyone I had heard of in the present world." Meanwhile, the Railway Employees' Department, financially decimated by the strike, had to downscale its operations. Once again out of a job, Gregg made up his mind to go to India.[19]

In his few years working for the federal government and the railway shopmen's union, Gregg had witnessed the disintegration of the American labor movement. He had taken part in government mediation that was apparently fair and open, but that lacked the power to enforce even its own moderate recommendations. Then he had participated in a strike that had twisted into an escalating spiral of destruction, only to end with a legal decision that seemed to restore order at the expense of justice. Neither the rational methods of legal professionalism nor the fearsome power of violent action had done much to solve the problems of modern society. Richard Gregg sailed for India on New Year's Day in 1925 to find a better way.

In the life of Mohandas Gandhi, Gregg must have seen a few parallels to his own. The man he hoped to meet had also discovered both the inadequacy of law and the uncontrollable nature of violence. Born in 1869, Gandhi was already an established Indian leader by the time Gregg sought him out, but his path had been circuitous. He had originally planned to be a lawyer, training in London for that purpose. Although he established a successful practice in South Africa, he also encountered there a system of racial discrimination far worse than anything he had experienced in India or England. As a consequence, he found himself increasingly engaged in political activity on behalf of his fellow Indians, including some early attempts at the distinctive form on nonviolent resistance that became known as *satyagraha*. Translated loosely as "hold fast to the truth," the term came to refer both to Gandhi's philosophy of conflict resolution and to his method of militant nonviolent action. In 1920 his nationwide noncooperation campaign marked his first wholesale attack on British colonialism as a system. Yet the specter of violence stalked his efforts. Just as the American railway strike had devolved into an increasingly violent struggle, so Gandhi's campaign floundered as a result of government repression and rioting by his followers. In February 1922 he called off the effort, denouncing both the "organized violence of the Government" and the "unorganized violence of the people." Still, as Gregg's Chicago epiphany showed, the Indian leader's novel methods of political protest had already made a worldwide impact.[20]

To understand those methods, Gregg immersed himself in Indian culture for four years. He had previously visited the country in 1913, while working as a business secretary for his brother-in-law, but on that earlier trip, he later confessed, he had been "an ignorant tourist with the usual ideas as to the superiority of the white man." Now he went abroad "not as a missionary or business man, but to learn about India, the land, the people, the religion and philosophy, the attitude toward life." He "avoided white men as much as possible" in order to interact with Indians, "eating their food, wearing their kinds of clothes, trying to learn their language, adopting their customs so far as I could, travelling with them so far as I could in the third ('lowest') class railway carriages." One white man he did not avoid was Gandhi's friend Charles Andrews, who smoothed Gregg's path into the Mahatma's Sabarmati ashram, where he spent several months. Gregg also met the renowned poet Rabindranath Tagore and spent time at his school. Like Holmes, Eddy, and Page, he had the social status to gain access to people in positions of power.[21]

Yet Gregg faced considerable challenges as he sought to "learn about India." He contracted malaria and dysentery during his first year overseas and struggled with frequent health problems after that. During his recovery, he took a job teaching science in a Himalayan village, but this undertaking does not seem to have been particularly therapeutic. Though he had taught chemistry and mathematics in America for a year after graduating from college, he was unprepared for this very different task. His students, he found, had little experience with science and tended to explain the world in terms of "people, fate, magic, spirits or gods." They handled scientific instruments only with "a very great slowness, awkwardness and inaccuracy," their work proving "slovenly in almost every respect." In this context, he discovered that British, American, and even Indian textbooks were "almost useless," for in addition to being too expensive for rural schools, such guides "assume a familiarity with machinery of many kinds and with machine-made devices, appliances and products of all kinds." Gregg set to work translating scientific concepts into an idiom that his charges could comprehend.[22]

The result was *A Preparation for Science*, published in India in 1928. Though it did not discuss Gandhi or nonviolence, this teacher training manual marked Gregg's first attempt to imagine a countermodernity based upon his experience in India.[23] It described techniques and exercises that used ordinary objects from peasant life, such as pebbles and rice, to teach science. Gregg intended the book to present science as a systematic way of examining the world that was "not the same as machinery or Western technology."[24] Like Gandhi, who described himself as a modern researcher performing "experiments with truth" (as the title of his autobiography had it), Gregg respected scientific methodology even as he renounced many of the fruits of Western scientific knowledge. In his view, the technological, economic, psychological, and philosophical transformations wrought by science in the previous half-century could result in the creation of societies unlike those in the United States and Europe, societies that were not primitive or antimodern, but modern in a different way. *A Preparation for Science* also marked Gregg's initial foray into translating ideas between India and the West, the kind of translation he later performed in his writings on nonviolence.[25]

Gregg's next book, *Economics of Khaddar*, sought to divorce economics from Western capitalism, just as *A Preparation for Science* had separated science from Western technology. *Economics of Khaddar* was his first book about Gandhi, but it was not about nonviolent resistance. It was instead an analysis of the Mahatma's economic ideas. Much to the embarrassment of other Indian political leaders and most Western admirers, Gandhi championed a program of decentralized handicraft production as the key to his nation's prosperity. Specifically, he called each person in India to the daily task of spinning thread for the production of *khaddar* (handmade cloth), an endeavor that would, he contended, keep Indians employed in productive labor while also undermining the power of the British textile industry.[26]

Economics of Khaddar sought to defend Gandhi's scheme in economic terms. Gregg's belief that scientific means did not necessarily point to Western ends offered a justification for the project. "The khaddar movement," he argued, "is more and more using modern science and technology, but applying them to a different mode of power utilization and to a different type of machinery from that found in Western industrialism." Gregg tried to show how India's agrarian society required an economy different from that in Europe and America. For instance, he argued that the supply of cheap labor in India worked against the adoption of mechanized systems of production. He also believed that handicraft production was morally and aesthetically superior to Western capitalism, but he assumed that economic efficiency and moral superiority could go together. Though he presented his book specifically as a defense of *khaddar* in India, he argued that even in the West, decentralized production would be a more efficient and humane form of economic life. Gregg condemned the schemes of John Maynard Keynes for managing capitalism as "fundamentally and ultimately impossible," for capitalism itself was "contrary to the fundamental spiritual and moral unity of mankind." Once again Gregg was trying to imagine a countermodernity.[27]

Back in the United States, few members of the Fellowship of Reconciliation resolved to take up their spinning wheels and follow Gandhi. Even his most enthusiastic supporters saw the idea of *khaddar* as an ill-advised reversion to tradition. "In my praise of Gandhi," Edmund Chaffee admitted, "I would make one modification." The Mahatma's rejection of Western technology was a mistake: "We can't go back. . . . We must not abandon machines—we must develop enough power of the spirit to control them." Reinhold Niebuhr, while allowing that "small-scale organization . . . may be possible in an agrarian civilization just emerging into industrialism," dismissed the spinning wheel with an unintentionally apt metaphor. "We cannot turn back the wheels of time," he insisted in answer to Gregg and Gandhi. "It is useless to abolish the machine or circumscribe its range. It must be mastered." For most of the FOR leaders, some form of industrial production was the only reasonable future of economic organization.[28]

Gregg's idea that decentralized, small-scale production was something more than "going back" looks more compelling in our own age of ecological crisis, but *Economics of Khaddar* had corollaries in American social thought even at the time of its publication. Critics such as Lewis Mumford and Ralph Borsodi frequently defended the merits of a less urban, less industrial society, while the economist Stuart Chase, usually remembered as an advocate of large-scale economic planning, wrote sympathetically about the cultural and economic advantages of handicraft production in Mexico. Even for supporters of American capitalism, the technologies that defined the 1920s, particularly electricity and the automobile, seemed to promise a reversal of the processes of consolidation that had defined American society since the Gilded Age. Amazingly, Henry Ford argued that his River Rouge factories, built well outside the metropolis of Detroit, represented an exercise in decentralization that sought a "balance between industry and agriculture."[29] That Richard Gregg cited, in support of his views, the builder of the largest factory in the world shows not only Gregg's eclecticism but also the unsettled character of economic thought in this period. *Economics of Khaddar* was unorthodox, to be sure, but it fit into a larger pattern of misgivings about industrial capitalism at the moment of its apparent triumph just before the onset of the Great Depression.

A Preparation for Science and *Economics of Khaddar* had little apparent relation to Gregg's writing on nonviolent politics. Because they were published in India, few Americans ever read them. Yet these works first articulated his idea that modern discoveries had proven the usefulness of social practices deemed primitive, irrational, or antimodern. His writing shared the contemporaneous cultural relativism of the anthropologist Franz Boas and his supporters. In fact, Boas's student Margaret Mead published *Coming of Age in Samoa* in 1928, the same year that Gregg's first two books appeared. Though Gregg and Mead approached their subjects from very different perspectives, both writers studied non-Western cultures with seriousness rather than condescension, then used their findings to suggest the possibility of alternative paths for their own societies. Combined with his scientific bent, Gregg's uncommon empathy led him to produce an American interpretation of Gandhian nonviolence more innovative than anything that had come before.[30]

Neither Mohandas Gandhi nor Richard Gregg invented nonviolent resistance. People lacking power have probably employed "weapons of the weak" as long as social inequalities have existed in human societies. In the U.S. context, black slaves in particular used forms of sabotage and subterfuge short of open revolt to assert their autonomy and improve their material conditions. Yet by its nature such "everyday resistance" was clandestine, not confrontational.[31] Closer to Gregg's own theories was the approach of the radical pacifist and abolitionist William Lloyd Garrison in the 1830s and 1840s. Garrison's colleagues in the New England Non-Resistance Society, while promising to "repudiate all human politics, worldly honors, and stations of authority," placed great faith in the power of public opinion. An 1839 article in one of their journals described the peculiar advantage that nonresistants held over attackers: "The aggressor of a nonresistant will be placed in the wrong; he will be condemned by himself, by byestanders [sic], by the public." Indeed, the Garrisonians proved adept at dramatizing their principles through public spectacle, particularly on the issue of slavery.[32]

Nonetheless, these earlier dissenters ultimately saw their stance as the product of an inner compulsion to do right regardless of political consequences. In general, religious pacifists—and before the twentieth century virtually all pacifism was religious—tended to view their condemnation of violence as a matter of personal conviction. Its effect upon others, though sometimes profound, was ultimately irrelevant to the believer's own determination to follow God's will. The incendiary "propaganda of the deed," whether in its European anarchist form or adapted to the anarcho-syndicalism of the American Industrial Workers of the World, held little attraction for these devoted Christians, who made mass persuasion subordinate to religious integrity.[33]

During World War I, Harold Gray and Evan Thomas interpreted their conscientious objection in terms of this inner conviction, writing long, tortured letters defending the supremacy of the individual's moral sense over the dictates of the state. Notably, they did not seek media attention for their hunger strikes and other extreme actions, even if their families and friends sometimes did. At the same time, Gray and Thomas did make bemused references to their plight as a "game" and a "performance," and Gregg elaborated these aspects of nonviolence into his own theory of strategic political action. By focusing on attackers and onlookers, he downplayed the nonviolent resister's own convictions, thereby reinventing pacifism as a pragmatic method of social change.

Gregg saw his writing on nonviolence, like his earlier books on science and economics, as a work of translation. Admitting that Gandhi's ideas sounded "preposterous to Westerners," Gregg adopted the role of cultural broker, endeavoring "to state in Western concepts and terminology the principles and practice of non-violent resistance." For all his practicality, he believed in a kind of Emersonian unity that underlay cultural differences. Names and labels were only surface adornments. "The Oriental terminology may be different from ours," Gregg explained, "but that does not make the conclusions less wise." He argued that the "dense population and intense social experience of India, China and other Asiatic civilizations brought about an insight and realization of the psychological validity of non-violent resistance." Now Westerners were beginning to "realize the same truth."[34]

Gregg's interpretations of Gandhi differed from those of Holmes, Eddy, and Page, even though he shared their belief that the Mahatma was revealing universal truths. Gregg published three books on nonviolence: *The Psychology and Strategy of Gandhi's Non-Violent Resistance* in 1929, *Gandhiji's Satyagraha or Non-Violent Resistance* in 1930, and *The Power of Non-Violence* in 1934. These were less a trilogy than a continuing revision of the same general themes and arguments. The titles, with their invocations of "strategy," "resistance," and "power," show how Gregg, despite his early association of the Indian leader with Jesus Christ, became more interested in Gandhi's political techniques than in his status as a transcendent modern saint. The saintly image proliferated during the Gandhian moment. Page's 1930 pamphlet asked *Is Mahatma Gandhi the Greatest Man of the Age?*, echoing the question in Holmes's earlier sermon "Who Is the Greatest Man in the World Today?" (Holmes's "one absolute is Gandhi's perfection," Reinhold Niebuhr once complained). Gregg, too, greatly admired Gandhi personally, but he wrote fairly little about the Indian leader's status as a "great man."[35]

Discussions of nonviolence, Gregg thought, needed to be less rousing and more rigorous. He wanted to extricate pacifism "from the profitless atmosphere, on the one hand, of warm adjectives, and on the other, of vague mysticism, futile protests, or confused and incomplete thinking."[36] This critical tone was by no means unique. Pacifist writers had for decades presented their work as more practical, more thorough, and more substantial than anything that had come before. Still, Gregg was more effective than most in this regard, cultivating a diffident writing style that contrasted sharply with the confident, sometimes overheated language of Page, Eddy, and Holmes. He was always hedging, acknowledging to the reader that he might be "mistaken" or even "wrong." Gregg's style was an organic part of his argument, for he believed that a practitioner of nonviolence, like a theorist of it, "recognizes that no matter what his beliefs and convictions are, he may possibly be mistaken or at fault." He borrowed this tone from Gandhi himself, who insisted that "a devotee of Truth . . . must always hold himself open to correction." Gregg tried to move pacifists away from their emphasis on moral absolutes and toward a more contingent, strategic politics.[37]

THE GANDHIAN MOMENT 99

"Let us . . . try," Gregg suggested, "to understand first how non-violent resistance works." In each of the three books on nonviolence, he presented a pair of dramatic scenes. First, he asked readers to imagine two men, one who attacks violently and another who defends himself by the same method. Such combatants, he explained, implicitly consent to a common set of moral values, despite their apparent opposition. Both believe in the efficacy and appropriateness of using physical force to settle disputes. Then Gregg changed the scene, portraying a violent attacker who faces a nonviolent resister. In failing to defend himself, the second person intentionally disrupts the attacker's value system. He employs "a sort of moral jiu-jitsu" that causes the attacker to "lose his moral balance." This was a psychological contest, and Gregg counted on the violent attacker to cave in from a sense of pity, sympathy, or sheer bewilderment. He suggested that the nonviolent conversion of an opponent was "analogous to . . . religious conversion, though in this case the change is moral rather than religious." More often, though, he drew on modern psychological models to explain how it happened. Gregg's use of psychological theories was opportunistic and eclectic, equally likely to employ Freudianism, the early behaviorism of John B. Watson, or the James-Lange theory of emotion to make a case. The larger point was that scientific authority could validate the methods that Gandhi explained in moral and spiritual terms. Just as modern economics had shown the unlikely rationality of hand spinning, so modern psychology proved the efficacy of standing defenseless before an enemy's assault.[38]

The nonviolent method, while a sincere expression of moral conviction, was also a public performance intended to persuade an audience. Gregg's construction of nonviolent action rested on the power of sympathy. "Undoubtedly," he wrote, "the sight of another person voluntarily undergoing suffering for a belief or ideal moves the assailant and beholders alike and tends to change their hearts and make them all feel kinship with the sufferer." Gregg's books elaborated on what the sociologist Edward Ross had in 1923 suggested only in passing—that "the spectacle of men suffering for a principle *and not hitting back* is a moving one." Gregg proposed two reasons for this phenomenon. One was physiological: humans had evolved to react to one another's pain. "Hence the sight of suffering, in all probability, causes an involuntary sympathetic response in the nervous system of the beholder, especially in the autonomic nervous system," Gregg wrote. The other reason stemmed from a psychological desire for vicarious experience. Gregg observed that "everyone wants, in his heart, to be strong and brave." At the sight of a nonviolent resister, "we wonder if we could do so well, and perhaps we even unconsciously identify ourselves with him."[39]

Spectators played a critical role in the victory of the nonviolent resister. Gregg, who was fundamentally optimistic about human nature, believed that a violent attacker would indeed convert, but he also thought that third parties could assist the process. "If there are onlookers," he wrote, "the assailant soon loses still more poise. Instinctively he dramatizes himself before them and becomes more aware of his position." The "audience," Gregg thought, became "a sort of mirror," reflecting back to the attacker his egregious violation of moral standards.[40]

This view of social life had affinities with older Enlightenment conceptions of the moral sense. Just as Gregg tried to modernize traditional Christian pacifism, so Adam Smith, in his 1759 work *The Theory of Moral Sentiments,* had attempted to explain Protestant conscience in the terms of Enlightenment reason. Downplaying the views of Martin Luther and John Calvin, who saw conscience as a proxy for God's judgment rooted deeply in the individual, Smith stressed the social character of conscience and emphasized the force of sympathy in spurring moral action. When we see another person in pain, Smith wrote, "we conceive ourselves enduring all the same torments, we enter as it were into his body, and become in some measure the same person with him." This self-conscious dramatization also applied to judging one's own actions. When we act according to conscience, Smith explained, "we endeavour to examine our own conduct as we imagine any other fair and impartial spectator would examine it." If the older Protestant view saw obeying one's conscience as a profoundly individual act, *The Theory of Moral Sentiments* saw it as the process of imagining oneself to be someone else.[41]

Smith, seeking the motives of individual character, had centered his inquiry on the hypothetical "impartial spectator" who served as an internalization of social values. Gregg was crafting a new political technique, and so he focused more on the roles of actual spectators in augmenting the power of nonviolence. He believed that mass media had created a global audience, a global *conscience,* for both nonviolent resisters and their violent opponents, citing "the propaganda in the World War" to show "the increasing importance of public opinion in large conflicts." Though Gregg did not use the phrase, Gandhian nonviolence became the "propaganda of truth" that pacifists had been searching for since the war. Under modern conditions, Gregg explained, "ruthless deeds tend to become known to the world at large." He acknowledged the existence of state censorship but maintained that it could be overcome. "Newspaper reporters are always keen for scenting a 'story,'" Gregg opined, "and as soon as they learn of a censorship anywhere they are still more eager." Whatever its moral import, the scene of defenseless men and women voluntarily succumbing to vicious assaults made a fascinating "story." Nonviolent resistance "makes wonderful news," he noted. "It is so unusual and dramatic." He even compared the power of a nonviolent resister's appeals to the persuasive effects of "commercial advertising." Gregg concluded, with both prescience and unwarranted optimism, that the threat of bad publicity would give the practitioners of nonviolence a decisive advantage over their violent opponents.[42]

The force of public opinion pressured nonviolent resisters as well as their oppressors. Gregg warned that practitioners of nonviolence could "break through the censorship of governments, press associations, or popular disdain" only if they "conducted themselves with high excellence, discipline, unity, coherence, cleanness and courage so as to compel respect, admiration and wonder."[43] Here again Gregg followed Gandhi, who saw decolonization not only as the expulsion of British political authority but also as a purification of Indian character. Gregg would devote much time in the late 1930s to the question of "discipline," for he believed that proper training made the difference between an unruly mob and a nonviolent army. He left ambiguous the motives for such discipline and "high excellence." Did a nonviolent resister act out of internal moral imperatives, or only to more effectively sway public opinion? Such unresolved tensions permeated Gregg's revisionist work.

His pragmatic theories led Gregg to the daring argument that "nonviolent resistance is perhaps . . . more like war than we had imagined." Other pacifist works at this time, such as Devere Allen's 1930 *The Fight for Peace*, also called for a more aggressive opposition to war, but few engaged military strategy itself as extensively as Gregg's did. Certainly no other peace advocate had ever gone so far as to write a book whose opening chapter was titled "The Truths and Virtues of Militarism," as in *Gandhiji's Satyagraha*. Gregg opposed the violence of war, but he accepted the necessity of conflict in social life. So he quoted extensively from Carl von Clausewitz and Napoleon Bonaparte, and he called nonviolence a "weapon," sometimes implying that, like poison gas or machine guns, it was an innovation in the history of warfare. Nonviolent resistance became a kind of war without killing, for Gregg thought that killing was unnecessary to achieve war's goals. "Though war uses violence," he explained, "the effect it aims at is psychological. Non-violent resistance also aims at and secures psychological effects, though by different means." If non-violent action was a kind of conflict and not a retreat from the world, it needed to draw on the "truths and virtues of militarism." Following Gandhi, Gregg's work suggested that nonviolent action had many of the characteristics of war. It relied on courage, loyalty, and other martial virtues, it required attention to strategy, and it depended on moral, emotional, and psychological elements, not solely physical ones.[44]

By linking nonviolence so closely to war, Gregg believed that he had answered the classic challenge to pacifism thrown down by the philosopher William James. In his 1910 essay "The Moral Equivalent of War," James had argued that armed conflict fulfilled deep psychological needs. The modern world of progress and comfort had no place for risk, pain, or danger, but people still craved extreme experience, turning to war as an antidote for the increasing banality of everyday life. "Showing war's irrationality and horror is of no effect," James insisted. "The horrors make the fascination." By contrast, the conflict-free world that pacifists imagined was maddeningly dull. As a solution, James proposed to keep some of the attractions of war by instituting an "army enlisted against *Nature*" that would engage in national improvement projects.[45]

Gregg agreed with James's general assessment, suggesting that the romance of war could be attractive "partly because our ordinary life of alleged peace is so often dull, trivial, monotonous and devoid of fine purpose." He was not the first pacifist to suggest that his enterprise was in fact the "moral equivalent of war," but he did so in an especially detailed and convincing way. With its promise of physical danger and even death, Gregg's technique offered an opportunity to demonstrate courage, endurance, and discipline. Furthermore, Gregg considered nonviolent resistance to be "much superior" to James's civil service plan, "in that it does not require State organization, direction or assistance," which Gregg the decentralist greatly distrusted.[46]

Gregg also diverged from James in the religious basis of his work. Despite all his language of "psychology and strategy," he was explicit about the spiritual imperative at the heart of his rejection of violence. Gregg closed both *Gandhiji's Satyagraha* and *The Power of Non-Violence* by stating that nonviolent action was "the practical instrument by which we can make very great progress" toward creating the "kingdom of God . . . here on earth" (an "ideal," he admitted, "that few now really believe"). With that language, he evoked the Social Gospel tradition that sought to usher in the millennium through human progress. Still, always attentive to issues of strategy, he generally avoided religious language in his books, believing that he could gain wider attention by appealing to secular explanations for his views. He did so, he explained in a letter to John Nevin Sayre, on the assumption that "readers who were religious would immediately link up my secular reasoning with the precepts of the New Testament and other religious thinking."[47]

Such readers could "link up" because Gregg's ideas admitted of both religious and secular interpretations. He insisted that "values," not material conditions, constituted the basis of reality. "Deeper than rulership by political governments, banks, and classes is the control coming from ideas and sentiments,—a scheme of values, a set of ideals or activities which people desire and believe to be right," he wrote. Clearly, this view had affinities with the Christian belief in a spiritual reality that transcended the physical world, but his focus on the importance of symbolic action spoke to modern secular concerns as well. The discoveries of modern physics, the increasing pervasiveness of mass media, and the findings of psychology (all of which Gregg incorporated into his work on nonviolence) had highlighted the active role of the observer in constituting reality. Gregg's attention to the place of values and symbols spoke to such awareness of the subjective components of human experience.[48] By attending to their primacy, he believed that he could help solve the crisis of democracy that threatened America and the world. If Gregg had only reshaped the contours of American pacifist thought, that alone would have been remarkable. In fact, his work went beyond pacifism to raise the most profound questions about the place of individuals in modern democratic societies.

Gregg was alarmed by the values that sprung from the large, impersonal structures of Western modernity. Indeed, the place of the individual in the new mass society became a central problem in the politics and culture of the interwar period. Walter Lippmann's *Public Opinion* (1922) had been an early statement of the pessimistic view that ordinary citizens were now subsumed in a simple-minded mass, an assessment that found confirmation in the hysterical reaction to Orson Welles's 1938 *War of the Worlds* broadcast. More optimistically, John Dewey, in his 1930 book *Individualism Old and New,* acknowledged the "submergence of the individual" but hoped that a modern form of individuality might arise. On film, King Vidor's *The Crowd* (1928) depicted the humble office worker dwarfed in the modern city, while *Modern Times* (1936) showed Charlie Chaplin's body contorted in the gears of an indifferent machine. It was a mark of Franklin D. Roosevelt's political astuteness that he proclaimed himself the champion of "the forgotten man." These American visions were responses not only to fears of runaway capitalism and mass culture at home, but also to the powerful collectivist dreams of Communism and Fascism abroad.[49]

Even the peace movement had not entirely resisted the trend toward impersonality. Christian nonviolence had always placed the individual at the heart of its program, but Fellowship leaders such as Kirby Page actually spent much of their time debating various schemes of world government and increased state intervention in the economy, sometimes extending to socialism. Such programs were not necessarily inconsistent with a commitment to individual fulfillment, but they did at times tend to squeeze human agency out of the picture. Pacifists, Gregg explained to Page, should concentrate less on "Leagues of Nations, international relations, disarmament, etc." and more on "individual attitudes and relationships." He recalled that "very few of the members of the Carnegie Peace Foundation or other similar formal peace organizations went to jail as conscientious objectors during the war." Rather, the objectors "were more apt to be people who had thrashed it all out as an individual problem."[50]

Other radical religious dissenters shared Gregg's concern. In 1933, the Catholic convert Dorothy Day and her French adviser Peter Maurin started the Catholic Worker movement in New York City. Catholic Workers shared Gregg's commitment to nonviolence, his agrarian and decentralist predilections, and, as the group's name implied, a preference for the laboring classes. Day's "Houses of Hospitality" offered free food and shelter to anyone, modeling an egalitarian "personalist" theology that stood against both capitalism and Marxism. Gregg had no significant contact with Day's movement during its early years, but by the 1940s some Catholic Workers and FOR members would find common ground in the vanguard of nonviolent action.[51]

Like Dorothy Day, Gregg tried to restore individual dignity in an inhospitable world. *A Preparation for Science* sought to provide Indian children with the cognitive tools to accept or reject Western innovations on their merits, while *Economics of Khaddar* suggested that every person could engage in meaningful work that would also benefit the Indian nation as a whole. Similarly, in his writings on nonviolence, Gregg proposed a style of politics that would depend upon and dramatize the worth of the human person. Against peace plans proposing "something that 'ought' to be done by governments, by statesmen, by educators, by great bankers, or the like," Gandhian nonviolence offered "every single individual" the chance "do something real and immediate and continuous for the cause of peace."[52]

Relying as it did on the individual, nonviolence cut across social divisions. "It may be practised," Gregg insisted, "and skill may be acquired in it in every situation of life, at home and abroad, by men and women of any and all races, nations, tribes, groups, classes, or castes, young and old, rich and poor." He considered it "important" that women could participate, observing that "they are more effective in it than most men." Again he drew directly from Gandhi, who insisted that "even a man weak in body is capable of offering this resistance. . . . Both men and women can indulge in it."[53] Gregg attributed much of the success of the 1930 salt march to the fact that "a great many more women are taking active part in this struggle than was the case in 1920–21." He did not address the potential difficulties for women of a form of political action modeled on the decidedly masculine institution of war. In the decades to come, militant nonviolence would offer important opportunities for female participation in the public sphere, but its dependence on martial virtues would also reinforce a masculine ideal of strenuous heroism.[54]

Despite his relative lack of attention to questions of gender, Gregg anticipated later feminist theory in his attention to the political significance of the body. Gandhi's own body proved a source of constant fascination and wonder to the outside world. The fasts, the dietary experiments, the practice of *brahmacharya* (celibacy), the loincloth, and the emaciated form itself—all this was inseparable from the Mahatma's philosophy and politics. Holmes and Page were thinking of such oddities when they warned Gandhi not to visit America, while later interpreters have seen the bodily experiments of the Indian leader as manifestations of deep psychological needs or traumas.[55] Such approaches miss the importance of the body as a site of social power, part of a decolonization project that involved cultural politics as well as formal diplomacy. In his own body, Gandhi sought to forge the countermodernity that defined his vision for India. Gregg was sympathetic to this project. The American and the Indian often shared ideas about health reform, and Gregg once sent Gandhi a book by the American health reformer John Harvey Kellogg. Unorthodox experimenters such as Kellogg viewed their work as scientific, so here, too, Gandhi and Gregg drew on an alternative science in the service of building a new society.[56]

Gregg did not endorse all of Gandhi's corporeal experiments—he seems to have had little interest in the Mahatma's promotion of celibacy, for example. Also, though he was personally intrigued by Gandhi's health reform program, Gregg did not write much about it when he translated nonviolence for the West. What Gregg did adopt, and what many psycho-analytic readings of Gandhi have missed, was the idea that the physical body could play a central role in political action. He emphasized that Gandhi's program "is more of action than of talk." "Mere words or pleas are not enough," he wrote. "They are only a part of our total language." Non-violence "uses the expression of the face, glances of the eyes, tones, inten-sities and modulations of the voice, movements and postures of the limbs and body,—just as in all personal communication." Most of all, the use of physical bodies dramatized the state's dependence upon the cooperation of its citizens or subjects. The body could cut through the machinations and evasions of politics, undermining the subtle systems of bodily disci-pline that Michel Foucault has identified as the defining feature of mod-ern power relations. Though nonviolence would not abolish legislatures, it "controls them, puts them in their proper place, and renders them less capable of doing harm." In this way it could be the "key to liberty in the modern State."[57]

Liberty, but what about democracy? What Gregg dismissed as "mere words" was the reasoned discourse that formed the lifeblood of represen-tative government. Later critics of nonviolence would suggest that Gan-dhian "direct action" short-circuited the deliberative process, leading ei-ther to anarchy or to the tyranny of implacable minorities. In this view, citizens ought to act through their representatives, not by personally chal-lenging the law. Gregg's response sprung from his experiences on the ragged margins of Anglo-American governance. "There is an essential preliminary to the act of governing," he noted, "namely, obtaining the consent of those who are to be governed." He had spent his career in arenas where governments had failed to serve their constituencies. In his work with the NWLB, he had witnessed the state's capitulation to busi-ness interests. Then he had lived under a colonial regime that depended more on force than on parliamentary procedure. Gregg also noticed the plight of African Americans in his home country, where racial terror over-powered legislative authority. For workers, Indians, and black Americans, representative government was failing by the 1930s. Gregg thought that the nonviolent method could serve a variety of political purposes, but he thought that these three groups had the most to gain.[58]

Gregg was sure that the labor movement had made a tragic mistake by countenancing the violent tactics that he had witnessed in the 1922 railway strike. "I am inclined to believe," he wrote, "that one reason why so many strikes fail in Western countries is because both employers and employees, capitalists and proletariat, are snared in the same net of ideas and valuations, those of money and of violence."[59] He believed that most violence originated with employers and with the state, not with labor, but he also thought that workers had to transcend brutality rather than repay it. Gregg extolled the "non-violent strike" as the way for them to achieve their goals. Though he was not involved in the Fellowship of Reconciliation's postwar debate over the ethics of strikes, he addressed some of the issues raised at that earlier moment. Frankly admitting that strikes involved a measure of "coercion," he denied that "all coercion is violence," accepting the reality of conflict in the world as one of the "truths of militarism." He was also the most accommodating of reformers. "If any conservatives are anxious lest there might be a 'tyranny of labor,'" Gregg offered, "let them remember that they also have the privilege of using non-violent resistance" (he did not explain the logistics).[60] Gregg's own sympathies were with labor, so in 1930 he sent one of the first two copies of *Gandhiji's Satyagraha* to Andrew Furuseth, the venerable founder of the International Seaman's Union, whom Gregg had probably met while working briefly for the U.S. Shipping Board during the war.[61]

Gregg viewed the strike primarily as a performance, not as a battle over material goods. Workers resorted to violence ("in those relatively rare cases where there is no provocation from strike breakers or policemen") not to do their employers material harm, but to "dramatize the issues" involved in a dispute. Other social critics had the same idea. In language similar to Gregg's, the American Marxist Sidney Hook maintained that violence appealed to subordinate groups because "it symbolizes in dramatic fashion the issues involved" in a social conflict. Yet although Gregg admitted that violence was the "surest form of melodrama," he argued that "non-violent resistance, if well managed, is still more surprising and dramatic."[62] Workers could win strikes not by financially crippling a business enterprise, but by gaining the sympathy of the public and, hopefully, of the employer. Gregg believed that strikes took place primarily in the realm of symbols and values, which could be acted out.

Other writers on the left also emphasized the role of publicity and performance in the labor movement. One Fellowship member who worked on labor issues explained that "organized labor . . . is increasingly realizing the importance of the publicity director." The shift began as early as the 1912 textile strike in Lawrence, Massachusetts, when police brutality against women and children had turned many reporters' sympathies to the workers. The next year, Greenwich Village denizens John Reed and Mabel Dodge organized the Paterson Pageant, a theatrical production that featured New Jersey silk workers performing their own strike in Madison Square Garden.[63] For his part, Gregg sought to collect material on nonviolent strikes into pamphlets, suggesting that these could provide "thrilling reading," and perhaps even the basis for "some little one-act plays." He hoped to inspire "both leaders and workers in the labor struggle and perhaps also . . . Negroes in the inter-racial struggles."[64]

Gregg thought that nonviolence could solve the problem of racial discrimination, so he mailed the other copy of *Gandhiji's Satyagraha* to W. E. B. Du Bois at the *Crisis*. He sent along a letter explaining that he thought it "more important for Negroes and Labor to understand this new method of handling conflict than for any other groups of the population." The two had corresponded while Gregg was in India. Du Bois sent him the *Crisis* as well as a copy of his book *Darkwater,* and Gregg, in turn, mailed *Economics of Khaddar* and argued for its relevance in America. "I think the movement has something that all our farmers and unemployed can profit from, especially those in the South," he wrote. Apparently Du Bois did not have much interest in the spinning wheel, but he did reprint Gregg's letter about *Gandhiji's Satyagraha* in the *Crisis*.[65]

Several members of the FOR saw the Indian situation as relevant to American racial politics. Devere Allen understood that Gandhi's early career in South Africa led him into "much the same sort of experience an American Negro would meet if he forgot the color line and Jim Crow cars in Mississippi." John Haynes Holmes once put Gandhi's work on behalf of Untouchables in abolitionist terms: "As Garrison freed the slave, so would Gandhi free the pariah." The analogies were muddled: did black Americans suffer under something like a colonial regime, or did they instead resemble the victims of a rigid caste system?[66] Regardless, Gandhi offered hope to the victims of Jim Crow. That was the view of Howard Thurman, the most prominent black FOR leader in these early years. Thurman was a key popularizer of Gandhi's ideas among African Americans, eventually traveling to India in 1935–1936 for a meeting with the Mahatma that was widely covered in the African American press. Gregg was not alone, then, in seeing the importance of the Indian movement for antiracism elsewhere in the world.[67]

Gregg believed that racial inequality, like labor conflict, centered on a question of values. "More than ever," he wrote to Du Bois, "I am convinced that in essence it is a spiritual and moral attitude which is at fault, and that the only real solution must be in the realm of the spirit." This "attitude" had global ramifications. In *Gandhiji's Satyagraha*, Gregg discussed racial violence against blacks in Africa as well as the United States, arguing that in "Asia and other countries the white race is treating colored races in ways which are violent in spirit and result, if not in outward form." Colonial regimes involved "a denial of choice or preference to the tropical peoples, and are therefore a form of violence." Again Gregg linked issues of individual participation and self-determination to his reinvention of pacifism. Nonviolent resistance could supply the power that would end imperialism and racial violence.[68]

In these conjectures, Gregg drew on racialist assumptions that were then common across the political spectrum. In his writing on Gandhi, Gregg occasionally relied on a dichotomy that set an arrogant, aggressive West against a submissive East. Similarly, in order to critique white racism and imperialism, and in order to legitimate this particular application of nonviolent action, Gregg sometimes imagined opposing "white" and "colored" characteristics. "The Negroes," he explained, "are a gentle race, accustomed to marvelous endurance of suffering. Their gentleness and humility would be towers of strength to them in any campaign of nonviolent resistance." These traits, he believed, marked "all colored races." The white race, in contrast, was destroying itself through its own "pride." Gregg argued that "we as a race cannot escape from our own chains without the help of our colored brothers and sisters." This racialist view, then, was another element of Gregg's countermodernity, a modernity that incorporated elements outside the white West.[69]

Upon his return to the United States in 1928, Gregg became a leading American analyst of Indian affairs and advocate of independence. Having learned the importance of winning over public opinion in a political conflict, he set out to do just that. With J. B. Matthews and Roger Baldwin, he helped start the American League for India's Freedom, one of several proindependence groups then springing up. The league published bulletins promising "up-to-date and accurate news regarding the Indian struggle for independence," particularly "what does not appear commonly in the press."[70] Gregg also wrote about India for various liberal journals and tried to promote the tenets of nonviolence through a short-lived tenure as director of Pendle Hill, a Quaker school ("calm yourself," he wrote a friend, "because I have not become a Quaker"). Like Gandhi, Gregg had long since abandoned his legal career and committed himself instead to developing the theory and applications of nonviolent action.[71]

In 1934 Gregg published *The Power of Non-Violence,* an extensively revised version of *Gandhiji's Satyagraha,* the work he had sent to Du Bois. This was the first book that he published in America, rather than India. It became, in the words of John Nevin Sayre, "the 'Bible' of non-violence." In the foreword, the eminent Quaker leader Rufus Jones pronounced *The Power of Non-Violence* "a new kind of book" that employed "practical wisdom" as a corrective to pacifism's airy abstractions. A reviewer in the *Christian Century* congratulated Gregg for undertaking the "monumental task of spelling out ABC and working out one-two-three a language and ethics actually utilizable in all social groups from homes and schools to factories, parades and international conclaves." Across the ocean, the Anglican minister Dick Sheppard made Gregg's ideas the guiding principles of the Peace Pledge Union, the most important English pacifist group of the 1930s. Aldous Huxley, a prominent Peace Pledge Union member, contended that "the only practical way of dealing with the problem of war is the organization of what Gregg in his recent book on the subject calls Non-Violent Coercion." Not surprisingly, the book's pragmatic orientation was its most frequently noted feature.[72]

The Power of Non-Violence created communities of readers and activists as it entered the Christian pacifist print culture that had blossomed during the 1920s. Gregg expected his work on nonviolence, like his science textbook, to serve as a practical guide for action. The FOR frequently advertised the book in its new journal *Fellowship,* and Gregg himself led discussion groups on it. The back of the 1935 edition contained "Questions for Study" intended for such groups, and in some cases, study led to action. In Columbus, Ohio, for instance, an interracial FOR group held regular meetings to discuss Gregg's book while also working to resolve a case of housing discrimination at Ohio State University.[73]

Not every reader was enamored of Gregg's practical pacifism. In a trenchant review of *The Power of Non-Violence,* Reinhold Niebuhr clarified what was at stake in a focus on the strategic qualities of nonviolent action. Niebuhr, who had quit the FOR the year before, showed his increasing skepticism about the moral authority of the pacifist position. While acknowledging that Gregg had "written the most authoritative book on non-violence yet published in this country," he wondered if *The Power of Non-Violence* did not place its author in an impossible bind. "Since his

THE GANDHIAN MOMENT   III

defense of non-violence is consistently pragmatic," Niebuhr reasoned, "it prompts the question whether it is possible to condemn violence so absolutely within the framework of a pragmatic position." Gregg "may have proved that it is important to reduce violence to a minimum," but "he has not thereby proved that force may not be necessary in a final crisis." If political effectiveness was the measuring stick, then the absolute condemnation of violence as a transgression of spiritual laws had no validity. If nonviolence was a better kind of war, then its essential difference from war became unclear. Given Gregg's pragmatic tone, Niebuhr found the "unqualified character of his loyalty to the principle of non-violence" to be "confusing." Gregg had tried to clothe the absolute values of religious pacifism in the relativist garb of scientific politics. But could one really maintain both principle and pragmatism?[74]

In writing about the strategy of nonviolence, Gregg had never meant to suggest that strategy was everything. Still, his explicitly instrumental focus raised the possibility of political actors who chose nonviolence purely on the grounds of political expediency. Gregg had intimated that nonviolence was in part a performance, but could it be *only* a performance, with loaded guns hidden just offstage in case the audience failed to respond sympathetically? He had begged these questions by eschewing the rhetoric of absolute moral values, creating a tension between principle and spectacle that would mark nonviolent action wherever it was used in the years to come.

In the end, Richard Gregg had produced the first substantial theory of nonviolence as an autonomous technique. His ideas first emerged out of his experiences in labor and anticolonial movements, not out of any close connection to the peace movement. As a result, his conception of nonviolence had less to do with ending international war than with bringing power to oppressed social groups. Gregg's colleagues in the Fellowship of Reconciliation had mixed feelings about his broad agenda for achieving a countermodernity, but they enthusiastically seized on the Gandhian method that he put forth in *The Power of Non-Violence*. In the 1930s, the task of proving pacifism's efficacy became especially urgent, for Christian nonviolence faced a new threat, this time from the left. The Fellowship's encounter with Communism led to further transformation of the absolute pacifism that had emerged during the years of the Great War.

4   Gandhism and Socialism

By 1934, the year that Richard Gregg published *The Power of Non-Violence*, the figure of Gandhi had become an important touchstone in discussions of violence, religion, and democratic politics. So the time was as ripe as it would ever be for Thornton Wilder to invent George Marvin Brush, undoubtedly the only Middle Western Gandhian traveling salesman in all of American literature. Though Wilder was no pacifist, his interest in Gandhi made sense. The son of a diplomat, he had spent much of his youth in the Asian missionary network that shaped so many of the leaders of the Fellowship of Reconciliation. Furthermore, religious themes pervaded Wilder's writing throughout his career. He first won attention, and a Pulitzer Prize, for *The Bridge of San Luis Rey*, which told the story of an eighteenth-century Peruvian monk who explores the meaning of an apparently random tragedy. Wilder's most lasting fame came from his elegiac portrayal of American village life in *Our Town*, but his first major work set in the United States was the satirical novel *Heaven's My Destination*, and his first American protagonist was George Brush.

Wilder understood that American readers were now familiar with Gandhi's ideas, an assumption borne out by the selection of *Heaven's My Destination* for the January 1935 Book-of-the-Month Club. The book gestures toward such classic works as *Don Quixote* and *Candide*, on one hand, and toward Sinclair Lewis's chronicles of American simple-mindedness on the other. George Brush is a devout Christian who holds an amalgam of liberal and conservative ideals, believing that followers of Jesus should oppose both banks and strong liquor, both Jim Crow and the theory of evolution. Above all, Brush attempts to spread the Gandhian doctrine of *ahimsa,* or nonviolence. The novel follows him along his travels as he attempts to make the world conform to his lofty standards, while meeting mostly incredulity, ridicule, and misunderstanding. He closes his bank account and announces his intention to live by a vow of "voluntary poverty, like Gandhi," but this only leads to a run on the bank by panicky investors. Believing that the use of force even to prevent injustice is immoral, he refuses to stop a thief who is robbing a store, but finds himself charged as an accomplice in the crime. In short, Wilder took for granted that his audience knew not only about Gandhi's nonviolence, but about many of his other beliefs and practices as well.

As itinerant Gandhian missionary and textbook salesman, Wilder's protagonist symbolized the emerging tension in radical pacifism between absolute values and instrumental tactics, between sincerity and artifice. Much to the bewilderment of readers, *Heaven's My Destination* never resolved that tension, for it satirized both George Brush's uncompromising devotion to principle and the shallow hypocrisy of the novel's other characters. In fact, the book seemed at times to be nothing more than a farce. "Just how far Mr. Wilder meant to go in seriousness of purpose is difficult to judge," one reviewer conceded.[1]

This puzzle had another dimension, for Wilder had written *Heaven's My Destination* in the wake of a protracted literary feud. In 1930, Michael Gold, an American Communist and champion of the new "proletarian literature," had dismissed Wilder in a *New Republic* essay as a "prophet of the genteel Christ." He thought that the spiritual explorations in Wilder's early novels added up to "a pastel, pastiche, dilettante religion . . . a daydream of homosexual figures in graceful gowns moving archaically among the lilies." Gold challenged him to write a book that would engage the social realities of modern America. This essay began a furious debate in the *New Republic* and other journals about the relationships between literature and political radicalism. Many observers saw *Heaven's My Destination* as an attempt to address Gold's critique. Though Wilder himself denied that the book was such a riposte, citing instead his interest in *Don Quixote,* it does appear to be in dialogue with the growing influence of social politics, and Marxism more specifically, in American literature. But what kind of response was it? The Gandhian apostle George Brush could be read as a tragic hero, a fool, or perhaps a surrogate for the author himself. The eminent literary critic Edmund Wilson suggested that Brush had "something in common" with A. J. Muste.[2] Whatever the case, Wilder mocked both American commonsense conservatism and visionary agendas for social transformation. So was Gandhi some kind of answer to Marx, or only a caricature of him?[3]

In the years before Wilder's book appeared, that question had become an urgent one for the Fellowship of Reconciliation. For the first time, it faced a formidable new adversary on the left. Marxist theory and Communist politics challenged Christian nonviolence in two major ways. First, Communists argued that the fundamental fact of modern society was the material reality of class conflict, not the spiritual reality of human unity. In 1928, the Comintern announced the beginning of a catastrophic "Third Period" of capitalism's demise, a prediction soon buttressed by worldwide economic depression. Third Period Communists condemned the Fellowship's brand of dissent as a class ideology that disguised the realities of power in a haze of spiritual goodwill. Michael Gold attacked "Christian Socialists" as frail, effete, and ultimately irrelevant. They were "not real Socialists," he claimed, but "wealthy Tolstoyans" who sought to maintain an impossible "neutrality in the class struggle."[4] As this diatribe suggests, the economic views of the Fellowship circle were becoming as significant as its opposition to international war. In the years between the Great Crash and the Spanish Civil War, Communist criticism would force the pacifists to extend the principles, and conundrums, of nonviolence to the question of class war.

Marxism also challenged the pacifist dream of overcoming violence with truth. John Nevin Sayre had argued for a nonviolent "propaganda of truth," but Communists were frank about their use of calculated strategies, truthful or otherwise, to foment workers' revolution. The world of American Communism was an endlessly shifting array of party lines, front organizations, secret meetings, and pragmatic alliances in the service of social transformation. The radical Christian pacifists might maintain that the example of Jesus prohibited such opportunistic measures, but Marxists insisted that the pacifists were impossibly naïve. For their part, the pacifists thought that the Communists' most dangerous deception was their attempt to smuggle violence into modern society under the auspices of social justice. The clashes between these rival visions offers a new window on Depression-era radicalism, one that goes beyond the Communist-focused notion of a "Red Decade." The Fellowship's religious radicalism formed an alternative tradition of American dissent, one that has long been overlooked by both celebrants and critics of the Old Left. That tradition put the relationship between power and violence at the heart of social thought and political culture in the thirties.[5]

For conservative anticommunists, the distinctions between Communists and pacifists hardly mattered. Many of them believed that religious radicals and Red revolutionaries were part of the same ominous conspiracy against American democracy. Foreshadowing the techniques of Joseph McCarthy in the 1950s, these "professional patriots" alleged sinister Communist influence in a wide variety of left-wing causes. Christian pacifists, they thought, were often the unwitting dupes of a dangerous enemy. The Fellowship leaders were used to this tactic of guilt by innuendo, for they had been through a similar experience during the Great War, when the enemy was German rather than Russian. Yet the attempts by conservatives to paint the Fellowship Red had important effects on pacifist strategy.[6]

Elizabeth Dilling's *The Red Network,* first published in 1934, became one of the most ambitious attempts to expose the naïveté and even outright subterfuge of left-leaning American Christians, especially pacifists. The Fellowship of Reconciliation was featured prominently in this encyclopedic tome, with almost every one of the group's leaders making an appearance (Dilling left out only Richard Gregg, though she included his mentor Mohandas Gandhi). Surprisingly, the book had relatively little to say about the workings of the actual Communist Party in the United States. The entry on Kirby Page, for instance, was longer than those on the Communist Party leaders Earl Browder and William Z. Foster put together, revealing Dilling's interest in the supposed extension of the "Red network" to the most unlikely places. Religious groups were not the book's only target, but they were an important one, for nothing spoke more strongly of Communism's devilry than its infusion into the nation's spiritual life. In chapters such as "So-Called 'Pacifism'—Is It Christian or Red?," Dilling put forth assertions that would have astonished Michael Gold. "As one becomes familiar with the names in the various Red organizations," she explained, "the truth becomes apparent that 'Christian' Socialism and Communism are branches of the same movement." This was not the worst. The respectable deportment that religious radicalism affected was especially dangerous, Dilling warned, "for no hate filled grimy Communist, however sincere, cursing God and capitalism from a soap box, could ever lure the Church-going 'bourgeoisie' into Marxism as can a truly sincere and altruistic 'Christian' Socialist." The Fellowship leaders, in this view, were at best "sincere and altruistic" fools, perhaps even devious frauds.[7]

The increasing popularity of the conspiratorial "Red network" style of anticommunism led to what Page later remembered as "one of my most unpleasant and at the same time exhilarating experiences." Though he was among the most virulent anticommunists in the FOR, Page attracted a disproportionate amount of the ire of the "professional patriots." His high profile, attained through his frequent speaking engagements and his constant stream of pamphlets, probably made him a good target. In the spring of 1932, he planned to give the commencement address at Baylor University, a Baptist school in his native Texas. J. Frank Norris had other ideas. Pastor of a large Baptist church in Fort Worth, Norris was the archetype of "fighting fundamentalism." The fundamentalist movement, which had emerged during the first years of the twentieth century as a fairly moderate critique of liberal Protestant theology, had by the 1920s become increasingly isolated, strident, and reactionary. Norris was at the extreme even in this climate, not simply because he denounced evolution, alcohol, Catholicism, the New Deal, and even the more mainstream Southern Baptist Convention as dangers to true religion, but because he did so in a style so bombastic and vindictive that even other fundamentalists cringed. Certainly not many of them offered to expose "The Ten Biggest Devils in Ft. Worth, Names Given," as Norris did in one sermon. Probably not one other had shot and killed a man in the church office, as Norris had (a jury ruled that he had acted in self-defense, and his congregation refused to accept his resignation). By 1932 Norris was the most powerful fundamentalist in the South. He was not about to let Page speak at his alma mater without a fight.[8]

"International Red Communist and Atheist to Deliver Commencement Address at Baylor University," read the headline of Norris's journal the *Fundamentalist* on April 8, 1932. Norris, like Dilling, sought to defeat Christian pacifism by insisting that it was not what it claimed to be. He began a campaign of letter-writing, publishing, broadcasting, and public speaking to prevent Page's appearance. Baylor president W. S. Allen soon contacted Page to explain that he disagreed with Norris but, given the force of the attack, hoped that Page could "make one of your great inspirational spiritual addresses rather than to go into a discussion of political and economic problems." Page promised a speech that would be acceptable to all parties, yet the onslaught continued and Baylor authorities grew more worried. On April 21, Allen informed Page that the Board of Trustees had decided not to grant him the honorary degree that he had been scheduled to receive.[9]

Finally, the week before commencement, the *Fundamentalist* struck again. The paper carried a large picture, not of Page, but of Egbert Ethelred Brown, an African American member of the *World Tomorrow* staff. Page "carries his communism into practical application by repeatedly advocating social equality with negroes," Norris charged. The transformation was complete: Kirby Page, the white Christian pacifist, had become a black atheist agent of Soviet Russia.[10]

In the end, Page gave his speech on June 1 to an enthusiastic audience. He found that "the student body was seething with indignation against the tactics of Dr. Norris." Nonetheless, in his address, titled "Religion and Social Progress," Page apparently heeded Allen's warnings against discussing radical political or economic reform, and he did not in the end receive his honorary degree.[11] Meanwhile, despite Norris's partial victory, his inability to prevent Page's visit only heightened his fanaticism. Soon after Page left Texas, Norris preached a sermon called "The Red Menace of Communism," during which he produced a Russian flag and called several knife-wielding young men to the front of the church to cut it apart and trample it. Page, for his part, continued to suffer from rumors of mistaken identity. While preparing to give an address in California a few years after the Baylor speech, he received a letter from a minister there asking for "some of those notices with your picture such as you enclosed with your last letter. . . . You are being unofficially announced as a pagan Negro."[12]

The shameless attempts by his conservative opponents to turn Kirby Page into a black man had a certain peculiar logic. The Fellowship leaders, mostly white at this time, believed that people of all races and nations were children of God and therefore must receive equal treatment. Page and Sherwood Eddy spoke to black and white groups all over the country, "repeatedly advocating social equality with negroes," as Norris had charged. "Jesus," Page explained, "was a radical on race questions." The pacifists tried to cross racial divides in physical as well as rhetorical ways, sometimes making an interracial "spectacle" of their "principle," to use Edward Ross's prescient terms. When he went to India, Richard

Gregg "avoided Americans, English and Europeans" and started "living with Indians, eating their food, wearing their kinds of clothes." John Haynes Holmes boasted that his Community Church contained not only Jews, Catholics, and "several Hindus," but also black members who "sit in our congregation alongside the white folks."[13] In addition, the Fellowship rather self-consciously billed its annual conferences as sites of amazing diversity, attracting men and women from around the world. So the Christian nonviolent vision required, for many, a willingness to put whiteness in jeopardy by personally associating with those of other races and nationalities. For the pacifists, this project was the expression of a fundamental truth about human unity, but to their conservative opponents, interracialism was evidence of a sinister duplicity, a duplicity entangled with a growing Communist threat.

Outside hostility and repression pushed the FOR away from the Communists. To allow racial justice to go forward as a political project, to say nothing of pacifism itself, many religious radicals felt that they had to avoid Red influence entirely. Even in 1935, when the Communist Party began to reach out to other groups on the left, Page warned that "cooperative action with communists plays into the hands of persons who lump together all opponents of the status quo—communists, socialists, pacifists, anarchists, and reds."[14] Fear of repression, though, was not the primary reason that the Fellowship kept its distance from the disciples of Marx and Lenin. More fundamentally, the Marxist outlook struck at the heart of the Christian nonviolent worldview. These religious radicals shared the Communists' passion for social justice, and in developing a modern form of nonviolence, the Fellowship would draw heavily on Marxist insights into the nature of class conflict and power. Nonetheless, the pacifists ultimately believed that the willingness to use violence, justified by a strident atheism, was Communism's fatal flaw.

The Fellowship leaders, like many left-leaning Americans, had initially hailed the Russian Revolution as a victory for freedom and progress. It was "the greatest event of modern times," John Haynes Holmes declared. To a remarkable degree, Holmes and his colleagues suppressed their pacifist instincts to support the Bolsheviks, overlooking political violence and religious repression to focus instead on the economic and social promise of the new regime. Their selective vision was an early manifestation of the ongoing tension in the FOR between support for the political left and allegiance to absolute pacifism, a tension that would resurface during the anticolonial struggles of the 1950s and 1960s. The dilemma was less acute in 1918, when the Bolsheviks' withdrawal from World War I seemed to suggest that the new regime shared the pacifists' abhorrence of war.[15]

A few FOR leaders actually came to believe that Communism was the better way. In 1927, the Fellowship lost two of its most talented women leaders to the Communist Party. Anna Rochester and Grace Hutchins had the typical backgrounds of radical Christian pacifists: Rochester had worked as a reformer in the prewar Christian socialist milieu, while Hutchins served as a missionary in China. Both came to oppose the Great War and found their way to the FOR. After the war, they started a short-lived women's "Community House" in Manhattan with the pacifist poet Sarah Cleghorn, published a book on religion and social problems called *Jesus Christ and the World Today,* and became editors at the *World Tomorrow.* In 1925, though, a dispute broke out on the editorial board of the journal. Details are sketchy, but a new plan to involve Kirby Page with the journal certainly upset the two women, probably because Page would turn the publication in a more explicitly Christian and anticommunist direction. Whatever their reasons, they left New York somewhat distraught for a world tour, during which they met with Gandhi and also visited Soviet Russia. Upon their return, Hutchins and Rochester cut ties with the FOR and joined the Communist Party. In addition to their interpersonal conflicts with the *World Tomorrow* leadership, the two women came to see Communism as the only ideology promoting economic justice. "I do not feel," Rochester wrote to Page and Devere Allen, "that either of you in your own thinking analyzes the basic industrial situations today and the problems of the immediate future in a way which lines up your intentions *with* the working class and not against it." Hutchins became one of the most prominent women in the Party, particularly after the publication of her 1934 book *Women Who Work,* while Rochester, too, became an important Communist researcher and writer. Michael Gold was undoubtedly pleased.[16]

Many other religious radicals who did not go over to full-fledged Party membership supported the Communists to a degree that the FOR circle did not. These sympathizers cohered in organizations such as the National Religion and Labor Foundation, which included prominent workers' advocates Jerome Davis and Willard Uphaus, as well as the Methodist Federation for Social Service, led by Harry F. Ward and Winifred Chappell.[17] Such groups cooperated with the Fellowship at times, but the differences between them were real. The Methodist Federation in particular

waged heated debates with the anticommunists in the Fellowship. "Inas-
far," Chappell wrote to Page, "as you pick out from the whole Communist
program violence—and, in my judgment, distort the picture by not recognizing the underlying philosophy—I . . . think . . . that you are on the
wrong track." This was, Chappell insisted, "not a superficial criticism but
a fundamental one."[18]

Ward, a professor at Union Theological Seminary, had a particularly
bitter falling-out with Page. The latter had greatly respected the older Social Gospel leader and had convinced him to write the introduction to his
first book on pacifism, *The Sword or the Cross*. "There are few men in the
country from whom I would rather have an introduction than Professor
Ward," Page declared.[19] In the 1930s, though, Ward consistently defended
Soviet Russia. Then, in 1934 he became the head of the American League
Against War and Fascism, a peace group with significant Communist
membership, and remained in that position until the organization dissolved in the wake of the 1939 Nazi-Soviet Pact. Page and Ward argued vehemently over the extent and significance of Communist influence in the
League, with Page finally concluding that he had to give up on the man he
had so much admired. "Harry Ward," he wrote to a friend, "seems to me
to be more and more a pathetic and tragic figure."[20]

As this feud suggests, the Christian pacifists adopted a more negative
view of Soviet Russia as the new regime consolidated power. To be sure,
they held the United States and Europe culpable for many of the problems that they identified. The FOR repeatedly insisted that America's opposition to the Communist government was building dangerous resent-
ments, but whoever was to blame, Russia seemed to be falling short of
the ideal that many had envisioned. Sherwood Eddy's conundrum was
typical. "I find myself," he wrote after three weeks in Russia in 1923, "in
sympathy with much of their economic policy, utterly opposed to their
religious attitude and divided on their political program." Eddy, like many
observers, suspended final judgment by insisting that Bolshevik rule remained an open-ended "experiment." However, Christian pacifist criticism focused with increasing intensity on three major aspects of the Soviet program: religious repression, a more general denial of civil liberties,
and violence.[21]

The Fellowship leaders saw Communism through the lens of their
Christian faith. They were willing to give Soviet atheism the benefit of the
doubt, for they believed that spiritual life under the czars had been hor-
rendous. "The type of religion developed in Russia," Eddy explained, "was

an esthetic mysticism" that, while "beautiful," was "lacking . . . in moral fiber and in social vision." John Haynes Holmes thought that czarist Russia had preserved "spiritual tyrannies" left over from "the darkness of the Middle Ages." To these Protestants, the Russian Orthodox Church may have resembled Roman Catholicism, which many of them still viewed with suspicion.[22]

Eventually, though, the Communist antipathy toward religion became too powerful to ignore. Eddy was an important authority on Soviet developments for the pacifists. During the 1920s and 1930s, he visited Russia several times as part of his "American Seminars," educational trips across the Atlantic intended to promote international understanding. In his 1931 book *The Challenge of Russia*, Eddy offered a sympathetic but critical account, praising the nation's economic planning but lamenting some political and social developments. His sharpest dissent came on the subject of religion. "Russia is the only civilized land . . . where no Christian Student Movement or religious student meeting of any kind whatever is permitted," Eddy charged. A student could not "openly profess his religious faith and remain unmolested." This persecution was disturbing, given the importance of his electrifying campus meetings to Eddy's religious politics. In 1926, he had actually arranged a debate in Russia on "Theism versus Atheism." The event turned into a raucous five-hour affair, with Christians and atheists loudly jeering each other. Five years later, though, Eddy lamented that "things have 'tightened up.' . . . and no such debate would be permitted or be possible today."[23] In their most combative moments, American Communist leaders promised to bring militant secularism to the United States. In describing a future "Soviet America," William Z. Foster explained that church "buildings will revert to the State," while "religious schools will be abolished and organized religious training for minors prohibited." Such unremitting hostility toward religion, however unlikely its possibility of realization, dismayed the Fellowship's committed Christians.[24]

For the pacifists, the repression of Christianity formed part of a broader Communist disregard for civil liberties. The Soviets practiced an "intolerant dogmatism," Eddy asserted in *The Challenge of Russia*. Edmund Chaffee felt that American Communists treated the underpinnings of democratic society with recklessness and cynicism, particularly his ideal of the open forum. The pacifists never extended their dissatisfaction with Communists to the point of actually arguing that they should be suppressed. As Page's experience showed, an attack on one strain of radicalism could have wide effects, as any American dissenter might find himself or herself labeled an "International Red Communist and Atheist." However, the Communists repeatedly angered Fellowship leaders by failing to respect their principles of open debate. Labor Temple, where Chaffee had attempted to create a sphere of unfettered free speech, became a key site of conflict. The Reds would often "howl down" anti-Soviet speakers, he complained, and factional groups tried to disrupt meetings. On February 26, 1929, Stalinists packed a speech by the Trotskyist James P. Cannon, leading to a fracas that forced Chaffee to call the police and the Trotskyists to cancel the event. Labor Temple allowed the group to schedule another date, and this time the meeting was successful, though it began, Chaffee explained, only after "several disturbers had been ejected from the hall, and the police had battled vigorously to keep the streets in front clear."[25] He counted this a victory, for he believed that he could incorporate the Communists into his ideal of open debate, and he insisted that others, too, try to deal with them through discussion rather than with "police clubs." Yet he still occasionally asked for police protection at Labor Temple during meetings involving Communists. "The Communist group is an exceedingly difficult group to deal with," he admitted, "and one that is most annoying and trying."[26]

The most "trying" part of Communist ideology was its belief in the liberatory effect of revolutionary violence. The pacifists' fears about religion and civil liberties under Communism were also connected to their belief in nonviolence, but world revolution put bloodshed at the center. Eddy diagnosed a peculiar "alchemy of communism" that sought to "sow violence and destruction only to reap lasting peace and brotherhood ever afterward." Moreover, the armed force employed by the Soviet regime was looking less uniquely revolutionary and more like the ordinary violence of its neighbors. John Haynes Holmes praised the Bolsheviks for building "a workers' republic" and promoting "the idea of a cooperative economic brotherhood," but denounced "nationalism" as the "great curse" of Russian society. "The same blight rests upon Communist Russia as upon capitalist America," he argued. "We see there the same pride in armies, which is militarism; the same quest of power, which is imperialism; the same passion for victory, which is patriotism. . . . I simply can't discover that nationalism is any different, or any better, in Russia than it is in America." The Soviet rhetoric of workers' revolution, in this view, served increasingly as a cover for the same old national chauvinism that had vexed the pacifists during the Great War.[27]

Christian nonviolence balanced precariously on the anticommunist left. Conservatives attacked the FOR as part of the "Red network" of Communism, but more troubling for the pacifists were the liberal and radical associates who scored them as a nest of intolerant Red-baiters in radical costume. Confronted by pro-Soviet radicals such as Harry Ward and Grace Hutchins, the Fellowship leaders realized that criticizing Russia was not enough. They had to put forth their own distinctive ideas, not only for avoiding international war but for addressing the economic disasters that now consumed American, and global, society. The ferment of Christian nonviolence in the Depression decade sprung from an attempt to incorporate Marxist insights without succumbing to Marxism wholesale. For a decade after the Great War, peace had been common sense. The Fellowship's "propaganda of truth" assumed the "truth" of nonviolence; the main question was how to get the word out. The thirties brought new efforts to rethink what nonviolence meant and what exactly it could, and could not, do.

Among the pacifists, Richard Gregg's answer diverged most drastically from the Communist model. Gregg was as staunch an anticommunist as anyone in the FOR, though he was temperamentally averse to the bombastic rhetoric produced by Page and Holmes ("in your devotion to Russia," Holmes once wrote a Communist opponent in a published letter, "you have just made your mind a piece of mush"). Furthermore, Gregg thought that the Russian Revolution contained crucial insights for pacifists. In *The Power of Non-Violence,* he quoted Lenin and Trotsky to bolster his case against moderate, ineffectual peace efforts, while in *Gandhiji's Satyagraha* he wondered if the Bolsheviks might have effectively used nonviolent resistance, despite their contempt for religion. "Mr. Gandhi would say that at least the leaders" of a nonviolent movement "must be religiously minded people," Gregg noted, but then suggested that "an apparently irreligious man, such as Lenin, who nevertheless had utter devotion and passion for the welfare of the common people, would probably make an excellent leader of non-violent resisters, if he once came to understand and believe in the method." Gregg was ambivalent about this possibility, and when he included a similar passage in *The Power of Non-Violence* four years later, he dropped Lenin's name and mentioned instead "a good Chinese Confucianist or an apparently irreligious man."[28] Gregg admired the Bolsheviks for their discipline, persistence, and social idealism, but like his friends in the Fellowship he regarded the acceptance of bloodshed as Communism's great weakness. He thought that the violence of the revolutionaries, "slight as it was at the beginning," had provided the pretext for fierce opposition by the regime's enemies both inside and outside the country, beginning an apparently endless spiral of brutality. "I believe," he wrote to John Nevin Sayre, "that non-violent resistance skilfully wielded would have brought far happier results with much less suffering and loss of life and a really bigger and more permanent [sic] advance." For Gregg, as for other pacifists, the Russian Revolution had been an opportunity lost.[29]

Gregg went beyond the Fellowship's standard anticommunist position to look askance at any form of centralized organization. He had, after all, audaciously championed Gandhi's program for handmade cloth production in *Economics of Khaddar*. "I myself," he admitted, "do not think that Socialism or Communism are radical enough to create the kind of world that I would want, or even radical enough to do away permanently with many of the evils of capitalism." At a time when the left, including the FOR, was painstakingly parsing the differences among varieties of socialism, Gregg simply employed the term as a loose catchall phrase to describe any state-controlled economic system. Though all of the FOR leaders had aversions to centralization, Gregg's opposition to state power was unrelenting. "All observers recognize," he insisted, "that compulsion, intimidation and violence have been and still are a very large and perhaps predominating element in the State." A "socialist oligarchy," he told Reinhold Niebuhr, would be no better than a capitalist one.[30]

For Gregg, the primary forces in society were not means of production, but rather the complicated systems of myths, symbols, and values that were in this period becoming known as *culture*. Gandhi offered the promise of a cultural transformation.[31] Gregg made the case in a pamphlet called *Gandhism and Socialism*, which was published in India in 1931, then in a revised version titled *Gandhiism Versus Socialism*, which came out in America the next year. This kind of rhetorical juxtaposition was not uncommon in the FOR at this time. Edmund Chaffee's sermon "Gandhi or Dynamite?" held up the Indian leader's autobiography against *Dynamite*, Louis Adamic's history of labor violence, while John Haynes Holmes preached a sermon entitled "Lenin and Gandhi—Apostles of Utopia." Gregg also saw two major alternatives to the status quo.[32]

He began by explaining that power stems ultimately not from political or economic structures but from "ideas and sentiments,—a scheme of values, a set of ideals or activities which people are induced to desire and accept as right, fitting and praiseworthy." Society functioned under a set of symbols that governed its conduct, an outlook also developed around this time by the political theorist Thurman Arnold in *The Symbols of Government* and *The Folklore of Capitalism*. Though some symbols were necessary at all times, Gregg explained, "yet, in order to keep them from making trouble, they must be periodically criticized, corrected, adjusted, or completely changed to meet changing insights and new circumstances and new truths." The symbols that Gregg saw dominating modern society were "money," "physical violence," "social rank and flattery," and "parliamentarianism." In the revised American edition, he added "large-scale organization," a "value prevalent all through the West, in Communist Russia as well as in capitalist Europe and America." These phenomena were not, at bottom, forms of political or economic power, but aspects of culture.[33]

Gregg saw "socialism" as deeply implicated in most of the same values that governed capitalist culture, particularly "violence values." "Socialism, especially as exemplified in Russia, clings to military and police violence and their symbols, as a prime control of society," but Gandhi's program went deeper. In their celebration of poverty, in their simple dress, in their decentralist and producerist values, and in their commitment to nonviolence, Gandhi's followers promised a more complete transformation of the social order. The "change of inner systems of values and of the symbols that go with them," Gregg announced, would be true "revolution."[34]

On principle, Gregg refused to lay out a definite political or economic program. The pacifist elevation of means over ends had traditionally derived from religious sources. The believer's allegiance to the divine stood higher than any political or social project, which invariably involved compromise with forces of corruption and deceit. Gregg, trying to create a modern pacifism, used science rather than religion to justify his own philosophy. In a letter to the Indian leader Jawaharlal Nehru, he argued that "the triumphs of the scientific method and the changes it has created during the last two or three hundred years" offered models for the Indian independence movement. "The early scientists," Gregg observed, "did not draft any picture of the future world of science and technology. They paid great attention, however, to the method of science and applied that as strongly as they could. Since the method was effective, look at the results." This lesson applied to the United States as well. At a moment when Communists preached the inevitability of revolution and liberals embraced centralized economic planning, Gregg extolled "Gandhism" precisely for its unmanageable open-endedness.[35]

Gregg's ideas anticipated those of the New Left and the counterculture in significant ways. E. F. Schumacher's 1973 book *Small Is Beautiful* popularized Gandhian economics in the spirit of Gregg, but far more successfully. In the thirties, Gregg was a political outlier in the Fellowship circle. Christian pacifists venerated *The Power of Non-Violence,* but its author's broader social outlook seemed too fearful of technology, too nonchalant about class conflict, and generally too nebulous to be useful. Against Gregg's juxtaposition of "Gandhiism Versus Socialism," most FOR leaders thought that radical nonviolence and "socialism" went together pretty well.

The Socialist Party offered a way for Christian pacifists to maintain their political and economic radicalism without having to swallow the contradictions they saw in Communism. The autonomy of the FOR prevented any kind of rigid alliance, but Norman Thomas consistently won the Fellowship vote. In 1932, a poll of the FOR membership showed three out of four respondents voting for Thomas, while Roosevelt gained only three percent. Even in 1936, when the Democrats had begun to co-opt large segments of the left, Thomas beat Roosevelt by a wide margin among respondents to a Fellowship questionnaire.[36] Some FOR leaders not only voted Socialist but participated actively in the Socialist Party. Reinhold Niebuhr ran for New York State Senate as a Socialist in 1930, FOR Southern Secretary Howard Kester was on the Socialist ticket for the U.S. Congress two years later, and Devere Allen was, for a time, an influential leader in both the Socialist Party and the FOR.

Some of the pacifists' allegiance to the Socialist Party sprang from traditional and personal sources. The FOR leaders envisioned themselves as heirs to a pre–World War I legacy of Christian socialism, closely linked to the Social Gospel movement, that included religious reformers such as Walter Rauschenbusch as well as more secular figures such as Henry George. This tradition had culminated in the presidential campaign of Eugene Debs in 1912. The young A. J. Muste, for instance, became an enthusiastic Debs supporter at that time, boasting some forty-five years later that he had "never subsequently voted for any Democrat or Republican for any major state or national office." Many radical Christian pacifists transferred their allegiance from Debs to Thomas, as when Kirby Page proclaimed that "the mantle of Debs has fallen upon Thomas."[37] Furthermore, Thomas was in some sense one of the Fellowship's own. Educated at Union Theological Seminary, he had been a cosecretary of the organization during the crucial years of American participation in the Great War and remained friends with most of the FOR leaders. He had left the Fellowship shortly after the war because he no longer shared its Christian viewpoint, but he still spoke a moral language that resonated with religious radicals.

The FOR leaders supported Thomas for political as well as personal reasons. They admired his economic agenda, which promised to eliminate waste and poverty through efficient state planning. Both Edmund Chaffee and Kirby Page wrote books in 1933 that essentially promoted the Socialist Party program of economic transformation. They tried to distinguish their vision from the New Deal, which they saw as a failure in its capitulation to capitalism, yet some observers thought that they protested too much. Henry Seidel Canby, reviewing Page's *Individualism and Socialism,* confided that "Mr. Page's socialism is not very different from the New Deal proposed by the liberals in Mr. Roosevelt's administration." Of course, the same could have been said of Thomas himself.[38]

Still, Norman Thomas championed political projects that Roosevelt could not. The Democratic coalition depended upon the support of Southern segregationists, so the New Deal consistently refused to confront racism in any direct way, a sharp contrast with Thomas's consistent denunciations of racial violence and discrimination. He worked for justice in the Scottsboro case, in which nine black youths were accused of raping two white women in Alabama. He also dealt extensively with sharecroppers in the South and criticized Roosevelt for failing to protect labor organizers and unions there.[39]

Most importantly, Norman Thomas and the Socialist Party stood for international disarmament and peace. Standard histories of the Roosevelt administration in the Depression years focus on the domestic New Deal, not on foreign policy, but the pacifists had a broader perspective. "On the various aspects of international relations, Franklin Roosevelt is probably the worst major party candidate in years," the *World Tomorrow* warned.[40] As assistant secretary of the Navy during the Great War, Roosevelt had been an enthusiastic proponent of preparedness and American intervention. During the 1930s he looked, to the pacifists, to be deliberately provoking Japan by increasing U.S. military presence in the Pacific, leading Chaffee to claim midway through the president's first term that "this administration drives steadily ahead toward war."[41] In contrast, Thomas frequently collaborated with the FOR on peace projects and seemed to be dedicated to the eradication of international violence.

In the end, perfect synergy never existed between the Socialist Party and the pacifists. Fellowship types liked to portray the transformation to

socialism as a peaceful affair. Kirby Page asserted that "the Socialist program of persuasion and social coercion through economic and political
pressure" was surely superior to "the Communist strategy of violent class
war," but he glossed over the fact that some Socialist Party members were
Marxists who accepted the principle of bloody revolution even though
they rejected Moscow's direction. Allen cautioned Page that "there can
be no such sharp differentiation between Communists and Socialists on
violence as pacifists often make." Some Socialists had preached class violence, while others had "cheerfully followed the old capitalist parties on
[p]reparedness and war." Pacifists tolerated these differences as best they
could. What became more troubling was the dissension growing within
the Fellowship of Reconciliation.[42]

Among the pacifists, some new voices insisted that the Fellowship had
to adjust to Marxist theory and Communist practice by focusing more
centrally on class conflict. Two of the Fellowship's traveling secretaries,
Charles Webber and Howard Kester, were among the strongest proponents of this view. Webber, who had worked in the labor movement in
Denver and New York and also taught at Union Theological Seminary, became the FOR's industrial secretary in 1929, an appointment that marked
the organization's growing interest in the labor movement. Each summer,
the Fellowship sent him to an industrial city to try to mediate a strike
or to organize unemployed workers. Webber became one of the most important liaisons between the FOR and organized labor, but he also discovered that, in many cases, Christian nonviolent methods appealed neither
to capitalists nor to workers nor to the Communists who competed with
him for the workers' allegiance. In 1931 he went to Allentown, Pennsylvania, where over five thousand silk workers were on strike under the
auspices of the American Federation of Labor's United Textile Workers
Union. Soon after arriving, he found the strikers enraged by a company
guard who had shot and wounded one of their number. Webber narrowly
averted further violence by talking the workers out of exacting revenge,
but his problems became worse when, after some unproductive negotiations, "a truckload of Communists came to Allentown from Paterson,
N.J." This group began to counsel the workers to use violence against the
mill owners, dealing harshly with Webber when he opposed this tactic.
After one particularly difficult meeting, Webber reported, the Communists "seized me and hurled me down a flight of stairs." Eventually the
strikers did attack the mills, bringing a brutal response by state police. Yet

FIGURE 4.1   Fellowship of Reconciliation Interracial Student Conference at Le Moyne College, Memphis, Tennessee, organized by Howard Kester in 1932. Howard Kester is fourth from left in front row; Alice Kester is sixth from left in middle row. (Howard Anderson Kester Papers #3834, Southern Historical Collection, Wilson Library, University of North Carolina at Chapel Hill.)

when the fighting began, Webber noted bitterly, "the Communist leaders . . . got about a block away from the clubs." He continued to advocate pacifism, leading nonviolent picket lines in front of one of the mills. The Communists persisted, too, but following a riot at a strike meeting, many workers gave up and went back to their jobs. The strike collapsed, with the Fellowship and the Communist Party apparently battling to a stalemate.[43]

Howard Kester, the FOR's Southern Secretary, also endured some harrowing experiences in defense of nonviolence. Kester was part of a fairly small but remarkably active network of black and white religious radicals in the South during the 1930s.[44] More than perhaps any other FOR leader, he moved freely across the color line. He was close friends with the black scientist and educator George Washington Carver, whom he called "the greatest inspiration in my life." Kester's attempt to represent radical Christian pacifism to black and white groups in the South was seldom appreciated, leading him into difficulties that were completely foreign to the Northern FOR leadership. When he tried to form a Socialist Party branch in Nashville, he could find only five other comrades in addition to himself and his wife, Alice.[45] For his public commitment to interracialism, he faced constant threats and harassment from white racists and suspicious police; before he delivered an Easter sermon on the Scottsboro case in Birmingham, Alabama, uniformed officers stood outside the church attempting to record the names of those who entered. Kester faced intermittent hostility from black audiences as well. After speaking in Greensboro, North Carolina, he wrote to Alice that "many . . . look upon me as a preacher of Pacifism, Patience and Peace just because I'm white. There are those who scowl and scorn and laugh." Kester provided the Fellowship with a close-up and often uncomfortable look at the realities of racial division in the Jim Crow South.[46]

In 1931, as Webber was battling Red influence in Allentown, Kester discovered increased Communist power below the Mason-Dixon line. "A year ago," he reported to FOR headquarters in New York City, "Communism was a relatively unknown term among most Negroes, especially of the lower South. This is no longer true." The Communists, Kester noted, had begun to organize black workers with considerable success, gaining a higher profile as a result of the legal defense they had provided in the Scottsboro case. Kester thought that the Communists' "questionable tactics" in that case might actually cost them support, but he also believed that "the tightening of the economic struggle may force the Negroes into their hands." For Kester, the ideologies of the Communist Party and the FOR were in direct competition. "The Communists and the Fellowship have this much in common, we both accept the Negro and the white on the same basis, with no discrimination whatsoever. The question," he concluded ominously, "is which will win." To prevent a Communist victory and racial violence, Kester insisted "that those of us of the Fellowship must seek more closely to identify ourselves with Negroes (and all those who suffer under our present system)." Commitment to racial justice became the proof of Christian pacifism's legitimacy.[47]

The experiences of Webber and Kester on the front lines of American battles over labor and race did not lead them, at this point, to the strident anticommunism of Kirby Page. Rather, as Kester's prescription shows, they sought to make Christian nonviolence itself more radical and class-conscious. Like-minded Fellowship leaders sought in various ways to move the organization toward a broader vision of social transformation and a deeper identification with the working class. However, this effort forced them to confront the allegiance to absolute pacifism that guided the Fellowship. Their conclusions varied widely. Richard Gregg argued that a more radical form of absolute pacifism was actually defensible as a political program. In *The Fight for Peace,* a critical history of the American antiwar movement, Devere Allen agreed. Pacifists, he found, had been both too willing to compromise their ideals and too reluctant to align themselves with organized labor. For others, however, the wholesale condemnation of violence itself looked more and more like a sentimental conceit. At this self-critical moment, Reinhold Niebuhr put forth the most searching exploration of the limits of the pacifist project. In 1932, his book *Moral Man and Immoral Society* dared to suggest that the moral superiority of absolute pacifism was nothing more than an illusion.

Niebuhr's journey to the FOR offered variations on a familiar story. Like Sherwood Eddy, Edmund Chaffee, and A. J. Muste, he had been raised in a devout Protestant home in the American heartland. The son of a minister who had emigrated from Germany, Niebuhr was around the same age as Kirby Page, Evan Thomas, and Harold Gray, who had gone to work for the YMCA in Europe during the Great War and returned as absolute pacifists. However, Niebuhr's German heritage pushed him along a different path. Condemning his ethnic community as benighted and provincial, he became a thoroughgoing Wilsonian and supported U.S. intervention. Then, somewhat like Eddy, he categorically renounced war in the aftermath of Versailles.[48] During the 1920s, as a pastor at Detroit's Bethel Evangelical Church and as a popular speaker on the college circuit, Niebuhr established himself as an aggressively intelligent promoter of social Christianity, a liberal Christian celebrity along the lines of Page and Eddy. In 1928, he moved to New York to join the faculty at Union Theological Seminary and the staff at the *World Tomorrow.* He also rose to prominence in the FOR, serving as chair of the group in 1931 and 1932.[49]

Niebuhr believed that religion's future depended more on its ethical relevance than on its metaphysical plausibility, a view succinctly encapsulated in the question that formed the title of his first book: *Does Civilization Need Religion?* This was a strong challenge to conventional Christian apologetics. During the last third of the nineteenth century, secular and religious thinkers held protracted arguments over the theological implications of modern archeology, psychology, and evolutionary biology. By the time that Niebuhr's cohort of liberal Protestants came to maturity, though, this so-called warfare of science with theology had largely played itself out among intellectuals, with the 1925 Scopes "monkey trial" as a kind of farcical final act. Certainly the members of the FOR still discussed religion and science, but hair-splitting epistemological debates sounded increasingly extraneous to the urgent human crises of the 1930s. "The curse of modern religion," Niebuhr remarked, "is that it is so busy adjusting itself to the modern mind that it can find no energy to challenge the modern conscience." Christians had spent so much time proving the mere existence of God that they had forgotten to determine whether or not he was worth having around. In fact, the prewar Social Gospel had targeted the "modern conscience" before Niebuhr and the FOR, but he dismissed that earlier movement as altogether too optimistic about the possibilities of social progress.[50]

The downplaying of religion in Niebuhr's early books, and particularly in *Moral Man and Immoral Society*, fit with the general approach of the FOR. The small amount of theology and biblical criticism that the Fellowship leaders produced in the 1920s and 1930s was mostly vague, half-hearted, and derivative. This lack of attention to traditional apologetics led some of their opponents to characterize them as irreligious, while certain secular allies wanted them to stop talking about Jesus entirely. That had been the wish of Harry Elmer Barnes in *The Twilight of Christianity* and the hope of Norman Thomas when he called the use of the Bible to address modern political and economic questions "an unscientific waste of time." Against these detractors, the pacifists believed that they had a conscious strategy to revitalize Christianity in the modern world. Ethical reconstruction, they thought, was the most pressing task of religious radicals, and such reconstruction required that religious people become conversant in social, economic, and political questions. Kirby Page suggested that modern ministers set aside two hours every day to research economic problems ("some pastors have concluded that four hours of daily study is the minimum"). Indeed, Page intended his pamphlets, with their endless quotations and statistics, to give such ministers easy access to information about pressing contemporary issues.[51]

In 1932, *Moral Man and Immoral Society* joined this contentious debate over religion's ethical relevance. Later, during the Cold War, liberal "realists" would see in the book's justification of violence a rationale for their own campaigns against Nazi Germany and the Soviet Union, an interpretation made plausible by its author's own political trajectory. This teleological reading, though, ignores *Moral Man*'s original context. When Niebuhr wrote it, he was a socialist and a Christian pacifist, trying to reconcile Jesus and Marx in a revolutionary world. He broke with the FOR a few years after the publication of *Moral Man*, but his decade in the Chris-

FIGURE 4.2
Reinhold Niebuhr,
1930s. (Archives of the
Burke Library at Union
Theological Seminary in
the City of New York.)

tian nonviolent avant-garde shaped his religious politics in the most fundamental ways.

Niebuhr stated his provocative thesis in the first sentence of *Moral Man*: "A sharp distinction must be drawn between the moral and social behavior of individuals and of social groups, national, racial, and economic; and . . . this distinction justifies and necessitates political policies which a purely individualistic ethic must always find embarrassing."[52] "Moral man" and "immoral society" were incommensurable. The inherent selfishness of nations, races, and classes would always spoil the aspirations of the "moralists, both religious and secular," who believed that education, rationality, or religious goodwill were ushering in the good society. Niebuhr believed that he was facing up to the realities of power that such "moralists" sought to evade, resembling in this sense Richard

Gregg, who would call his seminal revision of pacifism *The Power of Non-Violence*. Yet by modifying the idea of an altruistic human nature, which even Gregg had assumed, Niebuhr struck at the core of the Christian non-violent faith. He tended to think that "moral man" was naturally good, but he rejected the idea that this goodness carried over into the aggregate "immoral society." Niebuhr's juxtapositions—between the individual and society, between morality and politics—implied that the example of Jesus, the Fellowship's lodestar, was not always a reliable guide in the modern world. *Moral Man* said all this in a detached, seemingly omniscient tone that contrasted sharply with both the rousing rhetoric of John Haynes Holmes and Gregg's tentative, contingent language. Gregg liked to point out that he "could be mistaken"; such a phrase in Niebuhr's writing is virtually unimaginable.

Though he was savvy enough to call out the eminent John Dewey in the opening pages of *Moral Man*, Niebuhr's real interlocutors were the less famous "moralists" in the Fellowship of Reconciliation.[53] In fact, he had been part of a profound rethinking of the nature of coercion that engaged the Fellowship in the years before *Moral Man* was published. In 1928, Edmund Chaffee preached a sermon that asked whether "unethical methods" could play a role in the achievement of a just society ("Decidedly No" was his answer). At the FOR summer conference that year, attendees discussed "The Relation of the Individual to the Group" and "The Struggle for Power," themes that were virtual subject headings for *Moral Man*.[54] The structure of Niebuhr's thesis reflected the debate within the FOR over how to implement religious values on the national or international scene, how to apply the intense individual commitment of a conscientious objector on a scale large enough to make a societal difference.

The word that bound Niebuhr to Christian nonviolence and also moved him past it was "hypocrisy." A key term in *Moral Man*, it was also one of the common ways that the pacifists described the modern condition. They had come to see the world as a place riddled with deceptions, shams, and false pretenses, from Woodrow Wilson's "war to end all wars" to the pious platitudes of rapacious capitalists. Niebuhr shared the pacifist belief that power relations expressed in modern capitalism, nationalism, and racism betrayed human ideals of unity and wholeness.

Indeed, much of Niebuhr's unmasking of modern hypocrisy was in the FOR mode, though his later repudiation of pacifism obscured this fact. His writing had a hard edge not found in the work of more upbeat peace propagandists such as Kirby Page, but his attacks on war, nationalism, and imperialism were in the same vein. "Perhaps the most significant moral characteristic of a nation is its hypocrisy," Niebuhr wrote. He got more specific. "The Spanish-American War offers some of the most striking illustrations of the hypocrisy of governments as well as of the self-deception of intellectuals." The Treaty of Versailles was a stew of "dishonesties and hypocrisies." America tried to justify its "imperialistic policy in Latin-America and the Caribbean" by giving its actions a specious "halo of moral sanctity." Though "realist" liberals later used Niebuhr's thought to justify the use of force in international relations, *Moral Man* was in fact unremitting in its criticism of modern warfare.[55]

Niebuhr's analysis of social class, too, fit within a broader Christian nonviolent critique. Devere Allen, Richard Gregg, and Kirby Page all extolled the importance of the working class for social transformation and censured elite groups for their complicity in systems of economic oppression. When Niebuhr wrote that the "moral attitudes of dominant and privileged groups are characterised by universal self-deception and hypocrisy," he was not saying anything new to the FOR circle. Like other Christian pacifist writing around this time, *Moral Man* devoted considerable attention to class struggle and the possibility of a revolutionary proletariat.[56]

Niebuhr also continued the Christian pacifist effort to interpret Marxism in ethical and religious terms. He believed that Marxism was as partial and imperfect as any other ideology, but he argued that it had produced critical insights into the present crisis by exposing the realities of economic power. More importantly, Marxism had put forth "a dramatic, and to some degree, a religious interpretation" of the future. Marx had produced a faith, not a science. "His economic theory of labor value may be impossible," Niebuhr acknowledged, but his view of history was "in the style of great drama and classical religion." In *Moral Man*, Marx was a prophet who called down judgment on privileged groups and their attendant "moralists."[57]

Cold War liberals, including Niebuhr himself, largely ignored the sections of the book discussing Marxism and economic power, but in 1932 many readers thought that his evaluation of class violence was extremely important. This was especially true of his fellow Socialists, for whom *Moral Man*'s cavalier treatment of Marx was probably attractive. Norman Thomas considered the chapters on class struggle and the proletariat "among the best that [Niebuhr] has written," while Devere Allen praised his chapter entitled "The Ethical Attitudes of Privileged Classes" as "far and away the best thing I have ever seen in print" on the subject.[58] Such reviews showed that *Moral Man's* more famous justification of violence was inseparable from its analysis of class politics.

Niebuhr's indictment of modern hypocritical power structures was familiar to the pacifists, but he carried the idea of hypocrisy much further, into the individual personality itself. "Moral man," it turned out, was not above reproach. Rather, "self deception and hypocrisy is an unvarying element in the moral life of all human beings." Morality was often a "disguise" for power, and one could "never be quite certain whether the disguise is meant only for the eye of the external observer or whether, as may be usually the case, it deceives the self."[59] The idea of morality as a disguise mirrored, in an ominous way, Richard Gregg's notion that nonviolent resisters could turn moral action into a performance. Both writers seemed at times to treat morality less as an inner conviction and more as an outward method of persuasion.

From here Niebuhr assailed the family, which had served as the pacifists' most important model for social transformation. At different points in *Moral Man,* he made three related critiques. First, he claimed that although families manifested admirable moral qualities, these could not apply to larger social groups. The bonds of affection and obligation that linked parents and children, husbands and wives, or brothers and sisters were greatly attenuated, if they existed at all, among members of nations, classes, or races. Second, *Moral Man* argued that the moral logic of the family, with its inward focus, might inevitably weaken the forces of cohesion in those larger groups. All this was a flagrant rejection of pacifist ideals, but Niebuhr's third line of criticism went even further by claiming to find hypocrisy in the domestic sphere itself. The family could be a "means of self-aggrandisement," he noted. A father's special treatment of his wife and children "grows naturally out of the sympathy, which intimate relations prompt. But it is also a projection of his *ego.* Families may, in fact, be used to advertise a husband's and father's success and prosperity."[60] In the context of the FOR, such observations bordered on the perverse, and Niebuhr himself seemed more interested in sheer provocation than in a systematic analysis of domestic relations. Still, his message was clear. Pacifists had universalized a sentimental family ideal as a way to evade hard questions about power relations.

Moral Man did not quite accuse Mohandas Gandhi of hypocrisy, but it did try to clear up the Indian leader's "confusion." Gandhi was an American radical's Rorschach test, so Niebuhr saw him as a fascinating example of the way that moral discourse alternately justified, augmented, and obscured political power. He criticized Gandhi (and, by implication, American Gandhians) for finessing the question of coercion. The Mahatma had an "unwillingness, or perhaps . . . inability, to recognize the qualifying influences of his political responsibilities upon the purity of his original ethical and religious ideals of non-resistance." Gandhi tried to portray himself as a suffering saint, despite his use of "physical resistance, civil-disobedience, boycotts and strikes."[61] To be sure, Richard Gregg had also analyzed the practical political aspects of Gandhi's project, but *The Power of Non-Violence* had smoothed over the possible contradictions between the Indian leader's moral rhetoric and the requirements of power politics.

Intermingled with this discussion of Gandhi, Niebuhr emphasized the need for coercion in African Americans' struggle for equality. Because historians have overemphasized Niebuhr's influence on Martin Luther King Jr., they often credit *Moral Man* as a uniquely prescient anticipation of black nonviolent resistance. In fact, like so much else in the book, the remarks on black freedom revised earlier discussions rather than breaking new ground. Black Americans had already been discussing Gandhi's applicability to the United States for a decade when *Moral Man* appeared. Even among white commentators, Gregg had previously stated that "mass non-violent resistance" could help end racial violence and discrimination, while other Christian pacifists occasionally mentioned this possibility as well. Niebuhr essentially agreed with Gregg that nonviolent resistance would be far more efficacious than either "pure moral suasion" or violence, but he thought that this choice was purely a tactical one. On one hand, he doubted that the strategy of personal interracial contact, which was still at least as popular in the FOR as mass nonviolent action, could effect any substantial change. "However large the number of individual white men who do and who will identify themselves completely with the Negro cause," Niebuhr argued, "the white race in America will not admit the Negro to equal rights if it is not forced to do so." On the other hand, black use of violence against more powerful opponents would result in a "terrible social catastrophe."[62] Niebuhr shared the Fellowship's conviction that only nonviolent action could end discrimination against African Americans, but he left open the possibility that different means might be more effective under different conditions.

Niebuhr's pacifist colleagues could assimilate or simply overlook his critiques of the family or of Gandhi or of racial sentimentalism, but they were shocked by his contention that violence itself was not "intrinsically immoral." Niebuhr boldly insisted that the absolute pacifism of the FOR was yet another form of hypocrisy. He did not deny that the older tradition of nonresistance, exemplified in medieval monasticism and in Protestant sects such as the Mennonites, represented a legitimate moral stance that stood as a necessary critique of the political order, but he rejected the call by Gregg and other revisionists to turn nonviolence into a modern political program. While acknowledging the tremendous potential utility of nonviolent action in specific cases, Niebuhr observed that politics depended on compromise and the weighing of relative goods. *Moral Man* asked pacifists to confront the easy association they had made between peace and justice. "If a season of violence can establish a just social system and can create the possibilities of its preservation, there is no purely ethical ground upon which violence and revolution can be ruled out," he insisted.[63] Despite the later use of this argument as a defense of just wars, the violence that Niebuhr thought was a tragic necessity was the revolutionary violence of the working class. The absolute values of religious pacifism, he charged, resulted in a hypocritical defense of peace in a world of economic crisis.

Moral Man became most audacious in its instrumentalist view of religion. Niebuhr acknowledged its importance as a check on political ruthlessness and as a source of emotional and psychological strength. The problem, for his Christian readers, was that he seemed to see religion in the same pragmatic way that he viewed all other ideologies, that is, as a producer of "resources" (another important term in the book). "Contending factions in a social struggle," he wrote, "require morale; and morale is created by the right dogmas, symbols and emotionally potent oversimplifications."[64] In his focus on the power of symbols, Niebuhr again echoed Richard Gregg, but on a gloomier note. Niebuhr dared to call the insights of religion "illusions." The end of *Moral Man* was almost a parody of the great works of the Social Gospel tradition, which usually ended with stirring calls to bring religious ideals into practice. Even the levelheaded Gregg closed his books on nonviolence by encouraging his readers to help create "the kingdom of God . . . on earth." The closing of *Moral Man* was different. Rather than invoking the kingdom of God, Niebuhr called for "new illusions" to aid the process of social transformation. "The most important of these illusions," he continued, "is that the collective life of mankind can achieve perfect justice." Such a myth was "valuable," but also "dangerous." The book closed with a hope that human reason could control but not destroy the myth of justice.[65]

This was too much for many readers. In his review of *Moral Man,* Norman Thomas lashed out: "Mark, it is on this minor note, this qualified hope, that mankind may have enough illusion without having too much, that this gallant search after the truth comes to an end!" John Haynes Holmes thought that the book countenanced "the acceptance of the defeat of all man's best aims and hopes." Holmes and Thomas wondered how Niebuhr could claim a religious basis for his thought. Though "a religionist, he says that religion must fail," Holmes complained. "The word *God* appears frequently," Thomas added, "but one gets no idea what Mr. Niebuhr means by God or what power God may bring into the universe, including human society."[66] Thomas did not even consider himself a Christian, but he felt that *Moral Man* had crossed a line or, perhaps, drawn one. Niebuhr had suggested that religion in a political struggle would invariably become a strategic weapon as well as a source of ultimate allegiance. He also admitted frankly that deception and pretense might play a role in achieving a just society. In short, he threatened the roots of the Christian nonviolent project.

His most astute readers sought to engage Niebuhr on his own ground of pragmatism. Norman Thomas and Devere Allen both agreed that violence and nonviolence theoretically existed as points on a continuum rather than as opposites, but they accused *Moral Man* of failing to be even more realistic. "One great distinction," Allen wrote to Niebuhr, "between violence and non-violent coercion . . . is the extent to which violence, when initiated, so speedily becomes *uncontrollable.*" *Moral Man* posited an idealized picture of violence that could be doled out in predetermined quantities, for "a season." That tidy vision underestimated the messiness of real armed force, leading Thomas to wish that Niebuhr "had brought his incisive intelligence to bear more realistically on the grim meaning of wholesale violence in the modern world." Given the horrors of actually existing violence, perhaps absolute pacifism was the most clear-eyed realism.[67]

Edmund Chaffee was sure that he had heard it all before. "It was very interesting to me to note," he wrote to Holmes after a speaking engagement, "that Dr. William Adams Brown came up to Niebuhr and congratulated him but was rather upset by what I had said. Niebuhr is giving us substantially the same thing as was said at Union Seminary in 1917."[68] Union Seminary had been a leading supporter of Woodrow Wilson's decision to intervene in the Great War, with Brown helping to organize liberal Protestant churches to support the effort. Niebuhr actually viewed Wilson as the mistaken idealist par excellence, but the pacifists in the Fellowship thought that he was replicating, albeit in a different key, the late president's endorsement of the carefully bounded use of violence in the quest for justice. The Fellowship of Reconciliation had long debated that position with its friends and enemies, but during the winter of 1933–34, the debate would consume the organization itself.

The quarrel was as much personal as ideological. The cosecretaries leading the Fellowship at this time could hardly have been more different. John Nevin Sayre was a wealthy, well-connected Episcopal minister who joined the Fellowship during the Great War and had never since wavered from strict adherence to absolute nonviolence. The other cosecretary was Joseph B. Matthews, a volatile, charismatic figure who had only recently become prominent in the organization. Raised in Kentucky, Matthews had come under the spell of John R. Mott and the Student Volunteer Movement and gone to Java as a missionary. He had supported Wilson's position during the war, then turned pacifist after Versailles. In the 1920s, he became a bold voice for economic justice and racial equality in the upper South, thereby losing his teaching job at Scarritt College in Tennessee. His boundless energy and his interests in internationalism, labor, and race appeared to fit well with the Fellowship's own concerns, but appearances were deceptive. His appointment was a disaster. Matthews unapologetically promoted cooperation with Communists and served briefly as the first chair of the American League Against War and Fascism. Some thought that he himself was a covert Communist attempting to infiltrate the Fellowship. This was untrue, but Matthews had other liabilities. In a group so dedicated to personal character, he manifested what one prominent member called "a lack of grace." He antagonized the other FOR leaders by belittling the Christian basis of the organization and even participated in a nudist club. His pacifist colleagues were soon searching for a way to depose him.[69]

The growing threat of Communism, filtered through growing antipathy toward Matthews, pushed the FOR to resolve the issue of absolute pacifism with respect to "class war." On November 22, 1933, the FOR Council sent out a questionnaire to all members. The first question dealt with the Christian basis of the organization. The most controversial questions, though, asked members to define the character of their pacifism with respect to "the struggles of workers or other under-privileged groups." The six positions that members could choose ranged from exclusive reliance on "love, moral suasion and education" through "organizing the workers into unions and . . . leading them in strikes" and ended with "arming . . . workers" in "anticipation of the general class struggle." The position that proved most divisive, known as "II-5," asserted that the respondent, in extreme circumstances, would "consent to the use of armed force if necessary to secure the advantage of the workers, but regretfully and only while the necessity for it continues." Essentially, this was Niebuhr's position that limited use of violence in the service of justice could be morally acceptable. In their responses, most members stopped short of this position, and the Council decided that no FOR secretary could go as far as II-5 and maintain his post. After much dispute, three secretaries resigned after failing to endorse absolute pacifism—Charles Webber, Howard Kester, and the notorious J. B. Matthews. Reinhold Niebuhr also reluctantly quit the Fellowship, despite his close ties to many leaders of the group. His "political convictions," he wrote to Page, were with Matthews, but his "personal friendships" were "on the other side." He felt, he admitted, "like a lonely soul."[70]

The Fellowship questionnaire had several layers of meaning. At the first and most obvious level, it was sheer lunacy. The idea that these ministers, professors, and miscellaneous reformers might soon have to choose whether or not to "urge workers to acts of violence and participate with them in such acts" during an imminent state of "general class warfare" showed a lack of realistic analysis all around, as some observers at the time noted. From Nashville, Howard Kester's wife, Alice, who was perhaps enough of an outsider to see the points involved with more clarity, denounced the whole debate as "far-fetched and cloud-laden." Her husband had taken position II-5, but only with a sense of confusion and resentment. "While the whole issue may be a burning question in New York," she wrote to Nevin Sayre, "it is far from that here." Why not talk about the present rather than "the way-off future" of fantastic revolutions? Alice Kester accused the FOR Council of turning a personal dispute over Matthews into a bizarre ideological litmus test.[71]

Her complaint was unassailably correct in its substance, but the dispute in the Fellowship was not wholly "cloud-laden." These religious radicals sought to rethink Christian nonviolence in the light of the simultaneous rise of Fascism and Communism, a puzzle that occupied peace advocates both in the United States and abroad. The War Resisters League, the Fellowship's secular cousin, debated class war at this time, while in the Socialist Party the ascendant Militant faction squabbled with the Old Guard, who thought that the Militants were too sympathetic to

Russia and too amenable to the possibility of seizing power by armed force. In France, Romain Rolland, an eminent pacifist, early biographer of Gandhi, and hero of John Haynes Holmes, allowed that a socialist war might be morally defensible. Most ominously, in the year before the Fellowship dispute, Hitler had come to power and smashed the small German peace movement along with the rest of the vaunted German left. The felt imperative to choose sides was a product of this rapidly deteriorating political scene.[72]

Closer to home, the FOR disagreement reflected a larger consideration of the character of the American working class. In 1931 Louis Adamic had published *Dynamite: The Story of Class Violence in America,* an encyclopedic account of labor battles from the Molly Maguires and the Homestead Strike to the Industrial Workers of the World and Sacco and Vanzetti. The lesson of American labor history was impossible to miss: violence was the defining feature of modern capitalism, and it was on the rise. Norman Thomas took a contrary view. "Mr. Adamic," he wrote, "would have given a fairer picture in *Dynamite* if he had pointed out that the whole labor struggle in England and America since the beginning of the industrial revolution . . . has thus far been carried on with only a tithe of the violence which marked a single day when all was quiet on the western front." Workers, by the use of strikes, were developing "a comparatively nonviolent means of struggling for justice" that offered a hopeful contrast to the destructive patterns of international warfare. Thomas criticized Niebuhr's work on these same grounds, arguing that the picture of a revolutionary proletariat in *Moral Man* was an "oversimplification" that neglected present conditions. The working class, then, became a symbol for talking about the future of violence in the modern world and, by implication, the future of Communism and pacifism in America.[73]

For Howard Kester, the working class was more than a symbol, as his wife, Alice, had so angrily tried to explain to Sayre. In his own series of written exchanges with Sayre just before the questionnaire controversy, Kester revealed how pacifist theory mapped onto social conditions in the Depression-era South. The debate began when he mentioned in a report to FOR headquarters that he had used bodyguards while supporting a brutal miners' strike in Wilder, Tennessee. He also told Sayre that he relied on informants connected to the Ku Klux Klan to warn him about possible threats to his activities. Sayre responded by stating that it was "seriously wrong" for a Fellowship secretary to rely on armed guards for protection, advising Kester to work "alone, unarmed, or with a group of friends who will also go unarmed and be prepared, like Gandhi's follow-ers, to offer no violence themselves to opponents who may beat or shoot them down." Sayre also criticized Kester's infiltration of the KKK. "Un-less the Fellowship can fight its battles by holding onto truth and refusing deception and under-cover crookedness, and unless we can do our work without the support of armed guards, I think we are licked before we be-gin," he chided. Here again the specters of hypocrisy and deceit threat-ened the pacifist project.[74]

Kester asserted his commitment to nonviolence, but accused Sayre of being unrealistic about the South. "I have never entered Wilder or any other dangerous situation possessing arms or in any way relying upon the arms of associates or friends for protection," he insisted. At the same time, he asked Sayre to face facts. "Every man, woman and child in the moun-tains of Tennessee knows the use of firearms," he explained. "While most of the strikers possessed arms they scarcely ever used them as they knew it was not to their interest to do so." Kester tried to avoid violence when-ever possible, but he felt that he could not adopt the absolutist positions of some in the Fellowship. "What you say about Gandhi . . . leaves me cold," he admitted to Sayre. Gandhi's movement was largely irrelevant, he thought, in gun-owning, industrial America. As for his infiltration of the Klan, Kester wrote that he relied only on tips from friends in the orga-nization, not actual spies. "You may call this deception and 'under-cover crookedness' but I call it hard common sense," he retorted.[75]

Sayre was partly reassured. "I see you can not insist that the men of Wilder shall throw away their guns," he conceded. "Probably very few of them belong to the Fellowship." He was also satisfied with Kester's ex-planation concerning the KKK, but he still urged the Southern Secretary to insist that "guns are useless for winning the strike" and to "stand one hundred percent for a non-violent way of life." He suggested, too, that Kester had underestimated Gandhi, sending as proof one of Richard Gregg's pamphlets. Then, just as the matter seemed to cool down, the questionnaire debate forced Kester out of the organization. He could not believe, he wrote Sayre, that the FOR leaders had "become so damnably intolerant that they embark on a heresy hunt." In Wilder, Tennessee, the violence of the class struggle was more than a theoretical proposition.[76]

To other pacifists, the questionnaire was a referendum on the legacy of the Great War. The main defenders of absolute pacifism—Sayre, Holmes, Page, and Chaffee—had adopted their stance during the war, while those on the other side had played little or no role in antiwar activity. When faced with the critiques of Niebuhr and others, the absolute pacifists returned to those early days. "Our position," Chaffee emphasized to Niebuhr, "was something deeper than a mere fastidiousness about our wars." Though he was "quite ready to champion the cause of the workers in season and out of season," Chaffee would "use only those methods which are consistent with the maintenance of an attitude of good will on my part. Such," he explained, "has been the position of the Fellowship from its very origin."

To abandon the unique characteristics of the Fellowship would make its existence pointless, Chaffee thought. "If we are willing to apply a different standard to class warfare than we are willing to apply to international warfare our position loses its point. It becomes merely Marxian and there are plenty of organizations following that line." Similarly, jettisoning the Christian basis of the FOR "would be to become merely another pacifist, radical organization without any special reason for existence." Religious pacifism was a coherent position, Chaffee argued, and could not be reduced to some other ideological or political stance.[77]

Richard Gregg took an analogous tack, though he spoke in characteristically pragmatic language. Gregg was uninterested in political allegiances, Marxian or otherwise. For him, the function of the FOR was to promote the method of nonviolent resistance, and he resorted to the metaphor of war to describe his position. "A military drill master," Gregg offered, "can do his job equally well whether he is a republican, a democrat, a socialist, a Nazi, a communist, or a British Labor Party man. Military tactics and drill are all the same, substantially, in all countries and for any party policy." Gregg did not seriously consider the likelihood of nonviolent Nazis, but his point was that people could bring a wide range of ideological coloration to the task of developing nonviolent methods. If Matthews was dedicated to the technique, he should remain in the Fellowship regardless of his political beliefs. However, the group must maintain its emphasis on technique, not goals. Gregg pointed out that "many . . . organizations are interested in the class struggle and in helping the working class into greater power." The "unique thing" that the FOR stood for was "the thinking and working out of a certain technique," the technique of nonviolence.[78]

Ultimately, the furor over the questionnaire proved somewhat anticlimactic. Few Fellowship members actually left. In a short time, the names of Howard Kester and Charles Webber again appeared in connection with FOR projects. The two remained generally committed to nonviolence; Kester wrote to Gregg in 1937 to say that he had found *The Power of Non-Violence* "most stimulating and helpful." He also became increasingly hostile to Communist influence in the South. Webber, on the other hand, did continue to advocate a united front for a while, warning in 1935 that strong opposition to the American League Against War and Fascism would "divert" the Fellowship's "energies to fighting communism instead of just fighting war and fascism." Yet Kester and Webber were still willing to work in accordance the general principles of the FOR.[79]

The other leaders of the revolt over "class war" took different paths. Niebuhr tried to forge a nonpacifist religious radicalism in the Fellowship of Socialist Christians and in a new journal called *Radical Religion*. However, with his support of American intervention in World War II he began to embrace a new kind of "realist" liberalism that eventually distanced him from the American left. For him, Marxism had provided a bridge out of pacifism into a liberalism that condoned just wars. Having first accepted the morality of "class war," he was eventually able to justify other kinds of violence as well. Matthews, fittingly, took the most eccentric course. After a short period in the united front, he became a prominent anticommunist and eventually worked for the House Un-American Activities Committee. So the splinters from the "class war" controversy in the FOR never added up to any new challenge on the Christian left.[80]

The Fellowship of Reconciliation rejected class warfare, but the encounter with Marxism profoundly reshaped Christian nonviolence. It was now more radical, more class-conscious, and more sophisticated in its understanding of the realities of power. Pacifism today is virtually inseparable from soft-focus images of daisies and doves, but these radicals displayed a stubborn resilience. They had to be tough. In 1917 they had told prowar liberals that violence could not secure peace or justice, then argued the same point in the thirties with their Socialist allies and Communist foes on the left. Both of those disputes had been wrenching, but after 1934 the political landscape shifted dramatically. Antifascism replaced labor as the most urgent political cause, and somehow the defenders of nonviolence ended up fighting everyone at once.

My friends asked, whether there were any Americans?—any with an American idea,—any theory of the right future of that country? . . . I said, "Certainly yes;— but those who hold it are fanatics of a dream which I should hardly care to relate to your English ears, to which it might be only ridiculous,—and yet it is the only true." So I opened the dogma of no-government and non-resistance, and antici- pated the objections and the fun, and procured a kind of hearing for it. I said, it is true that I have never seen in any country a man of sufficient valor to stand for this truth, and yet it is plain to me, that no less valor than this can command my respect. I can easily see the bankruptcy of the vulgar musket-worship,—though great men be musket-worshippers;—and 'tis certain, as God liveth, the gun that does not need another gun, the law of love and justice alone, can effect a clean revolution. ·   —Ralph Waldo Emerson, English Traits*

5 Tragic Choices

In the tumultuous period that began with the Spanish Civil War and ended with the atomic destruction of two Japanese cities, Christian nonviolence faced its bleakest hours. In retrospect, the acrimonious de- bate over class warfare must have seemed like a luxury. Now the ques- tion was not about which degree of nonviolence was most ethical, but whether any kind of nonviolence had anything at all to say amid the new cataclysms. The Fellowship of Reconciliation actually grew from 8,600 members in 1937 to over 14,000 near the end of the war, but the num- bers were highly deceptive.[1] They represented not a slowly rising tide of opposition to war, but rather the consolidation of the few remaining ab- solutists still unwavering in the face of an unprecedented national con- sensus. In fact, the Second World War devastated the Fellowship, not only because people were again killing each other by the millions, but because sophisticated liberals, progressives, and radicals offered moral and even religious justifications for the slaughter, concluding that peace and justice had become tragically irreconcilable. Most painfully, some talented FOR leaders adopted this view and turned to support the war.

Against all odds, the Fellowship survived this dark night of the pacifist soul. Amid the devastation, a new generation of creative young radicals quietly laid the groundwork for the resurgence of Christian nonviolence in the decades after the war. This group included the future black civil rights leaders Bayard Rustin and James Farmer, the white Methodists George Houser, Glenn Smiley, John Swomley, and Jay Holmes Smith, and even Caleb Foote, an atheist. These figures admired the Fellowship's longstanding commitment to radical dissent. Several of them were less sure about the organization's devotion to Christianity, and some wondered if eliminating war was the most urgent task for pacifists. The development of nonviolence as an active method of social change, particularly in the arena of race relations, became the new cohort's highest priority. These innovators, mostly ignored in their time, turned out to be the vanguard of the more famous nonviolent movements of the 1960s.

Presiding over the ruin and rebirth of Christian nonviolence was A. J. Muste. That was unexpected. Muste had become a pacifist during the Great War, when he was forced out of the ministry and ended up in the Lawrence textile strike. During his years at Brookwood Labor College, he had served as a key connection between the Fellowship and the labor movement. As he plunged deeper into militant industrial unionism, though, he had drifted away from both religion and pacifism. He remained aloof from the Fellowship during the controversy over class warfare, focusing instead on radical labor politics. After a bitter internal dispute led to his departure from Brookwood in 1933, he formed the revolutionary American Workers Party with Sidney Hook and a number of other left-wing intellectuals. However, he soon lost control of the new party to the Trotskyists. By the time he left for Europe with his wife, Anna, in June 1936 to recover from a serious case of influenza, Muste had endured some of the most intense factional infighting on the American left.

Despite his troubles with the Trotskyists, the Mustes had a cordial visit with Leon Trotsky and his wife in Norway. The couple moved on to Switzerland, then to Paris, where A. J. entered the Church of St. Sulpice. While sitting inside, he heard a voice say: "This is where you belong, in the church, not outside it." With that mystical experience in a French Catholic cathedral, the American immigrant from Holland decided to break with the Russian exile in Norway and return to the religion of Jesus Christ.

Muste's conversion was a profound religious act of conscience, but it was also a kind of performance, retold in numerous speeches, letters, and essays. "I do think," the civil libertarian Roger Baldwin mused years later, "that he . . . has an actor's sense of always wanting to be part of the act when the act is sufficiently dramatic." As with most individual

FIGURE 5.1
A. J. Muste, 1945.
(DG 40, Box 1, Records of
the War Resisters League,
Swarthmore College Peace
Collection.)

religious experiences, the profoundly ambiguous occurrence in France
was open to vastly different interpretations, forcing Muste's audiences to
make their own decisions about him. Old Marxist colleagues rolled their
eyes, with Trotskyist James P. Cannon later writing that his old collaborator had been ruined "because of that terrible background of the church."
Mainstream media expressed detached bemusement, with *Time* magazine commenting that although Muste "has recanted the barricades, he is
still vaguely Marxian."[2] On the other hand, his old associates in the FOR
welcomed him back with enthusiasm. Muste became director of Labor
Temple in 1937, replacing Edmund Chaffee, who had died suddenly the
year before. From his new position, Muste brought the institution even
further into the Fellowship orbit than Chaffee had, while also providing
counsel for growing numbers of disillusioned ex-Marxists. In 1940, he
left Labor Temple to join John Nevin Sayre as cosecretary of the Fellowship of Reconciliation.[3]

Muste became, once again, a staunch defender of absolute pacifism rooted in Christian faith, insisting that "pacifism must be, is, religious." Hook, his old collaborator, maintained that he "could not have been very well versed in either" Marxism or Christianity to be able to switch back and forth so quickly, but Muste did have a theological foundation for his philosophy.[4] At its center was a transcendent God who was the source of ultimate reality and ultimate values. Muste was fully aware of the oddity of a radical intellectual turning to Christianity. "Men consider it a child-ish thing," he conceded, "something educated and sophisticated people do not do, to bow the knee before God and to be 'humble followers of the gentle Jesus.'" Still, the alternative was not a life of freedom, for secular-ists ended up worshiping "Hitler, Mussolini, Stalin, some political boss, some social arbiter or some other idol," or they lapsed into "disillusion-ment" and "cynicism." The point was that "if men really come to believe that they are the highest beings in existence, that there is no moral reality beyond them, they do not for long trust or respect themselves or each other." This amoral outlook, Muste decided, had been the fatal weakness in the labor radicalism he had recently abandoned.[5]

Muste excoriated his former colleagues for their short-sighted neglect of human values. In his view, the result of their myopia had been the self-destruction of the labor movement, which was now riddled with "the phi-losophy of power, the will to power, the desire to humiliate and dominate over or destroy the opponent, the acceptance of the methods of violence and deceit, the theory that 'the end justifies the means.'" Labor radicals had brought "the methods, standards and motivations of war . . . inside the labor movement, with consequent divisions and weakening." Not sur-prisingly, the movement had failed to promote international peace. The moderate trade unions had become mere appendages of the state, rally-ing around their respective national flags in times of war. Meanwhile, the revolutionary Marxist wing of the movement had countenanced ruthless violence in the class war, while the Soviet Union had become as belliger-ent as any other nation. Muste held that the ethical imperatives of Chris-tian nonviolence made it the only viable form of radicalism.[6]

At another level, Muste's surprising about-face stood as a stark rejec-tion of the emerging Popular Front. He heard the voice in Paris just a year after the American Communist Party's own conversion from the combative Third Period to a new phase of coalition-building. During the second half of the 1930s, the party sought to work with other progressive groups that shared the common aim of defeating Fascism. It even ended up supporting Franklin Roosevelt. The pacifists had seen precursors of this move a few years earlier in the more tentative United Front, which saw the Communist Party and the Socialist Party cooperating on certain projects. At that time the Fellowship, with anticommunists such as Kirby Page and John Haynes Holmes in the lead, had rejected any meaningful alliance, though the question had been a difficult one. "Effective cooperation is not possible" between pacifists and Communists, Page had insisted.[7] The more expansive Popular Front, which attracted so many non-Communist progressives, actually made the Fellowship's position clearer, for Popular Front politics soon elevated antifascism above peace and embraced the goal of collective security. The formation of the Popular Front, followed in a few years by the Nazi-Soviet nonaggression pact, then by Stalin's invasion of Finland, made Muste's point beautifully. In a crisis, the secular left maintained no moral high ground, but was just as mendicant and opportunistic as everyone else. Pacifism had to cling to unchanging religious ideals to retain its distinctive identity.

Even Muste's fellow believers, though, must have been shocked by his audacious declaration at a Quaker meeting in the summer of 1940, around the time that the Nazis marched into Paris. "If I can't love Hitler," he said, "I can't love at all." It was an outlandish, an unthinkable thing to say, even if, as a witness later claimed, he was not "preaching or confessing" but only "saying something to himself." Considered on its own, it can only be a statement of pure saintliness, or pure foolishness.[8]

In Muste's historical context, though, his assertion made a peculiar kind of sense. Many individuals and groups had claimed to want peace, but the outbreak of the Second World War had shown them all to be guilty of hypocrisy, to use a favorite pacifist term. American Communists had by 1940 abandoned the Popular Front to talk again of peace rather than antifascism, the bizarre turn a result of the Nazi-Soviet pact signed the year before. In March an exasperated FOR Executive Committee had issued a response, drafted by Muste. "In outward form," he wrote, the new Communist line "resembles that of pacifists," but no one should forget that "the Communist Party rejects pacifism in principle." A few months later, from a very different position, President Roosevelt declared himself a "pacifist" in a public address, but then added that he would, nonetheless, "protect and defend by every means at our command . . . our American freedom and our civilization." Muste's stated attempt to "love Hitler" exposed the superficiality of such political and linguistic contortions. Amid the cynical invocations of peace from the most unlikely quarters, whether the Communist Party or FDR, his comment stressed the ethical consistency inherent in the Christian pacifist position. His words highlighted, in the midst of a global clash of ideologies, the primacy of moral truth over temporary political expediency.[9]

Reinhold Niebuhr, who had abandoned the FOR just a few years before Muste came back to it, took issue with the Fellowship's claims to religious superiority. Muste preached that the followers of Jesus ought to be pacifists, but Niebuhr denounced this view as a "Christian heresy." Though by 1940 he had moved from a sui generis Marxist Christianity to a position of liberal "realism," Niebuhr's fundamental argument against pacifism had not changed since the publication of *Moral Man and Immoral Society* in 1932. The "non-violent resistance" of modern pacifists was much different from the older "non-resistance" of "sectarian perfectionism," he argued. The ascetics and the sectarians, Jesus included, "disavowed" politics in order to offer a moral critique from above the temporal fray. In contrast, the radical Christian pacifists sought the perfectionism without the renunciation, an end to violence within the realm of politics. The "*reductio ad absurdum* of this position," Niebuhr charged, "is achieved in a book which has become something of a textbook for modern pacifists, Richard Gregg's *The Power of Nonviolence*." Niebuhr's attack was little different from his review of Gregg's book in 1934. He maintained that no clear line separated violence from nonviolence. By entering into politics, pacifists had to relinquish their allegiance to absolute values. The alternative was "the morally absurd position of giving moral preference to the non-violent power which Doctor Goebbels wields over the type of power wielded by a general." Modern pacifism was a "religious absolutism" that led its proponents into a "preference for tyranny" over war. In contrast, Niebuhr advocated a pragmatic acceptance of the immoral compromises essential to the secular realm of politics, an acceptance that led him to support U.S. intervention in the world conflict.[10]

From a very different perspective, the practitioners of what Niebuhr called traditional "non-resistance" agreed that Muste and Gregg were up to something new and dangerous. Guy Hershberger, a Mennonite professor at Goshen College, explained that Mennonites practiced nonviolence because God had commanded it, not because it might effect social change. The Bible emphasized "*doing justice* rather than . . . *demanding justice*." Using the example of the apostle Paul's imprisonment, Hershberger declared it "impossible to believe that Paul would have . . . engaged in a hunger strike or similar means of forcing the government's hand." Yet "modern pacifists" since William Lloyd Garrison had adopted methods of political pressure that privileged social transformation over Christian love. Hershberger maintained that "there is no difference in principle between so-called nonviolent coercion and actual violence. There may be no bloodshed, of course, but the spirit, the aim, and the purpose are the same." Like Niebuhr, Hershberger accused the pacifists of trying to maintain an impossible balance. They would eventually slip into an apolitical religious witness or fall headlong into a pragmatic politics that abandoned nonviolence. The attention that these two very different writers paid to modern Christian nonviolence showed that the FOR had achieved a distinct place on the religious and political landscape.[11]

The intellectual debates over religion, politics, and violence came to a head during three conflagrations that led up to World War II. The pacifists in the Fellowship had long argued that a new world war was on the horizon, but Japan's 1932 seizure of Manchuria intensified the debate over the use of force among nations. As pacifists simultaneously debated the role of violence in the class struggle, the meaning of pacifism in the international arena came under renewed scrutiny. Reinhold Niebuhr, still in the FOR but moving away from absolute pacifism, called for an economic boycott against Japan. So did Kirby Page, who argued that such a step would be "ethical coercion" analogous to a "non-violent strike" or the "non-violent pressure" of Gandhi's movement. The cautious John Nevin Sayre retorted that a boycott would, on the contrary, be an incitement to war. This difference of opinion was only a minor skirmish, but the question of economic sanctions raised for the first time a serious practical question about the line between violence and nonviolence in the international arena.[12]

Italy's takeover of Ethiopia in 1935 brought real strain to the pacifist coalition. Sherwood Eddy, for one, quit the FOR in that year. Eddy, like Niebuhr, had come late to the Fellowship circle after the Great War, and now he was one of the first to countenance the use of armed force in the fight against Fascism. "I am a pacifist," he wrote to Page, "and will take part in neither a world war, a capitalist war nor a labor war." However, Eddy did approve "economic sanctions" and "would also favor defending . . . any points attacked by Mussolini, if necessary with all the force of Great Britain, France and other powers, at the request of the League [of Nations]." He stressed that he favored "the use of force" only under international auspices because it would then be "police power," not "war." Page objected, informing his old mentor that "a good many people" interpreted his views "as an abandonment of the pacifist position."[13]

Soon the team of Eddy and Page, which had done so much to promote social Christianity since the mid-1920s, came apart. In 1941, eight hundred people at the University of Mississippi heard the two take opposite sides in a public debate over U.S. intervention.[14] The next year, the seventy-one-year-old Eddy wrote a letter regarding his literary estate in which he explained that Reinhold Niebuhr should be given the opportunity to write his biography. "I would think of Kirby Page," he added, "were it not that he is such an absolutist as a pacifist, that he could not write the book in any satisfactory way, nor do I think he would care to do so." In 1941, Eddy became a sponsor of *Christianity and Crisis*, Niebuhr's new journal supporting intervention, though in 1955 he would still refer to Page as his "dear friend."[15]

The most crushing blow to the old Christian nonviolent network was the outbreak of the Spanish Civil War in 1936. Unlike the previous two events, the Spanish conflict drove a wedge between the FOR and most of its allies on the American left, as support for the Loyalists became the cause célèbre of the American Popular Front. Communists promptly formed the Abraham Lincoln Brigade to fight in Spain, but this was no threat to pacifist self-identity, for Communists had never shunned violence. More egregious, in the Fellowship's view, was the plan for a parallel Eugene Debs Column by the Socialist Party. Socialist Party members had always held widely varying views on the use of force, with absolute pacifists working alongside Marxists who dreamed of the violent overthrow of capitalist rule. Norman Thomas had held the factions together by leaving ambiguous the specifics of both pacifism and Marxism, a strategy that worked because the respective positions on violence had never been tested. American Socialists had found no wars, international or industrial, that seemed particularly worthy of their support. When Spain forced a reckoning, the Socialist Party chose to fight.

The pacifists in the party were shocked. John Haynes Holmes warned Thomas that he could not "stand by the party if this goes on." The FOR Executive Committee released a statement calling the formation of the Debs Column a "tragic decision" that was both morally indefensible and practically ineffectual. The Fellowship statement also attempted to link the Socialist Party's endorsement of violence abroad with a future predilection toward violence at home: "The logic of its present course will lead it to espouse violent revolution as the 'way out' also in the United States, unless it fearlessly and flatly renounces that course." Thomas returned the attack, pointing out that the pacifist position was "wholly negative" and offered no alternative to armed conflict. He maintained that war was an acceptable means of defeating the ominous threat of Fascism. The FOR, he thought, was trying to foist its own absolutist views onto an organization that had never professed to share them. The Socialist Party, Thomas explained, would "use to the uttermost non-violent methods consistent with true democracy," but "non-violence is not its first and last commandment." Devere Allen, a member of both the FOR and the Socialist Party, managed to mollify the pacifists enough to keep them in the Socialist ranks, while the plan for the Debs Column fizzled. But when the party adopted a policy of "critical support" for the Allies in World War II, many Fellowship members relinquished their identity as "Norman Thomas Socialists."[16]

Distancing themselves from proponents of intervention in Europe, the radical Christian pacifists were no more comfortable among the isolationists. Howard Brinton, director of the Quaker Pendle Hill School, explained that "pacifism and isolationism are polar opposites. Pacifists must clearly distinguish their position from that of the isolationist, and avoid alliances which we may later have cause deeply to regret." FOR leaders considered themselves consummate internationalists, but conservative isolationists such as Charles Lindbergh eschewed pacifism in favor of maintaining an impenetrable defense of the United States, while often sympathizing with anti-Semitism and other reactionary causes that were anathema to the Fellowship. Still, the two antiwar factions occasionally crossed paths. John Haynes Holmes once gave an invocation at a Lindbergh meeting, while A. J. Muste defended his own participation in a rally with Lindbergh by claiming that "there is no other basis for a mass movement against involvement." Such tentative cooperation soon dissolved, pushing the pacifists further to the fringes of American politics.[17]

The Fellowship leaders were well established in their positions before December 7, 1941. Pearl Harbor produced no major reversals of allegiance, but rather a rededication to first principles. Most of those who renounced pacifism had done so years earlier. The FOR Executive Committee pronounced itself "shocked . . . by the manner in which the Japanese-American conflict was precipitated," but only by the "manner." In fact, back in 1935 Holmes had written an antiwar play called *If This Be Treason* that imagined the United States brought to the brink of war by a

Japanese attack on the Philippines. No careful observer of world politics, pacifist or otherwise, could have been surprised that the United States eventually joined the global struggle. Recalling its stand in World War I, the Fellowship vowed to stay the course. Holmes wrote that pacifists should think of themselves as a "saving remnant" amid a return of the "Dark Ages." When the Communists switched positions to support the Allies after Hitler's invasion of Russia, Christian nonviolence stood virtually alone on the left in its opposition to the war. By 1944, even Muste's son John had signed up for naval training. "It is pretty tough," the father admitted, "to see him take this position." Abandoned by just about everyone, the Fellowship leaders engaged the "good war" primarily as critics.[18]

Both the strengths and the weaknesses of the Fellowship's criticism grew out of its belief in moral equivalence. Niebuhr had been right about one thing: pacifists were not especially concerned with making distinctions. As in 1917, they stressed the culpability of all the major powers. Sidney Hook overstated the case when he later complained that Muste "made no distinction between Hitler's world, with its total terror, and . . . the democratic world." Still, while seldom actually saying that an Allied victory and an Axis victory would be equivalent in their effects, Fellowship members did tend to see the two possibilities in the same general terms. "The worst outcome of this war," John Haynes Holmes argued, "would be a victory for the Nazis. Next to this would be a victory for the United Nations." Holmes equated "Nazi barbarism" with "British-American imperialism," maintaining that "both would lead to future wars, as the first World War led to the second."[19]

In setting forth the idea that all nations were more or less equally at fault, the pacifists were fighting, or rather fighting against, the last war. In World War I, the cause of the conflict was murky, the rival nationalisms of England, France, Germany, and, to some extent, the United States appearing almost interchangeable. Despite the long rise of Fascism during the 1930s, pacifists refused to admit that the new ideological dimensions of the war required any alteration in their position. "I can't see the situation a particle different from that of 1914–18," Holmes confessed as he tried to convince Eddy to stay with the pacifist cause. The Fellowship leaders' belief in the moral equivalence of all combatants developed well before the discovery of the concentration camps, but even at the beginning of the war many saw it as the weak point in their interpretation of the international scene. The liberal Protestant minister Ralph Harlow became disgusted with Christian nonviolence when he heard a Fellowship leader state that "it does not matter a bit who wins this war, England or Germany, it will all be the same." Harlow wrote to Muste that he "recognized then that I was not truly a pacifist any longer. For me it DID matter, very much."[20]

Their refusal to make distinctions led the pacifists to predict that something like Hitler's dictatorship would come to the United States. They were not alone in promoting this idea. Across the American political spectrum, dire forecasts came forth in the years following the Nazi rise to power, despite the fact that the United States had little organized Fascist activity. Republicans countered Roosevelt's 1940 campaign with the ominous slogan "Third Reich, Third International, Third Term." On the left, Sinclair Lewis's 1935 novel *It Can't Happen Here* described the ascension of a homegrown Fascist government. Pacifists, too, were insistent that Fascism was springing up around them. Richard Gregg took an especially somber view, predicting that "we are almost certain to have in America as well as in all Europe, some form of dictatorship, and here it will be fascist." He suggested gloomily that his FOR colleagues look at the life and teachings of Jesus, "in one sense, as being advice for living under a dictatorship." Such warnings fit well with the idea of moral equivalence, for they suggested that Fascism, like war, was a sin of every civilized nation, less a foreign military threat than a domestic political one.[21]

Today, the pacifists' use of moral equivalence as a justification for opposing American intervention seems overdrawn, even embarrassing. However, their singular vision led them to offer some of the most penetrating critiques of American intervention in World War II, critiques that make it impossible to dismiss Christian nonviolence as Hitler-loving mysticism. At their most trenchant, the Fellowship leaders accused "realists" like Niebuhr of being insufficiently realistic about the results of modern war. Hook claimed that Muste's style of pacifism showed a "reckless disregard of consequences," but that was a misinterpretation. Consequences actually weighed heavily in the moral thought of the Fellowship, for as Niebuhr and Hershberger had noted, the group was not a monastic order extolling transcendent virtue for its own sake. Rather, pacifists believed that good consequences could come only through moral action that aligned with the external source of morality—God, for most, though a few used terms such as "the universe." Pacifists therefore stressed that the immoral methods of war brought immoral results. In the case of World War II, those results included the militarization of American society, an acceptance of racism and imperialism, and the brutalization and dehumanization of the war's participants.[22]

Pacifists charged that prowar "realists" had failed to reckon with the costs of establishing war as an institution in American life. Muste, Gregg, and their colleagues overreached when they invoked the specters of "Fascism" and "dictatorship." Nevertheless, the war did produce greater powers for the president, the national government, large corporations, and especially the military, a shift exemplified by the opening of the enormous new Pentagon building in 1943. Pacifists demanded an honest reckoning with this reorientation of political and economic structures. They found particular cause for alarm in President Roosevelt's plan to make the United States into an "Arsenal of Democracy," a term that conveyed both a commitment to opposing Fascism and a desire to expend as few American lives as possible in the fight (an "Arsenal" was not an "Army"). Pacifists contended that the policy made the nation less an "Arsenal of Democracy" than a "Merchant of Death," recycling the term used to describe munitions makers after World War I.[23]

Muste wondered how the two terms—"Arsenal" and "Democracy"— could be compatible. He argued that the United States, as an "Arsenal," would gain the power to force compliance at gunpoint with "our ideas of what constitutes support of democracy." Furthermore, with the "Arsenal policy, the idea of democracy and of the defense of our own interests, markets, etc., are, to put it mildly, all mixed together." Although "we are asked to believe that somehow when the war is over . . . we shall scrap our armaments," such a course would be untenable. Instead, the emergent "armament economy" would continue to be a vital source of employment after the war, so no politician would dare to dismantle it. The wartime "Arsenal" would grow into a "Super-Arsenal," a permanent part of American society and an unstoppable weapon in furthering global American interests, democratic or not. The pacifists were some of the first Americans to identify what Dwight Eisenhower would later name the "military-industrial complex."[24]

Turning abroad, the Christian nonviolent position stressed that Allied nations, particularly Britain, were guilty of expansionist and imperialist aims. This critique, too, was rooted in an attempt at "realism," in this case an accurate assessment of the Allies' commitment to democracy, which prowar liberals tended to praise rather indiscriminately in promoting their vision of World War II as a global democratic revolution. In contrast, the FOR recalled American and British imperial ventures in Asia that had given Japan both a model and a motive for its current aggression. As early as the Japanese takeover of Manchuria in 1932, the *World Tomorrow* condemned the invasion but noted that Japan "was merely following in the steps of other aggressive powers who by force of arms have changed the maps of the world," not least the United States in the Philippines. The Fellowship's connections to the Protestant missionary network in Asia, as well as its special interest in the homeland of Gandhi, ensured that these pacifists would assess the war with colonized populations in mind. Calling again for Philippine and Indian independence, the Fellowship leaders saw more clearly than most prowar liberals that imperialism could not survive the war against Fascism intact.[25]

These radicals also maintained that Americans in general, and "realist" liberals in particular, failed to understand the uncontrollable quality of violence. A few critics had leveled this charge at Niebuhr's *Moral Man and Immoral Society* a decade before, arguing that while the book made a compelling theoretical case for the limited application of violence to achieve justice, it evinced no sense of the random, unpredictable, and irrepressible cycles of devastation that defined actual modern warfare. The debate resurfaced in response to the "area bombing" of German cities, primarily by British bombers, though the United States would unleash a similar campaign against Japan late in the war. Ostensibly undertaken to destroy enemy morale and shorten the war, area bombing's intentional targeting of civilians was, to the Fellowship, proof of the doctrine of moral equivalence. According to Alfred Hassler, who would later serve as executive secretary of the FOR during the Vietnam War, the bombing campaign showed that "a nation that gives its approval to participation in modern war, begins a process of progressive moral deterioration that leads eventually to the sanction of the most dreadful acts of torture and destruction."[26]

In March 1944, the FOR journal *Fellowship* reprinted "Massacre by Bombing," an exposé by the English pacifist Vera Brittain that described in detail the Allied strategy. Brittain presented her essay as a work of truth-telling that could overcome the dishonesty of war communication. She scorned the "carefully chosen phrases" used to describe the bombing: "*softening up* an area, *neutralizing the target, area bombing, saturating the defenses,* and *blanketing an industrial district.*" In contrast, she aimed to force a moral reckoning by relaying the "facts" of the campaign, echoing John Nevin Sayre's old notion of a "propaganda of truth." A foreword, condemning the bombing and calling Brittain's essay "a call to repentance," was signed by Holmes, Page, and other prominent FOR members.[27]

The signers had a reasonable case, if previous standards of wartime conduct were any guide. Until World War II, aerial bombing was still a fairly novel military innovation, and its recent effects in Manchuria, Ethiopia, and, especially, Spain had horrified pacifists and nonpacifists alike. On September 1, 1939, the day that Hitler invaded Poland, Franklin Roosevelt called on the major European powers to foreswear the practice. "The ruthless bombing from the air of civilians," the president declared, ". . . has sickened the hearts of every civilized man and woman, and has profoundly shocked the conscience of humanity." Indeed, international law and military tradition had long proscribed deliberate attacks of any kind on noncombatant populations. After the war, the famous Nuremberg trials would cite the murder of civilians in wartime as one of the Nazis' "crimes against humanity," but the Allies were clearly guilty of the same charge.[28]

In noting the moral exceptionalism implicit in area bombing, the pacifists provoked a heated response. Arguments raged in newspapers and magazines across the country, with the New York Times giving front-page coverage to the protest. Walter Lippmann defended the strategy as "a military operation to achieve a military objective," maintaining that it was the only way to "disarm" Germany. Niebuhr was more ambivalent. He saw the condemnation of the bombing as a sign of the pacifist "inability to understand the tragic necessities of history," but worried that the Allies were counting "increasingly upon the purely physical instruments of victory" to the exclusion of "moral and spiritual" aspects. Because the pacifists understood the war in terms of moral equivalence, they were among the first to suggest that the amoral logic of modern warfare could overcome the ideals for which any particular war was fought.[29]

At the same time, the bombing protest put the pacifists in a dilemma that would haunt them in all their efforts during World War II. In the Christian nonviolent view, Niebuhr shrewdly observed, "the whole war is rejected as well as the bombing." The Fellowship had tried to criticize a particular war strategy, but such criticism seemed to necessitate an acceptance of the war itself. The result was an awkward balancing act. As John Nevin Sayre put it, "we do not for a moment consider that a Christian conscience which is alive can be appeased by . . . 'humanitarian' rules of war" such as noncombatant immunity. Rather, pacifists had to wreck "the whole war method." This double criticism (we're against war, but even if we weren't . . .) muddied the pacifists' position while casting doubt on their authority. The FOR had raised the issue of the bombing, but seemed powerless to effect any alternative.[30]

In fact, as Norman Thomas had recognized, the Christian nonviolent criticism of the war was "wholly negative." Lippmann taunted the signers of the bombing protest: "If any one knows any easier way of defeating the German fighter force . . . , he ought to say so." The pacifists were astute critics of international affairs, but they had few compelling plans of action, as they themselves occasionally acknowledged. Bayard Rustin, who joined the FOR as a youth secretary in 1941, remarked that in "the last generation" the group had done "a superb job of causing men to fear, dislike, and to see the waste of war." However, the pacifists had "failed" to promote "a creative, capable, workable means of dealing with force and injustice." Without that program, they had no compelling retort to Niebuhr's depiction of war as a "tragic necessity."[31]

The plight of European Jews brought pacifist ethics to its limits. The Fellowship had long battled anti-Semitism. In 1929, Kirby Page had written that Jewish persecution by Christians "constitutes one of the most ghastly stories in all history." Christian pacifists participated in a variety of interfaith dialogues. John Haynes Holmes maintained a lifelong friendship with the eminent Reform rabbi Stephen Wise, who became one of the most outspoken critics of the Nazi regime. When Wise held one of the first major American anti-Hitler rallies in New York City, he made an exception for Holmes to march at the head of the otherwise all-Jewish event. The FOR itself even had a few Jewish members by the time of World War II, despite its Christian orientation.[32] The pacifists in the Fellowship, with their international and interfaith connections, were more aware than most Americans of the terror unleashed by the Nazis on Europe's Jewish population. The case for violence on behalf of that population looked incontrovertible, as even Mohandas Gandhi admitted. "If there ever could be a justifiable war in the name of and for humanity," he wrote in 1938, "a war against Germany, to prevent the wanton persecution of a whole race, would be completely justified."

"But," the Mahatma continued, "I do not believe in any war." Neither did his American admirers, who struggled to defend their faith. Holmes, in a 1940 essay entitled "Should Jews Be Pacifists?," argued that the war would unleash a torrent of anti-Semitism even worse than that propagated by the Nazis. Once again, though, pacifism offered no convincing alternative to violence. Gandhi advised the Jews to undertake nonviolent resistance, but an American Jewish leader dismissed that prescription with the remark that a "Jewish Gandhi in Germany" would last "about five minutes."[33] John Nevin Sayre took a different tack by trying to bring some European refugees to America, but the FOR lacked the resources to make much difference.[34] In the end, the course of the war erased from national memory the Fellowship's heroic stand against anti-Semitism in the 1920s and 1930s. Although few non-Jewish Americans had wished to fight a war for the Jews in 1941, the most powerful retroactive defense of World War II as a just war was the liberation of the concentration camps—by guns, not by Gandhi.

At this point, an earlier generation of scholars left the Christian nonviolent tradition for dead. War was the "tragic choice," the historian Donald Meyer wrote in 1960, and the Niebuhrian "realists" had the courage to choose correctly. That interpretation of events, begun by Niebuhr himself and continued by Arthur Schlesinger Jr., Meyer, and many others, draws on a compelling metanarrative of individual growth, a path from youthful idealism and naïveté to mature wisdom and discretion. World War II was in many respects a tragedy, but the "realist" account is simplistic and misleading. It tends to downplay cogent pacifist critiques, but more importantly, it remains within the limits of early Cold War foreign policy concerns. Meyer wrote before the March on Washington, before Vietnam, before "nonviolence" became a keyword of the New Left. He failed to notice that Christian pacifists, apparently defeated and discredited, were preparing to reshape the political morality of the postwar years.[35]

A new generation of Fellowship leaders rescued Christian nonviolence from its protracted crisis. Born too late to remember much of the Great War, this cohort was a product of the 1930s Fellowship, with its emphasis on labor, race, and Gandhian resistance. These younger men were certainly antiwar, but they effectively ceded the problem of stopping Hitler to others in order to concentrate on building actual nonviolence. Jay Holmes Smith, one of the young innovators, complained that "our brothers who are not CO's [conscientious objectors] are being led as sheep to the slaughter not because they believe in war but because they see no adequate alternative." Confronting an overwhelming prowar consensus and their own feelings of ineffectiveness, Smith and the rest of the second-generation vanguard changed the subject from condemning the war to practicing nonviolence in the arenas of conscientious objection, Japanese American internment, and, most importantly, African American equality. In these new projects, total mobilization for war heightened pacifism's paradoxes, as absolute pacifists made common cause with nonpacifists. Yet the Fellowship's work in the war years laid the foundation for the astonishing success of nonviolence in decades to come.[36]

The World War II generation broke down some of the religious and cultural strictures that had distinguished the FOR in previous decades. The specifically Protestant character of the organization began to shift, especially with the general decline in anti-Catholicism among liberal Protestants and the emergence of the nonviolent Catholic Worker movement in the mid-1930s. Furthermore, although most Fellowship leaders remained squarely in the Christian tradition, a few of the young members failed to display any faith in God. Caleb Foote admitted that he "did not . . . believe in any supreme being," while Farmer eventually called himself a "humanist." Social proscriptions fell, too. Many older Fellowship members were strict teetotalers, but the younger generation relaxed the alcohol proscription. Sexual mores met a similar fate, particularly in the case of Rustin's homosexuality, which was an open secret among the FOR staff. Much aesthetic and cultural conservatism remained, but the attenuation of the religious and ascetic standards of the Fellowship was a striking trend.[37]

Conscientious objection, for this younger generation, gained a meaning beyond the mere repudiation of violence. The most well-known conscientious objector was Henry David Thoreau, who was imprisoned in 1846 for refusing to pay his poll tax. He had withheld it to protest the Mexican War, which he regarded as an undertaking backed by the forces of imperialism and slavery. In his famous essay "Resistance to Civil Government," he parlayed his opposition to war into a more general attack on government. "The objections which have been brought against a standing army," he wrote, "may also at last be brought against a standing government." Thoreau maintained that extreme acts of individual integrity against the corruptions of the state were the best way to bring about social and moral improvement.

Thoreau's apparently clear stance hid a more complicated set of circumstances. Though his position sprang from opposition to war, he was not a pacifist and later became an enthusiastic champion of John Brown's bloody raid on Harper's Ferry. Then, too, his friends paid his poll tax and bailed him out of jail the day after his arrest. The issues raised by Thoreau's essay and by his life—about the connections between war and the state, about the relationship of conscientious objection to absolute pacifism, and about the possibility of complete noncooperation with govern-

mental authority—defined the experience of the Fellowship of Reconciliation's conscientious objectors nearly one hundred years later.[38]

Closer at hand, Richard Gregg tried to imagine a blueprint for a radical pacifist vanguard. Along with Muste, Gregg was the World War I–era
pacifist who had the greatest influence on the new FOR generation. He
had always been suspicious of conventional political protest, so the failure
of the antiwar movement in the years before World War II gave him a
certain authority. In a 1937 pamphlet called *Training for Peace,* which he
billed as "A Supplement to 'The Power of Non-Violence,'" he warned that
"war is no simple excrescence which can be removed merely by having
large numbers of people petition the government or just refuse to fight,
or by passing legislation." Instead, Gregg proposed a plan for individual
regeneration. If pacifists really wanted to eliminate war, they should recognize that "great changes in our lives must precede that accomplishment
in order to make it possible." He suggested that opponents of violence
concentrate on disciplining themselves and influencing their immediate
surroundings rather than worrying about national politics.

Gregg's plan was a combination of a religious community and a
Trotskyist cell. He encouraged pacifists to form teams containing "from
five to twelve members—no more and if possible no less," with members dedicating themselves to respectable and virtuous conduct. A team
had several tasks. Members should study pacifist theory, particularly *The
Power of Non-Violence.* They should build group cohesion through sing-
ing, folk dancing, and meditation. Reflecting Gregg's faith in handicraft
production, the peace team was also to engage in manual labor and community service, preferably to help the unemployed. "If people say it is
nonsense to do knitting or hand-spinning in this machine age," Gregg
wrote, "the reply is that it is no more nonsense than for soldiers in their
training to be required to march and counter-march in this age of the motor car, motor bus, tank and airplane." This was "training for peace" and
it had to be as rigorous as training for war. Only after "several months"
of such training should a team attempt any kind of nonviolent resistance.
In short, the members of a peace team were conscientious objectors, not
merely to war, but to the materialism and selfishness of modern society
itself. Their modest actions took on the gravity of religious rituals that
both modeled a new order and insisted that, in some nascent form, that
order already existed in their midst.[39]

Such theoretical developments intersected with more immediate concerns as the war's opponents tried to effect a lenient policy for actual con-

scientious objectors. The Fellowship opposed conscription, of course, but after the passage of the Selective Training and Service Act in September of 1940 it quickly refocused on the rights of dissenters. Few of the radical Christian pacifists, whatever their belief in the power of redemptive suffering, could have wished to relive the harrowing experience of the Great War. Then, provision for objectors had been on an ad hoc basis, with the caprice of army officers often making the difference between tolerable confinement and inhuman treatment. Norman Thomas and John Nevin Sayre had made personal appeals to Woodrow Wilson to improve the objectors' plight, but that was hardly a viable model. Connections to powerful political figures were still useful, to be sure. In 1940 Gregg secured a meeting with Eleanor Roosevelt to discuss the issue of conscientious objectors, and he also wrote a letter on the subject to Attorney General Francis Biddle, an old Harvard classmate. The goal of such entreaties, though, was to produce a more systematic and rational way to deal with those who refused to fight.[40]

Led by the "historic peace churches" (the Mennonites, Brethren, and Quakers), religious groups lobbied hard for civilian-controlled alternative service for conscientious objectors. The result was the Civilian Public Service (CPS) system, which placed objectors in camps where they would perform "work of national importance." In exchange for authority over the camps, the peace churches agreed to fund them. Representatives from major religious groups including the Fellowship formed a governing body called the National Service Board for Religious Objectors, though in the end Selective Service gained substantial control over CPS administration and the government even opened some of its own camps. The structure of the CPS system catered to the theology of the peace churches, particularly the Mennonites, who were the most conservative and the most numerous among conscientious objectors. Few Mennonite pacifists sought to abolish conscription, believing instead that God's people should suffer willingly the necessary evils undertaken by the secular state. The peace churches sought mainly to provide a haven for their pacifist members, not to attack the draft itself.[41]

Within this framework, young men had three main options to avoid killing in war, not counting exemptions for ministers, theological students, and a few other special cases. They could choose noncombatant service, such as providing medical care for wounded soldiers. This route never received much attention in FOR circles because it still left noncombatants under military jurisdiction. Debate centered on the other two choices: alternative service in a CPS camp or complete refusal to cooperate, resulting in a prison sentence. The moral question highlighted the ambiguities of absolute pacifism. Had the CPS system been a victory for the Christian nonviolent lobby, or was it rather a timid compromise with a proto-Fascist state?

Many men saw CPS as capitulation, so for them the site of resistance shifted back to the point of registration. The nonregistrants who ended up in prison included many of the most talented young Fellowship secretaries, including Bayard Rustin, George Houser, Caleb Foote, and Glenn Smiley. Most famously, Houser and nineteen other students at Union Theological Seminary announced in 1940 that they would refuse to register with Selective Service, even though, as theological students, they would have received draft exemptions. Twelve eventually changed their minds, but the remnant that would come to be known as the "Union Eight" persisted in its absolutist course. In fact, Muste, Gregg, and a number of other older FOR leaders also refused to register when the Selective Service law was expanded in 1942, but the government elected not to prosecute them.

The official refusal to pursue the older nonregistrants was probably wise, for the Union Eight showed the power of absolute pacifism as media spectacle. Though the students had distributed a mimeographed statement explaining their stand, they had not anticipated the storm of publicity that followed their action. Houser discovered that he was front-page news in both of his hometown newspapers in Denver, as well as in the *New York Times*. Newsreels showed the story, and it received radio coverage as well. Looking a bit like Gregg's imagined peace team, this small cluster of dedicated pacifists achieved a visibility out of all proportion to its small size.[42]

The Union Eight protest was audacious even by the Fellowship's standards. Those pacifists who chose to register and join a CPS camp seldom made the newspapers, but they, too, had to deal with affronts to their ideals. In order to assuage public opinion, CPS men received no compensation for their work, leading some to complain that they labored under a system of slavery or Fascism. Furthermore, while most camps were racially integrated, some in the South operated along Jim Crow lines. So with regard to the flashpoints of labor and race, CPS allowed egregious violations of radical pacifist principles. Soon an argument raged in the Fellowship over the value of the alternative service system.[43]

John Haynes Holmes, still a prominent minister at the Community Church in New York City, was appalled by the dissatisfaction with CPS.

"It only goes to show," he grumbled, "how utterly corrupting it is to succeed!" Using the Great War as a reference point, he pointed out that "the Government's handling of the pacifist problem, more particularly that of conscientious objection to war, has up to now been well in advance of the Government's treatment of conscientious objectors in 1917 and 1918." Holmes opposed conscription and wished for more accommodating draft laws, but he also insisted that opponents of war had won important concessions. He could not abide the grievances of the conscientious objectors, which he regarded as petty. One of the oldest FOR leaders when the war began, Holmes complained that "the whole state of mind of conscientious objectors these days seems to be one which is directed toward the exacting of privileges, rather than the fulfillment of duties, and the offering of sacrifices." Holmes's views were extreme within the FOR; when he used several of his regular columns in *Fellowship* to admonish the conscientious objectors, the editors published a statement refuting him and stressing that the CPS system did have significant problems.

Holmes had a salient point, however much his irritation owed to generational animus. He recognized that the new conscientious objectors were, as Thoreau had, shifting the locus of their dissent from armed combat to political injustice. "In the fight against war," Holmes wrote, "opposition to conscription must be kept in its place. Such opposition is incidental, subordinate, and, in the hour of crisis, non-essential." Draft resistance was the expression of a mere "political philosophy," while war resistance was a "religious conviction." Conscription was no inherent evil, Holmes argued. Pacifists might theoretically choose to support some forms of it, perhaps as part of the national service plan once proposed by William James in "The Moral Equivalent of War." Yet even allowing that conscription was an expression of totalitarian tendencies, it remained peripheral. "The pacifist's objection is not primarily to tyranny but to *war*—else might he be taking up arms in this war against Adolf Hitler, one of the most dangerous tyrants of all time," Holmes fumed. "*Keep the issue clear!* Don't confuse pacifism with rebellion against government." He sensed that, for many younger Fellowship members, the idea of conscientious objection as a general form of resistance to injustice and oppression was beginning to take priority over the dictates of absolute opposition to war.[44]

At the other pole on the conscientious objector question was Evan Thomas. During the Great War, while Holmes had tried to make pacifism palatable for his diverse congregation, Thomas had defined the limits of absolute resistance as a conscientious objector. After the war, he became a physician, serving as a family doctor for Muste and other prominent pacifists but playing no leadership role in the peace movement. With the emergence of another military draft, though, he burst back onto the scene, joining the staff of the War Resisters League and playing an important, though lesser, role in the FOR.[45]

Like Holmes, Thomas was sure that pacifists lacked the inner fortitude that they had displayed in World War I. Using the same historical reference point, the two nonetheless drew opposite conclusions. While Holmes argued that conscientious objectors were too selfish to accept the inconveniences of alternative service in CPS camps, Thomas accused them of using the camps as a "way out" of real sacrifice. Counseling objectors on how to deal with Selective Service boards, Thomas found them interested only in "whether the powers that be will be impressed with their answers" and grant their requests for conscientious objector status and alternative service. "The C.Os [conscientious objectors] with whom I associated in the last war were not like this," he insisted. "We were not interested primarily in answering arguments but in stubbornly standing for what we regarded as principles."[46]

Thomas displayed the same "stubborn" devotion to what he "regarded as principles" that had made him the scourge of the American military two decades before. "If pacifists are to have any permanent effect in the revolutionary task of bringing humanitarian and moral values into the social and political life of nations," he declared, "they cannot afford to engage in the kind of practical politics encouraged by the N.S.B.R.O." The CPS system had initially seemed to Thomas to be a matter of "buying privilege," but the situation had actually turned out far worse. Citing the lack of compensation for CPS workers, Thomas accused the pacifists of "paying for concentration camps or government labor camps, whichever label one wishes to choose." Thomas implicitly challenged Holmes's attempt to separate war from conscription, contending that the camps drew on "the entire coercive power of a government at war." He urged conscientious objectors to refuse cooperation with Selective Service and demanded that the FOR abandon the CPS system.[47]

A. J. Muste and John Nevin Sayre, the cosecretaries of the Fellowship, had their hands full. Their strength had always lain in their ability to appease all sides in a disagreement, and Muste in particular tried to do this with regard to the conscientious objector issue. Before the war, he maintained that the CPS program "holds great possibilities for democracy and for the pacifist movement." In early 1942, he sounded almost like Holmes when he complained that objectors "ought to display more initiative and have a more positive attitude in dealing with the camp situation." However, Muste supported the Union Eight as well and refused to register for the draft himself. Probably due to his influence, the FOR Executive Committee issued a statement soon after America entered the war that expressed support for *both* registering and nonregistering conscientious objectors.[48]

As the war continued, Muste, and the FOR in general, became more skeptical of the CPS system. In 1943 the National Council of the Fellowship took an informal vote on whether the organization should continue to assist in supervising the camps as a member of National Service Board for Religious Objectors. Muste, joined by young militants James Farmer and Bayard Rustin, voted to withdraw, but they were outnumbered by Holmes, Sayre, and others who wished to remain in the CPS program. The issue dominated the FOR agenda for the next year. Disgusted by this equivocation, Evan Thomas resigned from the organization, leading Muste to publish a conciliatory letter in *Fellowship* to prevent other members from following suit. Finally, on December 9, 1944, the Council voted to leave the Board of Directors of the National Service Board for Religious Objectors, while continuing in a "consultative relationship." The FOR continued to help conscientious objectors during and after the war, but its cooperation with the CPS system effectively ended. Once again, the FOR distinguished its own religious radicalism from the less militant pacifism of the peace churches.[49]

The debate at the Fellowship's New York headquarters did not always take full account of the nonviolent innovation happening on the ground. Despite its problems, and because of them, the system that the government and religious groups cobbled together provided a variety of opportunities for objectors to take positive action in accordance with their principles, rather than simply saying "no" to war. In CPS camps, and even in prisons, the federal government quickly accomplished what years of pacifist organizing had failed to achieve: it concentrated the country's most dedicated pacifists into groups and gave them a lot of spare time. The result was an ironic fulfillment of Gregg's vision in *Training for Peace*. As he had suggested, CPS participants read and discussed pacifist literature, which the FOR and other peace groups sent to the camps, while also performing manual labor and humanitarian service. Different men took different views of what their convictions required. Some considered their unpaid "work of national importance" to be a form of religious sacrifice,

FIGURE 5.2 Bayard Rustin addressing conscientious objectors at the Civilian Public Service camp in Powellsville, Maryland. (CDGA Rustin, Bayard, Bayard Rustin Papers, Swarthmore College Peace Collection.)

while others who were less content organized work slowdowns, sabotage, and other forms of nonviolent resistance. At the Germfask camp in Michigan, for instance, campers took sick days in alphabetical order. Only a small number of the men in the camps were FOR members, but they participated disproportionately in these kinds of protests. Whatever the objectors chose to do, they found a sense of solidarity in collective action.

Prison, too, became a laboratory of nonviolent resistance. At the Danbury, Connecticut, facility, the Union Eight undertook strikes to end racial segregation. Bayard Rustin tried personally to integrate the Ashland, Kentucky, prison by listening to the radio with some white FOR members. A white inmate objected and began to beat Rustin with a long stick. The other conscientious objectors tried to disarm the man, but Rustin ordered them to stop and absorbed the blows without resisting. The man soon ceased his assault, and Rustin's friends considered the incident a victory for nonviolent resistance, "a perfect example," a fellow conscientious objector thought, "of what Richard Gregg described in his POWER OF NONVIOLENCE."[50]

In these crucibles, Christian nonviolence continued its ambivalent relationship to American gender norms. The prison ordeal of Glenn Smiley shows how conscientious objectors built an alternative masculine identity even as they rejected the soldier's uniform, the era's irrefutable marker of manhood. Born in Texas in 1910, Smiley settled in Los Angeles and worked as a Fellowship secretary there during the war. Like many in the younger generation, he bucked the stereotype of the gaunt, solemn ascetic. "My own first impression was not altogether favorable," John Nevin Sayre confided to Muste, "but this was purely superficial as to his rather large bulk." Along with his size, Smiley was also known for his irrepressible sense of humor, which must have served him well when he was sentenced in 1944 to McNeil Island Federal Penitentiary in Washington for refusing to cooperate with the draft.[51]

Leaving his wife, Helen, and their three children in Los Angeles, Smiley entered a new, all-male environment. "I had not realized before being imprisoned," he later reflected, "how much of a half-world the life would be." He was ill-at-ease in this setting, but it had its compensations. Pacifists in CPS camps and prisons had to undertake strenuous tasks such as building roads and fighting forest fires. Smiley described his own logging work at McNeil Island in heroic masculine terms: "Stripped to the waist, with sweat running in rivulets down the body, I took satisfaction in the reemergence of something resembling the physical condition of my earlier youth." He also took satisfaction in his prison baseball team. "We have," he boasted to Helen, "a Mexican third baseman, a Nisei short fielder, a Negro right fielder with the rest of us being colorless, which makes us the most colorful team in the League." Indeed, Smiley's antiracist efforts—he led desegregation of the prison dining room as well as the baseball diamond—occurred in a context of male sociability that mirrored that of military life. The Union Eight had a parallel experience in Danbury, Connecticut. One of their number, Don Benedict, became the star pitcher on the prison softball team and traded on his skills to ingratiate himself with the warden, whose desire to win games trumped his lack of sympathy for the pacifists. However much conscientious objectors dissented from the war, from racism, or from a proto-Fascist state, the camps and prisons formed a gendered "half-world," thereby ensuring that Christian nonviolence would share some of the masculine culture of war itself.[52]

Glenn Smiley's baseball players were not quite what Richard Gregg had meant by a peace team, but they did reveal something about the new connections that the war made between antiracism and pacifism. The "Nisei short fielder" could have been one of the many second-generation Japanese American draft resisters who were held at McNeil Island. As pacifists looked for evidence of creeping Fascism, they noticed not only their own treatment but that of men and women of Japanese descent. The fight against Japanese American internment, then against Japanese American conscription, deeply engaged the Fellowship, while revealing once again the paradoxes of pacifism in a nation united by war.

The FOR had been criticizing American attitudes toward Japan long before internment. Because of the organization's connections to missionary work in Southeast Asia, it displayed particular interest in the region and its populations. The radical Christian pacifists strongly condemned the immigration laws of the 1920s, which banned Asians from becoming naturalized citizens of the United States. After the war began, some pacifists would cite these measures as examples of "Nazi-like racism" and a cause of the conflict. Even before Pearl Harbor, they warned of the racial antagonism that a war with Japan would bring. In late 1940, John Nevin Sayre wondered if there was "anything we can do . . . , before the war arrives, to prepare things so that our Japanese citizens will be treated better than we treated the German-Americans in the last war." The Fellowship's growing presence on the West Coast, bolstered by Kirby Page's move to California in 1934 and the work of Smiley and Caleb Foote, further stirred interest in anti-Japanese animus. By the time the war began, the Fellowship even had a few members of Japanese descent, drawn from the substantial Japanese Christian population on the West Coast.[53]

The pacifists' attention to Japanese Americans also derived from their interpretation of World War II in terms of moral equivalence. The FOR often used the Pacific theater, rather than the European one, to talk about the meaning of the war. Niebuhr and other supporters of U.S. intervention liked to invoke the symbol of Munich, which represented for them the failures of a flaccid liberalism that sought a spurious peace through the strategy of appeasement, but the Pacific war undermined that narrative. There, the prewar strategy had been escalation and intimidation, not acquiescence.[54] Furthermore, sites of combat such as Hawaii and the Philippines recalled uncomfortable histories of American imperialism. Most disturbingly, the United States, fighting against Aryan supremacy in Europe, became simultaneously embroiled in a grotesquely racist "war without mercy," as one historian has labeled it. Smiley observed that "certain aspects of the war in the Pacific . . . look like a race war."[55] That war would end not with the liberation of Dachau and Buchenwald, but with the obliteration of Hiroshima and Nagasaki. To the FOR, the Pacific theater proved that all sides had succumbed to the logic of violence that led to war, imperialism, racism, and, in the end, total annihilation.

The Fellowship launched a vigorous campaign against the evacuation of Japanese Americans from the West Coast that began in the spring of 1942. Many of the group's leaders personally visited the relocation centers and publicized the plight of the internees.[56] After the spring of 1943, when the government instituted a "leave clearance" program that allowed selected persons to depart the camps for employment or educational opportunities, John Swomley led a Fellowship effort to find sponsors and funds. In an unprecedented move, Swomley hired two young Japanese Americans, Perry Saito and Kenji Okuda, to assist him. Saito, who had been interned at the Tule Lake camp in California, became a highly visible presence on the FOR speaking circuit, thereby embodying the organization's interracial ideal.[57] Meanwhile, Caleb Foote wrote a widely circulated pamphlet called *Outcasts!* condemning the evacuation. He emphasized that "racial prejudice," not military necessity, was behind the internment, warning that this government action placed every "unpopular minority" at risk. Ironically, *Outcasts!* went to press while Foote was in jail for refusing to register for the draft. The Fellowship also received assistance from one of its newer members, the San Francisco poet Kenneth Rexroth, later a prominent figure in postwar Beat culture. Rexroth and his wife, Marie, worked diligently with the FOR to secure educational passes that would allow Japanese Americans to move to the Midwest and South, out of internment's reach.[58]

In their denunciation of the treatment of Japanese Americans, the beleaguered Christian pacifists finally found a few allies. Some historians have insisted on describing the relocation centers as "American concentration camps," a term both technically accurate (contemporaries used it) and usefully provocative. However, this evocation of the Holocaust obscures the substantial resistance inside and outside the centers, resistance that limited both the duration and the severity of the internment in ways that contrasted sharply with the European situation. Many American religious leaders, along with some secular liberals, sharply criticized the project. Reinhold Niebuhr, Norman Thomas, and A. J. Muste, divided on so many aspects of the war, all agreed that internment was a serious mistake. Still, the Christian pacifist outlook made the FOR protest unique.[59]

For those in the Fellowship circle, the internment problem expanded the possibilities of conscientious objection. The odyssey of Gordon Hirabayashi, a young Japanese American FOR member, showed how Christian pacifist ideas and modes of resistance took on new meaning during the war. Hirabayashi was born near Seattle in 1918, the son of immigrants who belonged to a Japanese offshoot of the Quakers called the "Friends of the World." He was active in liberal Christian organizations in high school and then at the University of Washington, where he became an officer in the student Young Men's Christian Association. His YMCA work took him to New York in the summer of 1940, where he encountered the Fellowship's brand of militant pacifism. Impressed, he joined the organization and, upon his return to Seattle, registered for the draft as a conscientious objector. He would indeed become one, but not in exactly the way he supposed.[60]

In May 1942, Hirabayashi received an order to sign up for evacuation. He arrived at the FBI office in Seattle a few days later with a lawyer and a lengthy typed statement. Showing himself already adept at the radical Christian pacifist habit of producing exhaustive declarations of conscience, Hirabayashi argued that the evacuation program was at once an affront to religion and a denial of American political principles. His refusal to comply with the policy eventually became one of the four major cases testing the legality of the government's actions with respect to Japanese Americans during the war. Harold Evans, a Quaker lawyer and founding member of the FOR, ended up arguing the Hirabayashi case before the Supreme Court.

The case revealed the fault lines between the Fellowship's thoroughgoing condemnation of internment and the more moderate criticism of prowar liberals. The pacifists were deeply involved at every level of the Hirabayashi case. The FOR raised money for his defense, and Sayre and Rustin visited him in prison while he awaited trial.[61] Sayre and Holmes, members of the national committee of the American Civil Liberties Union, wished to use the case to challenge the constitutionality of evacuation. They opposed not only the racial basis of internment, but also the broader implication that the government might disregard basic human rights during wartime. Here the pacifists ran into trouble, for most of the ACLU leadership was supportive of Roosevelt and wary of opposing any aspect of the war effort. With a majority of the committee outvoting the more radical position of Holmes and Sayre, the ACLU decided to argue only that the evacuation had been racially based, not that it had

FIGURE 5.3
Gordon Hirabayashi as a
student at the University
of Washington. (Wing Luke
Asian Museum, Seattle,
Washington.)

been an inherently illegitimate use of federal power. The legal politics
of this choice meant that the organization did not give much support to
Hirabayashi until the case reached the Supreme Court. There, with Evans
arguing the limited race-based position, the justices upheld the conviction
on a legal technicality, refusing to address the larger constitutional issues
raised by evacuation.

After the conviction, Hirabayashi's personal experience took a turn toward the surreal. He was supposed to go to a work camp in Arizona to
serve his time, but federal authorities discovered that no money was ear-
marked for his transport. The convicted man offered to make the trip on
his own, and, amazingly, the government consented, perhaps reasoning
that a lone Japanese American man would be likely to traverse the hostile
territory of the American West as quickly as possible. He hitchhiked to
Las Vegas, then bought a bus ticket the rest of the way. When he finally
arrived, the prison had misfiled his papers and tried to send him away.

Refusing to give up, Hirabayashi finally served a short prison sentence, but he had not yet escaped the labyrinth of the wartime state.[62]

In early 1943, as a public relations maneuver, the U.S. government began to allow Nisei like Hirabayashi to volunteer for service in the army. The new policy sought to mollify opponents of evacuation by allowing Japanese Americans to join the national struggle. Officials also hoped that the new soldiers would pave the way for the end of internment by convincing suspicious whites that the men and women living under armed guard were actually loyal American citizens. Many internees, including those in the powerful Japanese American Citizens League, advocated for the opportunity to serve.

For Hirabayashi and other pacifists, though, the use of war service as the proof of true American allegiance was an outrage, particularly when the government actually began to draft internees in 1944. The cosmically unlucky Hirabayashi, refusing the draft just as he had refused evacuation two years before, went off to prison with other Japanese American resisters, this time on McNeil Island. There he met two of his would-be white liberators, Glenn Smiley and Caleb Foote. Undaunted, Hirabayashi challenged the segregation of Japanese American inmates in his new home, asking Smiley to get involved. "I went to see the Superintendent about the matter," Smiley recalled, and soon Hirabayashi was allowed to move into a nonsegregated section of the prison. Smiley, though, lost his plum job at the prison filtration plant, an act of retaliation for his interference, he thought.[63]

The new policy of recruiting, then drafting, internees brought the delicate politics of conscientious objection to the fore. The possibility of military service made the situation of pacifist Japanese Americans into a racially charged Catch-22 (a term inspired, of course, by World War II). Hideo Hashimoto, a graduate of Union Theological Seminary and a Japanese Methodist minister, was one relocated FOR member who felt his pacifism to be hopelessly entangled in the politics of war and race. Writing to his Fellowship colleagues from the Jerome relocation center in Arkansas, Hashimoto tried to convey the depth of the problem. "By not enlisting," he explained, "the Americans of Japanese ancestry maybe [sic] inviting suspicion. But enlisting now would be taken as the approval of segregation." Indeed, the government had refused to integrate Japanese American soldiers into the army as a whole, in part because of the effect such a move would have on the attitudes of segregated African American troops. Hashimoto added that as a pacifist he would not join the armed forces, even if "the Jim-crow features" were abolished. Most of his fellow internees, however, seemed willing to join the army if it were desegregated, and some would not even require this condition to fight for the United States. Hashimoto had decided to adopt the in-between stance of supporting "Selective Service without discrimination," though he was "unalterably opposed to conscription" in principle. "Am I being out of bounds as a pacifist?," he wanted to know. By this point, who could say for sure? Many white conscientious objectors were able to trade on their elite social status, but Japanese Americans possessed no such leverage. In their precarious social position, using the war to their advantage looked more promising than condemning it wholesale.[64]

For some Fellowship members both inside and outside the camps, the relocation offered a possible proving ground for the practice of non-violent direct action. Hashimoto wrote to John Nevin Sayre that he was "stud[y]ing Richard B. Gregg again," just as he had during FOR meetings in Fresno, California, before the war. Meanwhile, Caleb Foote proposed to Sayre the possibility of using "direct non-violent opposition" to fight the internment. Foote envisioned "camping outside one of the evacuation camps, sharing their living conditions and privations, and perhaps picketing the gates; or even lying down across the entrances so that army and other evacuation officials would be made to realise what they are doing." Such action, Foote predicted, would bring "an instantaneous response from some of the people" in the camps. Sayre was cautiously supportive, emphasizing that the "approach should not suggest overt resistance . . . to the Army and American Government but . . . should somehow dramatize an injustice which we are doing to the underdog and . . . instantly connect with the Christian motives of pity and compassion." He doubted "whether lying down before Army trucks at the gates of a camp" would be efficacious. "It could work in India," he acknowledged, "but is pretty foreign to American psychology." Sayre also worried that "Japanese who fear association with pacifism" might be "offended." In fact, the Fellowship's reputation continually thwarted its efforts to provide any kind of help to the interned Japanese Americans.[65]

Sometimes, the radical Christian pacifists seemed to cause more harm than good. A white California minister explained to Sayre that "the Japanese are definitely embarrassed by identification with pacifists" and that such identification "does not make good publicity for us or for them." Pacifists could hardly help the Japanese gain the nation's trust when they themselves were so widely distrusted for their refusal to support the war.

The most innocuous gestures could create suspicion and even panic. At a CPS camp in California, FOR members attempted to send a box of toys to interned Nisei children at the relocation center in Poston, Arizona. Poston was one of the more unruly camps. In previous months, inmates had staged a strike, and the president of Japanese American Citizens League had been beaten by fellow internees for his support of the draft. Perhaps this reputation helps explain why, as the package from the FOR made its way to Arizona, "rumors . . . spread . . . that the conscientious objectors were sending subversive material, guns, dynamite, or other contraband to the Japanese." Government officials ended up opening the box en route to examine its contents before sending it on.[66] Understandably, most Japanese kept their distance from the FOR. Caleb Foote argued vehemently that internees were actually wary not of "pacifists," but of "Caucasians" in general. Nevertheless, the best he could say was that "the mass of the Japanese" manifested "indifference towards the whole issue" of pacifism.[67]

Most Japanese Americans were more interested in ending internment than in adopting absolute pacifism, thus displaying a pragmatic bent that vexed the leaders of the Fellowship. FOR groups existed in every camp, but they were small and apparently without much influence in the face of prowar American patriotism on one hand, considerable anti-American sentiment on the other, and sheer "indifference" in between. Japanese Americans explained their reluctance to join the pacifist ranks in terms of both expediency and principle. One internee wrote to John Swomley: "There are only a few who dare to commit themselves [to pacifism], being afraid of public opinion outside." Another letter, though, showed conviction rather than fear: "I am not a Pacifist to the great extent to which Fellowship members pledge themselves. I believe one can be a true Christian and still go to war when his country is in danger and needs him."[68] Over and over, correspondents from the camps expressed their appreciation for the Fellowship's work but added reservations about nonviolence. Despite the internment, most Japanese Americans who identified with the United States felt that their freedom would come by participating in the war effort, not by opposing it. The same conundrums of war and race appeared in the radical Christian pacifists' most lasting effort during these years, as they tried to link pacifism with the cause of black freedom.

The Fellowship was a vanguard of interracial idealism before the war, though its efforts often underscored a lack of actual racial diversity. John Haynes Holmes recalled participating in acts of conscience at theaters during the early days of the National Association for the Advancement of Colored People, which he helped found in 1909. Holmes and his colleagues would purchase tickets in advance, then show up on the date of the performance "with one or two Negroes in our company. The Negroes were under strict instructions to say nothing, but to hold their places at any cost." The white contingent, meanwhile, protested the inevitable refusal of admittance to the segregated show. As the argument persisted, the other patrons would become agitated at the delay. Eventually the theater manager would call the police, allowing the reformers to challenge the segregation system through legal channels. These maneuvers anticipated the tactics of the civil rights movement in their nonviolent method and in their performative dimensions, yet they also framed the debate over racial justice as a moral struggle among whites, leaving the black participants largely silent. The white reformers, in Holmes's retelling, "were politely but firmly protesting," while the theater employee would occasionally "blurt out the truth—that they did not admit Negroes to their performances." As the other theatergoers grew more agitated, "shouts were raised, protests heard." Yet one party remained outside the general cacophony. "The Negroes were under strict instructions to say nothing." This approach undoubtedly had its tactical advantages, but it also exemplified the Christian pacifists' tendency to view white initiative as the key to achieving black equality.[69]

During the war years, black Americans gained a voice in the FOR as Christian nonviolence began to influence much of the ideology and strategy of the nascent civil rights movement. A disproportionate number of black civil rights leaders, including Bayard Rustin, James Farmer, James Lawson, and Martin Luther King Jr., were members of the Fellowship at key points in their careers. A. J. Muste played an enormous role in the organization's turn to issues of race in these years, hiring Rustin and Farmer to join the FOR national staff in 1941. Along with George Houser and Glenn Smiley, two white workers who Muste also selected around the same time, they defined the cutting edge of Christian nonviolence.

Bayard Rustin was a rare religious hybrid. He was raised by his grandfather and grandmother, who came from the African Methodist Episcopal and Quaker traditions, respectively. In the late 1930s, Rustin joined the Young Communist League, which at the time was a leading proponent of racial equality in America. However, when Hitler invaded Russia in 1941, the Communists reversed their position and rushed to support the Allies, now denigrating Rustin's attempts to end Jim Crow as an obstruction to the war effort. He left in disgust and soon joined the FOR. As in the case of A. J. Muste, the Fellowship reaped tangible benefits from the political incoherence of Marxist radicalism in the years leading up to the war.[70]

James Farmer's trajectory was more similar to that of other FOR leaders. Like so many of them, he gained religious and political awareness by joining liberal Christian youth organizations, quickly rising to top positions in the dynamic Methodist student movement. Like Rustin, Farmer was influenced by both religious and secular radicalism; his two most important mentors during theological school, he claimed, were the black FOR leader Howard Thurman and the worldly white radical V. F. Calverton. Farmer also shared with Rustin a remarkable ability to work effectively in predominantly white organizations, whether the National Conference of Methodist Youth, the Fellowship of Reconciliation, or, later, the early Congress of Racial Equality.[71]

Farmer in particular jettisoned much of the baggage of absolute pacifism in favor of a more pragmatic commitment to nonviolence. Even before the war, black members such as Thurman had been more interested in the Fellowship's commitment to racial equality than in its peace witness.[72] Farmer, Thurman's student, also took the FOR peace platform with a grain of salt. He did oppose the war, registering as a conscientious objector and receiving an exemption as a theological student, but he distanced himself from the older generation of absolutists. Explaining his differences with Muste, Farmer admitted: "Peace was number one for him, whereas for me the top priority was racial equality." He remembered a Fellowship meeting in New York, shortly before the United States entered the war, where Muste had prophesied that a "historic moment" for religious pacifism was at hand. To Farmer, it was all a bit overwrought: "Some of us would live to see the day, we were told, when they would call a war and no one would come. The international pacifist movement would bring that about. (I didn't believe that, but as I looked around the room, most heads were nodding in agreement.)" Farmer eventually left the Fellowship in 1945 because Muste felt he spent too much time on civil rights initiatives and not enough on building opposition to war.[73]

The patron saint of Farmer, Rustin, and their allies was a disciple of Gandhi named Krishnalal Shridharani. Born in 1912, Shridharani participated in the 1930 March to the Sea before coming to the United States in 1934 to study at Columbia University, a neighbor to the Fellowship's

FIGURE 5.4
James Farmer, ca.
1945–46. (James Leon-
ard Jr. and Lula Peterson
Farmer Papers, Center
for American History,
University of Texas
at Austin.)

Upper West Side stronghold, Union Theological Seminary. He was no Mahatma. Farmer, who met Shridharani in 1943, recalled that he "had expected a Gandhiesque figure—ascetic, bony, waiflike." Instead, he saw a "roundish, well-fed" man in a "three-piece Brooks Brothers suit," smoking a cigar.[74]

In his writing as in his life, Shridharani downplayed the religious and abstemious aspects of Gandhi's *satyagraha*. His 1939 work, *War Without Violence*, outlined a militant form of nonviolent direct action as a method of social change, just as Richard Gregg's *The Power of Non-Violence* had done five years earlier. However, where Gregg had ultimately finessed the question of whether nonviolence could be *only* a tactic without roots in deeply held pacifist convictions. Shridharani was unequivocal. "There being no universal and time-honored criteria for ethical values," he wrote, "it is useless to prescribe Satyagraha on the grounds of moral superiority, notwithstanding the efforts of Gandhi and his disciples." Rather, militant nonviolence had merit solely by virtue of its "higher efficiency."[75]

Shridharani accused American pacifists of exaggerating the spiritual dimensions of the "essentially secular" Indian movement. He maintained that the religious aspects of *satyagraha* were "there for propaganda and publicity reasons as well as for the personal satisfaction of deeply conscientious men like Gandhi" and a small number of his followers. The "multitudes" understood nonviolence as "a weapon to be wielded by masses of men for earthly, tangible, and collective aims and to be discarded if it does not work." *War Without Violence* could be glib in its analysis of the performative qualities of the Mahatma's asceticism. "As an originator of fashions," Shridharani quipped, "Gandhi can well be the envy of Hollywood stars." Notably, *War Without Violence* included a chapter on Gandhi's charismatic leadership, which Gregg's writing did not discuss in any detail.[76] Shridharani clearly viewed nonviolence as a modern construct particularly attuned to modern forms of mass media and mass spectatorship. He kept a certain distance from the FOR, particularly after he publicly declared that India might have to defend itself with armed force, but *War Without Violence* became enormously influential among Farmer and other members of the younger generation.[77]

Despite his impatience with much of the FOR culture, Farmer did engage the group's religious and intellectual traditions. In 1942, he authored an incisive articulation of the connections between the war, Christian nonviolence, and racial equality. In a *Fellowship* essay entitled "The Race Logic of Pacifism," Farmer worked to appropriate nonviolence for the cause of racial justice. The international conflict, he argued, had exacerbated racial hostility, creating "an obvious rise in discrimination against minority races, accelerated by the fear and hysteria which are the inescapable bedfellows of war." At the same time, African Americans had taken seriously the democratic rhetoric of the American campaign and become "increasingly outraged and . . . more actively indignant" in the face of discrimination. War abroad, as pacifists had always maintained, produced conflict at home, too.[78]

Historians have often taken this incendiary domestic climate as a sign of progress in the struggle for racial equality. The *Pittsburgh Courier*'s widely adopted "Double Victory" slogan, which called for the simultaneous defeat of racists at home and Fascists abroad, has served as the organizing trope for understanding African American politics during World War II.[79] For pacifists at the time, though, "Double V" was as alarming as it was inspiring. The war had led to conscription, militarism, and deliberate immolation of civilian populations, so how could it possibly be a model for achieving social justice? Rustin related a friend's complaint in 1942: "If we must die abroad for democracy we can't have, then we might as well die right here fighting for our rights." It was "a tragic statement," Rustin thought. "The Negro can attain progress," he went on, "only if he uses, in his struggle, non-violent direct action—a technique consistent with the ends he desires." Pacifists had failed to fashion a credible alternative to the global conflagration; now they sought to prevent a race war in their own country.[80]

In "The Race Logic of Pacifism," Farmer named two specific qualities of Christian nonviolence that gave it the power to end racism in the United States without bloodshed. The first was its universalism. Religious pacifists held to "the Judeo-Christian faith in the universal community, the world fellowship, the unity of the human family." The same principles that led pacifists to view all war as fratricide should also force them to oppose racial discrimination, Farmer maintained. The specific form of pacifist antiracism would also be an outgrowth of universalist principles. "Our approach must differ from that of numerous contemporary groups," he insisted, "in that it in no sense smacks of racial chauvinism." Pacifism's "race logic" required instead "a cooperative endeavor recognizing no distinctions of race and mobilizing men of conscience of every race in a comprehensive program to resist racism." Both Farmer and Rustin generally maintained this allegiance to inclusive interracialism throughout their careers.

Commitment to nonviolent methods was the second key aspect of pacifism's "race logic." Farmer saw conscientious objection, not war, as the model for achieving racial justice. The "Gandhian pattern" was the key to pacifist power. The practice of "non-cooperation," so familiar to conscientious objectors, now had to take on broader significance. "What we must not fail to see," Farmer contended, "is that conscience should imply not only refusal to participate in war, but also, so far as is humanly possible, refusal to participate in, and cooperate with, all those social practices which wreak havoc with personality and despoil the human community." On these grounds, pacifists should support only "those concerns, institutions, and organizations which make no discrimination on the basis of race, color, or creed." Here was a compelling attempt to link antiwar and antiracist projects, first through a common universalist worldview, then through a specific style of social action, alternately called "non-cooperation" or "conscientious objection." In Farmer's view, pacifists' experience in opposing the war left them uniquely equipped to lead the battle for racial equality.[81]

Despite Farmer's "race logic," pacifists sometimes discovered contradictions between promoting peace and fighting racism. Pacifism, in the antiwar sense of the word, and nonviolence turned out not to be synonyms, but highly unstable ideas that could contradict each other at critical points. A. Philip Randolph's proposed march on Washington exposed some of the fault lines. Aiming to end discrimination in the nation's defense industries, the venerable leader of the Brotherhood of Sleeping Car Porters planned to send thousands of African Americans to the capital in a mass protest. Truly frightened by this prospect, President Roosevelt convinced Randolph to call off the march by agreeing to implement the desegregation of war production. Randolph then tried to channel the energy generated by the proposed march into a sustained organization called the March on Washington Movement (MOWM), which would make broader attacks on racial segregation.[82]

Randolph had no allegiance to the Fellowship's religious pacifism, but in 1943 he began talking about MOWM as an experiment in Gandhian nonviolence. Muste was thrilled, writing to him that the venture "may well prove as epoch-making as Gandhi's own inauguration of a similar movement in South Africa in 1906." Muste even allowed Rustin and Farmer to suspend their FOR activities temporarily and assist with the project. Here, surely, was a great opportunity to put militant pacifism into action.[83]

Or was it? Certainly, the movement, which eventually barred whites from participation, ran afoul of Farmer's ideal of interracialism. More serious were concerns about the depth of the MOWM's nonviolence. Smiley wrote to Muste that he had been talking to African Americans in Los Angeles about Randolph's movement and felt optimistic about its prospects. He worried, though, "that for the negro of the street, it would be a matter of political expediency and not a way of life. Some of them say that they would be for it if and when it worked, but felt that force should be used also if it showed promise of working." His interviews had left him "confused." Pacifism could not triumph without "participation on the part of the 'common' man," so could thoroughgoing pacifists support the use of nonviolence as a mere technique, "hoping that by a demonstration of its effectiveness, converts will be gained for the cause? But what if it backfires, and becomes violent?" In a Fellowship meeting, Muste confessed that MOWM was "a challenge to us."[84]

Smiley and the other Randolph enthusiasts in the FOR had difficulty confronting the fact that the "race logic" of MOWM implicitly accepted the war's legitimacy. The original march, after all, was supposed to force the desegregation of defense industries, even though the pacifist view had always been that the manufacture of armaments should be abolished, not simply integrated. Randolph, constrained neither by the Fellowship's antiwar stance nor by its Christian orientation, designed the campaign to work within, not against, the context of total domestic mobilization. Muste, Rustin, and the other pacifists had to choose between two stances that had once seemed inseparable: absolute opposition to war and commitment to Gandhian nonviolence. Muste, as usual, tried to split the difference. Support for MOWM, he insisted, "does not involve any change in our opposition to war or imply that we would approve of Armed [sic] forces if only racial discrimination were not practised within them." Rather, he emphasized the importance of fighting "the evil of racism wherever it manifests itself, whether in churches, industry, unions, schools, public office, or the armed forces." He argued that "attention upon racial discrimination in the armed forces may be the way in which multitudes are made for the first time to realize the way in which this evil strikes at the very heart of a people's life." By making this claim, though, he clearly ran the risk of legitimating the "armed forces." Perhaps they were not essentially different from other established institutions such as "schools," "unions," or "public office."[85]

Rustin attempted an analogous maneuver in a statement to the Selective Service Board that explained his reasons for seeking conscientious objector status. His own conflicted "race logic" echoed Hideo Hashimoto's dilemma regarding Japanese American soldiers. Rustin expressed outrage at segregation in the armed forces, calling it "not only morally indefensible but also in clear violation of the [Conscription] Act." Then he admitted that his protest "does not, however, imply that I could have a part in conforming to the Act if discrimination were eliminated."[86] As in their condemnation of area bombing, the pacifists maintained absolute opposition to war while also trying to reform its conduct. Given the way that mobilization had invaded every aspect of American life, Rustin, Farmer, and the other young radicals had little choice. Their allegiance was to nonviolent action, so they were willing to allow some ambiguity at the edges of their opposition to war.

Jay Holmes Smith, a white Methodist, faced similar contradictions in his own pioneering antiracist initiatives. Smith had served as a missionary in India, where his enthusiastic support for Gandhi and independence led the British government to send him home. Back in the United States, Smith registered for the draft as a conscientious objector, eschewing the extreme stance taken by Rustin, Smiley, and the Union Eight. He made this choice, he explained, not because he was a moderate, but rather because the nonregistrant position put too much emphasis on war resistance. "The focus of pacifist strategy has moved on," Smith believed, "and we ought not to be so inflexible in our inveterate opposition to war as to fail to move with it." The emphasis now, he thought, should be on developing a positive alternative to war, and for this purpose Muste installed him as secretary of a new "Committee on Non-Violent Techniques" within the FOR. Sharing the militance of other younger pacifists, Smith saw a "choice . . . not between *peace* and *conflict,* but between *methods* of conflict." Shridharani approvingly labeled Smith's efforts "Kristagraha," a combination of Christianity and Gandhi's *satyagraha.*[87]

Smith worked to find American applications for Gandhian methods, even if he had to reach beyond the small circle of absolute pacifists. Inspired by Randolph's aborted march, Smith led fourteen black and white marchers in an "Interracial Pilgrimage" during the fall of 1942. Walking from New York to Washington, D.C., the group carried placards denouncing racial discrimination and held public meetings in towns along their route. Smith allowed nonpacifists to join the event if they respected the general tenor of the march. "Whatever may be the varying attitudes of the participants towards the international conflict," he wrote, "we must unite on the basis of adherance [sic] to non-violent methods in working for racial justice within our country." *Fellowship,* in a report on the event, noted that although "several" of the marchers were "non-pacifist," they had "gained more respect" for the pacifist position by the time the group reached Washington. The idea that nonpacifists would renounce force entirely after participating in successful nonviolent actions became an article of faith within the Fellowship.[88]

At least one participant, the black civil rights lawyer Conrad Lynn, was not converted. A nonpacifist and an atheist, Lynn was deeply moved by the march, but its nonviolent ethos made him "uneasy." "I had no doubt they were sincere," Lynn later wrote of the pacifists, ". . . but it seemed to me that the elevation of nonviolence and orderliness as means, often vitiated the desired end." He allowed that the pilgrimage had been effective as "catharsis for the white people who participated," but thought that the black walkers had undergone "suppression of indignation and a lesson in humility." Lynn "doubted that this was desirable." Indeed, his most vivid memory of the event was when a black worker swinging a pick had offered to defend the marchers from a group of hostile whites. For Lynn, the "race logic of pacifism" was uncomfortably close to passive acquiescence.[89]

Most of the marchers in the "Interracial Pilgrimage" had come from Smith's most elaborate venture, the Harlem Ashram. Ashrams are Hindu religious centers, and Gandhi established several over the course of his career. They appealed to the Fellowship's religious sensibilities as well as its decentralist and ascetic tendencies. By 1935, the American Methodist missionary E. Stanley Jones had established a "Christian Ashram" in India, a venture that included Smith among its members. In 1940, Jones returned to the United States, joined the FOR, and worked to build ashrams in America. They became an attractive form of alternative living for many Gandhian pacifists during the war. Dave Dellinger, for instance, helped start a "Newark Ashram" after his release from prison as one of the Union Eight. The ashrams were as varied in emphasis as the pacifists themselves, but they usually consisted of a small, racially diverse group that participated in religious worship, community service, nonviolent action, and some degree of communal life. They presented another variation on the intensive small groups that Gregg had proposed in *Training for Peace*.[90]

Smith's Harlem Ashram, on Fifth Avenue near 125th Street, was perhaps the most well known of these experiments. It opened in the winter of 1940–41 with eleven members, seven white, three black, and one Indian Hindu. Swomley and Farmer passed through, as did the peripatetic young Gandhian Pauli Murray. Spiritually, Smith explained, the ashram stood for the values of the FOR. "Economically," he went on, "we are trying to work out the principle evident in the original Christian community, 'From each according to his ability and to each according to his need.'" The group also sought to reach out to the surrounding neighborhood. It experimented with nonviolent action and held workshops on the subject. For many Fellowship members, the Harlem Ashram promised, as one put it, to overcome "traditionally individualistic urban ways of living" and "make pacifism a way of life."[91]

No group exemplified the new orientation of nonviolent action more fully than the Congress of Racial Equality, which had its New York chapter, for a time, at the Harlem Ashram. CORE's roots were in an interracial

FOR group in Chicago that consisted mainly of students and recent graduates, many with ties to the University of Chicago. Though mostly Protestant, the Chicago cell included James Robinson, a Catholic Worker who would later serve as executive secretary of CORE. In early 1942, the group secured a lease on a house owned by the wife of the poet Edgar Lee Masters in a white neighborhood near the university. The members intended to test the residential segregation that dominated the city, though their lease expired before the issue came to a head. Meanwhile, James Farmer was attempting to turn pacifism's "race logic" into a coherent program. He wrote a proposal for the Fellowship outlining a program of "Brotherhood Mobilization." Citing the ideas of Shridharani and the work of Jay Holmes Smith, Farmer suggested a program of nonviolent direct action along Gandhian lines to achieve racial equality. The membership would be "recruited from all sections of the country and from all ages, races, classes, and religions." Farmer soon fell in with the Chicago cell and became one of its leaders.[92]

Farmer's proposal raised once more the problem of absolute pacifism with respect to nonviolent social protest. Farmer, Houser, and most of the other CORE founders were adamant that the new organization must be open to nonpacifists. A. J. Muste, along with many of the more established FOR leaders, was wary of this idea, so wary that the FOR Council refused to embrace the new organization under Fellowship auspices, agreeing instead to fund Farmer's project as a separate entity. The Chicago group then played the lead role in creating CORE.

CORE showed more than a passing resemblance to its parent. Like the early FOR, and unlike established civil rights organizations such as the NAACP, CORE had a structure that was loose and decentralized, allowing considerable autonomy for individual members and local groups. As in the Fellowship, individual chapters were small, widely scattered, and often ephemeral. They drew on young populations in churches and colleges and also tended to have white majorities, despite CORE's explicit interracialism. The problem of attracting African Americans bothered its early leaders, this being one reason why Farmer had insisted that the new organization reject the pacifist label. "The masses of Negroes will not become pacifists," Farmer remembered telling Muste. "Being Negroes for them is tough enough without being pacifist, too" ("neither," he added, "will the masses of whites"). African Americans who did join CORE were often somewhat exceptional figures in the mold of Farmer and Rustin.[93]

Farmer's original "Brotherhood Mobilization" proposal not only included plans for nonviolent direct action, but also envisioned an alternative economic system. Reflecting the ideas of Gregg and others, he wanted to establish interracial "consumers' cooperatives," "housing cooperatives," "cooperative farms," and "eating cooperatives." Despite the Fellowship's lessened participation in the labor movement during the war, meaningful work still figured as an important element in a just society. Sounding like Gregg, Farmer suggested that "plans be developed for the cooperative production and cooperative marketing of *folk craft* and *art* by Negroes and whites alike." Such handicraft production "wo[u]ld supply to participants a tremendous spiritual value, by virtue of their working with their hands to produce useful objects." Farmer even ventured the Gandhian observation that these efforts would "supplement industrialization" and ease unemployment problems among the poor. The new movement would also, however, "work in close contact with unions."[94]

The attempt to build labor into CORE never went very far. Some residual legacies of the 1930s remained: the first CORE sit-ins were called "sit-downs," after the "sit-down" strikes of 1936 and 1937.[95] George Houser, a member of the original Chicago group, recalled being "impressed" by the "pretty nonviolent" tactics of the labor movement, particularly the United Auto Workers. From the beginning, however, Houser and the other CORE insurgents achieved success primarily in the arenas of consumption, recreation, and transportation, not at sites of production or distribution. Both Richard Gregg's vision of virtuous handicraft production and the industrial unionism of the thirties faded into the background as the younger FOR generation focused its energies on movie theaters, skating rinks, restaurants, and other institutions of American consumer culture.[96]

The Chicago cell's attempt to desegregate the Jack Spratt coffee house showed the power of nonviolence in a culture of consumption. Farmer and the white Catholic Worker James Robinson visited Jack Spratt and were refused service until Robinson made repeated complaints. Annoyed by their treatment, the two soon brought other members of the Chicago group to the restaurant to occupy seats at the counter. They were served after much delay, but upon paying their bill and leaving the establishment, the group turned to see the manager of Jack Spratt run out of the building and yell to them: "Take your money and get out!" With that, he threw their cash into the street. After months of fruitless negotiation with the restaurant, the group planned another action.

In May 1942, the Chicago cell undertook what Farmer later called "the first organized civil rights sit-in in American history." Twenty-eight people entered the restaurant in small mixed-race groups, filling all available seats. They were denied service. The standoff continued until a "well-dressed middle-aged woman" not associated with the group received her food but would not eat it. Meanwhile, a man who also received his meal passed it to a black person sitting next to him. Soon, Farmer remembered, several "customers, not in our groups, had stopped eating, too, or were eating very slowly; they did not want to miss any of this drama." Eventually, a restaurant employee called the police, whom Farmer had earlier notified of the demonstration. When an officer arrived but refused to make any arrests, the restaurant relented and served the sit-in participants (and this time kept their money). The Jack Spratt coffee house had been desegregated.[97]

The Jack Spratt project was a triumph of nonviolence as an act of conscience. As Farmer had predicted in "The Race Logic of Pacifism," the protests were interracial and nonviolent. The cell had successfully expanded "conscientious objection" and "non-cooperation" from the domains of war and imperialism into the arena of consumption. Also, the protestors gained the sympathy of spectators by dramatizing a consumer exchange. Farmer later alluded to the performative aspects of the confrontations. Preparing for the first action, he remembered feeling like "a young actor at a dress rehearsal before opening night of his Broadway lead." With the restaurant staff playing unwitting supporting roles, the young protesters had highlighted unfair treatment by dramatizing the component parts of the consumer experience that were usually taken for granted: entering a site of consumption, requesting a good or service, receiving that good or service, paying the bill. Finally, the Jack Spratt protest demonstrated an awareness of the coercive power of the state as a kind of final arbiter. Appeal to moral and religious values did not move the restaurant management. Only when the police refused to lower the curtain by arresting Farmer and his friends did Jack Spratt's staff give in. Downplaying absolute pacifism, practitioners of nonviolence proved willing to rely on this implicitly violent ally.

Before World War II, nonviolent direct action had been a promising outgrowth of the radical Christian pacifist opposition to war. During the war years, however, nonviolence outgrew its pacifist progenitor. Now, nonviolent action was not necessarily an expression of radical pacifist belief. The reverse was true: opposition to war became one of many causes that could employ the method of nonviolent action. Guy Hershberger, the Mennonite critic, thought modern pacifists had surrendered too much to the logic of war. Practitioners of "nonviolent coercion" to achieve racial justice, he warned, "are actually engaged in a race war; and the war may turn out to be a violent and bloody one before it is over." Hershberger raised a troubling question: how would nonviolence survive as a method without the absolute commitment of pacifism?[98]

When the century closes, Gandhi and his followers—whether in Asia, Africa or America—may go down as the influential men of our time, not because they revived religion, not even because they scored political successes, but because they were imaginative artists who knew how to use world politics as their stage.
          —Ved Mehta, "Gandhiism Is Not Easily Copied"

6   The Age of Conscience

On the evening of October 1, 1956, eight hundred black men and women packed the Hutchinson Street Baptist Church in Montgomery, Alabama. Such mass meetings, organized by the Montgomery Improvement Association (MIA), were a regular part of the bus boycott that had now been operating for several months. This assembly, though, marked a shift of emphasis for the boycott's organizers. They did not know for certain that the Supreme Court would soon rule bus segregation unconstitutional, but they sensed that the momentum of the struggle was turning their way. So, at the October 1 meeting, Martin Luther King Jr. and the other MIA leaders focused less on boycott strategy and more on preparing for the eventual integration of the buses. At Hutchinson Street, King conducted the first of a series of workshops on nonviolence that dramatized the situations that the boycotters might face as bus passengers. "Suppose," King asked the crowd, "you sat down next to a white person" who began "to make a fuss, calling you names, or even going so far as to shove you?" In answer, a woman from the audience admonished those gathered not to "get mad and strike back." "Now we've got this freedom," she asserted, but warned that "we will lose it" if white Montgomerians see that "we are incapable of acting like good Christian ladies and gentlemen." The church erupted in applause, which King followed with concluding remarks on the "Christian responsibility" of rejecting violence. Then the crowd settled in to watch the world premiere of *Walk to Freedom*, a seventeen-minute film about the Montgomery bus boycott produced by the Fellowship of Reconciliation.

Walk to Freedom, according to FOR staff member Robert Cannon, was a "howling success" at Hutchinson Street Baptist Church. During the first part of the film, which showed scenes from Montgomery, some of the men and women in the audience must have recognized their homes, their friends, and even their own likenesses onscreen. Early on, a shot of Rosa Parks appeared as a voice-over described how "a seamstress, tired after a hard day's work, got fed up with her forty years of living under Jim Crow." This scene, Cannon wrote in a letter to his FOR associates, "brought the house down" (one can only guess at the reaction of the real Rosa Parks, who was in attendance that evening). Then the film shifted course to place Montgomery in a global context. The bus boycott, the narrator intoned, had "rocked the cradle of the Confederacy and told the world a story of Negro people united for action without bitterness, without malice, without fear." The Hutchinson Street audience heard that they were "part of a struggle going on around the world, for the right to enjoy decent homes like anyone else, to work at better jobs for higher pay, and the right to live longer too, the right to an equal place in the family of man." The film moved through a montage of newsreel and television clips from colonized nations, then jumped back to an interview with King. Again the crowd at Hutchinson Street exploded in "ovation-like applause," according to Cannon. *Walk to Freedom* closed with a confident assertion of the global power of nonviolence: "They walked to freedom in Montgomery . . . and more and more they are walking in the same way throughout the world."

Cannon was ecstatic over the reception of the film. King, he reported, was "obviously deeply moved," and the crowd was electrified. "I have often thought," Cannon mused, "what it would be like to hear people cheer and applaud the virtues of nonviolence and Christian love the same way people go nuts over seeing 'our boys' march to war or the impressive fluttering of Old Glory in the winds. That night," he concluded, "my wondering was answered."[1]

The Montgomery bus boycott marked a turning point in Christian nonviolent acts of conscience, a dramatic reversal of the Fellowship's hardships during the Second World War. In the intervening decade, the culture of American dissent had changed dramatically. The postwar years were an age of conscience, a period deeply concerned with the sanctity of moral action amid the crushing force of destructive mass ideologies. The appeal to conscience might appear anywhere across the political spectrum, but the left was most likely to appeal to that individual moral compass as a guide for social change. In struggles over nuclear weapons, Communism, colonialism, and racial equality, radical Christian pacifists led the development of this new sensibility.

Although the nonviolent proponents of conscience eschewed the ideological strife of the Old Left, they were hardly apolitical. Their self-conscious moral dissent took place in public, thereby becoming both a religious ritual and, as Edward Ross had predicted in 1923, the "spectacle" of a "principle." The secular intellectual Dwight Macdonald, in his 1946 repudiation of Marxism, described the surprising result: "Individual actions, based on moral convictions, have *greater* force today than they had two generations ago."[2] The events in Montgomery typified the convergence of the moral, ritual, and political. As the narrator in *Walk to Freedom* put it, the bus boycott "told the world a story," a story that could be scripted, reported, recounted, and performed. The power of the tale depended on participants "acting like good Christian ladies and gentlemen," in the words of the unnamed woman at the Hutchinson Street meeting. Sitting in a church, thinking about what they would "act like," watching their own lives transformed into cinematic spectacle, black Montgomerians experienced individual moral action as religious ceremony and public performance. The creative tension between personal moral witness and the spectacle of that witness led Christian nonviolence to its greatest triumphs in these years and sowed the seeds of its future difficulties.

The age of conscience began on August 6, 1945. The atomic bombs dropped on Hiroshima and Nagasaki ended World War II, but at the same time they tainted the joy of victory with a vague sense of dread. Prowar liberals, Reinhold Niebuhr prominent among them, had argued that a limited application of violence might advance the cause of justice enough to be morally defensible. Now many of those same liberals shrank from the logic of destruction that threatened to annihilate democracy's moral victory at the very moment of the Allies' military triumph. Soon, a new Cold War consensus would obscure the guilt felt by the war's supporters, but for a few years after 1945 regret flowed freely. The historian and critic Lewis Mumford, one of those supporters, ruefully observed that "our methods of fighting have become totalitarian: that is, we have placed no limits upon our capacity to exterminate or destroy." The result was "moral nihilism," the "social counterpart of the atomic bomb." American religious groups produced some of the most emphatic dissent from the general national approval of the decision to use the Bomb. In 1946, a group of prominent liberal Protestants, including Niebuhr, issued "Atomic Warfare and the Christian Faith," a report that denounced the use of atomic weapons against Japan. Catholic periodicals such as *Commonweal* also condemned the bombings. Doubts surfaced in unusual places: *Life* magazine, no bastion of radical antiwar sentiment, published an editorial on August 20, 1945, that warned of a "reversion to barbarism" and championed the "individual conscience" as a safeguard against the atomic bomb.[3]

The Bomb presented overwhelming evidence of pacifism's failure, but also opened new space for pacifist criticism. The FOR took the lead in condemning the destruction of Hiroshima and Nagasaki. On one level, the new weapon cinched the case that the pacifists had made against area bombing the previous year. A Fellowship statement of protest, signed by A. J. Muste, John Haynes Holmes, Kirby Page, and a few dozen others, argued that even before the atomic horror the United States had "descended step by step" to the moral level of its enemy by systematically destroying Japanese cities with conventional weaponry. In this sense the Bomb was a new but not unprecedented result of the amoral logic that defined modern warfare.[4]

Despite these continuities, the atomic bomb marked a qualitative shift as well. It was, as the signers of the protest put it, "an atrocity of a new magnitude" that "has dragged the war and all of us with it, to a new low of inhumanity."[5] The Bomb reinforced the religious and moral language of pacifism by undermining the tenets of liberal "realism" in two interrelated ways. First, the incredible destructiveness of atomic weapons changed the rules of battle, casting doubt on the desirability or even the possibility of victory as traditionally defined. This was especially true after the United States and the Soviet Union began to amass nuclear stockpiles in the 1950s.[6] Second, and more amorphously, the weapon's actual operation served as a powerful metaphor. The Bomb was not simply a very large mass of explosives. Rather, its efficacy depended upon a series of physical reactions that were impossible for the average person to observe or even comprehend. The atom, infinitesimal but containing unimaginable power, was the negative image of the Christian nonviolent faith, with its assertion of strength through weakness, of social transformation through appeal to potent invisible forces.

A. J. Muste's *Not by Might* was the most penetrating defense of pacifism in the early atomic age. Published in 1947, Muste's book self-consciously eschewed realist discourse in favor of a language of God, love, and conscience. "It seems foolish today," he admitted, "that what we have to place against the atomic bomb is conscience and love. But we have to get away from the wisdom and realism which have brought us where we are, very far away from them and very quickly." Then he invoked the atom as metaphor: "We have to look in the opposite direction, at that which in its own order is perhaps as invisible to the naked eye, seemingly as devoid of power, as the atom." The figure of Jesus, who had achieved victory through meekness and suffering, offered a way out of global annihilation. In contrast, the realist neglect of the moral universe put humanity on a course of global disaster.[7]

The author of *Not by Might* was no orthodox believer, certainly no evangelical Christian, despite his Christ-centered language and imagery. Billy Graham would arrive on the national scene in just a few years, but Muste distanced himself from "the 'religious revivals' of which we hear so much in certain circles," insisting that he was not "writing of matters ecclesiastical or theological in the dogmatic sense." He was uninterested in leading readers to the promise of eternal life in heaven that revivalists offered, for the death of Jesus on the cross was less a sacrifice for the sins of humanity than a symbolic explanation of "the paradox at the heart of the universe. . . . Out of weakness comes strength; out of defeat comes victory. Out of death springs life."[8]

The transformative experience of the moral act lay at the center of Muste's spiritual politics. *Not by Might* owed much to the rise of existentialism, both Christian and secular, during the age of conscience. Muste posited the individual act of moral dissent as a moment of authenticity in an increasingly unreal world. "Man no longer believes in himself," he explained, and "can no longer feel that he, himself, is real, that he counts and 'belongs.'" In fact, atomic war may come because "inwardly men are not sure they want to survive." Muste argued that even the most thoughtful "realists" had only exacerbated the postwar miasma of anxiety. In an open letter to Niebuhr published the year after *Not by Might*, he charged his longtime critic with spreading "defeatism and despair." Themes of sin and fallibility in human action had come to loom so large in Niebuhr's theology that, as Muste saw it, he had given "to people the subtle suggestion that they are paralyzed, under a judgment which they cannot escape."[9]

For Muste, escape from the immobilizing weight of atomic despair came "in the moment when a man makes a moral decision . . . and when he acts upon his decision." Then "he is not troubled with this sense of his own unreality or of the illusoriness or emptiness of life." Rather, "he experiences himself as real." Here, Muste argued, was the true religious experience. "At the moment of moral decision, in the realm of the spirit, he is face to face with Reality" and "experiences this Reality as absolute, inexorable, inescapable, eternal. Such is the nature of the moral order." Breaking through to this moral order, he maintained, was the only hope for humanity's survival.[10]

The supremacy of the moral individual served as the basis for Muste's critique of world government as a solution to the atomic menace. The hope of "one world" that would overcome the threat of the Bomb dominated American public debate in the years immediately following World War II. The radical Christian pacifist response to schemes of international authority was mixed, just as it had been after the First World War. Muste allowed that he was "definitely in favor of federal world-government," but pointed out the impossibility of a global system under the antagonistic conditions existing between the United States and the Soviet Union. Peace had to precede world government, just as the moral universe preceded politics. The "stalemate" emerging by 1947 was, Muste argued, "proof that the crisis is deeper than politics. The real crisis is in the mind and spirit of man. The solution must be found on that level."[11]

The Fellowship circle viewed all state power with some degree of suspicion in the years after the war, particularly the newly dominant American and Soviet states. In part the radical Christian pacifist stance was an anticommunist move, a rejection of the doctrine of "peaceful coexistence" promoted by many American Communists. More often, the libertarian bent of the FOR led to a critique of the United States. As a conscientious objector and an advocate for interned Japanese Americans during World War II, Caleb Foote had special cause to be wary. Shortly before the elections of 1948, he wrote in *Fellowship* that the outcome of the vote was meaningless. Left-leaning Americans were sharply divided between the Democrat Harry Truman and the insurgent Progressive candidacy of Henry Wallace, but Foote was unmoved. "No matter who wins," he lamented, "the mandate of the voters will be used as an excuse to increase the power of centralized Big Government, strengthen the growing army of Federal bureaucracy, and move us toward the evolution of the police state which is the logical outcome of our historical situation." The only hope was to reconstruct society by "building freedom here and now—in ourselves, our families, our communities, and by attacking the Big State with the only weapons which at this late date make much sense: direct action and revolutionary noncooperation." Foote's view was extreme, leading one *Fellowship* reader to suggest archly that he ought to vote for the independent segregationist candidate Strom Thurmond, who "echoes all his major arguments" about the evils of the national government. Yet many in the FOR voiced skepticism about the state and therefore looked askance at "one world." The emphasis that Muste and Foote placed on individual dissent proved a compelling alternative.[12]

The radical moral action described in *Not by Might* was something like a mystical experience, but the process was not only inward looking. It involved a public dimension. In the same year that *Not by Might* was published, Muste joined George Houser, Bayard Rustin, David Dellinger, and other radical pacifists in the nation's first draft card burnings. The February 12 action was part of a vigorous campaign against the Truman administration's Universal Military Training proposal, which sought to replace the Selective Service Act with a more sweeping peacetime conscription law. In New York, a few hundred protesters met at Labor Temple, the Fellowship's venerable institutional ally, to hear speeches denouncing the plan. The subsequent immolation of the cards was not a flawless act of political theater. Informed by the fire department that they could start fires neither in the street nor in a kettle placed on the speakers' platform for the purpose, the protesters finally dropped the cards in a Greenwich Village incinerator late that night. Parallel actions occurred in Washington, D.C., and San Francisco. The radical pacifists could claim little credit for defeating Universal Military Training, which soon died quietly in committee, but they put themselves once again on the cutting edge of radical dissent.[13]

More widely noticed than the draft card burning was the pacifists' leadership of the Civil Defense protest held in New York on June 15, 1955. This demonstration deployed the spectacle of individual moral action to expose the absurdity of realist discourse, just as Muste had suggested in *Not by Might*. The Civil Defense exercises, begun in 1951, were ostensibly intended to minimize casualties in case of nuclear war, though many proponents also saw them as a way to bolster the American public's anti-Soviet resolve. When the air raid sirens sounded, residents had to take shelter immediately or face misdemeanor charges under state law. The drill continued every year, despite its obvious inadequacy as a defense against nuclear weapons. Officials released precise calculations of the number of New Yorkers killed and wounded in each "attack," unintentionally validating Muste's description of the unreal quality of life in the atomic age.[14]

In this setting, Muste, Rustin, and twenty-seven other pacifists, many of them Catholic Workers, decided to take a radical moral stance. The resulting protest was not a series of spontaneous individual decisions. It was a planned spectacle, preceded by a "morning meeting for meditation" and a luncheon. The pacifists assembled in City Hall Park and submitted to arrest after they firmly refused to take shelter at the appointed time. The judge at their trial referred to them as "murderers" responsible for the simulated deaths of millions of New Yorkers. However, this particular act of conscience eventually gained a victory, as the protest became an increasingly popular yearly ritual. By 1960, it drew hundreds of participants and inspired related actions on college campuses around the city. In 1962, the drill itself was permanently canceled. The pacifists, by laying bare the artificiality of supposedly realistic war preparations, made the Civil Defense illusion impossible to sustain.[15]

The principles expressed in Not by Might and the spectacles generated by the Civil Defense protests made the Cold War a spiritual problem, a question of conscience. By the 1950s, that spiritualization was happening across the political landscape. President Dwight Eisenhower, commenting on his meeting with a Soviet official, insisted in 1952 that "our form of government has no sense unless it is founded in a deeply felt religious faith" (notoriously adding "and I don't care what it is").[16] Congress signaled its agreement by adding the phrase "under God" to the Pledge of Allegiance and changing the nation's official motto from "E pluribus unum" to "In God We Trust." For many Americans, "belief" served as the fundamental sign of difference between their nation and Soviet Russia.[17]

Indeed, the "act of conscience," in all its shades of meaning, was the defining mode of anticommunist political culture during the early Cold War. The most intense intellectual and political arguments about Marxism as a system, and about Russian Communism as its political expression, had occurred two or three decades earlier. By the time of Joseph McCarthy's rise in 1950, ideas had receded into the background of the anticommunist drama, replaced by questions of loyalty, integrity, and betrayal. The tropes of conscience served both the anticommunist crusaders and their opponents. When Elia Kazan made a film about a young dockworker whose nagging sense of right and wrong leads him to expose a corrupt union in *On the Waterfront* (1954), many of his colleagues saw it as the director's defense of his cooperation with the House Un-American Activities Committee. Arthur Miller admitted that his 1953 play *The Crucible* drew on the moral theater of the committee's investigations. He found that the hearings, like the Salem witch trials, contained "an immaterial element," a "surreal spiritual transaction" based on "rituals of guilt and confession." In various ways, anticommunists and their foes defended their positions in terms of individual integrity, putting their consciences—whether tortured, guilty, or unyielding—on display for public consumption.[18]

Whittaker Chambers's *Witness* was a particularly elaborate attempt to link the question of Communism to the question of conscience. Chambers was not affiliated with Christian nonviolence, but his life bore peculiar connections to the FOR. His wife, the former Esther Shemitz, had worked on the staff of the old *World Tomorrow* before becoming a Communist fellow traveler. Chambers himself, in a pattern similar to A. J. Muste's turn from Marxism back to the Fellowship, had broken with Communism in 1938 and eventually become a Quaker, though not a pacifist one. *Witness,* Chambers's 1952 memoir of his life as a Communist, ex-Communist, and anticommunist, displayed the combination of spiritual precocity and spiritual humility that also defined the Fellowship's brand of politics. The title of the book itself blurred a secular legal identity with a religious one. Chambers was a witness in the espionage trial of Alger Hiss, but at another level he was, he explained, "a witness to each of the two great faiths of our time," which he called "Communism and Freedom." Going still deeper, he saw himself as "an involuntary witness to God's grace and to the fortifying power of faith." *Witness,* then, took the Cold War to be a matter of cosmic significance.[19]

Muste used the book to draw a sharp distinction between his own spiritualization of the Cold War and the vision of the anticommunists. In a long review of *Witness,* he admitted that it had a "special fascination" for him because of the parallels between Chambers's life and his own. Muste found the facts of the book to be "reliable, illuminating, and remarkably objective," its analysis of Communism "profound, and in my view, essentially correct." However, *Witness* put righteousness all on one side. "No real consideration is given," Muste complained, "to dealing with the evil in ourselves." Chambers had merely switched allegiances, changing from a Communist conspirer into a conspirer against Communists. He had not found a "secure moral ground" above both Communism and its reactionary opposition. Muste did not quarrel with the assertion in *Witness* that the issues defining the Cold War were at bottom religious, but he saw Jesus standing above America and Russia, not on one particular side.[20]

Political circumstances, as well as religious principle, necessitated a search for a way out of the Cold War dichotomy. With notable exceptions such as the Civil Defense protests, the Fellowship of Reconciliation could not effectively engage the leaders of the United States and the Soviet Union. Along with a repressive domestic climate, the insulation of Cold War policy from democratic control marginalized dissenting voices by relying upon espionage, classified military projects, and secret negotiations. Even given the horrifying threat of the atomic bomb, pacifists made little headway. Nuclear stockpiling began a few years after the war, and in 1950 the United States tested the first hydrogen bomb, a weapon far more powerful than the ones that had destroyed Hiroshima and Nagasaki. Meanwhile, Cold War strategy fostered or abetted violent coups, insurgencies, and proxy wars around the world. The issue was not simply that radical pacifism failed to prevent these developments, but rather that even after the most destructive war in human history nonviolence was not even up for discussion in crafting foreign policy. In his 1947 book *Gandhi and Stalin: Two Signs at the World's Crossroads,* the liberal journalist Louis Fischer wrote admiringly of the Mahatma as the epitome of democracy, the anti-Stalin, yet Fischer also observed that "Gandhi's ideas of democracy and Gandhi himself could not survive in a dictatorship. A dictator would simply order Mr. Gandhi removed into oblivion." In this widespread view, nonviolence was a luxury that Cold Warriors could ill afford.[21]

Under these conditions, the groups attracted to nonviolence tended to be those that had little other plausible recourse. Despite the pacifist insistence that nonviolence was more powerful than the atomic bomb, those who were capable of getting atomic bombs chose to do so, with Great Britain, France, and China soon joining the "nuclear club." Still, those who could not make bombs, in the Fellowship's view, offered a possible vindication for nonviolence. "Out of weakness comes strength," Muste had written in *Not by Might.* For both theological and practical reasons, radical Christian pacifism rededicated itself to anticolonialism.

Walk to Freedom, the Fellowship's film about the Montgomery bus boycott, showed how Christian nonviolence sought to move beyond Cold War dualisms toward an anticolonial, even postcolonial, outlook. The film placed Montgomery in a larger context by using newsreel footage that showed soldiers harassing colonized people, destroying their homes, and, in one case, shooting them. "Segregation, discrimination, prejudice, exploitation: in any part of the world the meaning is the same," the narrator intoned, "in Johannesburg or Nairobi, in Algiers or Dakar." One pacifist viewer thought that this broad scope resulted in a jumbled "hodgepodge," while the New York Times called the film "rather piecemeal." However, the intended point was to depict, on a low production budget, a global police state that transcended the differences between the two Cold War superpowers. The experience of colonized populations, was, for the pacifists, the prototypical experience of modern militarized life. Most of the scenes of brutality shown in the film, then, were generic rather than specific, for the Fellowship sought to unmask "the face of violence, not in colonial areas alone, but wherever there is conflict and struggle—in South America, in Finland, in East Berlin, in Italy, in the United States, in any part of the world."[22]

In a letter to Henri Roser, a leader of the small FOR branch in France, Muste made explicit what the film only implied, namely that a successful peace movement "would be a movement of those people in all countries who will start from the standpoint of unequivocal condemnation of Russian militarism and American militarism, of the new Russian empire and the new American empire." He called upon the FOR to help guide the revolutions in Asia and Africa along a nonviolent path, seeing nonviolent direct action against racism in the United States as a model for anticolonial movements in other lands. He applauded members of the younger generation such as George Houser and Bayard Rustin. They had "pioneered in trying out Gandhian methods in race conflict here at home," Muste explained, "and . . . we may by the grace of God be able, therefore, to make a critical contribution to African developments." In a sense, the anticolonial movements in Africa became the world political equivalent of the individual conscientious objectors in America; both were apparently weak entities that created troublesome disruptions in established power structures. Both, Muste hoped, could exert disproportionate influence in the quest for world peace.[23]

In retrospect, Muste's view of Third World independence movements as vanguards of nonviolence looks naïve. Frantz Fanon's words from The Wretched of the Earth seem far more relevant: "The naked truth of decolonization evokes for us the searing bullets and bloodstained knives which emanate from it." However, the early history of anticolonialism did raise hopes that militant nonviolence could defuse some of the brutality of the decolonization process. In the years after Indian independence, Gandhian nonviolence won unprecedented victories and became the model for many independence movements, especially in Africa. Inspired by the Indian example, Kwame Nkrumah in Ghana and Kenneth Kaunda in Zambia led insurgencies that ended British rule, while the African National Congress in South Africa began a "Campaign to Defy Unjust Laws" on the Gandhian model. Fanon's focus on violence in *The Wretched of the Earth* was in part a response to Gandhi's posthumous popularity. Its first chapter began as part of a debate with Nkrumah at the 1958 All-Africa People's Conference over the efficacy of nonviolence.[24]

George Houser, a founder of CORE and Rustin's partner on the leading edge of FOR race relations initiatives in the 1940s, threw himself into the cause of African independence. He first heard about the South African situation in 1952, when Bill Sutherland, a fellow pacifist and World War II conscientious objector, told him about the Defiance Campaign. Later that year, Houser organized Americans for South African Resistance, with Rustin, Conrad Lynn, Roger Baldwin, Norman Thomas, and A. Philip Randolph all serving on the Executive Committee. Using his position as executive secretary of CORE, Houser began to correspond with the leaders of the South African resistance movement, urging them to remain on the path of nonviolence. The next year, Houser founded the American Committee on Africa, which became the most important American organization dedicated to the anticolonial struggle in Africa, primarily in an educational and fundraising capacity. In 1955, Houser left the Fellowship of Reconciliation to work full time for the new organization.[25]

Houser's promotion of racial equality in South Africa drew on the anti-communist conscience-based politics of the Fellowship. "Although all our supporters were unalterably opposed to McCarthyism," Houser recalled, "we were not interested in joining forces with the Communists in a united front." His stance had little in common with McCarthy's hysterical Red-baiting. In 1956, W. E. B. Du Bois called the American Committee on Africa "right-wing" and "reactionary," but this gross mischaracterization revealed more about Du Bois's increasing sympathy for the Soviet Union than about the orientations of Houser and his fellow anticolonialists. Some historians have recently adopted the assessment of Du Bois more or less uncritically, romanticizing Communist anticolonialism while overlooking the religious radicalism exemplified in Houser's sit-ins, draft card burning, and imprisonment during World War II. Certainly, Cold War repression was a disaster for anticolonial movements. However, by the 1980s, when non-Marxist radicals such as Desmond Tutu and Václav

Havel helped lead astonishing political revolutions, the efforts of Houser and Rustin looked far more prescient than the obdurate faith in Communism exhibited by the aging Du Bois.[26]

That portentous year of 1956 offered proof to the pacifists that Soviet Communism, far from offering the promise of liberation, was only another form of imperialism. Spurred in part by Nikita Khrushchev's "secret speech" criticizing Stalin's rule, a new government took control in the Soviet satellite state of Hungary and called for independence from Moscow, only to be crushed by the Russian military. These events marked the first major public stirrings of discontent that led to the final breakup of the Soviet Union some thirty years later, but in the short term, the use of violent repression finished off Communism as a viable form of American radicalism, Du Bois and a few other diehards notwithstanding.

The Fellowship seized on the Hungarian uprising to show the moral bankruptcy of both sides in the Cold War. Comparing the Soviet repression in Hungary to the invasion of Egypt by Western nations (the so-called Suez crisis) during the same month, *Fellowship* opined that the "moral pretensions of the great powers on both sides have been stripped away." "For the first time since World War II," the editorial went on hopefully, "there are more than two contending centers of power." The Cold War could end only through the efforts of these independent nations and movements, a fact that might resuscitate nonviolent action. After all, violence by Hungarians would be futile: "Does anyone assume that ten million Hungarians, no matter how well equipped with planes and tanks and guns, could be victorious in a struggle with the Soviet Union?" Violence by America on Hungary's behalf would be even more catastrophic, resulting in "global, hydrogen war." For the many pawns in the Cold War chess match, nonviolence was not a mere affectation, but a grim necessity. Hungary did eventually throw off Soviet rule nonviolently, but it was the struggle for racial justice in the United States that brought the Fellowship its greatest success during the age of conscience.[27]

Houser and others regarded their work in support of African independence as a corollary of their efforts to achieve justice for African Americans. Between World War II and the Montgomery bus boycott, the Fellowship of Reconciliation and the Congress of Racial Equality worked out the strategies and styles of the full-fledged civil rights movement that began in 1956. This was the radical Christian pacifists' most resounding achievement, as the pacifist dissent that Muste described in *Not by Might* crossed over into the arena of racial politics. The quest for black freedom became, for the Fellowship, the transcendent moral force that stood in judgment over American society but rejected Soviet Communism as an alternative.[28]

Christian nonviolence brought to black freedom struggles the multivalent quality inherent in acts of conscience. On one hand, the FOR and CORE turned racial justice into a moral imperative that rose above political and economic interest, an imperative that the righteous individual had to obey without regard for temporal consequences. At the same time, the radical Christian pacifist influence led to a focus on the performance of justice. Rather than resort to violence, the FOR and CORE sought to deploy the weapons of representation. Houser, Rustin, and the other nonviolent innovators dramatized existential moral action against racism by rehearsing, staging, casting, and replaying it as both ritual and spectacle. In doing so, they helped transform the character of political morality itself.

The 1947 Journey of Reconciliation, an early version of the 1961 Freedom Rides, marked a watershed in the development of a sophisticated form of Christian nonviolence deployed on behalf of racial equality. The year before, in the *Irene Morgan* case, the Supreme Court had ruled that segregation of interstate travel was unconstitutional, but enforcement of the decision had been lax. The FOR and CORE sponsored an interracial team of volunteers who would ride interstate Greyhound and Trailways buses to determine whether the bus companies were abiding by the court's ruling. The plan was also a product of the increasing racial conflict fomented by the recent war, during which black military personnel had resisted riding Jim Crow in several publicized instances. In this climate, sending an interracial team on buses around the South to test compliance with the Supreme Court decision would be "striking a raw nerve," as Houser later put it.[29]

Before the Journey began, pragmatic considerations scaled back the proposed radical moral action in two ways. First, the travelers decided not to follow an originally proposed Baltimore-to-New Orleans route, but rather to focus on the upper South, where they thought that racial prejudice was milder. In fact, the FOR and CORE had few Southern connections in this period, and the organizers of the Journey struggled to find anyone from the region to ride with them (they eventually located three white North Carolinians). The second issue was the role of women in the Journey. The original action was open to women and men alike. Although several women volunteered, organizers later limited the venture to men only, "with the thought," Houser explained later, "that mixing the races and sexes would possibly exacerbate an already volatile situation," or in Conrad Lynn's more direct assessment, "some of us would certainly have been killed." Discussions concerning a subsequent "Women's Journey" came to nothing. Militant nonviolence, in this case as in so many others, ended up replicating the masculine character of war itself.[30]

With eight white and eight black volunteers in place, preparations began. Houser remembered that "extensive socio-dramas were enacted, sometimes quite violent, to help prepare us for any eventuality." The so-ciodrama was a CORE innovation. Participants in demonstrations prac-ticed nonviolence in controlled settings by adopting the roles of violent assailants, passive resisters, and ambivalent bystanders, thereby steel-ing themselves against verbal and physical provocation. For the Journey of Reconciliation, James Peck remembered that "participants would act the roles of bus drivers, hysterical segregationists, police—and 'you.'" Clearly, the refusal to retaliate that marked successful CORE actions did not spring solely from an upwelling of spontaneous courage, but rather from an application of discipline. Even for atheist riders such as Peck, that discipline served as a kind of ritual, much as Richard Gregg had de-scribed in *Training for Peace*. In the ritual world of the sociodramas, every-day reality was at once suspended and transcended as radical antiracists temporarily transformed themselves into rabid white supremacists. Indi-vidual selfhood (Peck's "you") gave way to a sense of common purpose in a collective enterprise. Simultaneously, the sociodramas were rehearsals for a dramatic performance in front of a demanding, and possibly hostile, audience. Indeed, Peck later wrote that the bus ride gave him a feeling of being "on stage."[31]

The Journey members set out on April 9, 1947, in two groups, divided between Greyhound and Trailways bus lines. The participants formed an auspicious assembly that included many of the leading pacifists and civil rights workers of the time, including Houser, Rustin, Lynn, Peck, Homer Jack, and Igal Roodenko. Much of the Journey went smoothly. On the Greyhound buses no arrests were made at all. However, one harrowing incident revealed a barely submerged threat of violence. In Chapel Hill, North Carolina, police arrested four members of the Trailways group, in-cluding Rustin and Roodenko, for violating Jim Crow seating. During the delay at the bus station, a taxi driver struck Peck, who absorbed the blow without retaliating. The group eventually retreated to the home of Charles Jones, a local Presbyterian minister and FOR staff member, but angry taxi drivers followed and threatened the group with rocks and sticks. Next, an anonymous caller told Jones to "get those damn niggers out of town or we'll burn your house down." The Journeyers called the police, then decided to leave town and drive, rather than ride the bus, to the next stop in Greensboro.[32]

The most common response to the riders was not this kind of extreme intimidation. "The one word," Houser and Rustin wrote later, "which most universally describes the attitude of police, of passengers, and of the Negro and white bus riders is 'confusion.'" The usual sources of segregationist authority became unreliable, leading to moments of what Gregg in *The Power of Non-Violence* had called "moral jiu-jitsu." Repeatedly, transportation officials tried to intimidate the riders, then reluctantly backed down in the face of their intransigence. Once, a bus driver called police, but when they arrived they refused to remove the Journeyers from their seats. Another bewildered driver defended his enforcement of separate seating by explaining "that he was in the employ of the bus company, not the Supreme Court." The Journey dramatized the everyday occurrence of segregation on the buses and forced racism's defenders to articulate their positions, which often turned out to be hopelessly muddled or simply embarrassing. Just as the Civil Defense protests called attention to the absurdities inherent in government defense preparations, so the Journey of Reconciliation exposed the preposterous assumptions that supported racial discrimination. Both pacifist projects employed the act of conscience as a nonviolent weapon.[33]

The Journey also highlighted the fastidious interracialism practiced by the advocates of Christian nonviolence, an ideal that was at once an individual ethic and a public aesthetic. In Houser and Rustin's written report on the Journey, white and black bodies shift and realign themselves on a kind of real-life backgammon board: "A white couple sat on the back seat of the Greyhound bus with two Negroes. A Negro woman sat beside a young white man in the center of the bus when she could have taken a vacant seat by a Negro man. Rustin gave his seat, third from front, to an elderly Negro woman, and then sat by a white lad directly behind the driver." This quasimathematical attention to the position of the riders underscored the Journeyers' hope that personal interracial encounters could help end racism. The Journey's line of attack was clear. "We did not allow a single situation to develop," Houser and Rustin wrote, "so that the struggle appeared to be between white and Negro persons, but rather that progressives and democrats, white and black, were working by peaceful means to overcome a system which they felt to be wrong." Christian nonviolence depended upon the fact and the image of interracial solidarity.[34]

From the beginning, the bus rides were performances, to be replayed and retold for a variety of audiences. The participants thought carefully about their media strategy, though it proved to be somewhat counterintuitive. Unlike the later Freedom Rides, the Journey of Reconciliation depended upon the element of surprise. Houser, Rustin, and their fellow riders wanted to travel on the buses like normal passengers, so they intentionally neglected to invite any photographers to record their actions. Thus, the only extant photograph from the Journey shows the assembled group before its departure.[35]

At the same time, the Journeyers arranged for reporters from two black newspapers, the *Pittsburgh Courier* and the *Baltimore Afro-American,* to accompany the riders while posing as ordinary travelers, thus ensuring that the project received wide coverage in the black press. After the Journey, the participants themselves also publicized their undertaking. In November 1947, a radio show presented a dramatized account of the completed Journey, while the FOR and CORE distributed Houser and Rustin's pamphlet account of the trip, *We Challenged Jim Crow!* These recreations of the event offered further opportunities to spread the word not only about the Supreme Court's ruling, but about the effectiveness of nonviolent moral action against racism.[36]

The retellings, presented as factual reports, contained more sophisticated narratives. *We Challenged Jim Crow!,* for instance, offered a subtle critique of white soldiers in the aftermath of World War II. The social tension created by returning combatants haunted American culture during this period. In the same year as the Journey of Reconciliation, the film *Crossfire* broached the troubling subject of prejudice by depicting an American soldier who murders a Jewish man. Soldiers in Houser and Rustin's narrative manifested similar negative traits. Two incidents recorded in the pamphlet questioned the heroic qualities of soldiers and, given the all-male cast of the Journey, opened space for alternative conceptions of masculinity. In one case, a "young Marine" responds to the interracial group by saying: "The K.K.K. is coming up again and I guess I'll join up." In the other scene, a soldier asks a bus driver why he did not force a black Journey participant to move, leading the driver to impugn the Supreme Court decision: "If you want to do something about this," he told the soldier, "don't blame" the black rider; "kill those bastards up in Washington." Soldiers who joined forces with the Klan, or even contemplated the slaughter of their own political leaders—these were the ostensible heroes of World War II, in the Christian nonviolent reckoning. By choosing these anecdotes, Houser and Rustin slipped a pacifist denunciation of war into their nonviolent antiracist story.[37]

The Journey raised difficult questions about the role of the "bastards up in Washington," or any government authority backed by armed force. After the trip, the FOR debated the ethical propriety of resorting to police protection, as in the case of the Chapel Hill incident. Rustin claimed that "he personally would not have been in favor of calling the police, but when some of the group do not take this position one cannot resist." Another member asked if the Journey's appeal to the Supreme Court and the Constitution "is a relative or absolute difference from relying on police power." In fact, the Journey of Reconciliation prefigured the later civil rights movement in its tacit acceptance of the violent power of the state as an ally of nonviolent direct action. Despite the libertarian tendencies in the FOR, pragmatic considerations prevailed in this aspect of militant nonviolence.[38]

The Journey of Reconciliation was only the most prominent in a series of FOR-CORE assaults on racism at sites of transportation, consumption, and recreation. Ironically, the radical Christian pacifists' focus on the existential drama of extreme individual action led to an emphasis on the nation's burgeoning consumer culture. The moral actions most easily and effectively dramatized occurred in the spheres of consumption. Sitting on a bus, eating in a restaurant, or swimming in a pool were all easy to attempt and easy to photograph, film, and narrate. Like the Journey of Reconciliation, they brought black and white bodies into close contact in public spaces, thus enacting the radical Christian pacifist interracial ethic and, at the same time, producing stark and memorable images of integration being embraced or resisted.[39]

The orientation toward arenas of consumption was especially clear in the Washington Interracial Workshops organized by Houser and Rustin. Each July from 1947 to 1954, a small number of dedicated reformers gathered in the nation's capital to promote interracial understanding (the 1948 session was held in Los Angeles). The 1949 Workshop was particularly active. Participants arrived in the middle of a sweltering Washington summer to find that racial clashes had forced the closing of a popular segregated public swimming pool, so Workshoppers cooperated with lo-

FIGURE 6.1   George Houser speaking at the 1951 Interracial Workshop in Washington, D.C. (CDGA CORE, Congress of Racial Equality Papers, Swarthmore College Peace Collection.)

cal officials to formulate a plan for promoting nonviolent integration at all public pools. Other Workshop members participated in a "sit-down" in the Greyhound bus station restaurant, which, after much pressure and negotiation, agreed to serve black patrons. Finally, the Washington Interracial Workshop participants picketed the white-only Trans-Lux movie theater before the opening of the World War II film *Home of the Brave*. This action, in particular, showed how Christian nonviolence sometimes submerged its pacifist origins.[40]

Houser thought that the theater protest came at a "strategic moment," since *Home of the Brave* had an "interracial theme." The film tells the wartime story of an integrated special unit, a plot device to get around the fact that regular army units operated on Jim Crow lines. The narrative makes an antiracist statement, depicting a white soldier who overcomes his bigotry and a black soldier who conquers his sense of racial inferiority. *Home of the Brave* is not, however, an antiwar film. On the contrary, the protagonists achieve interracial harmony through the shared experience of combat. Furthermore, the black-white reconciliation depends upon a common Japanese enemy, which lurks as an unseen, treacherous foe represented only by gunshots and eerie vocalizations. In its "strategic" choice of *Home of the Brave*, the Washington Interracial Workshop implicitly elevated nonviolence in the service of black equality over resistance to war, even over racialized depictions of military enemies. Formed to abolish war, the Fellowship of Reconciliation now promoted equal access to the consumption of images of war onscreen.

Housing was one final arena for the radical Christian pacifists' moralization of consumer choice. The postwar period saw the suburbanization of America. Between 1947 and 1953, the increase in suburban population outstripped the general population increase 43 percent to 11 percent. Despite the later view of the suburbs as bland and monotonous, the new communities had elements of a latent utopianism in these early years. For a number of developers and white homebuyers, racial homogeneity was part of the neighborhood ideal, so many suburbs, including William Levitt's famous Levittowns, initially barred black residents.[41]

Conversely, for the radical Christian pacifists, suburbanization offered an opportunity to create new communities representative of the diverse human family. Several FOR families, including those of Houser and Charles Lawrence, the first black chair of the Fellowship, created an interracial suburb outside New York City called Skyview Acres.[42] In 1954, FOR member Morris Milgram began a remarkable experiment by opening Concord Park, an intentionally integrated development near Philadelphia. After assembling an interracial board of directors, Milgram promoted his new development with advertisements that asked: "Is your Golden Rule in housing lacking a few inches?" Concord Park maintained a loose quota system that kept white and black home ownership on a roughly equal basis, thereby exhibiting the mathematical black-white equivalence that defined the Fellowship's antiracism. The success of the venture, Milgram wrote enthusiastically to A. Philip Randolph, provided "an exciting demonstration that new homes can be sold to both Negro and white buyers— Mr. Levitt to the contrary, notwithstanding." Milgram also directed the construction of Greenbelt Knoll, a second, more upscale development, along the same integrated lines.[43]

These suburban experiments remained anomalies. Unlike the draft card burning, the Journey of Reconciliation, and the sit-ins, they never became models for more widespread reform efforts. Though de jure residential discrimination became illegal a few years after Milgram's venture began, Christian nonviolence did not effectively challenge that most momentous of consumer choices: where to buy a house. In practice, the intractable fact of geographical segregation was difficult to undo and difficult to dramatize. If Fellowship leaders failed to take account of this grim reality, they were blinded in part by the shimmering promise of their other experiments. In the Montgomery bus boycott, that promise looked virtually limitless.

At the time of the Montgomery bus boycott, the Fellowship's faith in nonviolent direct action generally did not extend to the South. The most innovative work by FOR and CORE groups took place in Northern urban centers such as Chicago and New York or in border cities such as St. Louis and Washington, D.C. A substantial FOR presence did exist in Nashville, where Howard and Alice Kester had worked in the 1930s, but the outlook and techniques that Houser, Rustin, and Farmer had developed largely failed to penetrate further than that. FOR Southern Secretary Constance Rumbough wrote that, because of state segregation laws and intense prejudice, "most Southern leaders think that the nonviolent direct action technique is not advisable in this area." Indeed, some Fellowship members in the South thought that the organization had focused too single-mindedly on militant nonviolence, to the exclusion of other kinds of antiracist practices. Rumbough undertook less confrontational, though still risky, projects such as interracial summer camps. When she departed her post in 1944, the organization's failure to appoint a replacement sparked a spirited debate. Charles Lawrence, who would become FOR chair in 1955, insisted to Muste that the "Southern field is ripe for the harvest" and urgently needed Houser or some other energetic pacifist presence. No, retorted John Haynes Holmes, it is "a barren field, certainly to be cultivated if we have the resources, but not to the neglect of other more fertile fields." As it happened, the Southern office remained vacant, so news of a mass nonviolent protest in the heart of Alabama took the organization completely by surprise.[44]

The Montgomery bus boycott marked a culmination of Christian nonviolent ethics and politics, even though the FOR had no direct role in starting it. The refusal by Rosa Parks to surrender her bus seat was arguably the prototypical event in the age of conscience. The widespread confusion, persisting even now, over the character of Parks's action underscores the ways that individual conscience became a public and political matter. Some observers saw her decision as completely spontaneous, unconnected to the history of black freedom struggles, but in fact she had long been active in the National Association for the Advancement of Colored People. Others viewed her refusal as part of a carefully scripted plot by black community leaders, but this, too, was inaccurate. The truth was that a web of black political organizations in Montgomery, notably the NAACP and the Women's Political Council, turned Parks's unplanned moral action into a public spectacle. Black churches helped, too, including Dexter Avenue Baptist, where the young Martin Luther King Jr. had recently become pastor.[45]

King had more experience with Christian nonviolence than did the other leaders of the boycott. While a student at Crozer Theological Seminary, a liberal interracial school in Pennsylvania, he had attended a lecture by A. J. Muste, where he was, he recalled, "exposed for the first time to the pacifist position." Though he "was deeply moved by Dr. Muste's talk," he remained "far from convinced of the practicability of his position." A few years later, the young theological student wrote a paper critiquing Muste's views on the atomic bomb. King also encountered the FOR while working toward his doctoral degree at Boston University, studying under longtime Fellowship member Allan Knight Chalmers. Along with these FOR connections, the writing and preaching of African American ministers such as Benjamin Mays, Mordecai Johnson, and Howard Thurman had exposed him to the philosophy and career of Gandhi. By the time of Parks's arrest, King was acquainted with the tradition of Christian nonviolence, though he was not a part of the FOR-CORE network.[46]

Despite some superficial similarities, the boycott did not progress along the lines of the nonviolent direct action projects that the FOR and CORE had undertaken further north. The boycotters' refusal of violence was wholly pragmatic and conditional. They did not abandon the right of self-defense, as Houser and Rustin had urged in their own nonviolent protests. Guns were everywhere and bodyguards protected King's home. Coretta Scott King later insisted that "if Martin ever heard that someone in the Movement was armed, he made them get rid of their weapons." She also claimed that her husband enforced this policy "from the beginning," but this was certainly false. Other observers remembered several guns plainly visible in the King home. The boycotters made no apologies for their defensive preparations. Jo Ann Robinson, who played a key role in initiating the boycott as a leader of the Women's Political Council, remembered that black men "got their guns and placed them conveniently near their beds." Robinson herself procured a pistol, pronouncing it a "comfort" even though she "was afraid to shoot" it. On January 30, when King's home was bombed, boycotters assembled at the site of the attack with guns, knives, and broken bottles. Only King's calming words avoided an outbreak of violence.[47]

Black Montgomerians' readiness to use armed force resulted in part from a lack of alternatives. Police seemed unconcerned about the bombings that terrorized King and other MIA leaders. Furthermore, city officials soon alleged that the boycott itself was illegal, a violation of the Alabama Anti-Boycott Act of 1921. The exhilaration created by the early success of the undertaking soon turned to dismay as a Montgomery grand jury indicted 115 of the boycott organizers on February 21. Perhaps it was true, then, that legal and cultural barriers made militant nonviolent action impossible to implement in the South. On that same day, however, a new face appeared in Montgomery, a black man claiming to be a foreign newspaper correspondent. Bayard Rustin's arrival, funded by the pacifist War Resisters League, began to shift the whole course of the boycott.

Rustin was no reporter, nor was he a member of the Fellowship of Reconciliation in 1956. Though he had been one of the group's most dynamic and effective staff members, Muste banished him after he was arrested on a "morals charge" for performing a sex act with two other men in California in 1953.[48] The Fellowship, dependent on an image of moral rectitude, could not countenance Rustin's frequent public breaches of sexual norms, while a political strategy built on *choosing* to go to jail could not survive many involuntary arrests. Despite lingering interpersonal tensions, Rustin's break with the FOR did not exile him from the political projects of radical Christian pacifism for long. The same year as the boycott, he cofounded the left-wing journal *Liberation* with Muste. Rustin later claimed that, while advising King, he "never made a difficult decision without talking the problem over with A.J. first."[49] Nonetheless, after much debate, pacifist and civil rights leaders concluded that Rustin's presence in Montgomery was too dangerous, given his previous record. Within a week, the Fellowship decided to send in his place Glenn Smiley, a white Methodist minister and Southwest FOR Secretary (since no Southern Secretary existed). Rustin introduced Smiley to King and then was smuggled out of the city.

Rustin's work during his one week in Montgomery was pivotal in turning the boycott toward the Christian nonviolence of the Fellowship of Reconciliation. He was not a total stranger to the King family. Coretta recalled hearing him speak when she was in eighth grade, then again at Antioch College. Yet on his first visit to King's home, Rustin was appalled at the weapons assembled there. The firepower was technically nonviolent, for no actual shootouts had erupted on the streets of Montgomery, but the threat of bloodshed outraged Rustin's commitment to the principle of nonviolence. Furthermore, he thought that the weapons raised fear and suspicion in observers that outweighed the benefit of the protection they provided. Under Rustin's influence, King became committed to a more thoroughgoing nonviolent stance.

Rustin's guidance also deflated the plan to destroy the boycott by arresting its leaders. He suggested that the indicted boycotters turn themselves in voluntarily, wearing their Sunday clothes and smiling broadly. They adopted his plan, to the amazement of the local police. A large crowd turned out to witness the scene at the jail, producing "a mood of good-natured hilarity," in the words of one early chronicler. Deputies laughed and joked with the prisoners, finally leading an exasperated sheriff to bark: "This is no vaudeville show." His comparison was unintentionally apt, for under Rustin's guidance the formidable power of law that had threatened the MIA just a few days before now seemed only a game, a performance, a show. At the beginning of the boycott, Edgar D. Nixon, a labor organizer and a secularist, had excoriated ministers who were reluctant to take on leadership roles in the effort. "You said that God has called you to lead the people," Nixon fumed, "and now you are afraid and gone to pieces because . . . your pictures might come out in the newspapers." Montgomery's African American clergy were understandably wary of the local press, but after the mass indictment the dynamics of media power shifted to make the boycott a story that traveled far beyond its city of origin.[50]

The work of the Fellowship of Reconciliation, begun by Rustin and continued by Glenn Smiley and others, was pivotal in turning the local bus boycott into the national, even global, symbol of an emerging civil rights movement, with King as its spiritual leader. In the strictest sense, the Montgomery project was not particularly successful in achieving its objectives, as the bus company and the local government resisted the pressure of the boycott until a Supreme Court ruling forced integration. At a more fundamental level, though, the black and white leaders of the Fellowship, in cooperation with the boycotters, "told the world a story," one that would orient black freedom efforts in the next decade and beyond. Under FOR guidance, the Montgomery bus boycott became suffused with moral and Christian imagery, on one hand, and became dependent on the creation and manipulation of mass mediated spectacles, images, and illusions, on the other.[51]

Reinhold Niebuhr often appears in historical accounts as King's most important influence, but the radical Christian pacifists had far more effect on King in this period than did the apostle of Christian realism. Niebuhr was certainly a crucial figure for any educated American Protestant in the 1950s, and King referred often to his profound theological interpretations of love, hope, and sin. However, Niebuhr's specific influence is difficult to discover. He was a committed antiracist, but so were white pacifists such as Muste. A famous passage in *Moral Man and Immoral Society* predicted the use of nonviolent action by African Americans, but that book was written when Niebuhr was still a member of the FOR and in dialogue with several other pacifists who had similar visions of a pragmatic, militant form of nonviolent action deployed against racism. Actually, King in 1958 called his own stance "realistic pacifism," a label that described Richard Gregg far more accurately than it fit Niebuhr. Most importantly, it was the Fellowship that sent representatives to Montgomery and directly supported the MIA. In an essay on the boycott, Niebuhr himself wrote that it was "inspired by the principles of the Fellowship of Reconciliation, a pacifist organization." He admitted, somewhat patronizingly, that pacifists could be "impressive" in effecting social change when they did not become obsessed with "personal perfection." For his part, Niebuhr was no longer a pacifist and had little immediate sway over the specific style and strategies of the civil rights movement.[52]

Glenn Smiley, not Reinhold Niebuhr, was the white Protestant cleric who most directly affected the course of the Montgomery bus boycott. Since serving his prison time for resisting the World War II draft, Smiley had worked hard to spread the tenets of nonviolence as the Fellowship's Southwest Secretary. Based in Los Angeles, he participated in an early CORE chapter there. He also organized a twenty-six-mile "poster walk" opposing peacetime conscription, thereby opening himself to ribbing from FOR colleague John Swomley, who found humor in the long hike being led by "the weightiest member of our staff." In 1952, he and his wife visited East Berlin. There he found confirmation of the superiority of pacifism over Communism, noting that "we are not put in the position of defending our military, whereas they *must* defend theirs, and as a result find themselves in the same reactionary camp as those of every land who condone and use violence and warfare." Well before he arrived in Montgomery, Smiley had become a leading proponent of the Christian nonviolent politics of conscience.[53]

Smiley's new project posed unique challenges. In one sense, the boycott was a dream come true for the Fellowship: a Christian nonviolent mass movement for social justice. King, like Gandhi before him, seemed to have implemented Fellowship ideals more effectively than those within the organization itself. FOR chair Charles Lawrence wrote to him some-what ruefully : "I wish very much that you were one of us, for you have talked and acted more like we should like to than many of us could hope to do under similar pressure."[54] But King did not fit the FOR mold too easily, as Smiley soon discovered. The FOR secretary, like Rustin before him, was appalled by the arsenal that Montgomery's blacks had assem-bled, not to mention their ignorance of Gandhian methods. Smiley, him-self a native Southerner, began a project of education, providing King with Richard Gregg's *The Power of Non-Violence* and a number of other paci-fist works while also distributing FOR literature to black college libraries around the South. In addition, he assisted with the everyday details of the boycott. On one occasion, he and Rosa Parks procured a number of used bicycles from Atlanta for use as alternative transportation.[55]

The FOR influenced the course of the boycott in several ways. Under Smiley's guidance, King and the other leaders came to understand their struggle in more explicitly Gandhian terms. By November 14, 1956, when King spoke at a mass meeting to announce the Supreme Court decision and the end of the boycott, he had assimilated the Indian leader's lan-guage and ideas, often filtered through Fellowship interpreters. In this address, King urged the black community to practice nonviolence when returning to the buses, then drew the classic Gandhian distinctions sepa-rating cowardice, violence, and militant nonviolence: "Now I'm not ask-ing you to be a coward. If cowardice was the alternative to violence, I'd say to you tonight, use violence. . . . Cowardice is as evil as violence. . . . What I'm saying to you this evening is that you can be courageous and yet nonviolent." Richard Gregg had expressed the same idea in *The Power of Non-Violence,* minus the preacherly cadences: "Courageous violence . . . is better than cowardly acquiescence. Cowardice is more harmful morally than violence. . . . But he who has the courage to fight and yet refrains, is the true non-violent resister." Smiley's work had succeeded in making the bus boycott a Gandhian project.[56]

The nonviolence that King promoted in his November speech was a mark of internal fortitude, but it also had a public, performative element. "I tell you," he warned, "if we hit back . . . we will be shamed before the world."[57] To prevent such humiliation, the MIA adopted the CORE tech-nique of the sociodrama. After the Supreme Court ruled segregation on buses unconstitutional, the prevention of violence between white and black riders remained a difficult task. To smooth the transition, the black Montgomerians rehearsed various scenarios that they would encounter

on the buses. In the churches where MIA meetings were held, King recalled that boycott leaders "lined up chairs in front of the altar to resemble a bus, with a driver's seat out front." Then "actors" from the audience
came forward to fill the roles of driver and white and black passengers,
some pretending to be "hostile" and others "courteous." These "actors
played out a scene of insult or violence," and a general discussion among
the performers and the audience followed. The participants often played
their parts with the utmost conviction. "Sometimes," King admitted, "the
person playing a white man put so much zeal into his performance that
he had to be gently reproved from the sidelines." In other sessions, an
actor playing a black passenger would return insults or blows; "whenever
this happened we worked to channel his words and deeds in a nonviolent
direction." In the Montgomery sociodramas, churches became theaters
of social justice, bringing the religious and performative dimensions of
Christian nonviolence together in physical space.[58]

The overt purpose of these role-playing exercises was to desensitize
blacks to the insulting treatment they might receive on the buses, thereby
maintaining the image of the movement as a moral exemplar. Yet the sociodramas had another, less obvious function. They denaturalized racial
hierarchies by revealing their constructed and contingent qualities. Race
was, in this theatrical world, only an attitude that one adopted while playing a part. Indeed, 1956 was the year that the sociologist Erving Goffman,
unknown at the time, first published *The Presentation of Self in Everyday
Life*, which purported to analyze all social interaction as performance.
In Goffman's account, the social world comprised a bewildering array
of poses, façades, feints, and counterfeints. For their part, the early civil
rights workers imagined nonviolence as the self-conscious performance
of a role, but they did not believe in Goffman's surreal world of ever-
shifting appearances. Rather, the acting they did was symbolic of an underlying religious truth about the unity of humanity. The sociodrama was
a ritual that reinforced that truth.[59]

These elaborate preparations show that the mythologizing of the civil
rights movement did not begin with King's assassination in 1968, much
less with the observance of the first nationwide Martin Luther King Jr.
Day in 1986. Instead, self-conscious attention to the movement's image
was one of its key features from the beginning. The FOR played a seminal
role in shaping the meaning of the bus boycott and, through it, the meaning of the civil rights movement. Nowhere was the sophisticated strategy
of Christian nonviolence more apparent than in the Fellowship's retell-

ings of the Montgomery events in the film *Walk to Freedom* and in the comic book *Martin Luther King and the Montgomery Story*. In their combination of religious idealism and temporal strategy, these productions recalled nothing so much as John Nevin Sayre's old paradoxical notion of a "propaganda of truth."[60]

Walk to Freedom welded together Gandhi, King, and the Fellowship's Christian nonviolence. The film was not wholly unprecedented. Back in 1948, the year of Gandhi's assassination, FOR officials had floated the idea of making a filmstrip entitled "Mohandas K. Gandhi, General of a Bloodless War," though that project was apparently never carried out.[61] The 1956 venture was more ambitious, for it related the Mahatma directly to Montgomery. "India's millions," like Montgomery's thousands, had "walked to freedom," the film noted, calling to mind the famous 1930 March to the Sea. Gandhi and King were part of the same lineage of nonviolent action. "It has been called by many names: *satyagraha*, passive resistance, nonviolent resistance," the narrator explained. "In Montgomery, Alabama, Martin Luther King calls it simply Christian love." Such love did not preclude the confrontational tactics that had worried some FOR leaders in earlier decades. Nonviolence, in this presentation, was "proud and dignified action" that included "mass meetings and demonstrations, picket lines and boycotts, strikes and noncooperation, civil disobedience and defiance." The word choices were significant, subtly alluding to the Defiance Campaign in South Africa as well as to the pacifists' abiding concern with the labor movement. Indeed, the United Auto Workers bought six copies of *Walk to Freedom*.[62]

For the most part, though, the film became part of the culture of the civil rights movement, playing at African American churches and colleges in the South as well as some Northern venues. Wherever it ran, the Fellowship tried to influence its reception. Robert Cannon, who finally filled the Fellowship's Southern Secretary position, wrote that "a discussion leader for the film is indispensable," someone who could "make clear the intimate relationship in terms of leadership and participation the FOR has had" in Montgomery and elsewhere. Such directives assumed that Christian nonviolence would spread not by a mystical osmosis but through the dedicated work of its earthly proponents.[63]

Martin Luther King and the Montgomery Story manifested the same kind of self-conscious strategy, one quite distant from the stereotype of detached, otherworldly pacifism. Comic books were an important part of American popular culture in the postwar decades and had been used in

FIGURE 6.2 *Martin Luther King and the Montgomery Story* comic book, 1957. (Swarthmore College Peace Collection.)

political protests at least as early as the Scottsboro trials of the 1930s.[64] The Fellowship's publication contained three sections: one recounted the story of the bus boycott, a second discussed the Indian independence movement, and the last talked about nonviolence in a more general way. Notably, the comic book told the story of Gandhi using the framing device of a sermon by King. A similar kind of metaphorical trope had appeared in the boycott leader's first article in *Fellowship,* which was actually an edited interview with Smiley. There a sketch of King in a pulpit included a ghostly image of the Mahatma hovering over his left shoulder.[65]

Like the ecstatic response to *Walk to Freedom* at Hutchinson Street Baptist Church, the distribution of the comic book shows how Christian nonviolence became more than just a warm feeling created by and for white liberals, as some recent histories of civil rights sometimes imply. Alfred Hassler, the FOR official who was most responsible for the project, conceived of it as "directed primarily to Negroes," though he also thought that "it might . . . be read by whites with profit." Smiley tirelessly handed out copies to black and white churches, colleges, and reform organizations across the South, while Hassler provided detailed instructions for getting the comic books placed at "newsstands patronized by Negroes." These efforts bore fruit. The young John Lewis, who would become chair of the Student Nonviolent Coordinating Committee and an organizer of the 1963 March on Washington, read the comic book and remembered it "being devoured by black college students across the South." From Cape Town, South Africa, Brian Bunting, the white editor of a newspaper affiliated with the African National Congress, asked to reprint the comic book in serial form. Apparently nothing came of this request, perhaps because the pacifists were suspicious of Bunting's association with the South African Communist Party, but his interest shows the breadth of exposure that the tract received. The Fellowship also produced a Spanish edition, *Martin Luther King y la Historia de Montgomery,* though the intended audience for this is unclear.[66]

The comic book version of the Montgomery bus boycott was an interracial story. Black and white cooperation was not a prominent component of the event itself, at least not at the outset. Black Montgomerians started the boycott, assisted by only a few white mavericks such as the reformers Clifford and Virginia Durr and Robert Graetz, the pastor of a black Lutheran congregation. None of the city's white churches contributed financially to the effort.[67] Therefore, *Martin Luther King and the Montgomery Story* was as much a prescriptive tale about radical Christian pacifist hopes as it was a description of the boycott. The FOR sought to present the "Montgomery story" as something like the 1947 Journey of Reconciliation or Morris Milgram's integrated housing developments, with their carefully measured ratios of black and white participation. To create an interracial tale, the comic book highlighted white sympathy for racial equality in the few places where it did appear. Reaching back in time, one frame depicted a college-age King at a meeting of a student Christian organization, sitting at a table with other students who alternate seating according to race and listen to a white woman expressing her concern about discrimination. In depicting the boycott itself, the comic book included a prominent mention of Robert Graetz. A boycotter explains that Graetz "had been one of us right from the start," but left unstated is the fact that Graetz was the *only* white minister in Montgomery to join the MIA leadership. Most stunning is the picture that accompanies a discussion of the spirit of nonviolence later in the book. "God loves your **enemy**, too, and that makes **him** important to you," the text reads. "You have to see **him** as a human being, like yourself." An image shows a black man looking in a mirror, which reflects back a face with blond hair and white skin. The Fellowship could hardly have constructed a more potent, or a more unsettling, image of its commitment to interracialism.[68]

Smiley worked diligently to lend substance to the interracial story. When he attended a mass meeting of the MIA soon after his arrival, he found that the only other white people in attendance were three reporters. He was sometimes able to turn his anomalous position to his advantage. At least once he infiltrated a meeting of the Ku Klux Klan in order to relay information to the boycotters.[69] He soon became a trusted adviser to the MIA, exemplifying the radical Christian pacifists' penchant for crossing the boundaries of race, class, and nation in the name of God's universal family. Like A. J. Muste leading the Lawrence textile strike, Richard Gregg plunging into life at Gandhi's ashram, or Rustin and Farmer reorienting the mostly white FOR itself, Smiley excelled outside his own social milieu. He also connected the boycott to a network of white liberals and activists. Following his lead, several other white FOR and CORE members, including Homer Jack, James Peck, and Lillian Smith, visited Montgomery or wrote letters of support. This was, however, racial reconciliation from the outside. An integrated Montgomery remained mostly in the comic book world.[70]

The FOR's interracial vision, with all its promise and its difficulties, reached a milestone around 6:00 A.M. on December 21, 1956, when King

FIGURE 6.3   Ralph Abernathy, Martin Luther King Jr., Glenn Smiley, and unidentified passengers ride the first integrated bus in Montgomery, Alabama, December 21, 1956. (*New York World-Telegram* and the *Sun Newspaper* Photograph Collection, Library of Congress.)

and Smiley sat down side by side on the first integrated Montgomery bus. Here was the embodiment of the Christian nonviolent ideal of individual moral action serving as the motor of social transformation. Here, too, was the public spectacle of that moral action. Though no cameras appear in the famous photographs of King and Smiley that ran in *Life* magazine and elsewhere, King remembered that "several reporters and television men" boarded the bus along with the boycott leaders, while Smiley marveled that he had "never seen so many TV cameras and radio reporters and lights and so on in my life."[71]

The media coverage in Montgomery marked a turning point in the representation of black protest, partly as a result of the incompetent response of the city's white supremacists. During the boycott, local police harassed reporters and photographers and often refused to defend them from mob violence. At this crucial early stage in the civil rights movement, opponents of racial equality lost control of their image in the national press. The city's segregationists were baffled by the way that media images could reshape local dynamics of power. In fact, nonviolent demonstrators had won such astonishing victories by publicizing the violence of the white supremacist regime in Montgomery that it became possible to imagine, using the looking-glass logic of the boycott's opponents, that the violence itself was just part of the act. Astoundingly, many white Montgomerians came to believe that MIA leaders were intentionally bombing their own homes to influence public opinion. After an explosion at Graetz's residence, the mayor of Montgomery speculated on the record that "perhaps this is just a publicity stunt" perpetrated by the boycotters. Such conspiratorial visions were more than quaint demonstrations of racist idiocy. They were, in fact, the only way for many white Southerners to explain how radical religion had combined with mass media to make their unquestioned social dominance so suddenly vulnerable.[72]

In the end, the dazzling "TV cameras and radio reporters and lights and so on" were not omnipotent. Although King and Smiley appeared to realize the Christian nonviolent dream of interracialism, the latter was, in a sense, "playing a white man" in a real-life sociodrama, standing in for the actual white Montgomerians who would ride the buses on a daily basis. The same was true of the white *Look* reporter who posed for a picture with Rosa Parks on another bus that same day.[73] Actual white riders harassed, insulted, and struck black passengers, while some fired shots into the buses. The illusion of interracialism would prove difficult to sustain. More seriously, the spectacular, performative content of Christian nonviolence itself had a troubling ephemerality. In the midst of the bus boycott's unprecedented impact, it was left to Richard Gregg to suggest that the performance of moral action would not be enough.

Richard Gregg turned seventy-one in 1956. The years since the outbreak of World War II had been difficult for him, and not only because of the blows to pacifism leveled by the war and by the violent death of his friend Mohandas Gandhi. In 1943, Gregg's wife, Nonie, began to show symptoms of mental illness. As her condition worsened, she moved in and out of hospitals, becoming an increasing burden for Gregg. At one point, he attempted to cure her using a special vegetarian diet. When her condition improved temporarily, Gandhi asked Gregg to write an article for Indian readers documenting her recovery. But Nonie's health soon deteriorated again, and Gregg, abandoning his dietary treatments, had to commit her to a mental hospital until her death some years later. Amid these political and personal upheavals, he was also trying out a new career path. In 1941, as his country headed toward total war, Gregg had made another of his unpredictable shifts. He had become an organic farmer.[74]

Gregg's interest in agriculture represented another of his many attempts to create a countermodernity. His affinity for the natural world had been implicit in his critiques of machine civilization, in his attention to the emerging science of ecology, and in the organic metaphors he often used to talk about nonviolence.[75] He worked first at Kimberton Farm in Phoenixville, Pennsylvania, under the direction of Ehrenfried E. Pfeiffer, a European proponent of "bio-dynamic farming" who insisted that traditional organic methods were not only morally superior to the modern agricultural industry but also economically rational. After Kimberton, Gregg took brief jobs teaching and doing agricultural work before finally settling in 1948 on a farm in Vermont run by the venerable radicals Scott and Helen Nearing. There he spent the next eight years.[76]

In 1956, Gregg's personal fortunes turned around. He married his longtime friend Evelyn Speiden, whom he had known since his days at Kimberton Farm. He prepared to end his agricultural work and travel once more to India, where he would teach at a village school, just as he had three decades earlier. At the same time, Glenn Smiley brought *The Power of Non-Violence* to Montgomery.[77]

Gregg's book played a major role in turning King toward the Gandhian point of view. "I don't know when I have read anything," he wrote to Gregg, "that has given the idea of non-violence a more realistic and depthful interpretation." Soon after the bus boycott, an official at the NAACP asked King to name the books that had most affected his thinking. King listed *The Power of Non-Violence* alongside Gandhi's autobiography, Louis Fischer's biography of the Indian leader, Thoreau's essay on civil disobedience, and Walter Rauschenbusch's *Christianity and the Social Crisis*.[78] King was so impressed with Gregg's book that he wrote the foreword to a revised 1959 edition, in which he stated that the years since the first edition was published "have shown . . . how right Richard Gregg was." Gregg, for his part, was thrilled by the revival of Gandhi's methods in Montgomery. "I can tell you," he confided to King, "he would rejoice mightily to know you have chosen this way." When King decided to visit India in 1959, he asked Gregg to share his contacts there.[79]

The subtle influence of *The Power of Non-Violence* was evident in King's writings and speeches, particularly in "Pilgrimage to Nonviolence," his famous autobiographical essay published immediately after the bus boycott. "Pilgrimage" never mentions Gregg, but his ideas and sometimes his language appeared in King's explanation of his own philosophy. King stressed the militant, assertive qualities of nonviolence, as Gregg had, and he focused on the importance of emotions such as love, hate, and shame. At one point "Pilgrimage" even reproduced phrasing almost directly from *The Power of Non-Violence*. King wrote: "For while the nonviolent resister is passive in the sense that he is not physically aggressive toward his opponent, his mind and emotions are always active, constantly seeking to persuade his opponent that he is wrong." Gregg had earlier written of the nonviolent resister: "Toward his opponent he is not aggressive physically, but his mind and emotions are active, wrestling constantly with the problem of persuading the latter that he is mistaken." Gregg was only one of several black and white Gandhians whose ideas appeared in "Pilgrimage to Nonviolence," yet his seminal work clearly had a profound effect.[80]

The affinity between *The Power of Non-Violence* and the Montgomery bus boycott obscured an uncomfortable truth: Richard Gregg's idea of nonviolence went far beyond the program of the MIA. Gregg never lost faith that *labor* was a crucial aspect of social transformation. Seeking to mediate industrial disputes during World War I, studying Gandhi's plans for a decentralized agrarian economy, farming his way through World War II—Gregg's life was a long search for spheres of authentic, meaningful work under conditions of modern alienation and regimentation. He maintained a certain distance from the labor movement as such, particularly in its Communist varieties, but this was only because he saw workers' radicalism succumbing too often to the dehumanizing logic of industrial capitalism or the nihilism of violence.

This proponent of meaningful labor was the other Richard Gregg, the one not well represented by the political strategizing in *The Power of Non-Violence*. Gregg summarized his full vision of nonviolence in a 1953 *Fellowship* article entitled "The Structure of a Nonviolent Society." He began by noting that *The Power of Non-Violence* was only a "first step" that "would leave most people hanging in mid-air" without further elaboration of the "entirely new civilization" that nonviolent people would have to construct. Then Gregg listed the characteristics that he saw as essential to that civilization, noting with his usual modesty that they were "only one person's suggestions, incomplete and perhaps faulty." Most of the points were unchanged from his writings of the mid-1930s. He advocated "a strong emphasis on agriculture as the most important part of the life of the nation." Economic life would be marked by "simplicity of living," cooperatives, and "Henry George's principle of 'single tax.'" A new educational system would teach children "through some craft or productive and really useful manual work." Gregg hoped not merely for a nonviolent politics, but for a nonviolent world that would restore meaning and purpose to modern existence.[81]

In the Montgomery bus boycott, Gregg thought he saw the opportunity to effect a moral revolution that went even further than the elimination of racial segregation. Praising King's work thus far, he suggested to the boycott leader that he "try to get going among your community some constructive work, after the fashion of Gandhi's hand spinning." Gregg offered that "some sort of campaign of clean-up, paint-up, tidy-up, creation of sanitation and good physical order might do." Such a program "would add to people's self respect, increase their solidity, use their emotions and energy on permanent constructive self-help as well as the effort of protest." Gregg compared the Montgomery situation to India: "It was the districts where much work went on constantly which offered the strongest, purest and most enduring non-violent resistance to the British rule." In 1958, Gregg sent to King a copy of his new book, *A Philosophy of Indian Economic Development,* which laid out a decentralized economic plan based on agriculture and small-scale industry. Just as in 1928, when he sent *Economics of Khaddar* to W. E. B. Du Bois, Gregg thought that his work applied to the United States as well as India. Yet, like Du Bois, King seems to have disregarded Gregg's economic views. The nonviolence of the civil rights movement leaders was on the model of *The Power of Nonviolence.* Gregg's more thoroughgoing countermodernity never gained a wide following.[82]

In 1956, the power of authentic labor proved less efficacious than the power of representation. Christian nonviolence succeeded by developing sophisticated public spectacles in the service of ambitious moral demands. This was not unexpected. Gregg himself had repeatedly insisted that the foundations of society were in the realm of values and symbols, a realm traversed by both religion and mass media. In the actions of the radical Christian pacifists, the sacred world, with its signs, portents, and truths seen "through a glass, darkly" converged with the illusions, images, and spectacles of modern communication technologies. The Journey of Reconciliation, the sociodramas, the King-Smiley bus ride—all were feats of existential courage, all were religious rituals, and all were shrewd attempts to gain political power by securing the sympathy of spectators. To focus solely on the act of personal religious faith is to succumb to a sentimental belief in individual saintliness. To focus solely on the spectacular act performed for media audiences is to turn a tin ear to the real power of religious belief in the modern world. Christian nonviolent acts of conscience were at once transcendent and temporal, simultaneously spiritual and strategic. "Be ye therefore wise as serpents," Jesus once instructed his followers, "and harmless as doves." It was one of Reinhold Niebuhr's favorite biblical passages, but nowhere was the paradox lived out more fully than among the apostles of Christian nonviolence.

Before anything can be done, two questions must be put: "Do you or do you not,
directly or indirectly, want to be killed or assaulted? Do you or do you not, directly
or indirectly, want to kill or assault?"
                                   —*Albert Camus, "Neither Victims Nor Executioners"*

Conclusion

James Lawson was teaching at a Methodist missionary school
in India when he first read about the Montgomery bus boycott. Lawson,
who discovered Christian nonviolence during his college years in the late
1940s, had participated in some of the early sit-ins organized by the Fellowship of Reconciliation and the Congress of Racial Equality. True to
his beliefs, he spent a year in prison for refusal to cooperate with the
military draft during the Korean War. Then he traveled to India to learn
about nonviolence in Gandhi's homeland, obtaining upon his return a
job as a Fellowship field secretary. Lawson began to organize students,
develop civil rights initiatives, and teach nonviolent strategy with Glenn
Smiley and other FOR leaders. In 1959, he held workshops to prepare
for direct action in the city of Nashville, where the next year his students
held the most disciplined and effective sit-ins in a nationwide movement.
John Lewis, Diane Nash, and Lawson's other nonviolent foot soldiers desegregated Nashville stores and helped spark that tumultuous period of
political upheaval that became known as "the sixties."[1]

Christian nonviolence reached unprecedented heights in the decade
following the Montgomery bus boycott. Fellowship leaders and former
leaders, including Lawson, Smiley, A. J. Muste, Bayard Rustin, and James
Farmer, wove nonviolence so deeply into the fabric of the civil rights

movement that the two concepts are now inseparable in American historical memory. Martin Luther King Jr. also joined the FOR, though he never had a leadership role in the organization. The theory of strategic nonviolence developed by Richard Gregg and the Fellowship defined the shape of black freedom struggles in these years. The August 1960 newsletter of the Student Nonviolent Coordinating Committee, the most radical and adventurous civil rights group, listed Gregg's *The Power of Nonviolence* (the twenty-five-year-anniversary edition dropped the hyphen) at the top of its recommended reading list, just ahead of King's *Stride Toward Freedom*. King's own admiration of Gregg continued after the bus boycott. In response to a 1962 survey by the *Christian Century,* King included *The Power of Nonviolence* on a list of the ten books that had most influenced his "vocational attitude and philosophy of life." Gregg participated in several nonviolent training sessions for civil rights workers, and he was delighted by black Americans' embrace of his methods. In early 1961, on his seventy-sixth birthday, he wrote to his old friend John Nevin Sayre: "What especially thrills me these days is the wonderful courage, understanding, discipline, enthusiasm and tenacity of the Negroes in our South, especially the students. . . . The developments are going to be exciting, I think."[2]

The Fellowship's influence was not a matter of mere inspiration. The specific techniques and strategies of the movement followed the patterns of innovations developed years, even decades, earlier by the FOR and CORE. The sit-ins that began in 1960 used the same method that CORE had employed as early as World War II; the 1961 Freedom Rides were an update of the 1947 Journey of Reconciliation; and the 1963 March on Washington for Jobs and Freedom was the latest incarnation of an idea that went back to the 1940s, when Rustin, Farmer, and other FOR leaders worked with A. Philip Randolph in the March on Washington Movement. All of these efforts fused absolute religious imperatives with strategic, media-savvy forms of political action. The civil rights movement depended upon moral spectacles that held racist violence "imprisoned in a luminous glare," as King put it. With the new popularity of television in the postwar decades, that glare became brighter than the pacifists could have imagined during their comparatively modest efforts with newspapers, books, radio, and film.[3]

The long genealogy of nonviolence ought to refute some myths about its much-discussed role in the civil rights movement. First, nonviolence did not spring fully formed from the "black church," though African

American religious institutions were certainly crucial to its success in the 1950s and 1960s. The radical pacifist project was transnational and interracial, drawing on the contributions of whites (Muste and Gregg), blacks (Rustin and Farmer), Indians (Mohandas Gandhi and Krishnalal Shridharani), the occasional Japanese American (Gordon Hirabayashi), and many others. The Fellowship sought to put nonviolence into action against war, imperialism, and capitalism, not just against segregation and white supremacy. Christian nonviolence and black freedom struggles had their own histories that intersected each other but were not coterminous.

Nor was the nonviolence of the civil rights movement a uniquely pure form of political dissent. A spate of recent studies has demonstrated that the lines between violence and nonviolence in the movement were exceedingly blurry.[4] For instance, the Deacons for Defense and other armed black groups protected CORE protesters at night, epitomizing the ambivalence that ordinary African Americans felt toward the philosophy of nonviolence even as they admired its tactical successes. Then, too, a major goal of the movement was to draw down the overwhelming force of the federal government to violently compel racial equality if necessary. These paradoxes were hardly new. When Howard Kester defended the use of bodyguards in his efforts to organize Southern sharecroppers during the Great Depression, when Reinhold Niebuhr argued in *Moral Man and Immoral Society* that violence and nonviolence were not opposites but points on the same continuum of force, and when Muste and Rustin tried to square absolute opposition to World War II with their support for racial integration in defense industries, Christian nonviolence showed itself to be a self-conscious position fully enmeshed in the most intractable dilemmas of modern politics, not simply a mystical faith. Indeed the common distinction in the sixties between nonviolence as a "way of life" and as a "tactic" hardly encompassed the wide range of positions that its practitioners held.

New interpretations of the civil rights movement have gone a long way toward rebutting the old sanctimonious mythology, but have also left nonviolence a bit too diminished. "Nonviolence," in one scholar's dispiriting formulation, "was ultimately a coalition-based legislative strategy cloaked as religion" and imposed by outsiders who had "superior organizational and funding resources."[5] Here and in other recent work by self-styled realists, the nonviolence of the civil rights movement appears as a kind of conspiracy of the wealthy, the white, the pious, and the cautious. Such constructions ignore not just the interracial and transnational history of this complex form of political action but also its profoundly radical vision, a vision that went far beyond legislative solutions.

The recent detractors of nonviolence generally neglect the cultural aspects of civil rights politics, so they are unable to consider religion as anything more than a thin "cloak" hastily thrown over naked political ambition. In fact, religion was the heart of nonviolence and, for most Americans, the system of meaning that framed questions of racial justice. The elimination of religion from the civil rights story paves the way for glib psychological explanations of armed self-defense and, later, Black Power. These explanations hold that violent struggle, or at least the threat of violence, produced pride, self-respect, and even psychological liberation that the Fellowship of Reconciliation could not quite achieve. Such an assertion contains the bizarre implication that King, Lawson, Lewis, and others who retained their commitment to nonviolence were somehow maladjusted, even lacking in self-respect. Furthermore, it simply exaggerates the salutary effect of assaulting another human being. Belief in the liberating effects of violence had a long history among militarists, Communists, anticolonialist guerrillas, and other opponents of the Fellowship's brand of dissent, but that belief rested at bottom on political and moral assumptions, not on the essential nature of human psychology.[6]

Another recent claim, that nonviolence in the South was the work of outsiders and not indigenous, is largely true. As its critics insisted at the time, nonviolence was foreign to the traditions of Southern communities, black and white. Less often noted was the fact that it was foreign to the traditions of virtually all communities in the United States and probably the world. That was why, for a time, it worked so well. As Richard Gregg had predicted back in the 1930s, the refusal to hit back threw opponents off balance, breaking the grim impasse that had deadlocked Southern race relations for half a century. That this drama became a national media spectacle made it all the more powerful. The rifle-toting proponents of black self-defense may look at first like the ultimate realists, but the devotees of nonviolence astutely argued that power resided in media representations as well as armed force. All social movements since the 1960s, whether antiwar, environmentalist, or conservative evangelical, have had to reckon with the profound influence of the media on their attempts to foment social change. With its focus on the ethereal power of religion and mass communication, Christian nonviolence won victories that the advocates of armed self-defense could never have achieved alone.

The peace movement itself, though not as successful as the struggle for black equality, also enjoyed a resurgence beginning in the late 1950s. In 1957, radical pacifists organized a group called Non-Violent Action Against Nuclear Weapons, later renamed the Committee on Non-Violent Action. This organization became the vanguard of the antinuclear movement, undertaking bold initiatives that, along with the civil rights efforts, marked the pinnacle of American Gandhians' creativity. In 1958, Albert Bigelow sailed his boat, the *Golden Rule*, into a hydrogen bomb testing zone in the Pacific. Two years later, in the Polaris Action project, pacifists swam through frigid waters to board a nuclear submarine stationed at the military base in Groton, Connecticut. As these actions suggested, nonviolence retained its connection to displays of strenuous masculinity. Women were gaining new authority, though, by participating in the Committee on Non-Violent Action and through the organization of Women Strike for Peace, whose members shrewdly made a performance of female domesticity by self-consciously opposing war as mothers and wives. These groups tended not to share the common religious culture that distinguished the FOR, but they took from the tradition of Christian nonviolence a belief in the power of turning principles into spectacles.[7]

At a greater remove, Students for a Democratic Society (SDS) showed how the Fellowship of Reconciliation's outlook gained momentum in the New Left. The older pacifists had less direct influence on the secular SDS than on civil rights groups, though A. J. Muste and others played important supporting roles. More generally, though, the family resemblance between FOR and SDS was impossible to miss. The Port Huron Statement, which served as a New Left manifesto, decried the moral bankruptcy of modern culture and called for a radical transformation of human beings, not just human institutions. To this end, SDS eschewed the dogmatic radicalism of Communism, as radical pacifists had done back in the Old Left's heyday, in favor of a decentralized structure that strongly resembled that of the FOR and CORE. The general focus of the New Left on young people also resonated with the history of Christian nonviolence, whether the energetic college tours by Sherwood Eddy and Kirby Page in the 1920s or the dynamic advances in nonviolent action pioneered by young conscientious objectors during World War II.[8]

The Christian nonviolent avant-garde proved especially significant when the New Left turned its energies to ending the war in Vietnam. The methods of protest that defined the antiwar movement, including conscientious objection, draft resistance, and civil disobedience, had been part of the Fellowship's work for a long time. Radical Christian pacifists had helped started the Committee on Militarism in Education in 1925 to protest Reserve Officer Training Corps programs. In 1947, some of them had burned their draft cards. Not surprisingly, FOR leaders and former leaders were some of the earliest critics of U.S. military intervention in Vietnam. At an annual Easter disarmament rally in 1963, A.J. Muste, who had officially retired from the FOR a decade earlier but was still an active force, made a speech denouncing the conflict and helped push the issue into public consciousness during that year. In addition to public events, the Fellowship, drawing on its experience during World War II, performed difficult behind-the-scenes work advising young men who wished to resist the draft. The legal and moral support for conscientious objectors had expanded greatly since the anguished bewilderment of Evan Thomas and Harold Gray during the First World War a half-century earlier, a testament to the network of pacifists that the FOR had done so much to construct.

The FOR also pioneered the practice of traveling to Vietnam on peace missions. A Fellowship team led by Alfred Hassler and James Lawson

FIGURE CON.I   A.J. Muste speaking at an antiwar rally in New York City, December 19, 1964. (DG 50, A.J. Muste Papers, Swarthmore College Peace Collection.)

went to Saigon in July 1965, while Muste led his own delegation in April 1966, then flew to Hanoi the next year. These journeys to the war zone were among the first by members of the American left, predating by several years Jane Fonda's notorious 1972 visit, but they were nothing new for the Fellowship. Rather, they hearkened back to John Nevin Sayre's trip to Nicaragua in 1927 to attempt negotiations with the guerrilla Augusto Sandino. As in Sayre's visit, the Vietnam journeys enacted the Fellowship's dedication to public displays of individual moral commitment and suggested that efforts by private citizens could thwart the violent intentions of governments.[9]

Among the travelers on the Fellowship's 1965 Vietnam trip were a priest and a rabbi, signs of the organization's shift from a Christian basis to an interfaith one. Though a new statement of purpose formalized the changed identity that year, the metamorphosis had occurred gradually over the previous decades. The old animosities between Protestants and Catholics, and between Christians and Jews, eroded quickly after World War II, at least in liberal religious circles. In 1965, a Jewish Peace Fellowship became officially affiliated with the FOR. More recently, the organization has also nurtured a Buddhist Peace Fellowship and a Muslim Peace Fellowship.[10]

The most important of these FOR subsidiaries during the 1960s was the Catholic Peace Fellowship. Catholics had been the hardest religious people to attract to the Christian nonviolent vanguard, even harder than Jews. In the Fellowship's early decades, many of its Protestant leaders harbored lingering anti-Catholic sentiments, while the Catholic ecclesiastical hierarchy discouraged cooperation with the heirs of the Reformation. Furthermore, Catholics had virtually no modern tradition of pacifism, looking instead to the venerable just war tradition that stretched back to Augustine and Thomas Aquinas. By the sixties, though, the Catholic Worker movement begun by Dorothy Day had almost single-handedly created a new American Catholic left, producing a small but energetic stream of nonviolent religious radicals who joined with Fellowship leaders in early CORE actions and Civil Defense protests. Within the Catholic hierarchy, pacifism gained unprecedented legitimacy from the 1963 papal encyclical *Pacem in Terris* (Peace on Earth). There Pope John XXIII called for an end to the production of nuclear weapons and asserted that "men nowadays are becoming more and more convinced that any disputes which may arise between nations must be resolved by negotiation and agreement, and not by recourse to arms."[11]

Seeking to capitalize on this trend toward peace advocacy, the Fellowship tried throughout the early 1960s to organize a Catholic group under its auspices, one that would draw on Catholic Workers but focus more centrally on peace issues. In 1964 the attempt finally came to fruition, with prominent Catholic Workers James Forest and Thomas Cornell taking the lead in creating the Catholic Peace Fellowship. The pacifist monk Thomas Merton, himself a member of the FOR, encouraged the new group and allowed the Catholic Peace Fellowship to publish his pamphlet *Blessed Are the Meek: The Roots of Christian Nonviolence*. The organization performed many of the same functions as the FOR, holding antiwar rallies, counseling conscientious objectors, and engaging in relief work. Most importantly, this new group gave the FOR a direct connection to the cutting edge of radical Christian nonviolence, exemplified in the activities of two of the Catholic Peace Fellowship's most important early participants, Daniel and Philip Berrigan.[12]

The Berrigan brothers and their radical Catholic associates in the so-called ultraresistance pushed Christian nonviolence another step beyond the innovations of the civil rights movement and the early Vietnam protests. In October 1967, Philip Berrigan and three others, the "Baltimore Four," poured blood on draft files at a Selective Service office in Baltimore. The next May, the Berrigans formed part of the "Catonsville Nine," a group that stole files and burned them with homemade napalm while reciting the Our Father prayer. James Forest engaged in a similar action a few months later as part of the "Milwaukee Fourteen." These undertakings were all in the mode of earlier acts of conscience. They relied on bold individual action rather than organized mass pressure, they functioned as religious rituals, and they became media spectacles, as the protesters usually invited reporters to tag along on their raids of Selective Service offices.

At the same time, the ultraresistance went beyond previous acts of conscience in three ways. First, it cultivated a new aesthetic, combining the Fellowship's older performances of Christian decency with a shocking, and more specifically Catholic, emphasis on the dialectic between the sacred and the blasphemous, embodied in the arresting religious symbols of blood and fire. Second, the Berrigans reimagined the relationship of nonviolence to the law. With their brazen defiance of the federal government, not just the local and state ordinances that King and Lawson had challenged, the draft board raids brought to nonviolence a new audacity. In some ways, the Catholic protesters resembled the absolutist conscientious objectors of World War II, but while the Union Eight had simply refused to register and then submitted to arrest, Daniel Berrigan actually went underground in 1970 to avoid capture by the FBI. Third, the ultra-resistance redrew once again the zigzag line between violent and non-violent action. The Berrigans asserted that the destruction of property, "the burning of paper instead of children" in Daniel's memorable phrase, was not incompatible with the spirit of nonviolence. They also rational-ized their forcible restraint of draft office workers who tried to interfere with their actions, thereby suggesting that a little incidental physical force might be necessary to carry out successful nonviolent resistance. These ambiguities had roiled the nonviolent civil rights movement as well, but largely behind the scenes. The Berrigans, by contrast, put blatant illegal-ity and destruction of government property at the center of their acts of conscience while still claiming allegiance to nonviolence.[13]

Would A. J. Muste have supported the Berrigans' daring experiments, or worried that they had compromised the Christian nonviolent outlook? The answer can be only a matter of speculation. On January 9, 1967, the day after his eighty-second birthday, he arrived in Hanoi, where he toured villages and hospitals, met with American prisoners of war, and talked with Ho Chi Minh. Then, two weeks after the return of his entourage to the United States, Muste died unexpectedly in his sleep. He had over-seen, and exemplified, the twists and turns of Christian nonviolence for half a century. His passing, along with the assassination of King the next year, marked the beginning of its decline in the United States, the efforts of the ultraresistance notwithstanding. If the politics and culture of the sixties produced the heyday of Christian nonviolence, developments in that decade simultaneously sowed the seeds of trouble for the Fellowship of Reconciliation's spiritual radicalism.

The Fellowship's brand of dissent had been in crisis before, perhaps per-petually, but most notably in the 1933–1934 rift over revolutionary vio-lence and the descent into world war a few years later. Nonetheless, the new challenges of the 1960s proved especially intractable. Some of them resulted from the apparent failure of nonviolence in the face of shocking brutality, but on that score the violence of the 1960s was certainly less catastrophic than the violence of the 1940s. The most difficult dilemmas sprung paradoxically from the pacifists' success, particularly from the dif-ferences between practicing nonviolence as a small vanguard and apply-ing it in mass movements.[14]

As in previous decades, the context was global rather than national. For a decade, the shift away from nonviolence in anticolonial struggles abroad had provided a foretaste of things to come. The 1960 Sharpeville Massacre in South Africa, where police opened fire on a crowd of protesters, turned Nelson Mandela and the African National Congress away from the nonviolence of the earlier Defiance Campaign. Kwame Nkrumah, Kenneth Kaunda, and other African devotees of Gandhian methods began to accept the necessity of armed force, tempting some in the Fellowship circle to do the same. For George Houser, head of the American Committee on Africa, the predicament reached its height during France's war in Algeria. Though the American Committee on Africa, as an organization, was not pacifist and supported the armed resistance of the Front de Liberation Nationale, Houser had an "initial hesitancy" in the late 1950s because of his roots in radical pacifism. Yet he had to admit that "no Gandhi" existed in Algeria; the Front de Liberation Nationale was the only viable anticolonial force. "For the first time," he later reflected, "I found myself facing a conflict situation in which nonviolence was not a practical alternative." Houser finally told himself that the job of the American Committee on Africa was to educate Americans and affect the nation's foreign policy, "not to condone violence or give military aid." Thus, "somewhat uneasily," he was able to "rationalize" his support for one of the most vicious anticolonial struggles and still remain a pacifist. The conflation of nonviolent action and guerrilla warfare had a certain logic. Both phenomena grew out of power struggles between vastly unequal opponents, both relied on unconventional and surprising methods, and both sought to take full advantage of the psychological and symbolic aspects of conflict. Still, the "rationalization" of Third World wars of liberation by Houser and many other pacifists left the unique position of Christian nonviolence in doubt.[15]

Meanwhile, no Gandhi arose in Southeast Asia either. The Fellowship's solution to the Vietnam War was the same as its prescription for previous social and political conflicts: an independent, nonviolent, radical religious entity had to find a middle way between armed repression and armed insurrection. Politically engaged Buddhists could play the role of this "third force" in Vietnam, some FOR leaders thought. Alfred Hassler, a World War II conscientious objector who became head of the organization in these years, promoted the Buddhists as an alternative to both the American-supported Saigon government and the North Vietnamese Communists. Hassler worked to develop Buddhist connections on his trips to Vietnam, and the FOR sponsored an American tour by the Buddhist monk and author Thich Nhat Hanh in 1966. Unfortunately for the Fellowship, the Buddhist movement fell apart within a few years, and militant nonviolence never played much of a role within Vietnam.[16]

The slippage between nonviolence and guerrilla warfare contributed to the fragmentation of the left in the United States during the late 1960s. Without the tight Christian nucleus that had guided the Fellowship of Reconciliation, nonviolence was unable to sustain its astounding advances. SDS splintered into ideologically polarized factions, and a few of them, most infamously the Weatherman group, sought to turn the act of conscience into an act of violence. Proponents of Black Power, some of whom took over CORE and the Student Nonviolent Coordinating Committee in the late 1960s, broke with the more practical orientation of earlier black self-defense groups by actually seeking to supplant nonviolence rather than supplement it. Black Power borrowed and inverted Christian nonviolent motifs.[17] For example, Huey Newton, a founder of the Black Panther Party, coined the term *shock-a-buku,* which he explained as "a tactic of keeping the enemy off balance through sudden and unexpected maneuvers that push him toward his opponent's position." The word *shock-a-buku* echoed Gandhi's "*satyagraha,*" just as Newton's description was a variation on Richard Gregg's idea that nonviolence worked by "causing the attacker to lose his moral balance." Weatherman, the Black Panthers, and other radical groups in these years engineered spectacles of violence, just as the Fellowship had created spectacles of nonviolence. If the pacifists' dramatic acts had made nonviolence look far more powerful than it was, so these newer groups used symbols of violence to amplify their efforts, producing far more spectacle than actual killing. The militarist aesthetic of the Panthers stood as a clear repudiation of the FOR style, but its forms and assumptions depended upon radical Christian pacifist insights into the power of symbolic action undertaken by small groups of dedicated people.[18]

The logic of Christian nonviolence did not, in most cases, lead to the Black Panthers and Weatherman. Instead, less visible factors eroded the power of nonviolence. First, the Fellowship's mode of dissent encountered a growing skepticism about the prevalence of political spectacle in modern life. As early as 1961, the year of the Freedom Rides, Daniel Boorstin lamented the rise of "pseudo-events," artificial happenings created solely for their newsworthiness. Despite all of Richard Gregg's strategic thinking, his analysis of mass media now seems overly simplistic on this point.

Modern systems of representation and communication did not simply amplify political messages, but selected, framed, and helped create them. Mass media had an autonomous logic that the radical Christian pacifists did not fully recognize.[19]

Awash in these proliferating forms of communication, nonviolence came to depend increasingly on a culture of celebrity. Here again, *The Power of Non-Violence* fell short in its failure to confront the implications of charismatic leadership. Krishnalal Shridharani had discussed the effects of Gandhi's image in *War Without Violence,* but the Fellowship did not seriously consider the possibility that one charismatic person might become an individual spectacle of conscience. After the Montgomery bus boycott, the possibility became reality. Certainly some of the Fellowship leaders themselves had achieved minor celebrity status in limited circles: Sherwood Eddy and Kirby Page on college campuses, John Haynes Holmes among East Coast liberals, and A. J. Muste across the American left. However, none of them had received anything close to the attention from mainstream media that King garnered. By 1957, he had hired an agent to deal with the many offers he received to make books and films about the boycott. As Ella Baker and other critics would note, his status as the image of black freedom had ambivalent results, providing the quest for racial justice with unprecedented exposure but also leading to infighting, jealousy, and distortion of the character of the movement, particularly in regard to the contributions of women. The nonviolent celebrities of the New Left were even more problematic. In the case of SDS, the mass media anointed leaders in arbitrary ways that eventually tore the organization apart.[20]

As nonviolent leaders became celebrities, celebrities were getting in on nonviolence. One portent was the 1960 Civil Defense protest, when New York luminaries such as Norman Mailer joined the lesser-known radical pacifists in City Hall Park (Mailer's rationale for his participation— "Politics is like sex. You have to go all the way"—must have given some of the more staid Fellowship leaders pause). Famous actors, entertainers, and writers, including comedian Dick Gregory and musician Harry Belafonte, joined the civil rights struggle. Such figures lent important prestige and financial support to nonviolent social movements, but they moved acts of conscience closer to the world of mere acting.[21]

The practitioners of nonviolence were not the only ones who were changing. As civil rights protesters won more victories in the 1950s and 1960s, their opponents became more savvy, more aware of their place on a national or even global stage. Gregg's "moral jiu-jitsu" presupposed a clumsy opponent, one who would be unable to exert a counterclaim on the sympathy of spectators. Indeed, the canonical photographs of the civil rights movement reveal the stunning inability of white Southern segregationists to maintain control of their image in the media. The neo-Fascist police attacking defenseless blacks, the leering mobs of white youth, the highly photogenic dogs, clubs, and fire hoses—all of these characters and props played into the hands of nonviolent strategists.

The targets of nonviolent action, however, learned from their opponents' successes. In 1961, a coalition of civil rights groups began a large-scale project to dismantle racial discrimination in Albany, Georgia. Determined to thwart the movement, police chief Laurie Pritchett carefully studied *Stride Toward Freedom,* King's account of the Montgomery bus boycott. Based on his reading, Pritchett worked to defuse the acts of conscience that the practitioners of nonviolence wished to perform. He made mass arrests before demonstrations began and avoided the use of excessive force against civil rights workers, later calling this approach "our nonviolence." When King's imprisonment in Albany threatened to make him an object of public sympathy, Pritchett endorsed a clandestine scheme to have his bail paid so that he would have to leave the jail. The Albany Movement, confused and fragmented, eventually melted away with only modest accomplishments. Pritchett's method of refusing to participate in the act of conscience did not become widespread right away. A few years later, he tried to give advice to Birmingham's Eugene "Bull" Connor and Selma's Jim Clark, but they ignored him and instead provided the civil rights movement with its most powerful images of moral resistance to unjust authority. Yet containment and avoidance of confrontation eventually became formidable weapons in emaciating the power of nonviolence. In the last three decades, militant nonviolence has become a legitimate part of American political life, but police power has pushed it into increasingly conventional and predictable forms.[22]

As acts of conscience became more familiar, one response was to make them more audacious, as the Catholic ultraresistance demonstrated with aplomb. Nonviolent direct action depended upon novelty, for the "power of nonviolence" was, in part, the power to surprise an opponent. Gregg had assumed that an assailant faced with nonviolent resistance would become "insecure because of the novelty of the situation and his ignorance of how to handle it."[23] In 1934 he rightly deduced that mere refusal to fight would itself be sufficiently novel, but by the mid-1960s this was no longer true. As in the theater, repeat performances of militant nonviolence became increasingly mannered and unconvincing, so as nonviolent action became more widely used, it became more extreme or simply more bizarre, particularly among those unconnected to the Fellowship's tradition of Christian respectability. The most extreme innovation was the violent resistance of the Panthers and Weatherman, while the bizarre end of the spectrum encompassed such endeavors as Jerry Rubin's 1967 plan to levitate the Pentagon at an antiwar rally.

In the sixties, too, nonviolent resisters witnessed the uncomfortably close connection between sacrifice and suicide. Alice Herz, Norman Morrison, and Roger LaPorte set themselves on fire, in separate incidents in 1965, as acts of protest against the Vietnam War. These pacifists, two Quakers and a Catholic Worker, were not associated with the Fellowship of Reconciliation, yet their deaths carried Christian nonviolence, with its focus on individual public displays of suffering, to alarming ends. Evan Thomas, Bayard Rustin, and other radicals had engaged in hunger strikes and other severe measures, but they generally regarded suicide as a final limit that a resister should never reach. Now that limit was a matter of debate, as Daniel Berrigan compared the death of LaPorte to the sacrifice of Christ. A. J. Muste also defended the self-immolations, but Thomas Merton was appalled, seeing the suicides and the war as part of the same creeping moral nihilism.[24]

In the same year as those three fiery deaths, Rustin offered his own ideas about acts of conscience and their shortcomings, focusing less on immolation than on co-optation. His famous essay "From Protest to Politics: The Future of the Civil Rights Movement" implicitly downplayed his own storied career as the leading nonviolent innovator of the previous two decades. He insisted that direct action—"sit-ins, freedom rides, and the rest"—had "affected institutions which are relatively peripheral both to the American socio-economic order and to the fundamental condition of the Negro people." Militant nonviolence had successfully desegregated "hotels, lunch counters, terminals, libraries, swimming pools, and the like" because "in these forms, Jim Crow does impede the flow of commerce in the broadest sense: it is a nuisance in a society on the move (and on the make)." That kind of integration, Rustin came to believe, could reinforce rather than challenge American consumer society, while neglecting more difficult social problems such as poverty and unemployment. He advised black Americans to build political coalitions around broad economic issues, and for the last two decades of his life he became a labor organizer.

David Dellinger, Staughton Lynd, and other leaders of the peace movement excoriated Rustin for his silence on the question of Vietnam, which they interpreted as a craven attempt to curry favor with the administration of Lyndon Johnson. They should not have been too surprised, for Rustin had long been willing to finesse his antiwar beliefs to further the cause of racial equality. During World War II, he worked enthusiastically with A. Philip Randolph to desegregate war production, even though as a pacifist he claimed to oppose the very existence of armies, interracial or otherwise. Yet his dissociation from radical pacifism also suggests that it was losing some of its power.[25]

Christian nonviolence had ebbed and flowed throughout its history. The early FOR itself was an antidote to the outmoded pacifism of the early twentieth century. Then, in the 1940s, Rustin's generation had rescued the Fellowship's World War I cohort from the stalemate produced by the internecine rifts of the 1930s and the unprecedented bloodshed of the Second World War. By the late 1960s, though, changes in the patterns of American religious and political life made creativity more difficult to achieve within the Fellowship circle. The waning of liberal Protestantism in the second half of the twentieth century, coincident with the eclipse of political liberalism, is one of the great puzzles of modern American history, but whatever its complex causes, that trend damaged Christian nonviolence severely. The Fellowship leaders in this study were not exactly "liberal" in theology or politics. They criticized liberal Protestantism for its complacency, its socioeconomic and racial exclusiveness, and its often uncritical embrace of secular values. Nonetheless, the liberal Protestant tradition provided the institutional network of churches, seminaries, student groups, journals, and other forums that supported the Fellowship's activities and occasionally produced truly radical religionists. By the end of the sixties, that network was fraying.

The deterioration of Union Theological Seminary was symptomatic of the larger problem. Union had long been a national and international hub for bright young people who sought to apply their Christian faith to social and political problems. Most of the Fellowship leaders, from Norman Thomas and A. J. Muste in the early years of the century to the draft-resisting Union Eight, passed through the school at one time or another. In the first half of the 1970s, however, Union Theological Seminary entered a severe financial crisis from which it has never fully recovered. There was no better symbol of the diminution of liberal Protestantism's intellectual and institutional resources, at the same time that conservative evangelicals were organizing for a political resurgence that would culminate in the formation of Jerry Falwell's Moral Majority in 1979. Membership in the Fellowship of Reconciliation itself peaked in 1972 and declined thereafter.[26]

It would be tidy, but historically inaccurate, to characterize the last four decades as nothing more than the downhill half of the "rise and fall" of radical religious pacifism. In fact, nonviolence continued after the heady decade of the sixties. In the 1970s and 1980s, the antinuclear movement gained important victories through the use of nonviolent tactics, as did protests against U.S. policy in Latin America. New human rights organizations relied heavily on the creation of sympathy through the use of mass media images. Environmentalist groups such as Greenpeace expanded nonviolence beyond the human realm to include the natural world, while feminists drew links between violence and masculinity in ways that the early Fellowship leaders never had. Nonviolent actions are now a part of most major political events, from the World Trade Organization conference in Seattle in 1999 to the commencement of war in Iraq in 2003. Many of these efforts had more secular than religious leadership, but religious groups played important, and often underreported, roles. In addition, these later incarnations of nonviolence, however secularized, derived outlooks and approaches from the work done by the Fellowship's radical religious avant-garde.[27]

Even conservatives have deployed acts of conscience, thus fulfilling with a vengeance Gregg's prediction that militant nonviolence might become a strategy adaptable to a variety of political positions and philosophies. Perverse as it may seem to suggest that the pro-life movement was part of the genealogy of Christian nonviolence described here, the parallels are striking. As early as the 1970s, opponents of abortion studied the philosophies and consciously imitated the tactics of Martin Luther King Jr. and the Berrigan brothers. The new protesters juxtaposed their media-friendly nonviolent methods with what seemed to them horrific acts of violence; they fused a political agenda with a religious imperative; and they sought, paradoxically, to nonviolently compel the state to use its coercive power to end abortion. In response, their pro-choice adversaries charged that the ostensible nonviolence of the movement was encouraging antiabortion terrorism, just as segregationists had accused King of stirring up black violence. Debates over violent and nonviolent tactics occurred within the pro-life ranks as well. The ideological allegiances were scrambled, but the moral and political questions were little altered from the quarrels over the nonviolent civil rights movement and the Vietnam War protests. In fact, Daniel Berrigan was arrested in 1990 for joining a blockade outside a Planned Parenthood office.[28]

Nonviolence has made its greatest recent gains outside the United States. With the end of apartheid in South Africa and the overthrow of Communist regimes in Eastern Europe, acts of conscience achieved breathtaking victories, while certain failures, such as the 1989 Tiananmen Square protest in China and the 2007 demonstrations by Buddhist monks in Burma, have shown the continuing potency of public displays of individual moral commitment. Most of these efforts sprang from non-Christian sources, but even secularists such as Václav Havel acknowledged a transcendent component in their struggles. As Christianity becomes an increasingly non-Western religion, the radical religious innovations pioneered by the Fellowship of Reconciliation may gain new life. Indeed, the FOR itself continues to promote nonviolent solutions to social and political conflict around the world.[29]

All this is to say that the history of Christian nonviolence has contemporary relevance for people outside the minuscule ranks of absolute pacifism. Certainly that relevance is not a matter of merely copying specific methods of protest that are now a half-century old. The importance of the Christian nonviolent tradition lies deeper, in its thoroughgoing critique of power. By seeing politics and society through the lens of violence, the Fellowship unmasked the ideological assumptions behind reigning political and economic structures. They showed the limits of imperialism and war, even a "good war," as instruments of democratic progress. One need not be philosophically opposed to all violence to wish for an equally robust critique of the presuppositions underlying our current "war on terror."

Tempering their dour assessment of the pervasiveness of violence, though, was the Fellowship leaders' astonishing creativity in fighting it, another legacy that speaks to our own conundrums. They believed that the victory of nonviolence depended upon new ways of thinking and acting, with Christian religion functioning not as a mental straitjacket but as a spur to originality. If the violence of the twentieth century was beyond all comprehension, nonviolence, too, yielded some surprises. No one expected that Harold Gray and Evan Thomas, earnest young YMCA workers, would end up in jail for opposing the Great War, or that Richard Gregg, a Harvard-trained labor lawyer, would abandon his career to study Gandhi's movement firsthand, or that A. J. Muste would walk away from the Old Left's sectarian Marxism to craft his own religious pacifist vision. No one imagined how Christian narratives of suffering and redemption would fuse with mass media spectacles to create powerful new political forces in a century of supposed secularization. Amid the echo chambers of contemporary American politics, this history offers the promise of unrealized possibilities in the future as well.

The creative unpredictability of Christian nonviolence was what struck Reinhold Niebuhr in a 1967 *New York Times* review of Muste's published essays. Muste had just died, and the ailing Niebuhr had only four years to live. Perhaps a growing awareness of mortality led the great Christian realist to offer less a definitive rebuttal of his theological archrival than a respectful appreciation, almost as one old soldier to another, if the metaphor were not so patently inappropriate. Niebuhr pronounced his distinguished opponent a "revolutionary Christian" in the mold of William Lloyd Garrison, who had "combined social reform with pacifism exactly in the spirit of Muste." The tireless critic of the Fellowship could not resist tweaking Muste for his unreasonable faith in "a universal love that will solve all problems of community," but thought that he had mixed his "love perfectionism" with a "radical ethics of justice" that led him to noble action in an imperfect world.

"Perhaps," Niebuhr concluded, "an estimate of rigorous, if inconsistent, idealists is beyond the capacity of mere academic critics, who are obsessed with logical consistency, but who also never dared an interview with Ho Chi Minh."[30] The reference to Muste's Hanoi visit marked a surprising moment of humility from this bold thinker, who seldom let his interlocutors off the hook so easily. Niebuhr had to admit that an honest assessment of Muste and the Christian nonviolent tradition required a suspension of abstract logic, a frank acknowledgment that beyond the debates over pacifism, Marxism, capitalism, and religion stood an irreducible daring. In the end, Niebuhr was left to grapple with Muste's acts, those inspiring, irritating, audacious acts of conscience. So are we.

Acknowledgments

It is a gratifying and humbling experience to thank some of the many people who have contributed to this book. It began as a dissertation at Yale University, where I received expert guidance. I never stopped being amazed by Jean-Christophe Agnew's brilliance, which lit up new directions for my inquiries over and over again. Jon Butler's wise counsel, good humor, and midwestern virtues frequently saved me from despair. Michael Denning's insights clarified the big questions I was pursuing, while his enthusiasm reassured me that those questions were worth the effort. Nancy Ammerman and Robert Johnston helped me formulate and refine my ideas, while Glenda Gilmore and Harry Stout read my work with their usual incisiveness.

My graduate colleagues at Yale formed a vibrant intellectual community. Lila Corwin Berman, Robin Bernstein, Brian Herrera, Tavia Nyong'o, Aaron Sachs, and Roxanne Willis all read portions of the project, their remarks providing exactly the right proportion of encouragement and constructive criticism. Others who gave ideas and support include Brenda Carter, Rebecca Davis, Mark Krasovic, Adriane Lentz-Smith, and Mark Oppenheimer.

The American Studies department at George Washington University, where I completed this book, cultivated an environment both nurturing and intellectually electrifying. Melani McAlister and Tom Guglielmo gave incredibly smart comments on key sections of the manuscript. Chad Heap, Jim Horton, Jim Miller, Terry Murphy, and Phyllis Palmer provided invaluable assistance on matters both theoretical and practical.

I benefited from the contributions of many others as well. Maurice Isserman read and commented on the entire manuscript. Other scholars who enriched the final product include Scott Bennett, Charles Chatfield, Leilah Danielson, Matthew Hedstrom, Chuck Howlett, Joanne Meyerowitz, Nancy Roberts, Jo Ann Robinson, and Joan Shelley Rubin. Richard Deats and Ethan Vesely-Flad welcomed me at the Fellowship of Reconciliation, while George Houser shared his memories of the Fellowship's past. My friends Scott Baldwin, Erin Obermueller, and Mark Manassee helped as well.

Archivists and librarians provided invaluable aid and advice. I especially wish to thank Wendy Chmielewski and the staff at the Swarthmore College Peace Collection, Betty Clements and the staff at the Claremont School of Theology Library, and the staff in the following archives: Library of Congress, New York Public Library, Schomburg Center for Research in Black Culture, Special Collections Research Center at Syracuse University Library, Friends Historical Library, Wing Luke Asian Museum, Kautz Family YMCA Archives at the University of Minnesota, Disciples of Christ Historical Society, Southern Historical Collection at the University of North Carolina at Chapel Hill, Burke Library at Union Theological Seminary, Center for American History at the University of Texas at Austin, Harvard University Archives, and Beinecke and Divinity Libraries at Yale University. Nancy Godleski answered research questions and purchased material for me. Margaret Thompson and Josh Shugarts provided hospitality in Syracuse, and David Lee did the same in Los Angeles. Greg Miller tirelessly tracked down obscure sources for me in the Library of Congress collections.

I presented portions of this work in the following forums: the Writing History workshop at Yale University, the American Religious History colloquium at Yale, the "Limits of the Past" conference at Vanderbilt University, the History-American Studies colloquium at George Washington University, and conferences of the Peace History Society and the Organization of American Historians. I am grateful to the participants in those events for their thoughtful remarks. Generous funding came from a University Facilitating Fund grant from George Washington University, a Leylan Fellowship from Yale University, and a fellowship from the

Institute for the Advanced Study of Religion at Yale. A fellowship from the John W. Kluge Center at the Library of Congress gave me leave time to finish the book in a wonderful setting. The University of Illinois at Urbana–Champaign supplied a library carrel and borrowing privileges for a summer of research and writing.

I am grateful to the Burkybile, Taylor, Price, Johnson, Effinger, and Kosek families for their support. I first heard about A. J. Muste from Jane Richardson, who has since served as authority on religion, social reform, New York City, and much else. Joseph F. Kosek, Loraine Kosek, and the late Trudy Effinger taught me more about life in the exhilarating, catastrophic first half of the twentieth century than I learned from any book. Joe and Jan Kosek first taught me how to read, how to think critically, and how to work hard. From Koy I learned how to argue, something brothers often do better than scholars.

Elinor and Charlotte ensured a healthy balance of work and play. Anne did everything—she was my editor, counselor, financial supporter, and best friend. I owe her more than I can say.

Notes

Introduction

1. A.J. Muste to John Haynes Holmes, September 7, 1944, Box 55, John Haynes Holmes Papers, Library of Congress.

2. I focus specifically on the *leaders* of the Fellowship because, as in many voluntary organizations, they were more dynamic, dedicated, and articulate than was the general membership.

3. "For Pacifists," *Time*, July 10, 1939, http://www.time.com/. Previous work on these figures includes Patricia Faith Appelbaum, "The Legions of Good Will: The Religious Culture of Protestant Pacifism, 1918–1963" (PhD diss., Boston University, 2001); Peter Brock, *Twentieth-Century Pacifism* (New York: Van Nostrand Reinhold, 1970); Charles Chatfield, *For Peace and Justice: Pacifism in America, 1914–1941* (Knoxville: University of Tennessee Press, 1971); Charles DeBenedetti, *The Peace Reform in American History* (Bloomington: Indiana University Press, 1980); Paul R. Dekar, *Creating the Beloved Community: A Journey with the Fellowship of Reconciliation* (Telford, PA: Cascadia, 2005); Donald Meyer, *The Protestant Search for Political Realism*, 2nd ed. (Middletown, CT: Wesleyan University Press, 1988); James Tracy, *Direct Action: Radical Pacifism from the Union Eight to the Chicago Seven* (Chicago: University of Chicago Press, 1996); Lawrence Wittner, *Rebels Against War: The American Peace Movement, 1933–1983* (Philadelphia: Temple University Press, 1984).

4. On the British FOR, see Jill Wallis, *Valiant for Peace: A History of the Fellowship of Reconciliation, 1914–1989* (London: Fellowship of Reconciliation, 1991). For

other countries, see Peter Brock and Thomas P. Socknat, eds., *Challenge to Mars: Essays on Pacifism from 1918 to 1945* (Buffalo: University of Toronto Press, 1999), 101–16. On the International Fellowship of Reconciliation, see Lilian Stevenson, *Towards a Christian International: The Story of the International Fellowship of Reconciliation* (New York: Fellowship of Reconciliation, 1936).

5. Milton Mayer, "The Christer," *Fellowship* 18, no. 1 (January 1952): 1–10; Sidney Hook, *Out of Step: An Unquiet Life in the Twentieth Century* (New York: Harper and Row, 1987), 202. On just war theory, see Michael Walzer, *Just and Unjust Wars: A Moral Argument with Historical Illustrations*, 4th ed. (New York: Basic Books, 2006).

6. On the relevance of Cold War liberalism, see Peter Beinart, *The Good Fight: Why Liberals—and Only Liberals—Can Win the War on Terror and Make America Great Again* (New York: HarperCollins, 2006); and Kevin Mattson, *When America Was Great: The Fighting Faith of Postwar Liberalism* (New York: Routledge, 2004).

7. A. J. Muste, "What Is Left to Do?" *Fellowship* 17, no. 7 (July 1951): 11; Cheney quoted in Bob Woodward, "CIA Told to Do 'Whatever Necessary' to Kill Bin Laden," *Washington Post,* October 21, 2001, http://www.lexisnexis.com/.

8. Niall Ferguson, *The War of the World: Twentieth-Century Conflict and the Descent of the West* (New York: Penguin, 2006). For the statistics, see pp. 647–54.

9. The terminology related to nonviolence is byzantine, as befits its complex history. "Pacifism" is a twentieth-century term that has come to denote absolute opposition to all war, though in Continental Europe it could refer to a more moderate commitment to peace, as in the French *pacifisme.* "Non-resistance" and "passive resistance" were nineteenth-century terms for a nonviolent refusal to cooperate with unjust authority, William Lloyd Garrison's New England Non-Resistance Society being a notable example. "Non-violence" gradually replaced "non-resistance" during the middle decades of the twentieth century. It referred to a philosophy of life, but also a means of political action. The new word suggested that, against the concept of "non-resistance," practitioners of nonviolence *would* resist, but without deadly force, an approach exemplified in Richard Gregg's 1934 book *The Power of Non-Violence.* "Non-violence" also went beyond "pacifism" to address forms of organized violence other than international war, though the distinctions here were especially murky. This new approach gained a number of labels, including "nonviolent resistance," "militant nonviolence," and "nonviolent direct action," the latter term borrowing the phrase "direct action" from the anarcho-syndicalist tradition. Any attempt at rigid definitions in this realm is an exercise in rhetorical strategy, not scientific typology. I have generally used "nonviolence" simply because it is the most inclusive term, carrying both philosophical and tactical connotations. For an extensive effort at empirical classification of the varieties of nonviolence, see Gene Sharp, *The Politics of Nonviolent Action* (Boston: Sargent, 1973).

10. Walter Laqueur, *Guerrilla Warfare: A Historical and Critical Study* (New Brunswick, NJ: Transaction, 1998); Rupert Smith, *The Utility of Force: The Art of War in the Modern World* (New York: Knopf, 2007).

11. John Haynes Holmes, *My Gandhi* (New York: Harper, 1953). On violence and its representations, see Judith Butler, *Excitable Speech: A Politics of the Performative* (New York: Routledge, 1997); James Dawes, *The Language of War: Literature and Culture in the U.S. from the Civil War Through World War II* (Cambridge: Harvard University Press, 2002); Mark Juergensmeyer, *Terror in the Mind of God: The Global Rise of Religious Violence,* 3rd ed. (Berkeley: University of California Press, 2003); Jill Lepore, *The Name of War: King Philip's War and the Origins of American Identity* (New York: Knopf, 1998); Kevin Rozario, "'Delicious Horrors': Mass Culture, the Red Cross, and the Appeal of Modern American Humanitarianism," *American Quarterly* 55, no. 3 (September 2003): 417–55; Elaine Scarry, *The Body in Pain: The Making and Unmaking of the World* (New York: Oxford University Press, 1985); Susan Sontag, *Regarding the Pain of Others* (New York: Farrar, Straus and Giroux, 2003).

12. A. J. Muste, "Return to Pacifism," *Christian Century,* December 2, 1936, 1605.

13. Devere Allen, "Would Jesus Be a Sectarian Today?" *World Tomorrow* 11, no. 11 (November 1928): 458; Kirby Page, *Jesus or Christianity: A Study in Contrasts* (Garden City, NY: Doubleday, Doran, 1929), 44.

14. For extensive statements of Christian nonviolent theology, see A. J. Muste, *Non-Violence in an Aggressive World* (New York: Harper, 1940); and Page, *Jesus or Christianity.* On *ressentiment,* see Friedrich Nietzsche, *On the Genealogy of Morals,* in *Basic Writings of Nietzsche,* trans. and ed. Walter Kaufmann (New York: Modern Library, 2000).

15. Recent calls for a "religious left" include Michael Lerner, *The Left Hand of God: Taking Back Our Country from the Religious Right* (San Francisco: HarperSanFrancisco, 2006); and Jim Wallis, *God's Politics: Why the Right Gets It Wrong and the Left Doesn't Get It* (San Francisco: HarperSanFrancisco, 2005).

16. On pragmatism, see James Kloppenberg, *Uncertain Victory: Social Democracy and Progressivism in European and American Thought, 1870–1920* (New York: Oxford University Press, 1986); Louis Menand, *The Metaphysical Club* (New York: Farrar, Straus and Giroux, 2001); Robert B. Westbrook, *John Dewey and American Democracy* (Ithaca: Cornell University Press, 1991). For a more recent pragmatist argument against religious politics, see Richard Rorty, "Religion as Conversation-Stopper," in *Philosophy and Social Hope* (New York: Penguin, 2000), 168–74.

17. A. J. Muste, "Theology of Despair: An Open Letter to Reinhold Niebuhr," *Fellowship* 14, no. 8 (September 1948): 4–8.

18. Peter Brock, *Freedom from Violence: Sectarian Nonresistance from the Middle Ages to the Great War* (Buffalo: University of Toronto Press, 1991); Meredith Baldwin Weddle, *Walking in the Way of Peace: Quaker Pacifism in the Seventeenth Century* (New York: Oxford University Press, 2001).

19. Brent Dow Allinson, "'Quo Vadis,' Quaker?," *World Tomorrow* 6, no. 8 (August 1923): 246.

20. Thomas F. Curran, *Soldiers of Peace: Civil War Pacifism and the Postwar Radical Peace Movement* (New York: Fordham University Press, 2003); C. Roland Marchand, *The American Peace Movement and Social Reform, 1898–1918* (Princeton: Princeton University Press, 1972).

21. John Haynes Holmes, *I Speak for Myself: The Autobiography of John Haynes Holmes* (New York: Harper, 1959), 45–46; *Kirby Page, Social Evangelist: The Autobiography of a 20th Century Prophet for Peace*, ed. Harold E. Fey (Nyack, NY: Fellowship Press, 1975), 1–2.

22. Sherwood Eddy and Kirby Page, *The Abolition of War* (New York: Doran, 1924), 25.

23. John Haynes Holmes, "What Anyone Can Do," *World Tomorrow* 7, no. 2 (February 1924): 56. The question of nonviolence in radical abolitionism was more complex than pacifists assumed; see chapter 2 in this volume as well as Lewis Perry, *Radical Abolitionism: Anarchy and the Government of God in Antislavery Thought* (Knoxville: University of Tennessee Press, 1995); John Stauffer, *The Black Hearts of Men: Radical Abolitionism and the Transformation of Race* (Cambridge: Harvard University Press, 2002); Valarie Ziegler, *The Advocates of Peace in Antebellum America* (Bloomington: Indiana University Press, 1992).

24. On the Social Gospel, see Aaron Abell, *The Urban Impact on American Protestantism, 1865–1900* (Cambridge: Harvard University Press, 1943); Susan Curtis, *A Consuming Faith: The Social Gospel and Modern American Culture* (Baltimore: Johns Hopkins University Press, 1991); Gary Dorrien, *The Making of American Liberal Theology*, vol. 2: *Idealism, Realism, and Modernity, 1900–1950* (Louisville: Westminster John Knox, 2003), 73–150; Peter J. Frederick, *Knights of the Golden Rule: The Intellectual as Christian Social Reformer in the 1890s* (Lexington: University Press of Kentucky, 1976); C. Howard Hopkins, *The Rise of the Social Gospel in American Protestantism* (New Haven: Yale University Press, 1940); Ralph Luker, *The Social Gospel in Black and White: American Racial Reform, 1885–1912* (Chapel Hill: University of North Carolina Press, 1991); Henry May, *Protestant Churches and Industrial America* (New York: Harper, 1949); Kathryn J. Oberdeck, *The Evangelist and the Impresario: Religion, Entertainment, and Cultural Politics in America, 1884–1914* (Baltimore: Johns Hopkins University Press, 1999); Ronald C. White Jr., *Liberty and Justice for All: Racial Reform and the Social Gospel, 1877–1925* (San Francisco: Harper and Row, 1990).

25. Reinhold Niebuhr, *An Interpretation of Christian Ethics* (New York: Harper, 1935); Christopher Lasch, "Religious Contributions to Social Movements: Walter Rauschenbusch, the Social Gospel, and Its Critics," *Journal of Religious Ethics* 18, no. 1 (Spring 1990): 7–25.

1. Love and War

1. *Character "Bad": The Story of a Conscientious Objector*, ed. Kenneth Irving Brown (New York: Harper, 1934), 71. This assumption was mistaken; though exemption policy was often ambiguous, YMCA workers were eligible for the draft. See *Character "Bad,"* 101.

2. Harold Gray to family, September 20, 1917, in *Character "Bad,"* 74–77.

3. For an encyclopedic history of the American YMCA, see C. Howard Hopkins, *History of the Y.M.C.A. in North America* (New York: Association Press, 1951).

For the early history of the YMCA in the context of nineteenth-century reform, see Paul Boyer, *Urban Masses and Moral Order in America, 1820–1920* (Cambridge: Harvard University Press, 1978), 112–20.

4. On the rise of the student YMCA, see Hopkins, *History of the Y.M.C.A.*, 271–308; and David P. Setran, *The College "Y": Student Religion in the Era of Secularization* (New York: Palgrave Macmillan, 2007). On the secularization of the university in this period, see George M. Marsden, "The Soul of the American University: An Historical Overview," and Bradley J. Longfield, "From Evangelicalism to Liberalism: Public Midwestern Universities in Nineteenth-Century America"— both in George M. Marsden and Bradley J. Longfield, eds., *The Secularization of the Academy* (New York: Oxford University Press, 1992), 9–45, 46–73. On the Student Volunteer Movement, see Michael Parker, *The Kingdom of Character: The Student Volunteer Movement for Foreign Missions, 1886–1926* (New York: University Press of America, 1998); and Nathan D. Showalter, *The End of a Crusade: The Student Volunteer Movement for Foreign Missions and the Great War* (Lanham, MD: Scarecrow, 1998).

5. The standard biography of Mott is C. Howard Hopkins, *John R. Mott, 1865–1955* (Grand Rapids: Eerdmans, 1979). For the purest statement of Mott's evangelistic goals, as well as his frenetic style, see John R. Mott, *The Evangelization of the World in This Generation* (New York: Student Volunteer Movement for Foreign Missions, 1900).

6. J. B. Matthews, *Odyssey of a Fellow Traveler* (New York: Mount Vernon, 1938), 46.

7. Hopkins, *Mott*, 398–400; Hopkins, *Y.M.C.A.*, 635–36.

8. Hopkins, *Mott*, 418–21.

9. Sherwood Eddy to Frank Buchman, July 12, 1916, Box 2, George Sherwood Eddy Papers, Divinity Library, Yale University. For Mott's activities during the Great War and its aftermath, see Hopkins, *Mott*, 430–597; on Eddy's career, see Rick L. Nutt, *The Whole Gospel for the Whole World: Sherwood Eddy and the American Protestant Mission* (Macon, GA: Mercer University Press, 1997).

10. On Page's early life, see *Kirby Page, Social Evangelist: The Autobiography of a 20th Century Prophet for Peace*, ed. Harold E. Fey (Nyack, NY: Fellowship Press, 1975), 1–23; on his first interracial meal, see Kirby Page to M. Ivey Crutchfield, March 18, 1924, Kirby Page Papers, Special Collections, Library, Claremont School of Theology, Claremont, California (permission to quote from the correspondence written by Kirby Page has been granted by the repository). Page's correspondence with his brothers is in the Page Papers, Claremont. On the Church of Christ, see Michael W. Casey, "From Religious Outsiders to Insiders: The Rise and Fall of Pacifism in the Churches of Christ," *Journal of Church and State* 44, no. 3 (Summer 2002): 455–75, http://web.ebscohost.com/; and Richard T. Hughes, *Reviving the Ancient Faith: The Story of Churches of Christ in America* (Grand Rapids: Eerdmans, 1996).

11. Kirby Page to family, July 11 to July 20, 1916, Page Papers. On Gray, see *Character "Bad."* On Yergan, see David Henry Anthony III, *Max Yergan: Race Man, Internationalist, Cold Warrior* (New York: New York University Press, 2006).

12. On "muscular Christianity," see Gail Bederman, "'The Women Have Had Charge of the Church Work Long Enough': The Men and Religion Forward Movement of 1911–1912 and the Masculinization of Middle-Class Protestantism," *American Quarterly* 41, no. 3 (September 1989): 432–65; and Clifford Putney, *Muscular Christianity: Manhood and Sports in Protestant America, 1880–1920* (Cambridge: Harvard University Press, 2001).

13. Sherwood Eddy to Maud, August 1, 1916, Box 1, Eddy Papers; Sherwood Eddy to Mother, August 3, 1917, Box 1, Eddy Papers; Sherwood Eddy, *The Right to Fight: The Moral Grounds of War* (New York: Association Press, 1918); *Kirby Page, Social Evangelist,* 26, 69–70.

14. Harold Gray to family, October 22, 1916, in *Character "Bad,"* 23; Harold Gray to family, November 13, 1916, in *Character "Bad,"* 24.

15. Evan Thomas to Norman Thomas, November 12, 1915, Series I, *The Norman Thomas Papers* (New York Public Library; Alexandria, VA: Chadwyck-Healey, 1983), microfilm; Charles Chatfield, *For Peace and Justice: Pacifism in America, 1914–1941* (Knoxville: University of Tennessee Press, 1971), 42–49. Evan Thomas's World War I correspondence, along with some biographical information, has been edited and collected in *The Radical "No": The Correspondence and Writings of Evan Thomas on War,* ed. Charles Chatfield (New York: Garland, 1974).

16. Sherwood Eddy, *With Our Soldiers in France* (New York: Association Press, 1917), 9–10.

17. On the trauma of the Great War, see Paul Fussell, *The Great War and Modern Memory* (New York: Oxford University Press, 2000); and Modris Eksteins, *Rites of Spring: The Great War and the Birth of the Modern Age* (New York: Anchor, 1989). The "weak children" quote is from Garfield Powell, diary, July 23, 1916, quoted in Eksteins, p. 173.

18. Sherwood Eddy to Maud, August 21, 1916, Box 1, Eddy Papers; Eddy, *With Our Soldiers in France,* 111–26; Evan Thomas to Norman Thomas, November 12, 1915, Series I, *Thomas Papers;* Evan Thomas to Mother, May 9, 1916, Series VIII, *Thomas Papers.*

19. Kirby Page, report letter, September 2, 1916, Page Papers. On the language of the YMCA, see Mark Meigs, *Optimism at Armageddon: Voices of American Participants in the First World War* (New York: New York University Press, 1997). The effects of the war on the European experience of modernity were, of course, entirely different; see Fussell, *Great War and Modern Memory.*

20. Kirby Page, report letter, June 5, 1917, Page Papers; Kirby Page, report letter, August 8, 1917, Page Papers.

21. See Kirby Page, "The Sword or the Cross," [October 1917], Page Papers; *Character "Bad,"* 31–32, 46–54; Chatfield, *For Peace and Justice,* 42–49.

22. Harold Gray to family, January 1, 1917, in *Character "Bad,"* 28; Harold Gray to family, February 11, 1917, in *Character "Bad,"* 33–34; *Kirby Page, Social Evangelist,* 26.

23. Page, "The Sword or the Cross." On Page's liberal Protestant theological context, see Gary Dorrien, *The Making of American Liberal Theology,* vol. 2: *Idealism, Realism, and Modernity, 1900–1950* (Louisville: Westminster John Knox, 2003).

24. Harold Gray to family, May 6, 1917, in *Character "Bad,"* 56; Evan Thomas to Norman Thomas, January 15, 1917, *Thomas Papers*; Maxwell Chaplin to Thomas Evans, February 10, 1917, in George Stewart, ed., *The Letters of Maxwell Chaplin* (New York: Association Press, 1928), 119.

25. Sherwood Eddy to Kirby Page, telegram, August 17, 1918, Page Papers.

26. *Forty Years for Peace: A History of the Fellowship of Reconciliation, 1914–1954* (New York: Fellowship of Reconciliation, 1954); Hopkins, *Mott,* 469–72.

27. Vera Brittain, *The Rebel Passion: A Short History of Some Pioneer Peacemakers* (London: Allen and Unwin, 1964), 35.

28. Henry Hodgkin form letter, October 20, 1915, Box 1, Series A-1, Section II, Fellowship of Reconciliation Papers, Swarthmore College Peace Collection; "The Fellowship of Reconciliation: Its Origins and Development," [1920], Box 1, Series A-1, Section II, FOR Papers; Chatfield, *For Peace and Justice,* 19–21.

29. *Forty Years for Peace.*

30. *Statement of Purpose,* [1919?], Box 1, Series A-1, Section II, FOR Papers.

31. Minutes of the Garden City Conference of the Fellowship of Reconciliation, 1915, Box 1, Series A-1, Section II, FOR Papers.

32. Edward Evans to Norman Thomas, December 10, 1915, Series I, *Thomas Papers.*

33. On Thomas's knowledge of New York religion, see William Shriver to Ralph Diffendorfer, October 27, 1916, Series I, *Thomas Papers.* The most comprehensive biography is W. A. Swanberg, *Norman Thomas: The Last Idealist* (New York: Scribner, 1976); see also Harry Fleischman, *Norman Thomas: A Biography* (New York: Norton, 1969); Bernard K. Johnpoll, *Pacifist's Progress: Norman Thomas and the Decline of American Socialism* (Chicago: Quadrangle, 1970); Murray B. Seidler, *Norman Thomas: Respectable Rebel* (Syracuse: Syracuse University Press, 1967). On immigrant life in the vicinity of Thomas's American Parish, see Robert Orsi, *The Madonna of 115th Street: Faith and Community in Italian Harlem, 1880–1950* (New Haven: Yale University Press, 1985).

34. *I Speak for Myself: The Autobiography of John Haynes Holmes* (New York: Harper, 1959); and Carl Hermann Voss, *Rabbi and Minister: The Friendship of Stephen S. Wise and John Haynes Holmes* (Cleveland: World, 1964).

35. John Haynes Holmes, *The Revolutionary Function of the Modern Church* (New York: Putnam, 1912), 178, 200.

36. "Speaker in Church Boasts He's a Thief," *New York Times,* March 15, 1915, http://proquest.umi.com/.

37. Norman Thomas to Captain Brady, June 30, 1917, Series I, *Thomas Papers.*

38. Max Eastman to Norman Thomas, May 28, 1917, Series I, *Thomas Papers*; Swanberg, *Norman Thomas,* 53.

39. John Haynes Holmes, "The Ethics of Chastity," *Messiah Pulpit,* April 1917, 3.

40. On the formation of the American Union Against Militarism, see C. Roland Marchand, *The American Peace Movement and Social Reform, 1898–1918* (Princeton: Princeton University Press, 1972), 223–65; and Chatfield, *For Peace and Justice,* 15–41. The group went through a variety of names before settling on "American Union Against Militarism"; I use this title for convenience.

258   I. LOVE AND WAR

41. Thomas J. Knock, *To End All Wars: Woodrow Wilson and the Quest for a New World Order* (New York: Oxford University Press, 1992), 63–67.

42. Knock, *To End All Wars*, 85–104; Swanberg, *Norman Thomas*, 40, 44; Evan Thomas to Mother, November 14, 1916, Series VIII, *Thomas Papers*.

43. Woodrow Wilson, "An Address to a Joint Session of Congress," April 2, 1917, in Arthur S. Link, ed., *Papers of Woodrow Wilson* (Princeton: Princeton University Press, 1993), 41:519–27.

44. Robert B. Westbrook, *John Dewey and American Democracy* (Ithaca: Cornell University Press, 1991).

45. John Dewey, "Fiat Justitia, Ruat Cœlum," *New Republic*, September 29, 1917, in Jo Ann Boydston, ed., *John Dewey: The Middle Works, 1899–1924* (Carbondale: Southern Illinois University Press, 1980), 10:281–84.

46. William Adams Brown, *Is Christianity Practicable?* (New York: Scribner, 1916), 153, 175–80. For the liberal Protestant context of Brown's views, see William R. Hutchison, *The Modernist Impulse in American Protestantism* (Cambridge: Harvard University Press, 1976), 226–56; Susan Curtis, *A Consuming Faith: The Social Gospel and Modern American Culture* (Baltimore: Johns Hopkins University Press, 1991), 179–227; Dorrien, *Making of American Liberal Theology*, 2:21–72.

47. Jane Addams, *Peace and Bread in Time of War* (New York: Macmillan, 1922), 143, 150.

48. John Haynes Holmes, "A Statement to My People on the Eve of War," *Messiah Pulpit*, May 1917, 6, 12; "Holmes Won't Fight So Offers to Resign," *New York Times*, April 2, 1917, http://proquest.umi.com/; "Trustees Support Holmes," *New York Times*, April 3, 1917, http://proquest.umi.com/.

49. Later incarnations of the American Union Against Militarism continued into the early 1920s, but these did not attract the broad coalition of social reformers that had defined the original organization. See Marchand, *American Peace Movement*, 253–61.

50. John F. Piper Jr., *The American Churches in World War I* (Athens: Ohio University Press, 1985), 8–68; Swanberg, *Norman Thomas*, 59–60; Norman Thomas to Archibald McClure, March 9, 1917, Series I, *Thomas Papers*.

51. Hopkins, *Mott*, 474; Henry Hodgkin to John R. Mott, October 31, 1917, Box 41, John R. Mott Papers, Divinity Library, Yale University; Hopkins, *Mott*, 469–71.

52. See John Dewey, "In Explanation of Our Lapse," *New Republic*, November 3, 1917, in Jo Ann Boydston, ed., *John Dewey: The Middle Works, 1899–1924* (Carbondale: Southern Illinois University Press, 1980), 10:292–95.

53. Woodrow Wilson, "An Address to a Joint Session of Congress," 519–27; H. C. Peterson and Gilbert Fite, *Opponents of War, 1917–1918* (Madison: University of Wisconsin Press, 1957), 195, 45–47; Robert Justin Goldstein, *Political Repression in Modern America: From 1870 to 1976* (Urbana: University of Illinois Press, 2001), 103–36; Christopher Capozzola, "The Only Badge Needed Is Your Patriotic Fervor: Vigilance, Coercion, and the Law in World War I America," *Journal of American History* 88, no. 4 (March 2002): 1354–82, http://www.historycooperative.org/journals/jah/88.4/capozzola.html/.

54. Floyd Hardin to Edward Evans, August 5, 1917, Box 2, Edward W. Evans Papers, Swarthmore College Peace Collection.

55. This account is based primarily on the *Los Angeles Times*, September 27–October 7, 1917; and Norman Thomas, *The Case of the Christian Pacifists at Los Angeles, Cal.* (New York: National Civil Liberties Bureau, 1918). Other brief discussions of the case include Floyd Hardin, "An Account of the Conference of Christian Pacifists in California," 1917, Box 9, Series I, John Nevin Sayre Papers, Swarthmore College Peace Collection; William Emmett, "Mania in Los Angeles," *Nation*, January 17, 1918, 58–59; "The Conviction of the Christian Pacifists," *New World* 1, no. 1 (January 1918), 16.

56. "Patriots Rout the Pacifists," *Los Angeles Times*, October 3, 1917; Emmett, "Mania in Los Angeles"; "Billy Whacks the Pacifists," *Los Angeles Times*, September 28, 1917; untitled article in *Los Angeles Times*, October 2, 1918; "Billy Launches Big Drive on Saloon Evil," *Los Angeles Times*, October 1, 1917; Thomas, *Case of the Christian Pacifists*, 5.

57. "Miscellaneous," *News Sheet* 3 (July 1917); John Howard Melish, *Paul Jones: Minister of Reconciliation* (New York: Fellowship of Reconciliation, 1942); John R. Sillito and Timothy S. Hearn, "A Question of Conscience: The Resignation of Bishop Paul Jones," *Utah Historical Quarterly* 50, no. 3 (Summer 1982): 208–23; John R. Mott to John Nevin Sayre, May 11, 1917, Box 1, Series A, Sayre Papers; "A Minister and His Church in War," *Survey*, June 2, 1917, 228–9.

58. The other case where Wilson overruled Burleson involved an issue of the *Nation*, edited by FOR member Oswald Garrison Villard. On the *World Tomorrow* controversy, see Paul L. Murphy, *World War I and the Origin of Civil Liberties in the United States* (New York: Norton, 1979), 71–132; and Swanberg, *Norman Thomas*, 60–66.

59. Holmes, *I Speak For Myself*, 189.

60. On the history of civil liberties as a political issue, see Robert C. Cotrell, *Roger Nash Baldwin and the American Civil Liberties Union* (New York: Columbia University Press, 2000); Murphy, *Origin of Civil Liberties*; David M. Rabban, *Free Speech in Its Forgotten Years* (New York: Cambridge University Press, 1997).

61. Norman Thomas to Frederick Lynch, August 3, 1917, Series I, *Thomas Papers*.

62. On this broader resistance to the draft, see John Whiteclay Chambers II, *To Raise an Army: The Draft Comes to Modern America* (New York: Free Press, 1987), 210–17; and Jeanette Keith, *Rich Man's War, Poor Man's Fight: Race, Class, and Power in the Rural South During the First World War* (Chapel Hill: University of North Carolina Press, 2003).

63. "Fellowship Members and Exemption," *News Sheet* 3 (July 1917): 6; Minutes of FOR Executive Committee Meeting, July 3, 1917, Box 1, Series A-2, Section II, FOR Papers.

64. For the statistics, see Chambers, *To Raise an Army*, 216–17; and Gerlof D. Homan, *American Mennonites and the Great War, 1914–1918* (Scottdale, PA: Herald, 1994), 182–84. On Mennonite theology, see Perry Bush, *Two Kingdoms, Two Loyalties: Mennonite Pacifism in Modern America* (Baltimore: Johns Hopkins University Press, 1998).

65. Evan Thomas to Norman Thomas, June 8, 1918, Series I, *Thomas Papers;* Harold Gray to family, April 27, 1918, in *Character "Bad,"* 103–4.

66. Harold Gray to family, September 5, 1918, in *Character "Bad,"* 149. On the plight of the conscientious objectors, see Chatfield, *For Peace and Justice,* 68–87; Swanberg, *Norman Thomas,* 66–75; Norman Thomas, *The Conscientious Objector in America* (New York: Huebsch, 1923); *Radical "No"; Character "Bad."*

67. Harold Gray to family, October 6, 1918, in *Character "Bad,"* 169–70; Evan Thomas to Norman Thomas, July 28, 1918, Series I, *Thomas Papers;* Evan Thomas to Norman Thomas, July 29, 1918, Series I, *Thomas Papers;* Harold Gray to family, September 7, 1918, in *Character "Bad,"* 155–56.

68. John Dewey, "Conscience and Compulsion," *New Republic,* July 14, 1917, in Jo Ann Boydston, ed., *John Dewey: The Middle Works, 1899–1924* (Carbondale: Southern Illinois University Press, 1980), 10:260–64.

69. Norman Thomas, *The Christian Patriot* (Philadelphia: Jenkins, 1917), 34, 65.

70. John Nevin Sayre to Woodrow Wilson, April 27, 1917, Box 18, Series A, Sayre Papers; Woodrow Wilson to John Nevin Sayre, May 1, 1917, Box 18, Series A, Sayre Papers; Norman Thomas to John R. Mott, July 16, 1918, quoted in Hopkins, *Mott,* 529; Chatfield, *For Peace and Justice,* 85.

71. Erez Manela, *The Wilsonian Moment: Self-Determination and the International Origins of Anticolonial Nationalism* (New York: Oxford University Press, 2007). See also Alan Dawley, *Changing the World: American Progressives in War and Revolution* (Princeton: Princeton University Press, 2003), 237–43.

72. John Haynes Holmes, "O Beautiful, My Country," *Messiah Pulpit,* July 1917, 15; John Haynes Holmes, "This Enormous Year (1917): Its Terrors, Tragedies, and Triumphs," *Messiah Pulpit,* February 1918, 11; John Haynes Holmes, "Christ at the Peace-Table," *Messiah Pulpit,* Series 1918–1919, no. 5, 6.

73. "Peace and Honor Yet to Be Won," *World Tomorrow* 2, no. 6 (June 1919): 145–48; "Peace and the Financiers," *World Tomorrow* 2, no. 12 (December 1919): 327; "The Treaty a Flat Betrayal, Says Dr. Holmes," *World Tomorrow* 2, no. 6 (June 1919): 169. See also "What, Then, Shall We Do?," *World Tomorrow* 2, no. 10 (October 1919): 263–66.

74. Woodrow Wilson, "An Address at the University of Paris," December 21, 1918, in Arthur S. Link, ed., *Papers of Woodrow Wilson* (Princeton: Princeton University Press, 1993), 53:461–63; Stuart I. Rochester, *American Liberal Disillusionment in the Wake of World War I* (University Park: Pennsylvania State University Press, 1977), 73–77; "Some Questions for Liberals," *World Tomorrow* 1, no. 12 (December 1918): 295; see also "The One Course for Us Is Penitence," *New World* 1, no. 5 (May 1918): 100. Knock's *To End All Wars* stresses the relationship between wartime repression and the evaporation of liberal (not only pacifist) support for Wilson's peace proposals; see esp. pp. 236–39.

75. John Dewey, "The Discrediting of Idealism," *New Republic,* October 8, 1919, in Jo Ann Boydston, ed., *John Dewey: The Middle Works, 1899–1924* (Carbondale: Southern Illinois University Press, 1980), 10:180–85; "A Welcome Telegram from Los Angeles," *World Tomorrow* 1, no. 11 (November 1918): 285.

76. "The White Terror in America," *World Tomorrow* 2, no. 11 (November 1919): 306–7; Robert Whitaker, "The Anti-Japanese Agitation in California," *World Tomorrow* 3, no. 11 (November 1920): 329–30; Goldstein, *Political Repression*, 139–63.

77. Melvin Dubofsky, *We Shall Be All: A History of the Industrial Workers of the World* (Chicago: Quadrangle, 1969), 400–403; David Montgomery, *The Fall of the House of Labor: The Workplace, the State, and American Labor Activism, 1865–1925* (New York: Cambridge University Press, 1987).

78. Norman Thomas, "The Conscientious Objector: II—Conscience and the Church," *Nation*, August 23, 1917, 198–99; John Haynes Holmes, "Is Violence the Way Out? (2.) The Answer for Labor," *Community Pulpit*, Series 1919–1920, no. 6, 9.

79. Dubofsky, *We Shall Be All*. The Gurley Flynn quote is on p. 274.

80. Edward W. Evans to Robert Whitaker, March 3, 1920, Box 2, Evans Papers.

81. John Haynes Holmes, "Is Violence the Way Out?" *Community Pulpit*, Series 1919–1920, no. 5–7. The sermons were later revised and published in pamphlet form as John Haynes Holmes, *Is Violence the Way out of Our Industrial Disputes?* (New York: Dodd, Mead, 1920).

82. Norman Thomas, "The Strike, II: The Strike a Justifiable Form of Passive Resistance," *World Tomorrow* 3, no. 5 (May 1920): 133–35; Robert Whitaker, "The Strike a Release from Industrial Warfare," *World Tomorrow* 3, no. 6 (June 1920): 186; A. J. Muste, "The Two Tests," *World Tomorrow* 3, no. 7 (July 1920): 214; Evan Thomas, "The Strike a Necessary Compromise in a Practical World," *World Tomorrow* 3, no. 6 (June 1920): 177.

83. On Muste's early life and career, see A. J. Muste, "Sketches for an Autobiography," in Nat Hentoff, ed., *The Essays of A. J. Muste* (New York: Simon and Schuster, 1967), 1–54; Nat Hentoff, *Peace Agitator: The Story of A. J. Muste* (New York: Macmillan, 1963); Jo Ann Ooiman Robinson, *Abraham Went Out: A Biography of A. J. Muste* (Philadelphia: Temple University Press, 1981), 1–31.

84. Muste, "Sketches," 55–77.

85. On the Amalgamated Textile Workers Association, see David J. Goldberg, *A Tale of Three Cities: Labor Organization and Protest in Paterson, Passaic, and Lawrence, 1916–1921* (New Brunswick: Rutgers University Press, 1989).

86. See Goldberg, *Three Cities*.

87. *Radical "No,"* 224–30; Cedric Long, "The Consumer as Revolutionist," *World Tomorrow* 4, no. 11 (November 1921): 334–36; Harold Rotzel, "Pacifism in the Labor Field," *World Tomorrow* 9, no. 3 (March 1926): 81–83; Paul Jones to Marguerite Hallowell, November 11, 1921, Box 1, Series A-1, Section II, FOR Papers.

2. Social Evangelism

1. Clarence Marsh Case, *Non-Violent Coercion: A Study in Methods of Social Pressure* (New York: Century, 1923), introduction by Edward Alsworth Ross.

2. Statistics are from minutes of FOR Council and Executive Committee, Section II, Fellowship of Reconciliation Papers, Swarthmore College Peace Collection.

3. For a version of this outlook among secular radicals, see Christine Stansell, *American Moderns: Bohemian New York and the Creation of a New Century* (New York: Metropolitan, 2000).

4. Woodrow Wilson, "An Address at the University of Paris," December 21, 1918, in Arthur S. Link, ed., *Papers of Woodrow Wilson* (Princeton: Princeton University Press, 1993), 53:462; Kirby Page to Howard E. Sweet, February 3, 1918, Kirby Page Papers, Claremont School of Theology Library.

5. George Creel, *How We Advertised America* (1920; repr., New York: Arno, 1972). On Creel and the Committee on Public Information, see David M. Kennedy, *Over Here: The First World War and American Society* (New York: Oxford University Press, 1980), 59–75; and Stephen Vaughn, *Holding Fast the Inner Lines: Democracy, Nationalism, and the Committee on Public Information* (Chapel Hill: University of North Carolina Press, 1980).

6. Walter Lippmann, *Public Opinion* (1922; repr., New York: Free Press, 1949); Brett Gary, *The Nervous Liberals: Propaganda Anxieties from World War I to the Cold War* (New York: Columbia University Press, 1999), 15–53.

7. Kirby Page, *War: Its Causes, Consequences, and Cure* (New York: Doran, 1923), 44; Sherwood Eddy report letter, [1923], George Sherwood Eddy Papers, Divinity Library, Yale University.

8. Edmund Chaffee, "Biographical Sketch of Edmund B. Chaffee," [1925?], unpublished ms., Box 1, Series I, Edmund B. Chaffee Papers, Special Collections Research Center, Syracuse University Library.

9. Edmund Chaffee to Mother, March 29, 1917, April 19, 1917, and February 15, 1917, Box 1, Series I, Chaffee Papers.

10. Edmund Chaffee to Mother, June 30, 1918, Box 1, Series I, Chaffee Papers.

11. On the debate with the Industrial Workers of the World, see Charles Stelzle, *A Son of the Bowery* (New York: Doran, 1926), 126–27. On the history of Labor Temple, see James S. Armstrong, "The Labor Temple, 1910–1957: A Social Gospel in Action in the Presbyterian Church" (PhD diss., University of Wisconsin, 1974). For an interpretation of Stelzle that stresses his engagement with American consumer culture, see Susan Curtis, *A Consuming Faith: The Social Gospel and Modern American Culture* (Baltimore: Johns Hopkins University Press, 1991), 254–65. On Hughan's speech and the Anti-Enlistment League, see Scott H. Bennett, *Radical Pacifism: The War Resisters League and Gandhian Nonviolence in America, 1915–1963* (Syracuse: Syracuse University Press, 2003), 11–12.

12. Edmund B. Chaffee, "The Religious and Philosophical Basis of Free Speech," n.d., unpublished ms., Box 6, Series III, Chaffee Papers.

13. Henry Sloane Coffin to Edmund Chaffee, April 5, 1929, Box 21, Series I, Chaffee Papers; Henry Sloane Coffin to Edmund Chaffee, December 8, 1923, Box 4, Series I, Chaffee Papers.

14. Edmund Chaffee to Blanche Watson, December 11, 1925, Box 8, Series I, Chaffee Papers.

15. Edmund Chaffee to Theodore Savage, September 12, 1927, Box 13, Series I, Chaffee Papers; Edmund Chaffee to VanSantvoord Merle-Smith, September 23, 1927, October 24, 1927, and November 28, 1927, Box 13, Series I, Chaffee Papers.

16. Edmund B. Chaffee, "Ethics and Propaganda," n.d., unpublished ms., Box 3, Series III, Chaffee Papers; Edmund B. Chaffee, *The Protestant Churches and the Industrial Crisis* (New York: Macmillan, 1933), 203.

17. John Nevin Sayre, "Disarmament and Defense," *World Tomorrow* 5, no. 1 (January 1922): 3–7.

18. Kirby Page to Alma Page, November 23, 1917, Page Papers.

19. Sherwood Eddy report letter, July 10, 1920, Box 3, Eddy Papers; Sherwood Eddy, *A Pilgrimage of Ideas; or, The Re-Education of Sherwood Eddy* (New York: Farrar and Rinehart, 1934), 17–18; C. Howard Hopkins, *John R. Mott, 1865–1955* (Grand Rapids: Eerdmans, 1979), 621–22.

20. Kirby Page to Mother, June 4, 1914, Page Papers; Kirby Page to Alma Page, November 14, 1931, Page Papers.

21. Edward E. Spafford, National Commander of American Legion, to Albert L. Cox, December 20, 1927, Box 2, Eddy Papers.

22. On this point, see Richard Fox, *Reinhold Niebuhr* (San Francisco: Harper and Row, 1987), 75; and David P. Setran, *The College "Y": Student Religion in the Era of Secularization* (New York: Palgrave Macmillan, 2007), 221–43.

23. Sherwood Eddy report letter, March 6, 1924, Box 3, Eddy Papers.

24. Sherwood Eddy report letter, February 6, 1922, Box 3, Eddy Papers.

25. Sherwood Eddy report letter, April 8, 1924, Box 3, Eddy Papers.

26. *News Letter,* November 1929; Hillman M. Bishop to Edmund Chaffee, February 27, 1929, Box 20, Series I, Chaffee Papers; Frank C. Goodman to Edmund Chaffee, August 12, 1927, Box 12, Series I, Chaffee Papers; Edmund Chaffee to George L. Leonard, September 8, 1927, Box 12, Series I, Chaffee Papers; Linley Gordon to Kirby Page, November 24, 1930, Page Papers, Claremont; S. Theodore Granik to Kirby Page, December 24, 1930, Page Papers.

27. On Durant and middlebrow culture, see Joan Shelley Rubin, *The Making of Middlebrow Culture* (Chapel Hill: University of North Carolina Press, 1992).

28. Kirby Page, *Christianity and Economic Problems* (New York: Association Press, 1922); Kirby Page to Grace Hutchins and Anna Rochester, May 1, 1922, and Grace Hutchins and Anna Rochester to Kirby Page, May 2, 1922, Page Papers. On the new religious publishing, see Matthew Sigurd Hedstrom, "Seeking a Spiritual Center: Mass-Market Books and Liberal Religion in America, 1921–1948" (PhD diss., University of Texas at Austin, 2006).

29. On the importance of discussion in pacifist culture, see Patricia Faith Appelbaum, "The Legions of Good Will: The Religious Culture of Protestant Pacifism, 1918–1963" (PhD diss., Boston University, 2001), 170–73.

30. Fleming H. Revell Company to Kirby Page, December 28, 1917, Page Papers; Charles Clayton Morrison to Kirby Page, June 15, 1921, Page Papers; Kirby Page, *The Sword or the Cross: Which Should Be the Weapon of the Christian Militant?* (Chicago: Christian Century Press, 1921).

31. Kirby Page to Y. Last, February 25, 1925, Page Papers; James Maurer to Kirby Page, December 26, 1923, Page Papers; Kirby Page to Harold Gray, January 11, 1924, Page Papers; Kirby Page, *War: Its Causes, Consequences, and Cure*, abridged ed. (New York: Doran, 1923), back matter.

32. Paul Jones, "Editing Creatively," *World Tomorrow* 15, no. 6 (June 1932): 187; G. Bromley Oxnam to Kirby Page, January 3, 1924, Page Papers; Kirby Page, *Individualism and Socialism: An Ethical Survey of Economic and Political Forces* (New York: Farrar and Rinehart, 1933).

33. Kirby Page, *National Defense* (New York: Farrar and Rinehart, 1931). For Niebuhr's citations, see Reinhold Niebuhr, *Moral Man and Immoral Society* (1932; repr., New York: Scribner, 1960), 84, 93, 98, 108.

34. "Excerpts from the Report of Don M. Chase to F.O.R. Conference," unpublished report, Page Papers; *News Letter*, April 1927; *News Letter*, August 1927; Harold Moran to Kirby Page, July 20, 1931, Page Papers, Claremont; John H. Austin to Kirby Page, July 11, 1931, Page Papers.

35. Paula Fass, *The Damned and the Beautiful: American Youth in the 1920's* (New York: Oxford University Press, 1977), 334.

36. Brewer Eddy to Sherwood Eddy, September 22, 1924, Box 1, Eddy Papers.

37. Maxwell Chaplin to Kirby Page, February 4, [1926], Page Papers; Henry P. Van Dusen to Kirby Page, September 17, 1921, Page Papers.

38. Harry Elmer Barnes, *The Twilight of Christianity* (New York: Vanguard, 1929).

39. The Fellowship tried to compromise on the issue of religious commitment by spinning off the War Resisters League in 1923, under the leadership of charter FOR member Jessie Wallace Hughan. The War Resisters League became the major *secular* radical pacifist organization of the interwar period. Most of its leaders claimed some kind of personal religious affiliation, but the organization itself had no official requirements. Unlike the wide-ranging agenda of the FOR, the War Resisters League program in this period focused narrowly on the issue of international war. See Bennett, *Radical Pacifism*.

40. John Haynes Holmes, "Damaged Souls," *Community Pulpit*, Series 1923–1924, no. 5, 15; A. J. Muste, "Sketches for an Autobiography," in Nat Hentoff, ed., *The Essays of A. J. Muste* (New York: Simon and Schuster, 1967), 38; Edmund Chaffee, "Personal Virtues and the Social Gospel," n.d., unpublished ms., Box 5, Series III, Chaffee Papers.

41. Stansell, *American Moderns*.

42. Kirby Page, *Jesus or Christianity: A Study in Contrasts* (Garden City, NY: Doubleday, Doran, 1929), 1; Reinhold Niebuhr, *Does Civilization Need Religion? A Study in the Social Resources and Limitations of Religion in Modern Life* (New York: Macmillan, 1927), 46.

43. Kirby Page, "Building Tomorrow's World," *World Tomorrow* 9, no. 5 (October 1926): 168.

44. John Haynes Holmes, "Pacifism in Personal Relations," in Devere Allen, ed., *Pacifism in the Modern World* (Garden City, NY: Doubleday, Doran, 1929), 239–53. See also Sherwood Eddy, *Sex and Youth* (Garden City, NY: Doubleday, Doran, 1928).

45. Sayre, "Disarmament and Defense," 7; Norman Thomas, "Afterthoughts on the Suffrage Victory," *World Tomorrow* 4, no. 1 (January 1921): 20–21; V. L. Walker, letter to the editor, *World Tomorrow* 8, no. 2 (February 1925): 51.

46. On the Women's International League for Peace and Freedom, see Harriet Hyman Alonso, *Peace as a Women's Issue: A History of the U.S. Movement for World Peace and Women's Rights* (Syracuse: Syracuse University Press, 1993); Carrie A. Foster, *The Women and the Warriors: The U.S. Section of the Women's International League for Peace and Freedom* (Syracuse: Syracuse University Press, 1995); Linda K. Schott, *Reconstructing Women's Thoughts: The Women's International League for Peace and Freedom Before World War II* (Stanford: Stanford University Press, 1997).

47. Grace Hutchins, "Our Inferiority Complex," *World Tomorrow* 6, no. 12 (December 1923): 362–63; Nancy Kester Neale, interviewed by Dallas Blanchard, Documenting the American South, University Library, University of North Carolina at Chapel Hill, August 6, 1983, http://docsouth.unc.edu/; Alice Kester to Howard Kester, October 29, 1928, Series I, *Howard A. Kester Papers* (Glen Rock, NJ: Microfilming Corporation of America, 1973); *I Speak for Myself: The Autobiography of John Haynes Holmes* (New York: Harper, 1959), 286.

48. Hannah M. Stone to Edmund B. Chaffee, June 9, 1928, Box 17, Series I, Chaffee Papers; Edmund B. Chaffee to Hannah M. Stone, June 13, 1928, Box 17, Series I, Chaffee Papers; Edmund B. Chaffee to Abraham Stone, December 13, 1930, Box 25, Series I, Chaffee Papers; John Haynes Holmes, "The Ethics of Chastity," *Messiah Pulpit*, April 1917, 11. On the wider debate over companionate marriage in the 1920s, see Rebecca L. Davis, "'Not Marriage at All, but Simple Harlotry': The Companionate Marriage Controversy," *Journal of American History* 94, no. 4 (March 2008): 1137–63, http://web.ebscohost.com/.

49. Advertisement in the *World Tomorrow* 9, no. 3 (March 1926): 101; "To All Friends of the *World Tomorrow*," form letter, May 15, 1926, Box 2, Series C-4, Devere Allen Papers, Swarthmore College Peace Collection.

50. Ethelred Brown to Kirby Page, August 13, 1934, Page Papers. On Brown's career, see Ethelred Brown, "A Liberal Church for Negroes," *World Tomorrow* 12, no. 8 (August 1929): 379; Mark D. Morrison-Reed, *Black Pioneers in a White Denomination* (Boston: Beacon, 1984), 30–111.

51. Devere Allen to Grace Hutchins, March 27, 1927, Box 2, Series C-4, Allen Papers. On Thurman, see Eleonore van Notten, *Wallace Thurman's Harlem Renaissance*, Costerus New Series 93 (Atlanta: Rodopi, 1994).

52. Wallace Thurman to Langston Hughes, [1926], Box 155, Series I, Langston Hughes Papers, Beinecke Rare Book and Manuscript Library, Yale University.

53. For the broader context of religious reform in the twenties, see Paul A. Carter, *The Decline and Revival of the Social Gospel: Social and Political Liberalism in American Protestant Churches, 1920–1940* (Ithaca: Cornell University Press, 1954); Robert Moats Miller, *American Protestantism and Social Issues, 1919–1939* (Chapel Hill: University of North Carolina Press, 1958); Donald Meyer, *The Protestant Search for Political Realism, 1919–1941*, 2nd ed. (Middletown, CT: Wesleyan University Press, 1988).

54. Robert Goldstein, *Political Repression in Modern America: From 1870 to 1976* (Urbana: University of Illinois Press, 2001), 137–92; Irving Bernstein, *The Lean Years: A History of the American Worker, 1920–1933* (Boston: Houghton Mifflin, 1960); David Montgomery, *The Fall of the House of Labor: The Workplace, the State, and American Labor Activism, 1865–1925* (New York: Cambridge University Press, 1987).

55. Kirby Page, "United States Steel Corporation," *Atlantic Monthly*, May 1922, 585–93.

56. On the Dutchess Bleachery, see Benjamin M. Selekman, *Sharing Management with the Workers: A Study of the Partnership Plan of the Dutchess Bleachery, Wappinger Falls, New York* (New York: Russell Sage Foundation, 1924). On liberal Protestant views of capitalists, see Meyer, *Protestant Search for Political Realism*, 55–75.

57. Kirby Page to George Collins, October 30, 1923, Page Papers.

58. "Fellowship Made Dynamic," *Inquiry*, September 1925, 43.

59. On Brookwood, see Richard J. Altenbaugh, *Education for Struggle: The American Labor Colleges of the 1920s and 1930s* (Philadelphia: Temple University Press, 1990); Charles F. Howlett, *Brookwood Labor College and the Struggle for Peace and Social Justice in America* (Lewiston, NY: Mellen, 1993); Muste, "Sketches for an Autobiography," 84–154; Jo Ann Ooiman Robinson, *Abraham Went Out: A Biography of A. J. Muste* (Philadelphia: Temple University Press, 1981), 32–61. On the adult education movement in the 1920s, see Harold W. Stubblefield and Patrick Keane, *Adult Education in the American Experience: From the Colonial Period to the Present* (San Francisco: Jossey-Bass, 1994), 191–228.

60. Muste, "Sketches for an Autobiography," 86, 127; *Brookwood* (n.p., n.d.), pamphlet in Brookwood Labor College Papers, Tamiment Library, New York University.

61. Helen G. Norton, "Considering the Negro: Significant Symposium at Brookwood," *Labor Age* 16, no. 8 (August 1927): 11; Howlett, *Brookwood Labor College*, 247–48.

62. Howlett, *Brookwood Labor College*, 142–43, 176–80. On pacifist plays and pageants, see Appelbaum, "Legions of Good Will," 186–201.

63. Len De Caux, *Labor Radical: From the Wobblies to the CIO* (Boston: Beacon, 1970), 94. For Muste's inclusive vision, see A. J. Muste, "Revolutionary Movements: What They Have in Common," *World Tomorrow* 5, no. 4 (April 1922): 116–18; and A. J. Muste, "Can We Have Unity?" *World Tomorrow* 8, no. 1 (January 1925): 14–16.

64. *Threescore: The Autobiography of Sarah N. Cleghorn* (New York: Smith and Haas, 1936), 245–46. On Brookwood's political uses of language, see Susan Kates, *Activist Rhetorics and American Higher Education* (Carbondale: Southern Illinois University Press, 2001), 75–96.

65. Cedric Long, "Can Capital and Labor Get Together?" *World Tomorrow* 12, no. 9 (September 1929): 358–61; "Mr. Muste Takes Issue" and "Mr. Long Replies," *World Tomorrow* 12, no. 10 (October 1929): 426–28.

66. See, for instance, John Haynes Holmes, "Outlawry of War—A Policy of Abolition," *World Tomorrow* 9, no. 6 (November 1926): 204–7; [Kirby Page], "The

Point of View," *World Tomorrow* 10, no. 11 (November 1927): 434; John Nevin Sayre, "The Power of Opinion," *World Tomorrow* 8, no. 4 (April 1925): 105–7.

67. "Following Up the Peace Pact: A Symposium," *Inquiry,* February 1929, 26–31. On the antiwar movement in the twenties, see Charles Chatfield, *For Peace and Justice: Pacifism in America 1914–1941* (Knoxville: University of Tennessee Press, 1971); and Charles DeBenedetti, *Origins of the Modern American Peace Movement, 1915–1929* (Millwood, NY: KTO, 1978).

68. Page, *Jesus or Christianity,* 1–52; Devere Allen, "War Resistance as War Prevention," in Devere Allen, ed., *Pacifism in the Modern World* (Garden City, NY: Doubleday, Doran, 1929), 171–83.

69. Reinhold Niebuhr, "The Threat of the R.O.T.C.," *World Tomorrow* 9, no. 5 (October 1926): 154–56. On the early ROTC, see Michael S. Neiberg, *Making Citizen-Soldiers: ROTC and the Ideology of Military Service* (Cambridge: Harvard University Press, 2000), 11–34. On the Committee on Militarism in Education, see Committee on Militarism in Education Papers, Swarthmore College Peace Collection; and Chatfield, *For Peace and Justice,* 152–56. On the broader anti-ROTC campaign, see Fass, *Damned and the Beautiful,* 339–43. ROTC remained mandatory at many colleges until the 1960s; see Neiberg, *Making Citizen-Soldiers,* 54–58.

70. Sherwood Eddy and Kirby Page, *Makers of Freedom: Biographical Sketches in Social Progress* (New York: Doran, 1926), 272–82; Page, *Jesus or Christianity,* 25. On race and warfare in the twentieth century, see Niall Ferguson, *The War of the World: Twentieth-Century Conflict and the Descent of the West* (New York: Penguin, 2006).

71. Devere Allen, *The Fight for Peace* (New York: Macmillan, 1930), 462; Charles Ellwood to Kirby Page, April 14, 1921, Page Papers.

72. John Haynes Holmes, "Is America a Civilized Country?" *Community Pulpit,* Series 1922–1923, no. 14, 18; *With Head and Heart: The Autobiography of Howard Thurman* (New York: Harcourt Brace Jovanovich, 1979), 265.

73. *Character "Bad": The Story of a Conscientious Objector,* ed. Kenneth Irving Brown (New York: Harper, 1934); Edmund Chaffee to Mother, Jerusalem, June 27, 1919, Box 1, Series I, Chaffee Papers; Edmund Chaffee to George Fitch, April 11, 1921, Box 2, Series I, Chaffee Papers; Edmund Chaffee to James Nicol, April 11, 1921, Box 2, Series I, Chaffee Papers; Alden Clark to Edmund Chaffee, February 23, 1923, Box 4, Series I, Chaffee Papers; Edmund Chaffee to Clark, March 6, 1923, Box 4, Series I, Chaffee Papers; Edmund Chaffee to Harry Stock, December 29, 1924, Box 5, Series I, Chaffee Papers.

74. Reinhold Niebuhr, "Building Tomorrow's World: Missions and World Peace," *World Tomorrow* 10, no. 4 (April 1927): 170–71; Niebuhr, *Does Civilization Need Religion?,* 46.

75. On the wider crisis of American Protestant missions in the twenties, see William R. Hutchison, *Errand to the World: American Protestant Thought and Foreign Missions* (Chicago: University of Chicago Press, 1987); and Nathan D. Showalter, *The End of a Crusade: The Student Volunteer Movement for Foreign Missions and the Great War* (Lanham, MD: Scarecrow, 1998). On the Fellowship's support of Filipino independence, see Kirby Page, "The Danger of Drifting," *World Tomorrow* 10,

no. 2 (February 1927): 57–58; Kirby Page, "The Price of Philippine Independence," *World Tomorrow* 13, no. 4 (April 1930): 156–58; "Free the Philippines Now!" *World Tomorrow* 15, no. 3 (March 1932): 69–70.

76. Michel Gobat, *Confronting the American Dream: Nicaragua Under U.S. Imperial Rule* (Durham: Duke University Press, 2005); Neill Macaulay, *The Sandino Affair* (Chicago: Quadrangle, 1967).

77. On the Nicaraguan peace mission, see Paul Dekar, *Creating the Beloved Community: A Journey with the Fellowship of Reconciliation* (Telford, PA: Cascadia, 2005), 153–55; *Elbert Russell, Quaker: An Autobiography* (Jackson, TN: Friendly Press, 1956), 253–60; Charles F. Howlett, "Neighborly Concern: John Nevin Sayre and the Mission of Peace and Goodwill to Nicaragua, 1927–28," *Americas* 45 (July 1988): 19–46; Robert David Johnson, *The Peace Progressives and American Foreign Relations* (Cambridge: Harvard University Press, 1995), 126–40, 220–21; John Nevin Sayre, "A Try at Peace and Justice with Sandino," *World Tomorrow* 11, no. 3 (March 1928): 113–17.

78. Gobat, *Confronting the American Dream*, 236, 238; Macaulay, *Sandino Affair*, 84, 112–13; John Nevin Sayre, "Nicaragua: Test of the U.S.A." [1928], unpublished ms., Box 3, Series E, John Nevin Sayre Papers, Swarthmore College Peace Collection.

79. Sayre, "Try at Peace and Justice"; John Nevin Sayre diary, Box 4, Series E, Sayre Papers, Swarthmore College; Robert Cuba Jones, "The FOR-AFSC Joint Peace Mission to Nicaragua 1927–28," unpublished ms., Box 3, Series E, Sayre Papers; Johnson, *Peace Progressives*, 126–40, 220–21; Howlett, "Neighborly Concern."

80. Dana Munro to Secretary of State, December 31, 1927, Box 4, Series E, Sayre Papers; Sayre, "Try at Peace and Justice"; Howlett, "Neighborly Concern."

81. Gobat, *Confronting the American Dream*, 251–53; Macaulay, *Sandino Affair*, 95–96, 105–7, 111.

82. Sayre, "Try at Peace and Justice"; Dana Munro to Secretary of State, December 31, 1927, Sayre Papers.

83. Sayre diary, Sayre Papers; *Elbert Russell, Quaker*, 256. Partly as a result of these efforts, the American FOR formed a Latin American division under the direction of Charles Thomson.

84. "Marines Kill 14 in Nicaragua Fight," *New York Times*, January 12, 1928, http://proquest.umi.com/; Howlett, *Brookwood Labor College*, 151; [John Nevin Sayre], "Report of Western Trip of J. N. Sayre," [1928], unpublished report, Box 3, Series E, Sayre Papers; Sayre, "Try at Peace and Justice"; John Nevin Sayre, "The Making of Peace," [January 3, 1928], unpublished sermon, Box 3, Series E, Sayre Papers.

85. On Gandhi's peculiar "invisibility" in postcolonial studies, see Robert J.C. Young, *Postcolonialism: An Historical Introduction* (Malden, MA: Blackwell, 2001), 337–38.

86. Mohandas Gandhi, "The Law of Suffering," *World Tomorrow* 3, no. 9 (September 1920): 266–67; "Fellowship of Reconciliation in Conference," *Christian Century*, September 27, 1923, 1238; E. Stanley Jones to Kirby Page, February 6, 1926, Page Papers.

87. John Haynes Holmes, "Who Is the Greatest Man in the World Today?" *Community Pulpit*, Series 1920–1921, no. 19; John Haynes Holmes, *My Gandhi* (New York: Harper, 1953), 21–33; Alan Raucher, "American Anti-Imperialists and the Pro-India Movement, 1900–1932," *Pacific Historical Review* 43, no. 1 (February 1974): 83–110; Haridas Muzumdar, *Gandhi the Apostle* (Chicago: Universal, 1923), v; John Haynes Holmes to Gertrude L. Winslow, August 18, 1923, Box 4, John Haynes Holmes Papers, Library of Congress.

88. Edmund Chaffee, "Gandhi," n.d., unpublished sermon, Box 4, Series III, Chaffee Papers; John Haynes Holmes, "The World Significance of Mahatma Gandhi," *Community Pulpit*, Series 1921–1922, no. 15, 23; E. Stanley Jones, "The Soul of Mahatma Gandhi," *World Tomorrow* 7, no. 12 (December 1924): 367.

89. Gerald Studdert-Kennedy, *British Christians, Indian Nationalists, and the Raj* (New York: Oxford University Press, 1991). For an interpretation stressing the Protestant chauvinism that colored early endorsements of Gandhi, see Leilah Danielson, "'In My Extremity I Turned to Gandhi': American Pacifists, Christianity, and Gandhian Nonviolence, 1915–1941," *Church History* 72, no. 2 (June 2003): 361–88.

90. Holmes, "World Significance of Mahatma Gandhi," 9. On the debate over Christian uniqueness in this period, see Grant Wacker, "A Plural World: The Protestant Awakening to World Religions," in William R. Hutchison, ed., *Between the Times: The Travail of the Protestant Establishment in America, 1900–1960* (New York: Cambridge University Press, 1989), 253–77.

91. Holmes, "World Significance of Mahatma Gandhi," 16–19.

3. The Gandhian Moment

1. Judith M. Brown, *Gandhi and Civil Disobedience: The Mahatma in Indian Politics, 1928–1934* (New York: Cambridge University Press, 1977), 99–116; Louis Fischer, *The Life of Mahatma Gandhi* (New York: Harper, 1950), 263–75; D. G. Tendulkar, *Mahatma: Life of Mohandas Karamchand Gandhi* (Delhi: Ministry of Information and Broadcasting, Government of India, 1961), 3:20–51; Stanley Wolpert, *Gandhi's Passion: The Life and Legacy of Mahatma Gandhi* (New York: Oxford University Press, 2001), 144–51. The "great artist" quotation is in Fischer, *Life of Mahatma Gandhi*, 268.

2. Manoranhan Jha, *Civil Disobedience and After: The American Reaction to Political Developments in India During 1930–1935* (Meerut: Meenakshi Prakashan, 1973), 55, 179–80; "Indians Go to Quaker City," *New York Times*, January 27, 1931, http://proquest.umi.com/; Ferdinand Kuhn Jr., "Gandhi in Radio Plea Asks America to Aid," *New York Times*, September 14, 1931, http://proquest.umi.com/; "Text of Gandhi's Radio Speech," *New York Times*, September 14, 1931, http:// proquest.umi.com/. See also Haridas T. Muzumdar, *America's Contributions to India's Freedom* (Allahabad: Central Book Depot, 1962); and C. Seshachari, *Gandhi and the American Scene: An Intellectual History and Inquiry* (Bombay: Nachiketa, 1969). On Gandhi's importance among black Americans at this time, see

Sudarshan Kapur, *Raising Up a Prophet: The African-American Encounter with Gandhi* (Boston: Beacon, 1992). For a fascinating array of American primary documents concerning Gandhi, see Charles Chatfield, ed., *The Americanization of Gandhi: Images of the Mahatma* (New York: Garland, 1976); Chatfield's introductory essay (pp. 24–75) provides historical context.

3. John Haynes Holmes to Mohandas Gandhi, January 12, 1926, in S. P. K. Gupta, *Apostle John and Gandhi* (Ahmedabad: Navajivan, 1988), 147.

4. Gupta, *Apostle John and Gandhi*, 27–39, 145–77; Mahadev Desai, preface to *An Autobiography: The Story of My Experiments with Truth*, by Mohandas K. Gandhi (Boston: Beacon, 1993). The three volumes are C. F. Andrews, *Mahatma Gandhi's Ideas: Including Selections from His Writings* (New York: Macmillan, 1930); *Mahatma Gandhi: His Own Story*, ed. C. F. Andrews (New York: Macmillan, 1930); *Mahatma Gandhi at Work: His Own Story Continued*, ed. C. F. Andrews (New York: Macmillan, 1931).

5. Kirby Page to Mohandas Gandhi, April 21, 1931, Kirby Page Papers, Claremont School of Theology Library.

6. John Haynes Holmes, *My Gandhi* (New York: Harper, 1953), 51–55; "Gandhi to Visit Us If We Take Him Seriously; Holmes's Warning of Ridicule Deters Him," *New York Times*, October 9, 1931, http://proquest.umi.com/. On Einstein's visit, see József Illy, ed., *Albert Meets America: How Journalists Treated Genius During Einstein's 1921 Travels* (Baltimore: Johns Hopkins University Press, 2006).

7. "Gandhi to Visit Us," *New York Times*; John Haynes Holmes to Mohandas Gandhi, October 6, 1931, in *Apostle John and Gandhi*, 187.

8. Richard B. Gregg to John Nevin Sayre, July 17, 1957, Box 6, Series A, John Nevin Sayre Papers, Swarthmore College Peace Collection.

9. John M. Swomley Jr., "Richard Gregg," *Fellowship* 40, no. 4 (April 1974): 23; Mildred B. Young, "Richard B. Gregg, In Memoriam," *Friends Journal*, May 15, 1974, 303.

10. Richard B. Gregg to Ellis W. Bacon, April 9, 1934, Pendle Hill Papers, Friends Historical Library, Swarthmore College. Material on Gregg's college career is in the Harvard University Archives.

11. *Fiftieth Anniversary Report of the Harvard Class of 1907* (Cambridge, 1957), copy in Harvard University Archives; Richard B. Gregg to Ellis W. Bacon, April 9, 1934, Pendle Hill Papers.

12. On the fortunes of the labor movement in this period, see David Montgomery, *The Fall of the House of Labor: The Workplace, the State, and American Labor Activism, 1865–1925* (New York: Cambridge University Press, 1987). The progressive labor networks that Gregg worked in at this time are described in Leon Fink, *Progressive Intellectuals and the Dilemmas of Democratic Commitment* (Cambridge: Harvard University Press, 1997). On the role of Colorado Springs in the mining industry during Gregg's youth, see Elizabeth Jameson, *All That Glitters: Class, Conflict, and Community in Cripple Creek* (Urbana: University of Illinois Press, 1998).

13. Richard B. Gregg to A. J. Muste, August 18, 1940, Reel 6, *The Papers of A. J. Muste, 1920–1967* (Swarthmore College Peace Collection, Swarthmore, PA; Wilmington, DE: Scholarly Resources, 1991), microfilm.

14. Richard B. Gregg, "The National War Labor Board," *Harvard Law Review* 33, no. 1 (November 1919): 59.

15. Gregg, "National War Labor Board," 39–63; Valerie Jean Conner, *The National War Labor Board: Stability, Social Justice, and the Voluntary State in World War I* (Chapel Hill: University of North Carolina Press, 1983); Joseph A. McCartin, *Labor's Great War: The Struggle for Industrial Democracy and the Origins of Modern American Labor Relations, 1912–1921* (Chapel Hill: University of North Carolina Press, 1997).

16. Richard B. Gregg to Ellis W. Bacon, April 9, 1934, Pendle Hill Papers.

17. Montgomery, *Fall of the House of Labor*, 408.

18. On the strike, see Colin J. Davis, *Power at Odds: The 1922 National Railroad Shopmen's Strike* (Urbana: University of Illinois Press, 1997).

19. Richard B. Gregg to Ellis W. Bacon, April 9, 1934, Pendle Hill Papers.

20. Judith M. Brown, *Gandhi: Prisoner of Hope* (New Haven: Yale University Press, 1989), 7–175; Wolpert, *Gandhi's Passion*, 13–114. On *satyagraha*, see Joan Bondurant, *Conquest of Violence: The Gandhian Philosophy of Conflict* (Princeton: Princeton University Press, 1988). For Gandhi's statement, see excerpt from *Young India*, November 24, 1921, in *Collected Works of Mahatma Gandhi* (Ahmedabad: Publications Division, Ministry of Information and Broadcasting, Government of India, 1966), 21:465.

21. *Fiftieth Anniversary Report*, 272; Richard B. Gregg to W. E. B. Du Bois, November 19, 1926, Reel 18, *W. E. B. Du Bois Papers* (Sanford, NC: Microfilming Corporation of America, 1981), microfilm; Richard B. Gregg to Ellis W. Bacon, April 9, 1934, Pendle Hill Papers.

22. Richard B. Gregg, *A Preparation for Science* (Ahmedabad: Narahari Dwarkadas Parikh, [1928]), 6–9.

23. I borrow the concept of a Gandhian "countermodernity" from Robert J. C. Young, *Postcolonialism: An Historical Introduction* (Malden, MA: Blackwell, 2001), 317–34. See also the similar notion of "alternative modernity" in David Hardiman, *Gandhi in His Time and Ours: The Global Legacy of His Ideas* (New York: Columbia University Press, 2003), 66–93.

24. Gregg, *Preparation for Science*, 16.

25. On the quest for an Indian "alternative science," see Subrata Dasgupta, *Jagadis Chandra Bose and the Indian Response to Western Science* (New York: Oxford University Press, 1999); and Ashis Nandy, *Alternative Sciences: Creativity and Authenticity in Two Indian Scientists* (Bombay: Allied Publishers, 1980).

26. On Gandhi's economic ideas, see Brown, *Gandhi: Prisoner of Hope*, 176–213; Hardiman, *Gandhi in His Time and Ours*, 66–93; Wolpert, *Gandhi's Passion*, 115–26.

27. Richard B. Gregg, *Economics of Khaddar* (Madras: Ganesan, 1928), 142, 223–24. Gregg stressed the *moral* superiority of decentralized production over industrial capitalism in Richard B. Gregg, "The Morals of Machinery," *Current Thought*, February 1926, 172–79; Richard B. Gregg, "Aspects of Spiritual and Moral Beauty in Charkha and Khaddar," *Modern Review*, November 1925, 560–66.

28. Edmund B. Chaffee, "More About Gandhi," October 16, 1921, unpublished sermon, Box 5, Series III, Edmund B. Chaffee Papers, Special Collections Research Center, Syracuse University Library; [Reinhold Niebuhr], "Gandhiism Versus Socialism," *World Tomorrow* 15, no. 24 (December 1932): 607.

29. Stuart Chase and Marian Tyler, *Mexico: A Study of Two Americas* (New York: Macmillan, 1931); Henry Ford, *Today and Tomorrow* (Garden City, NY: Doubleday, Page, 1926), 135–49. On 1930s decentralist thought in general, see R. Alan Lawson, *The Failure of Independent Liberalism, 1930–1941* (New York: Putnam, 1971), 135–47; and Edward S. Shapiro, "Decentralist Intellectuals and the New Deal," *Journal of American History* 58, no. 4 (March 1972): 938–57.

30. Margaret Mead, *Coming of Age in Samoa* (New York: Morrow, 1928).

31. On "everyday resistance," see James C. Scott, *Weapons of the Weak: Everyday Forms of Peasant Resistance* (New Haven: Yale University Press, 1985); and James C. Scott, *Domination and the Arts of Resistance: Hidden Transcripts* (New Haven: Yale University Press, 1990). The literature on American slave resistance is enormous; see especially Ira Berlin, *Many Thousands Gone: The First Two Centuries of Slavery in North America* (Cambridge: Harvard University Press, 1998); and Eugene Genovese, *Roll, Jordan, Roll: The World the Slaves Made* (New York: Vintage, 1976). On African American "everyday resistance" in the twentieth century, see Robin D. G. Kelley, *Race Rebels: Culture, Politics, and the Black Working Class* (New York: Free Press, 1996).

32. William Lloyd Garrison, "Declaration of Sentiments, 1838," in Staughton Lynd and Alice Lynd, eds., *Nonviolence in America: A Documentary History*, rev. ed. (Maryknoll, NY: Orbis, 1995), 13–17; "Safety of the Non-Resistant Pledge," *Non-Resistant*, March 2, 1839, quoted in Valarie Ziegler, *The Advocates of Peace in Antebellum America* (Bloomington: Indiana University Press, 1992), 69.

33. On the "propaganda of the deed," see George Woodcock, *Anarchism: A History of Libertarian Ideas and Movements* (New York: Meridian, 1962), 18, 327–55.

34. Richard B. Gregg, *Gandhiji's Satyagraha or Non-Violent Resistance* (Madras, 1930), x; Richard B. Gregg, *The Power of Non-Violence* (Philadelphia: Lippincott, 1934), 77–78. One historian has described Gregg as "a kind of Transcendentalist"; see Charles A. Barker, introduction to *The Psychology and Strategy of Gandhi's Non-Violent Resistance*, by Richard B. Gregg (1929; repr., New York: Garland, 1972).

35. Kirby Page, *Is Mahatma Gandhi the Greatest Man of the Age?* (New York: K. Page, 1930). Niebuhr's remark appears in Reinhold Niebuhr to Kirby Page, February 13, 1932, Page Papers.

36. Gregg's three major works on nonviolence contain many passages that are identical or very similar. Where appropriate, I have cited the work quoted in the text first, then used *cf.* to indicate parallels in the other works. Gregg, *Gandhiji's Satyagraha*, xi; cf. *Power of Non-Violence*, 11.

37. Gregg, *Power of Non-Violence*, 210; Gandhi, *Autobiography*, 350. My account of Gregg's theories, especially his views of human nature, is indebted to the path-breaking analysis in Charles Chatfield, *For Peace and Justice: Pacifism in America, 1914–1941* (Knoxville: University of Tennessee Press, 1971), 202–12.

38. Gregg, *Psychology and Strategy*, 1–90; cf. Gregg, *Gandhiji's Satyagraha*, 8–79; and Gregg, *Power of Non-Violence*, 41–68.

39. Gregg, *Power of Non-Violence*, 57–58; cf. Gregg, *Gandhiji's Satyagraha*, 50–51; Edward Alsworth Ross, introduction to Clarence Marsh Case, *Non-Violent Coercion: A Study in Methods of Social Pressure* (New York: Century, 1923).

40. Gregg, *Power of Non-Violence*, 45.

41. Adam Smith, *The Theory of Moral Sentiments* (1759; repr., Amherst, NY: Prometheus, 2000), 3–5, 161–65. On this earlier debate over the nature of moral action, see Edward G. Andrew, *Conscience and Its Critics: Protestant Conscience, Enlightenment Reason, and Modern Subjectivity* (Buffalo: University of Toronto Press, 2001); and Lynn Hunt, *Inventing Human Rights: A History* (New York: Norton, 2007).

42. Gregg, *Power of Non-Violence*, 110, 99–100, 44. For more recent, less optimistic views of the power of sympathy, see Susan D. Moeller, *Compassion Fatigue: How the Media Sell Disease, Famine, War, and Death* (New York: Routledge, 1999); Kevin Rozario, "'Delicious Horrors': Mass Culture, the Red Cross, and the Appeal of Modern American Humanitarianism," *American Quarterly* 55, no. 3 (September 2003): 417–55; Susan Sontag, *Regarding the Pain of Others* (New York: Farrar, Straus and Giroux, 2003).

43. Gregg, *Power of Non-Violence*, 102.

44. Devere Allen, *The Fight for Peace* (New York: Macmillan, 1930); Gregg, *Gandhiji's Satyagraha*, 1–7; Gregg, *Psychology and Strategy*, 95. For a more recent analysis of the psychological and physical aspects of war, see Elaine Scarry, *The Body in Pain: The Making and Unmaking of the World* (New York: Oxford University Press, 1985), 60–157.

45. William James, "The Moral Equivalent of War," in Bruce W. Wilshire, ed., *William James: The Essential Writings* (Albany: State University of New York Press, 1984), 349–61.

46. Gregg, *Power of Non-Violence*, 116, 127–28.

47. Gregg, *Power of Non-Violence*, 294; cf. Gregg, *Gandhiji's Satyagraha*, 498; Richard B. Gregg to John Nevin Sayre, June 12, 1944, Box 6, Series A, Sayre Papers.

48. Gregg, *Power of Non-Violence*, 136. On values and symbols, see Edward Purcell, *The Crisis of Democratic Theory: Scientific Naturalism and the Problem of Value* (Lexington: University Press of Kentucky, 1973); and Warren Susman, "The Culture of the Thirties," in *Culture as History: The Transformation of American Society in the Twentieth Century* (New York: Pantheon, 1984), 150–83.

49. John Dewey, *Individualism Old and New* (New York: Minton, Balch, 1930), 33, 51; Richard H. Pells, *Radical Visions and American Dreams: Culture and Social Thought in the Depression Years* (Urbana: University of Illinois Press, 1998), 96–150.

50. Richard B. Gregg to Kirby Page, June 2, 1931, Page Papers.

51. On the Catholic Worker, see James Terence Fisher, *The Catholic Counterculture in America, 1933–1962* (Chapel Hill: University of North Carolina Press, 1989); Mel Piehl, *Breaking Bread: The Catholic Worker and the Origin of Catholic Radicalism in America* (Philadelphia: Temple University Press, 1982); Nancy L.

Roberts, *Dorothy Day and the* Catholic Worker (Albany: State University of New York Press, 1984).

52. Gregg, *Power of Non-Violence*, 226; cf. Gregg, *Gandhiji's Satyagraha*, 467.

53. Compare Gregg, *Power of Non-Violence*, 127; and Mohandas Gandhi, *Hind Swaraj and Other Writings*, ed. Anthony J. Parel (New York: Cambridge University Press, 1997), 94.

54. Richard B. Gregg, "Will Gandhi Win?" *Nation*, June 4, 1930, 661–63. See also Richard B. Gregg, "India Confronts Britain," *Nation*, June 18, 1930, 696–99. On the gendered aspects of radical pacifism, see Marian Mollin, *Radical Pacifism in Modern America: Egalitarianism and Protest* (Philadelphia: University of Pennsylvania Press, 2006).

55. The masterpiece of these psychoanalytic studies is Erik Erikson, *Gandhi's Truth: On the Origins of Militant Nonviolence* (New York: Norton, 1969).

56. Mohandas Gandhi to Richard B. Gregg, May 29, 1927, in *Collected Works of Mahatma Gandhi* (Ahmedabad: Publications Division, Ministry of Information and Broadcasting, Government of India, 1969), 33:396–98; Mohandas Gandhi to Richard B. Gregg, June 16, 1927, in *Collected Works of Mahatma Gandhi* (Ahmedabad: Publications Division, Ministry of Information and Broadcasting, Government of India, 1969), 34:13–14. My interpretation of Gandhi's health reforms draws heavily on Joseph S. Alter, *Gandhi's Body: Sex, Diet, and the Politics of Nationalism* (Philadelphia: University of Pennsylvania Press, 2000). On the politics of the body more generally, see Judith Butler, *Gender Trouble: Feminism and the Subversion of Identity* (New York: Routledge, 1990).

57. Richard Gregg, *Gandhism and Socialism: A Study and Comparison* (Madras: Ganesan, 1931), 27; Gregg, *Power of Non-Violence*, 60, 290, 155; Gregg, *Gandhiji's Satyagraha*, 292. Michel Foucault, *Discipline and Punish: The Birth of the Prison* (New York: Vintage, 1995). The physical beatings that nonviolent resisters courted bear an intriguing inverse relationship to the premodern punitive spectacles that Foucault has analyzed.

58. Gregg, *Power of Non-Violence*, 187. For critiques of nonviolent direct action as destructive of representative government, see Frank S. Meyer, "The Violence of Nonviolence," *National Review*, April 20, 1965, 327; and Lewis H. Van Dusen Jr., "Civil Disobedience: Destroyer of Democracy," *American Bar Association Journal* 55 (February 1969): 123–26.

59. Gregg, *Power of Non-Violence*, 151.

60. Richard B. Gregg to John Nevin Sayre, February 23, 1933, Box 6, Series A, Sayre Papers; Gregg, *Power of Non-Violence*, 152.

61. "The Browsing Reader," *Crisis*, October 1930, 341; *Fiftieth Anniversary Report*, 271.

62. Richard B. Gregg to Mary Van Kleek, March 17, 1936, Richard B. Gregg Papers, Swarthmore College Peace Collection; Sidney Hook, "Violence," in E. R. A. Seligman, ed., *Encyclopaedia of the Social Sciences* (New York: Macmillan, 1934), 15:264–67.

63. George L. Collins, "Pacifism and Social Injustice," in Devere Allen, ed., *Pacifism in the Modern World* (Garden City, NY: Doubleday, Doran, 1929), 111;

Martin Green, *New York 1913: The Armory Show and the Paterson Strike Pageant* (New York: Scribner, 1988).

64. Richard B. Gregg to Mary Van Kleek, March 17, 1936, Gregg Papers.

65. Richard B. Gregg to W. E. B. Du Bois, November 19, 1926, Reel 18, *Du Bois Papers;* and Richard B. Gregg to W. E. B. Du Bois, July 24, 1928, Reel 25, *Du Bois Papers*. Gregg's letter appears in "The Browsing Reader," *Crisis*, October 1930, 341. Charles Chatfield, because he based his discussion almost solely on the text of *The Power of Non-Violence*, erroneously claimed that Gregg "did not anticipate the use of the technique [of nonviolent action] in the American struggle for racial equality"; see Chatfield, *For Peace and Justice*, 209.

66. Devere Allen, *Fight for Peace*, 639; John Haynes Holmes, "What Is a Religious Life?" *Community Pulpit*, Series 1926–1927, no. 3, 14. On analogies between Indians and African Americans, see Daniel Immerwahr, "Caste or Colony? Indianizing Race in the United States," *Modern Intellectual History* 4, no. 2 (August 2007): 275–301.

67. On Thurman's interest in Gandhi, see Kapur, *Raising Up a Prophet*, 72–100.

68. Richard B. Gregg to W. E. B. Du Bois, November 19, 1926, Reel 18, *Du Bois Papers;* and Richard B. Gregg to W. E. B. Du Bois, July 24, 1928, Reel 25, *Du Bois Papers;* Gregg, *Gandhiji's Satyagraha*, 281, 241–43.

69. Gregg, *Gandhiji's Satyagraha*, 281.

70. *News Bulletin* 8 (July 1, 1932); Chatfield, *For Peace and Justice*, 203. A few issues of the *News Bulletin* and other documents from the American League for India's Freedom are in the Swarthmore College Peace Collection.

71. Richard B. Gregg to E. K. Hogan, January 29, 1936, Pendle Hill Papers.

72. John Nevin Sayre to Richard B. Gregg, January 26, 1942, Box 6, Series A, Sayre Papers; Rufus Jones, introduction to Gregg's *Power of Non-Violence*, 7–10; Frank C. Bancroft, "A Textbook of Revolution," review of *The Power of Non-Violence*, by Richard B. Gregg, *Christian Century*, November 7, 1934, 1414–15; Martin Ceadel, *Pacifism in Britain, 1914–1945: The Defining of a Faith* (New York: Oxford University Press, 1980), 219–20, 250–57. Huxley quoted in Alan Campbell Johnson, *Peace Offering* (London: Methuen, 1936), 154–55.

73. "Fellowship News," *Fellowship* 1, no. 2 (April 1935): 14.

74. Reinhold Niebuhr, "Militant Pacifism," review of *The Power of Non-Violence*, by Richard B. Gregg, *Nation*, December 19, 1934, 718.

4. Gandhism and Socialism

1. J. Donald Adams, "Mr. Wilder's Comedy of Virtue," review of *Heaven's My Destination*, by Thornton Wilder, *New York Times*, January 6, 1935, http://proquest.umi.com/.

2. Edmund Wilson, "Thornton Wilder in the Middle West," in *The Shores of Light: A Literary Chronicle of the 1920s and 1930s* (Boston: Northeastern University Press, 1985), 591–92.

3. Thornton Wilder, *Heaven's My Destination* (1934; repr., New York: Harper-Collins, 2003); Michael Gold, "Wilder: Prophet of the Genteel Christ," *New Republic*, October 22, 1930, 266–67. On Wilder's life and career, see Rex Burbank, *Thornton Wilder*, 2nd ed. (Boston: Twayne, 1978); and Gilbert A. Harrison, *The Enthusiast: A Life of Thornton Wilder* (New Haven: Ticknor and Fields, 1983).

4. Michael Gold, "Change the World," *Daily Worker*, October 27, 1934, 15. Gold echoed Vladimir Lenin himself, who had considered "Christian socialists" to practice "the worst variety of 'socialism,' and its worst distortion"; see Vladimir Lenin to Maxim Gorky, November 1913, in Vladimir Lenin, *Collected Works* (Moscow: Progress Publishers, 1976), 35:127–29, Marxists Internet Archive, http://www.marxists.org/. For a recent critique of pacifism in this vein, see Ward Churchill, *Pacifism as Pathology: Reflections on the Role of Armed Struggle in North America*, with Mike Ryan (Winnipeg: Arbeiter Ring, 1998).

5. For an overview of U.S. Communism in the thirties, see Harvey Klehr, *The Heyday of American Communism: The Depression Decade* (New York: Basic Books, 1984). On American Marxism more generally, see Paul Buhle, *Marxism in the United States: Remapping the History of the American Left*, rev. ed (New York: Verso, 1991).

6. On conservative anticommunism in this period, see Robert Goldstein, *Political Repression in Modern America: From 1870 to 1976* (Urbana: University of Illinois Press, 2001), 165–236; and Ellen Schrecker, *Many Are the Crimes: McCarthyism in America* (Boston: Little, Brown, 1998), 42–85.

7. Elizabeth Dilling, *The Red Network* (Chicago: Published by the Author, 1934). On Dilling's career, see Christine K. Erickson, "'I Have Not Had One Fact Disproven': Elizabeth Dilling's Crusade Against Communism in the 1930s," *Journal of American Studies* 36, no. 3 (December 2002): 473–89.

8. *Kirby Page, Social Evangelist: The Autobiography of a 20th Century Prophet for Peace*, ed. Harold E. Fey (Nyack, NY: Fellowship Press, 1975), 132. On Norris, see Barry Hankins, *God's Rascal: J. Frank Norris and the Beginnings of Southern Fundamentalism* (Lexington: University Press of Kentucky, 1996). On fundamentalism more generally, see George Marsden, *Fundamentalism and American Culture*, 2nd ed. (New York: Oxford University Press, 2006).

9. "International Red Communist and Atheist to Deliver Commencement Address at Baylor University," *Fundamentalist*, April 8, 1932; W. S. Allen to Kirby Page, April 11, 1932, and April 21, 1932, Kirby Page Papers, Claremont School of Theology Library; Kirby Page to W. S. Allen, April 14, 1932, Page Papers.

10. "Advocates the Overthrow of the Gover[n]ment by Force and Violence," *Fundamentalist*, May 27, 1932.

11. *Kirby Page, Social Evangelist*, 133; "Page Pleads for a New Civilization," *Waco Times-Herald*, June 1, 1932; W. S. Allen to Kirby Page, June 7, 1932, Page Papers.

12. Hankins, *God's Rascal*, 141; Royal H. Reisner to Kirby Page, December 11, 1937, Page Papers.

13. Kirby Page, *Jesus or Christianity: A Study in Contrasts* (Garden City, NY: Doubleday, Doran, 1929), 25; Richard Gregg to W. E. B. Du Bois, November 19,

1926, Reel 18, *W. E. B. Du Bois Papers* (Sanford, NC: Microfilming Corporation of America, 1981); "Preacher Without Authority: The Story of John Haynes Holmes," *World Tomorrow* 13, no. 3 (March 1930): 121; "A Fellowship Gathering, 1922," *News Letter*, no. 4 (September 1922).

14. Kirby Page, "The United Front," *Fellowship* 1, no. 1 (March 1935): 6–7.

15. John Haynes Holmes, "This Enormous Year (1917): Its Terrors, Tragedies, and Triumphs," *Messiah Pulpit*, February 1918, 13. For a survey of American views, see Christopher Lasch, *The American Liberals and the Russian Revolution* (New York: McGraw-Hill, 1972).

16. Anna Rochester to Devere Allen and Kirby Page, November 18, 1927, Box 2, Series C-4, Devere Allen Papers, Swarthmore College Peace Collection. On Hutchins and Rochester, see Janet Lee, *Comrades and Partners: The Shared Lives of Grace Hutchins and Anna Rochester* (Lanham, MD: Rowman and Littlefield, 2000). Some material regarding the dispute at the *World Tomorrow* is in the Allen Papers and the Page Papers.

17. These figures have received less scholarly attention than the FOR pacifists, with the exception of Harry Ward. On Ward, see Robert H. Craig, *Religion and Radical Politics: An Alternative Christian Tradition in the United States* (Philadelphia: Temple University Press, 1992), 174–228; David Nelson Duke, *In the Trenches with Jesus and Marx: Harry F. Ward and the Struggle for Social Justice* (Tuscaloosa: University of Alabama Press, 2003); Eugene P. Link, *Labor-Religion Prophet: The Times and Life of Harry F. Ward* (Boulder, CO: Westview, 1984); Donald Meyer, *The Protestant Search for Political Realism, 1919–1941,* 2nd ed. (Middletown, CT: Wesleyan University Press, 1988); Doug Rossinow, "The Radicalization of the Social Gospel: Harry F. Ward and the Search for a New Social Order, 1898–1936," *Religion and American Culture* 15, no. 1 (Winter 2005): 63–106. On Davis, see his autobiography *A Life Adventure for Peace* (New York: Citadel, 1967). On Uphaus, see his autobiography *Commitment* (New York: McGraw Hill, 1963). On Chappell, see Miriam J. Crist, "'Everybody on the Left Knew Her': Winifred L. Chappell" (MDiv thesis, Union Theological Seminary, 1979).

18. Winifred Chappell to Kirby Page, February 27, 1933, Page Papers.

19. Kirby Page to Charles Clayton Morrison, November 16, 1920, Page Papers; Kirby Page, *The Sword or the Cross: Which Should Be the Weapon of the Christian Militant?* (Chicago: Christian Century Press, 1921).

20. Kirby Page to Albert MacLeod, December 4, 1934, Page Papers. For a thoughtful comparison of Page and Ward, see Meyer, *Protestant Search*, 144–59. On Communism and the left in the thirties more generally, see Klehr, *Heyday of American Communism;* Judy Kutulas, *The Long War: The Intellectual People's Front and Anti-Stalinism, 1930–1940* (Durham: Duke University Press, 1995); Alan M. Wald, *The New York Intellectuals: The Rise and Decline of the Anti-Stalinist Left from the 1930s to the 1980s* (Chapel Hill: University of North Carolina Press, 1987); Frank A. Warren, *Liberals and Communism: The "Red Decade" Revisited* (Bloomington: Indiana University Press, 1966).

21. Sherwood Eddy to Mother and Brewer, September 12, 1923, Box 1, George Sherwood Eddy Papers, Divinity Library, Yale University. On American and

European responsibility for Russia's problems, see John Nevin Sayre, "Recognize Russia Now," *World Tomorrow* 13, no. 1 (January 1930): 8–9.

22. Sherwood Eddy, *The Challenge of Russia* (New York: Farrar and Rinehart, 1931), 157; John Haynes Holmes, "Leo Tolstoy," *Messiah Pulpit*, January 1911. Holmes's view of Russian Christianity was undoubtedly influenced by his reading of Tolstoy, who excoriated the Russian Orthodox Church in his religious writings; see Leo Tolstoy, *The Kingdom of God Is Within You*, trans. Aline Delano (1894; repr., New York: Scribner, 1911).

23. Eddy, *Challenge of Russia*, 166, 178–79. See also Sherwood Eddy, *Russia Today: What Can We Learn from It?* (New York: Farrar and Rinehart, 1934); Sherwood Eddy to Raymond Robbins, August 17, 1929, Box 2, Eddy Papers. On Eddy's American Seminars, see Rick L. Nutt, *The Whole Gospel for the Whole World: Sherwood Eddy and the American Protestant Mission* (Macon, GA: Mercer University Press, 1997), 201–17.

24. William Z. Foster, *Toward Soviet America* (New York: Coward-McCann, 1932), 316.

25. Eddy, *Challenge of Russia*, 211; Minutes of Labor Temple Committee, March 12, 1929, Box 19, Series I, Edmund B. Chaffee Papers, Special Collections Research Center, Syracuse University Library; Edmund B. Chaffee, "Do You Believe in Free Speech?" *Outlook and Independent*, May 15, 1929, 99; James S. Armstrong, "The Labor Temple, 1910–1957: A Social Gospel in Action in the Presbyterian Church" (PhD diss., University of Wisconsin, 1974), 153–55.

26. Edmund Chaffee to Lee W. Beattie, April 3, 1930, Box 22, Series I, Chaffee Papers.

27. Eddy, *Challenge of Russia*, 200; John Haynes Holmes, "What the World Owes the Bolsheviki!" *Community Pulpit*, Series 1927–1928, no. 3, 18, 22; Holmes, "America and Russia: When Shall They Be Friends?" *Community Pulpit*, Series 1927–1928, no. 7, 19–20.

28. John Haynes Holmes, letter to the editor, *New Masses*, April 20, 1937, 29; Richard B. Gregg, *Gandhiji's Satyagraha or Non-Violent Resistance* (Madras: Ganesan, 1930), 211; Richard B. Gregg, *The Power of Non-Violence* (Philadelphia: Lippincott, 1934), 260.

29. Richard Gregg to John Nevin Sayre, February 23, 1933, Box 6, Series A, John Nevin Sayre Papers, Swarthmore College Peace Collection.

30. Richard Gregg to John Nevin Sayre, February 23, 1933, Box 6, Series A, Sayre Papers; Gregg, *Power of Non-Violence*, 155; Richard Gregg to Reinhold Niebuhr, December 13, 1935, Box 48, Reinhold Niebuhr Papers, Library of Congress.

31. For another vision of cultural revolution in this period, see Michael Denning, *The Cultural Front: The Laboring of American Culture in the Twentieth Century* (New York: Verso, 1997).

32. Richard Gregg, *Gandhism and Socialism: A Study and Comparison* (Madras: Ganesan, 1931); Richard Gregg, *Gandhiism Versus Socialism* (New York: John Day, 1932); Edmund Chaffee, "Gandhi or Dynamite?" unpublished ms., Box 4, Series III, Chaffee Papers; John Haynes Holmes, "Lenin and Gandhi—Apostles of Utopia," *Community Pulpit*, Series 1927–1928, no. 5.

33. Gregg, *Gandhiism Versus Socialism*, 19; Thurman Arnold, *The Symbols of Government* (New Haven: Yale University Press, 1935); Thurman Arnold, *The Folklore of Capitalism* (New Haven: Yale University Press, 1938).

34. Gregg, *Gandhiism Versus Socialism*, 23, 7.

35. Richard Gregg to Jawaharlal Nehru, December 16, 1935, Pendle Hill Papers, Friends Historical Library, Swarthmore College.

36. 1932 poll in J. B. Matthews, *Odyssey of a Fellow Traveler* (New York: Mount Vernon, 1938), 70; 1936 poll in *Fellowship* 2, no. 8 (October 1936): 1.

37. Jo Ann Ooiman Robinson, *Abraham Went Out: A Biography of A. J. Muste* (Philadelphia: Temple University Press, 1981), 15; A. J. Muste, "Sketches for an Autobiography," in Nat Hentoff, ed., *The Essays of A. J. Muste* (New York: Simon and Schuster, 1967), 44; Page quoted in W. A. Swanberg, *Norman Thomas: The Last Idealist* (New York: Scribner, 1976), 125. On Thomas's popularity in the thirties, see Robert Cohen, *When the Old Left Was Young: Student Radicals and America's First Mass Student Movement, 1929–1941* (New York: Oxford University Press, 1993).

38. For the Fellowship's socialist vision, see Edmund Chaffee, *The Protestant Churches and the Industrial Crisis* (New York: Macmillan, 1933); and Kirby Page, *Individualism and Socialism: An Ethical Survey of Economic and Political Forces* (New York: Farrar and Rinehart, 1933). For the critique of the New Deal, see Edmund Chaffee, "Two Years of Roosevelt," unpublished ms., Box 6, Series III, Chaffee Papers. Canby reviewed Page's book in the *Book-of-the-Month Club News* (January 1934).

39. James Goodman, *Stories of Scottsboro* (New York: Pantheon, 1994); Swanberg, *Norman Thomas*, 158–63, 180–84. On the distinctions between Socialists and Rooseveltian liberals, see Frank A. Warren, *An Alternative Vision: The Socialist Party in the 1930's* (Bloomington: Indiana University Press, 1974).

40. "The Case Against Roosevelt," *World Tomorrow* 15, no. 12 (October 5, 1932): 320.

41. Chaffee, "Two Years of Roosevelt."

42. Kirby Page, "Class War and Religion," *World Tomorrow* 16, no. 10 (March 8, 1933): 228; Devere Allen to Kirby Page, August 27, 1933, Page Papers.

43. Charles F. Howlett, *Brookwood Labor College and the Struggle for Peace and Social Justice in America* (Lewiston, NY: Mellen, 1993), 109–16; "Report of Charles C. Webber, Summer 1931," Box 1, Series A-2, Section II, Fellowship of Reconciliation Papers, Swarthmore College Peace Collection.

44. On Kester and his Southern colleagues, see Craig, *Religion and Radical Politics*, 130–73; Anthony P. Dunbar, *Against the Grain: Southern Radicals and Prophets, 1929–1959* (Charlottesville: University Press of Virginia, 1981); John Egerton, *Speak Now Against the Day: The Generation Before the Civil Rights Movement in the South* (Chapel Hill: University of North Carolina Press, 1994); Robert F. Martin, *Howard Kester and the Struggle for Social Justice in the South* (Charlottesville: University Press of Virginia, 1991).

45. "Social Equality: Three Views by Southern Whites," *World Tomorrow* 9, no. 4 (April 1926): 117; Martin, *Howard Kester*, 45.

46. Dunbar, *Against the Grain*, 50; Howard Kester to Alice Kester, November 8, 1928, Series I, *Howard A. Kester Papers* (Glen Rock, NJ: Microfilming Corporation of America, 1973).

47. Howard Kester, "The Interracial Situation," October 1931, Box 1, Series A-2, Section II, FOR Papers. On African American Communism in the South, see Robin D. G. Kelley, *Hammer and Hoe: Alabama Communists During the Great Depression* (Chapel Hill: University of North Carolina Press, 1990).

48. Reinhold Niebuhr, *Leaves from the Notebook of a Tamed Cynic* (New York: Willett, Clark and Colby, 1929), 47.

49. My analysis of Niebuhr's early life and career relies heavily on Richard Fox, *Reinhold Niebuhr* (San Francisco: Harper and Row, 1987).

50. Reinhold Niebuhr, "Would Jesus Be a Modernist Today?" *World Tomorrow* 12, no. 3 (March 1929): 123; Reinhold Niebuhr, *Does Civilization Need Religion?* (New York: Macmillan, 1927). On the importance of ethics over metaphysics, see also John Haynes Holmes, "Religion's New War with Science," *Christian Century*, October 27, 1937, 1322–24; and J. B. Matthews, *Christianity the Way* (Garden City, NY: Doubleday, Doran, 1929).

51. Harry Elmer Barnes, *The Twilight of Christianity* (New York: Vanguard, 1929); Norman Thomas, "Religion at the End of an Epoch," *Christian Century*, November 4, 1931, 1375; Page, *Individualism and Socialism*, 311. In later years, Niebuhr focused more on theology; see Reinhold Niebuhr, *The Nature and Destiny of Man* (New York: Scribner, 1941).

52. Reinhold Niebuhr, *Moral Man and Immoral Society* (1932; repr., New York: Scribner, 1960), xi.

53. Robert Westbrook points out that Niebuhr's critique of Dewey happened "absent much direct engagement between the principals." See Robert B. Westbrook, *John Dewey and American Democracy* (Ithaca: Cornell University Press, 1991), 524.

54. Edmund Chaffee, "Can We Achieve an Ethical Society by Unethical Methods?" [1928], unpublished ms., Box 3, Series III, Chaffee Papers; "Summer Fellowship Conference," (1928), pamphlet in Box 15, Series I, Chaffee Papers.

55. Niebuhr, *Moral Man*, 95, 99, 107, 106.

56. Niebuhr, *Moral Man*, 117.

57. Niebuhr, *Moral Man*, 154. On Niebuhr's use of Marx, see Richard Pells, *Radical Visions and American Dreams: Culture and Social Thought in the Depression Years* (New York: Harper and Row, 1973), 140–47.

58. Norman Thomas, "Moral Man and Immoral Society," review of *Moral Man and Immoral Society*, by Reinhold Niebuhr, *World Tomorrow* 15, no. 22 (December 14, 1932): 565; Devere Allen to Reinhold Niebuhr, February 7, 1933, Box 2, Series C-4, Allen Papers.

59. Niebuhr, *Moral Man*, 95.

60. Niebuhr, *Moral Man*, 47.

61. Niebuhr, *Moral Man*, 241–49.

62. Niebuhr, *Moral Man*, 252–56.

63. Niebuhr, *Moral Man*, 179.

64. Niebuhr, *Moral Man*, 255, xv.

65. Niebuhr, *Moral Man*, 277.

66. Thomas, "Moral Man," 565; John Haynes Holmes, "Religious Defeatism," review of *Moral Man and Immoral Society*, by Reinhold Niebuhr, *New York Herald Tribune*, January 8, 1933.

67. Devere Allen to Reinhold Niebuhr, February 7, 1933, Box 2, Series C-4, Allen Papers; Thomas, "Moral Man," 565–66.

68. Edmund Chaffee to John Haynes Holmes, March 20, 1934, Box 42, Series I, Chaffee Papers.

69. Matthews's autobiography, *Odyssey of a Fellow Traveler*, describes his early career, though it is filtered through the lens of his later conservative anticommunism. See also Charles Chatfield, *For Peace and Justice: Pacifism in America, 1914–1941* (Knoxville: University of Tennessee Press, 1971), 191–97; Murray Kempton, "O'er Moor and Fen: J. B. Matthews and the Multiple Revelation," in *Part of Our Time: Some Ruins and Monuments of the Thirties* (New York: Simon and Schuster, 1955), 155–79. On Matthews's "lack of grace," see "Statement by Edward C. M. Richards Concerning the Special Council Meeting of the Fellowship of Reconciliation," March 3, 1933, Box 38, Series I, Chaffee Papers. On allegations that Matthews was a Communist in the 1930s, see John Nevin Sayre to Reinhold Niebuhr, August 21, 1953, Box 10, Series A, Sayre Papers.

70. The split is documented in Box 2, Series A-2, Section II, FOR Papers, which also contains a copy of the questionnaire. The *World Tomorrow* and the *Christian Century* carried extensive coverage, and some liberal religious and secular journals had stories as well. Scholarly accounts of the controversy include Chatfield, *For Peace and Justice*, 191–97; Fox, *Reinhold Niebuhr*, 154–59; Meyer, *Protestant Search*, 203–16. The "lonely soul" quote is from Reinhold Niebuhr to Kirby Page, December 25, 1933, quoted in Fox, *Reinhold Niebuhr*, 155.

71. Alice Kester to John Nevin Sayre, January 11, 1934, Box 9, Series A, Sayre Papers.

72. Scott H. Bennett, *Radical Pacifism: The War Resisters League and Gandhian Nonviolence in America, 1915–1963* (Syracuse: Syracuse University Press, 2003), 51–54; Warren, *Alternative Vision;* Norman Ingram, *The Politics of Dissent: Pacifism in France, 1919–1939* (New York: Oxford University Press, 1991), 153–60; Reinhold Niebuhr, "A Reorientation of Radicalism," *World Tomorrow* 16, no. 19 (July 1933): 443–44.

73. Louis Adamic, *Dynamite: The Story of Class Violence in America*, rev. ed. (New York: Viking, 1934); Norman Thomas, *As I See It* (New York: Macmillan, 1932), 56–57; Thomas, "Moral Man," 567.

74. "Annual Report of Howard Kester," October 1933, Box 2, Series A-2, Section II, FOR Papers; John Nevin Sayre to Howard Kester, October 30, 1933, Box 9, Series A, Sayre Papers. See also Dunbar, *Against the Grain*, 1–15; Martin, *Howard Kester*, 41–60.

75. Howard Kester to John Nevin Sayre, November 2, 1933, Box 9, Series A, Sayre Papers.

76. John Nevin Sayre to Howard Kester, November 21, 1933, and Howard Kester to John Nevin Sayre, January 16, 1934, Box 9, Series A, Sayre Papers.

77. Edmund Chaffee to Reinhold Niebuhr, March 3, 1933, Box 38, Series I, Chaffee Papers.

78. Richard Gregg to John Nevin Sayre, February 23, 1933, Box 6, Series A, Sayre Papers; Minutes of FOR Council Meeting, December 16, 1933, Box 2, Series A-2, Section II, FOR Papers.

79. Howard Kester to Richard Gregg, July 28, 1937, Series I, *Kester Papers;* Minutes of the FOR Council Meeting, February 5, 1935, Box 2, Series A-2, Section II, FOR Papers.

80. Fox, *Reinhold Niebuhr;* Matthews, *Odyssey of a Fellow Traveler;* Heather Warren, *Theologians of a New World Order: Reinhold Niebuhr and the Christian Realists, 1920–1948* (New York: Oxford University Press, 1997). For Matthews's later career as a Red hunter, see Schrecker, *Many Are the Crimes.*

5. Tragic Choices

1. "Annual Report of the Executive Secretary, Sept. 26, 1936–Sept. 11, 1937," Box 2, Series A-2, Section II, Fellowship of Reconciliation Papers, Swarthmore College Peace Collection; "Composite Staff Report," May 29–30, 1944, Box 2, Series A-2, Section II, FOR Papers.

2. Baldwin quoted in Nat Hentoff, *Peace Agitator: The Story of A. J. Muste* (New York: Macmillan, 1963), 115–16; James P. Cannon, *The History of American Trotskyism: Report of a Participant* (New York: Pioneer, 1944), 171; "Muste to Temple," *Time,* May 10, 1937, http://www.time.com/.

3. These events are described in A. J. Muste, "Sketches for an Autobiography," in Nat Hentoff, ed., *The Essays of A. J. Muste* (New York: Bobbs-Merrill, 1967), 1–174; Hentoff, *Peace Agitator;* Jo Ann Ooiman Robinson, *Abraham Went Out: A Biography of A. J. Muste* (Philadelphia: Temple University Press, 1981); Jo Ann Ooiman Robinson, "The Pharos of the East Side, 1937–1940: Labor Temple Under the Direction of A. J. Muste," *Journal of Presbyterian History* 48, no. 1 (1970): 18–37. On Muste's silence during the split in the FOR, see A. J. Muste to John Nevin Sayre, September 17, 1936, Box 11, Series A, John Nevin Sayre Papers, Swarthmore College Peace Collection.

4. Sidney Hook, *Out of Step: An Unquiet Life in the Twentieth Century* (New York: Harper and Row, 1987), 199.

5. A. J. Muste, "Return to Pacifism," *Christian Century,* December 2, 1936, 1605; A. J. Muste, *Non-Violence in an Aggressive World* (New York: Harper, 1940), 6.

6. Muste, "Return to Pacifism," 1604–5. On Muste's theological and political ideas at this time, see Robinson, "Pharos of the East Side."

7. Kirby Page, "The United Front," *Fellowship* 1, no. 1 (March 1935): 6–7.

8. Milton Mayer, "The Christer," *Fellowship* 18, no. 1 (January 1952): 1–2.

9. Maurice Isserman, *Which Side Were You On? The American Communist Party During the Second World War* (Urbana: University of Illinois Press, 1993); Minutes of Executive Committee Meeting, March 12, 1940, Box 2, Series A-2,

Section II, FOR Papers; Franklin D. Roosevelt, "Radio Address Before the Eighth Pan American Scientific Congress, Washington, DC," May 10, 1940, in John T. Woolley and Gerhard Peters, *The American Presidency Project,* Santa Barbara: University of California (hosted), Gerhard Peters (database), http://www.presidency .ucsb.edu/ws/?pid = 15948.

10. Reinhold Niebuhr, "Why the Christian Church Is Not Pacifist," in *Christianity and Power Politics* (1940; repr., n.p.: Archon, 1969), 1–32. On the debates over the war within American Christianity, see Gerald L. Sittser, *A Cautious Patriotism: The American Churches and the Second World War* (Chapel Hill: University of North Carolina Press, 1997).

11. Guy Hershberger, *War, Peace, and Nonresistance* (Scottdale, PA: Herald, 1944).

12. Richard Wightman Fox, *Reinhold Niebuhr: A Biography* (San Francisco: Harper and Row, 1987), 132–34; Kirby Page, "Is Coercion Ever Justifiable?" *World Tomorrow* 15, no. 6 (June 1932): 173–75; John Nevin Sayre, "Why We Are Squeamish," *World Tomorrow* 15, no. 7 (July 1932): 214.

13. Sherwood Eddy to Kirby Page, October 15, 1935, Kirby Page Papers, Claremont School of Theology Library; Sherwood Eddy to family, October 28, 1935, Page Papers; Kirby Page to Sherwood Eddy, October 30, 1935, Page Papers.

14. "News from the Field," *Fellowship* 7, no. 6 (June 1941): 93. *Kirby Page, Social Evangelist: The Autobiography of a 20th Century Prophet for Peace,* ed. Harold E. Fey (Nyack, NY: Fellowship Press, 1975), 110.

15. Sherwood Eddy form letter, June 9, 1942, Box 2, George Sherwood Eddy Papers, Divinity Library, Yale University; Sherwood Eddy, *Eighty Adventurous Years* (New York: Harper, 1955), 110. On Eddy's move away from pacifism, see Rick L. Nutt, *The Whole Gospel for the Whole World: Sherwood Eddy and the American Protestant Mission* (Macon, GA: Mercer University Press, 1997), 284–94. In fact, Page did write a biography of Eddy, but it was never published; meanwhile, Eddy lived long enough to publish his own memoir.

16. John Haynes Holmes to Norman Thomas, December 28, 1936, Box 186, John Haynes Holmes Papers, Library of Congress; "We Will Not Fight in Spain: Statement of Executive Committee Fellowship of Reconciliation on Socialist Party Recruiting for Spanish War," *Fellowship* 3, no. 1 (January 1937): 10; "Norman Thomas Replies: Socialist Party Head Answers F.O.R. Indictment of Debs Column," *Fellowship* 3, no. 2 (February 1937): 13. On this controversy, see Scott H. Bennett, *Radical Pacifism: The War Resisters League and Gandhian Nonviolence in America, 1915–1963* (Syracuse: Syracuse University Press, 2003), 50–68; W. A. Swanberg, *Norman Thomas: The Last Idealist* (New York: Scribner, 1976), 210–13; Frank Warren, *An Alternative Vision: The Socialist Party in the 1930's* (Bloomington: Indiana University Press, 1974), 152–57.

17. Howard H. Brinton, "Pacifist Not Isolationist," *Fellowship* 6, no. 6 (June 1940): 91; Carl Hermann Voss, *Rabbi and Minister: The Friendship of Stephen S. Wise and John Haynes Holmes* (Cleveland: World, 1964), 308; A. J. Muste to Lucille B. Milner, October 30, 1940, Reel 6, *The Papers of A. J. Muste, 1920–1967*

(Swarthmore College Peace Collection, Swarthmore, PA; Wilmington, DE: Scholarly Resources, 1991), microfilm. On isolationism, see Manfred Jonas, *Isolationism in America, 1935–1941* (Chicago: Imprint Publications, 1990).

18. "The Course Before Us: Statement of F.O.R. Executive Committee, December 10, 1941," *Fellowship* 8, no. 1 (January 1942): 2; John Haynes Holmes and Reginald Lawrence, *If This Be Treason* (New York: Macmillan, 1935); John Haynes Holmes, *Out of Darkness* (New York: Harper, 1942); A. J. Muste to Caleb Foote, May 9, 1944, Box 2, Series A-3, Section II, FOR Papers; Hentoff, *Peace Agitator*, 144.

19. Hook, *Out of Step*, 201; John Haynes Holmes, "From My Standpoint," *Fellowship* 8, no. 8 (August 1942): 126.

20. John Haynes Holmes to Sherwood Eddy, October 17, 1939, Box 188, Holmes Papers; Ralph Harlow to A. J. Muste, August 5, 1949, Box 2, Eddy Papers.

21. Richard Gregg, "The Next Two Years," *Fellowship* 5, no. 5 (May 1939): 4–5. On fears of a fascist America, see Benjamin Alpers, *Dictators, Democracy, and American Public Culture: Envisioning the Totalitarian Enemy, 1920s–1950s* (Chapel Hill: University of North Carolina Press, 2003); Alan Brinkley, *The End of Reform: New Deal Liberalism in Recession and War* (New York: Knopf, 1995); R. Alan Lawson, *The Failure of Independent Liberalism, 1930–1941* (New York, 1971), 91–95; Leo Ribuffo, *The Old Christian Right: The Protestant Far Right from the Great Depression to the Cold War* (Philadelphia: Temple University Press, 1983).

22. Hook, *Out of Step*, 201. On pacifist moral reasoning, see Cynthia Eller, *Conscientious Objectors and the Second World War: Moral and Religious Arguments in Support of Pacifism* (New York: Praeger, 1991), 121–53. On the Socialist Party's critique of World War II, which paralleled that of the pacifists in many ways, see Warren, *Alternative Vision*, 158–75.

23. Harold Fey, "Again the Merchant of Death," *Fellowship* 6, no. 3 (March 1940): 44. On the "Arsenal of Democracy," see David Kennedy, *Freedom from Fear: The American People in Depression and War, 1929–1945* (New York: Oxford University Press, 1999).

24. A. J. Muste, "U.S.A.—Arsenal," *Fellowship* 7, no. 4 (April 1941): 59–60.

25. "Statement on Far Eastern Situation by the 1938 Conference of the Fellowship of Reconciliation," *Fellowship* 4, no. 8 (October 1938): 2; "A Statement by the Council of the Fellowship or Reconciliation: Foreign Policy and Neutrality Legislation," *Fellowship* 5, no. 3 (March 1939): 14–15. On the liberal view of the war as a democratic revolution, see Frank A. Warren, *Noble Abstractions: American Liberal Intellectuals and World War II* (Columbus: Ohio State University Press, 1999).

26. R. Alfred Hassler, "Slaughter of the Innocent," *Fellowship* 10, no. 2 (February 1944): 19–21.

27. Vera Brittain, "Massacre by Bombing," *Fellowship* 10, no. 3/2 (March 1944); John Nevin Sayre, "American Postscript," *Fellowship* 10, no. 3/2 (March 1944): 63–64. For the final version of Brittain's tract, see Vera Brittain, *Seed of Chaos: What Mass Bombing Really Means* (London: New Vision, 1944).

28. Franklin D. Roosevelt, "An Appeal to Great Britain, France, Italy, Germany, and Poland to Refrain from Air Bombing of Civilians," September 1, 1939,

in John T. Woolley and Gerhard Peters, *The American Presidency Project*, Santa Barbara: University of California (hosted), Gerhard Peters (database), http://www .presidency.ucsb.edu/ws/?pid = 15797.

29. "Obliteration Raids on German Cities Protested in U.S.," *New York Times*, March 6, 1944, http://proquest.umi.com/; Walter Lippmann, "The War in the Air," *New York Herald Tribune*, March 11, 1944; Reinhold Niebuhr, "Is the Bombing Necessary?" *Christianity and Crisis*, April 3, 1944, 1–2. On American bombing strategy, see Conrad C. Crane, *Bombs, Cities, and Civilians: American Airpower Strategy in World War II* (Lawrence: University Press of Kansas, 1993); and Ronald Schaffer, *Wings of Judgment: American Bombing in World War II* (New York: Oxford University Press, 1985). For a recent attempt to revive the moral debate over area bombing, see A. C. Grayling, *Among the Dead Cities: The History and Moral Legacy of the WWII Bombing of Civilians in Germany and Japan* (New York: Walker, 2006).

30. Niebuhr, "Is the Bombing Necessary?" 1; Sayre, "American Postscript," 63–64.

31. Lippmann, "War in the Air"; Bayard Rustin, Report of Youth Secretary, September 12, 1942, Box 3, Series A-2, Section II, FOR Papers.

32. Kirby Page, *Jesus or Christianity: A Study in Contrasts* (Garden City, NY: Doubleday, Doran, 1929), 136; Voss, *Rabbi and Minister*; John M. Swomley to Dixon Miyauchi, October 1, 1942, Box 16, Series E, Section II, FOR Papers.

33. Mohandas Gandhi, "The Jews," *Harijan* 6, no. 42 (November 26, 1938): 352; see also Mohandas Gandhi, "Jews in a World of Violence: A Symposium, I: 'Death Has No Terror,'" *Jewish Frontier*, March 1939, 9–11. John Haynes Holmes, "Should Jews Be Pacifists?" *Opinion*, September 1940, 6–8; Hayim Greenberg, "Jews in a World of Violence: A Symposium, II: We Are Treated As Subhumans—We Are Asked to Be Superhuman," *Jewish Frontier*, March 1939, 11–15. On the context of Gandhi's ideas about World War II, see Louis Fischer, *The Life of Mahatma Gandhi* (New York: Harper, 1950), 341–49.

34. John Nevin Sayre, "Some I Can Save," *Fellowship* 4, no. 9 (November 1938): 4–5; see also the material on Sayre's refugee work in Box 13, Series E, Sayre Papers.

35. Donald Meyer, *The Protestant Search for Political Realism, 1919–1941*, 2nd ed. (Middletown, CT: Wesleyan University Press, 1988).

36. J. Holmes Smith, "Why J. Holmes Smith Registered," *Conscientious Objector*, March 1942, 3; George Houser, "Reflections of a Religious War Objector (Half a Century Later)," in Larry Gara and Lenna Mae Gara, eds., *A Few Small Candles: War Resisters of World War II Tell Their Stories* (Kent: Kent State University Press, 1999), 130–51.

37. For an early endorsement of the Catholic Worker movement by the FOR, see A. J. Muste, "Catholic Workers Unite," *Fellowship* 3, no. 6 (June 1937): 5–6. Farmer describes himself as a "humanist" in James Farmer, *Lay Bare the Heart: An Autobiography of the Civil Rights Movement* (New York: Arbor, 1985), 172. On Foote's atheism, see Eller, *Conscientious Objectors*, 104.

38. Henry David Thoreau, "Resistance to Civil Government" (1849), repr. in David A. Hollinger and Charles Capper, eds., *The American Intellectual Tradition*, 5th ed. (New York: Oxford University Press, 2006), 1:401–14.

39. Richard B. Gregg, *Training for Peace: A Program for Peace Workers* (Philadelphia: Lippincott, 1937). On Gregg's vision, see also Patricia Faith Appelbaum, "The Legions of Good Will: The Religious Culture of Protestant Pacifism, 1918–1963" (PhD diss., Boston University, 2001), 201–14. On the "cell" idea in left-leaning Christian social thought during this period, see Eugene McCarraher, *Christian Critics: Religion and the Impasse in Modern American Social Thought* (Ithaca: Cornell University Press, 2000), 57–88. On the meanings of religious ritual, see Clifford Geertz, "Religion as a Cultural System," in *The Interpretation of Cultures: Selected Essays* (New York: Basic Books, 1973), 87–125.

40. Richard Gregg to A. J. Muste, August 4, 1940, and September 5, 1940, Reel 6, *Papers of A. J. Muste;* Richard Gregg to Francis Biddle, September 5, 1940, Reel 6, *Papers of A. J. Muste.*

41. Mulford Q. Sibley and Philip E. Jacob, *Conscription of Conscience: The American State and the Conscientious Objector, 1940–1947* (Ithaca: Cornell University Press, 1952); Perry Bush, *Two Kingdoms, Two Loyalties: Mennonite Pacifism in Modern America* (Baltimore: Johns Hopkins University Press, 1998), 56–128; Hershberger, *War, Peace, and Nonresistance.* Not all peace church members refused to fight in World War II. A large percentage of drafted Quakers, Brethren, and Mennonites joined the military; see Sibley and Jacob, *Conscription of Conscience,* 19–43.

42. On the Union Eight, see Andrew E. Hunt, *David Dellinger: The Life and Times of a Nonviolent Revolutionary* (New York: New York University Press, 2006), 37–61; James Tracy, *Direct Action: Radical Pacifism from the Union Eight to the Chicago Seven* (Chicago: University of Chicago Press, 1996), 1–46; Houser, "Reflections of a Religious War Objector"; George Houser, interview by author, April 21, 2007.

43. Sibley and Jacob, *Conscription of Conscience,* 156–60.

44. John Haynes Holmes to Frank Olmstead, December 16, 1942, Box 7, Series A, Sayre Papers; Holmes, "From My Standpoint" column in the following issues of *Fellowship:* September 1942, January 1943, April 1943, August 1943. For the editors' rebuttal, see "An Open Letter to John Haynes Holmes," *Fellowship* 9, no. 9 (September 1943): 167.

45. *The Radical "No": The Correspondence and Writings of Evan Thomas on War,* ed. Charles Chatfield (New York: Garland, 1974); Muste, "Sketches for an Autobiography," 79–80.

46. Evan Thomas to A. J. Muste, November 18, 1940, Reel 6, *Papers of A. J. Muste.*

47. Evan Thomas to FOR National Council, September 14, 1944, Box 3, Series A-2, Section II, FOR Papers; Evan Thomas, "CPS and the Second Mile," *Fellowship* 10, no. 2 (February 1944): 28.

48. A. J. Muste, "The First and Fourth of July," *Fellowship* 7, no. 6 (July 1941): 115–16; A. J. Muste, "Comments on General Perspective and Program," April 10, 1942, Box 3, Series A-2, Section II, FOR Papers; "Extension of Draft," *Fellowship* 8, no. 2 (February 1942): 28.

49. Minutes of FOR National Council Meeting, December 6, 1943, Box 3, Series A-2, Section II, FOR Papers; Evan Thomas to FOR National Council, September 14, 1944, Box 3, Series A-2, Section II, FOR Papers; A. J. Muste, "Fellowship

in Discovering Truth," *Fellowship* 10, no. 9 (November 1944): 188–89; "FOR Changes Its Relationship to NSBRO," *Fellowship* 11, no. 1 (January 1945): 11.

50. "Excerpts from Letter to Doris Grotewohl from Eleanor Clark, May 3, 1944," and "Excerpts from Letter to Doris Grotewohl from Bayard Rustin, May 5, 1944," Reel 1, *Bayard Rustin Papers, 1942–1987* (Library of Congress; Frederick, MD: University Publications of America, 1988), microfilm. On Rustin's wartime experiences, see Jervis Anderson, *Bayard Rustin: Troubles I've Seen* (New York: HarperCollins, 1997), 99–108; John D'Emilio, *Lost Prophet: The Life and Times of Bayard Rustin* (New York: Free Press, 2003), 72–120; Daniel Levine, *Bayard Rustin and the Civil Rights Movement* (New Brunswick: Rutgers University Press, 2000), 40–48. On Civilian Public Service camps and prisons as laboratories for nonviolence, see Scott H. Bennett, *Radical Pacifism: The War Resisters League and Gandhian Nonviolence in America, 1915–1963* (Syracuse: Syracuse University Press, 2003), 69–133; Gretchen Lemke-Santangelo, "The Radical Conscientious Objectors of World War II: Wartime Experience and Postwar Activism," *Radical History Review* 45 (Fall 1989): 5–29; Patricia McNeal, *Harder Than War: Catholic Peacemaking in Twentieth-Century America* (New Brunswick: Rutgers University Press, 1992), 49–70; Sibley and Jacob, *Conscription of Conscience;* Tracy, *Direct Action,* 1–46; Lawrence Wittner, *Rebels Against War: The American Peace Movement, 1933–1983* (Philadelphia: Temple University Press, 1984), 62–96.

51. John Nevin Sayre to A. J. Muste, October 21, 1942, Box 4, Series A-3, Section II, FOR Papers. On Smiley, see Margaret Cavin, "Glenn Smiley Was a Fool: The Use of the Comic as a Strategy of Nonviolence," *Peace and Change* 26, no. 2 (April 2001): 223–42. On the wartime masculine ideal, see Steve Estes, *I Am a Man! Race, Manhood, and the Civil Rights Movement* (Chapel Hill: University of North Carolina Press, 2005), 11–38; Christina Jarvis, *The Male Body at War: American Masculinity During World War II* (DeKalb: Northern Illinois University Press, 2004). On pacifism and gender during World War II, see Rachel Waltner Goossen, *Women Against the Good War: Conscientious Objection and Gender on the American Home Front, 1941–1947* (Chapel Hill: University of North Carolina Press, 1997); and Marian Mollin, *Radical Pacifism in Modern America: Egalitarianism and Protest* (Philadelphia: University of Pennsylvania Press, 2006), 9–43.

52. Glenn Smiley, "Calendar of Exile," unpublished ms., Box 2, Series A-1, Section II, FOR Papers. On the Union Eight softball team, see Houser, "Reflections of a Religious War Objector"; and Hunt, *David Dellinger,* 57–60.

53. "A Statement by the Council of the Fellowship of Reconciliation: Foreign Policy and Neutrality Legislation"; "Report of John Nevin Sayre, September 1940 to December 1940," Box 2, Series A-2, Section II, FOR Papers.

54. See Michael C. C. Adams, *The Best War Ever: America and World War II* (Baltimore: Johns Hopkins University Press, 1994), 20–42; and Greg Robinson, *By Order of the President: FDR and the Internment of Japanese Americans* (Cambridge: Harvard University Press, 2001), 8–44.

55. John W. Dower, *War Without Mercy: Race and Power in the Pacific War* (New York: Pantheon, 1986); Glenn Smiley, *F.O.R. Facts and Figures* 2, no. 5 (June 27, 1944), Reel 2, *Rustin Papers.*

56. A typical FOR condemnation of the internment is Kirby Page, "Empty the Relocation Centers!" *Christian Century*, June 16, 1943, 715–16.

57. John M. Swomley, *Confronting Systems of Violence: Memoirs of a Peace Activist* (Nyack, NY: Fellowship Publications, 1998), 19–20. See also the material on resettlement work in Box 9, Series E, Sayre Papers; for instance, Dorothy A. Nyland to John Nevin Sayre, May 13, 1943. On Perry Saito, see Klancy Clark de Nevers, *The Colonel and the Pacifist: Karl Bendetsen, Perry Saito, and the Incarceration of Japanese Americans During World War II* (Salt Lake City: University of Utah Press, 2004).

58. Caleb Foote, *Outcasts! The Story of America's Treatment of Her Japanese-American Minority* (New York: Fellowship of Reconciliation, [1943?]); Linda Hamalian, *A Life of Kenneth Rexroth* (New York: Norton, 1991), 102–29.

59. For the "concentration camp" approach, see Roger Daniels, *Concentration Camps USA: Japanese Americans and World War II* (New York: Holt, Rinehart and Winston, 1971). On the problems of terminology, see Robinson, *By Order of the President*, 260–61. On the attitudes of American churches toward internment, see Sittser, *Cautious Patriotism*, 169–78. On the widespread religious and secular opposition, see Robert Shaffer, "Cracks in the Consensus: Defending the Rights of Japanese Americans During World War II," *Radical History Review* 72 (Fall 1998): 84–120.

60. This account of the Hirabayashi case relies heavily on Peter Irons, *Justice at War: The Story of the Japanese American Internment Cases* (Berkeley: University of California Press, 1983).

61. John Nevin Sayre to Gordon Hirabayashi, November 9, 1942, Reel 2, *Rustin Papers*.

62. Irons, *Justice at War*, 250–51; "45 Years Later, An Apology from the U.S. Government," *Newsletter of the University of Washington College of Arts and Sciences*, Winter 2000, http://www.artsci.washington.edu/.

63. Smiley, "Calendar of Exile," FOR Papers. On the conscription of Japanese Americans, see Eric L. Muller, *Free to Die for Their Country: The Story of the Japanese American Draft Resisters in World War II* (Chicago: University of Chicago Press, 2001). On Foote, see Eller, *Conscientious Objectors*, 35.

64. Hideo Hashimoto form letter, February 8, 1943, Box 9, Series E, Sayre Papers; Muller, *Free to Die*, 49.

65. Hideo Hashimoto to John Nevin Sayre, March 10, 1943, Box 9, Series E, Sayre Papers; Caleb Foote to John Nevin Sayre, June 1, 1942, Box 9, Series E, Sayre Papers; John Nevin Sayre to Caleb Foote, June 3, 1942, Box 9, Series E, Sayre Papers.

66. William Meyer to John Nevin Sayre, May 31, 1942, Box 9, Series E, Sayre Papers; "Gifts to Nisei Children Arouse Town's Ire," *Fellowship* 9, no. 2 (February 1943): 36. On the unrest at the Poston camp, see Muller, *Free to Die*, 40, 44.

67. Caleb Foote to Paul Comly French, October 15, 1942, Reel 2, *Rustin Papers*.

68. Royden Susu-Mago to John Swomley, December 16, 1942, and Florence Sato to John Swomley, April 8, 1943, Reel 2, *Rustin Papers*.

69. *I Speak for Myself: The Autobiography of John Haynes Holmes* (New York: Harper, 1959), 198.

70. Anderson, *Bayard Rustin*, 1–77; D'Emilio, *Lost Prophet*, 7–38.

71. On Farmer's career, see Leilah Danielson, "The 'Two-Ness' of the Movement: James Farmer, Nonviolence, and Black Nationalism," *Peace and Change* 29, no. 3–4 (July 2004): 431–52; and Farmer, *Lay Bare the Heart*.

72. *With Head and Heart: The Autobiography of Howard Thurman* (New York: Harcourt Brace Jovanovich, 1979), 265–66.

73. Farmer, *Lay Bare the Heart*, 84–86.

74. Farmer, *Lay Bare the Heart*, 112.

75. Krishnalal Shridharani, *War Without Violence: A Study of Gandhi's Method and Its Accomplishments* (New York: Harcourt, Brace, 1939), 315. On Shridharani's life, see Krishnalal Shridharani, *My India, My America* (New York: Duell, Sloan and Pearce, 1941).

76. Shridharani, *My India, My America*, 276; Shridharani, *War Without Violence*, 220–47. The "Hollywood" quote is on p. 230.

77. Muste was disappointed by Shridharani's rejection of absolute pacifism. See A. J. Muste, review of *My India, My America*, by Krishnalal Shridharani, *Fellowship* 7, no. 12 (December 1941), 194; and Shridharani's reply: "Has Not Renounced Satyagraha," *Fellowship* 8, no. 1 (January 1942): 15.

78. James Farmer, "The Race Logic of Pacifism," *Fellowship* 8, no. 2 (February 1942): 24–25.

79. See Estes, *I Am a Man!* 11–38; Lauren Rebecca Sklaroff, "Constructing G.I. Joe Louis: Cultural Solutions to the 'Negro Problem' During World War II," *Journal of American History* 89, no. 3 (December 2002): 958–83; Ronald Takaki, *Double Victory: A Multicultural History of America in World War II* (Boston: Little, Brown, 2000); Timothy B. Tyson, *Radio Free Dixie: Robert F. Williams and the Roots of Black Power* (Chapel Hill: University of North Carolina Press, 1999).

80. Bayard Rustin, "The Negro and Non-Violence," *Fellowship* 8, no. 10 (October 1942): 166–67.

81. Farmer, "Race Logic of Pacifism."

82. Lucy G. Barber, *Marching on Washington: The Forging of an American Political Tradition* (Berkeley: University of California Press, 2002), 108–40; Paula F. Pfeffer, *A. Philip Randolph: Pioneer of the Civil Rights Movement* (Baton Rouge: Louisiana State University Press, 1990), 45–168; Cynthia Taylor, *A. Philip Randolph: The Religious Journey of an African American Labor Leader* (New York: New York University Press, 2006), 128–75.

83. Minutes of FOR Executive Committee, February 21, 1943, Box 3, Series A-2, Section II, FOR Papers. On the Gandhian turn in the March on Washington Movement, see A. Philip Randolph, "Randolph Tells Technique of Civil Disobedience," *Chicago Defender*, June 26, 1943, http://proquest.umi.com/.

84. Glenn Smiley to A. J. Muste, February 13, 1943, Box 4, Series A-3, Section II, FOR Papers; Minutes of FOR Executive Committee, January 12, 1943, Box 3, Series A-2, Section II, FOR Papers.

85. Minutes of FOR Executive Committee, September 14, 1943, Box 3, Series A-2, Section II, FOR Papers; Anderson, *Bayard Rustin*, 83–87.

86. Bayard Rustin to Local Board No. 63, November 16, 1943, Reel 1, *Rustin Papers*.

87. J. Holmes Smith, "A Missionary Leaves India," *Christian Century*, April 10, 1940, 485; Haridas T. Muzumdar, *America's Contributions to India's Freedom* (Allahabad: Central Book Depot, 1962), 7; Smith, "Why J. Holmes Smith Registered"; Minutes of FOR Executive Committee, February 11, 1941, Box 3, Series A-2, Section II, FOR Papers; J. Holmes Smith, "Non-Violent Direct Action," *Fellowship* 7, no. 12 (December 1941): 207; Shridharani, *My India, My America*, 304.

88. "Memo on the Pilgrimage to the Lincoln Memorial," attachment to Minutes of FOR Executive Committee, May 12, 1942, Box 3, Series A-2, Section II, FOR Papers; "Interracial Group Marches to Washington," *Fellowship* 8, no. 11 (November 1942): 192.

89. Conrad Lynn, *There Is a Fountain: The Autobiography of a Civil Rights Lawyer* (Westport, CT: Lawrence Hill, 1979), 84–91.

90. On E. Stanley Jones's Christian ashram, see Serena G. Shapleigh, letter, *Fellowship* 1, no. 5 (September 1935): 2; and E. Stanley Jones, "I Join the Fellowship," *Fellowship* 6, no. 10 (December 1940): 150. On the Newark Ashram, see David Dellinger, *From Yale to Jail: The Life Story of a Moral Dissenter* (New York: Pantheon, 1993); and Hunt, *David Dellinger*, 37–83.

91. Swomley, *Confronting Systems of Violence*, 15–16; J. Holmes Smith, "Our New York Ashram," *Fellowship* 7, no. 1 (January 1941): 2; John Swomley, "Youth News and Plans," *Fellowship* 7, no. 4 (April 1941): 63; Donovan E. Smucker, Report of Youth Secretary, September 1939 to September 1940, Box 2, Series A-2, Section II, FOR Papers.

92. On the founding of CORE, see August Meier and Elliott Rudwick, *CORE: A Study in the Civil Rights Movement, 1942–1968* (New York: Oxford University Press, 1973), 1–39. Farmer has argued that the Meier and Rudwick account understates the influence of his Brotherhood Mobilization proposal; see Farmer, *Lay Bare the Heart*, 104. It is probably fruitless to try to untangle the intricacies of CORE's founding. Clearly, both the activities of the Chicago FOR cell and the Farmer prospectus played central roles.

93. Meier and Rudwick, *CORE*, 1–39; Farmer, *Lay Bare the Heart*, 101–16.

94. James Farmer to A. J. Muste, February 19, 1942, repr. in Farmer, *Lay Bare the Heart*, 355–60; Minutes of FOR Council, April 11, 1942, Box 3, Series A-2, Section II, FOR Papers.

95. Meier and Rudwick, *CORE*, 6.

96. Houser, interview by author, April 21, 2007.

97. Farmer, *Lay Bare the Heart*, 90–108.

98. Hershberger, *War, Peace, and Nonresistance*, 229.

6. The Age of Conscience

1. Robert L. Cannon to Alfred Hassler and Glenn E. Smiley, October 3, 1956, in Clayborne Carson, ed., *Papers of Martin Luther King, Jr.* (Berkeley: University

of California Press, 1997), 3:388–91; *Walk to Freedom* (Fellowship of Reconciliation, 1956; Colorlab, 2002). Videocassette copy in Swarthmore College Peace Collection.

2. Dwight Macdonald, *The Root Is Man* (1946; repr., New York: Autonomedia, 1995), 147.

3. Lewis Mumford, "Program for Survival," in *Values for Survival* (New York: Harcourt, Brace, 1946), 78–130. For the influence of atomic weapons on cultural and intellectual life, see Paul Boyer, *By the Bomb's Early Light: American Thought and Culture at the Dawn of the Atomic Age* (Chapel Hill: University of North Carolina Press, 1994). On the origins of the antinuclear movement, see Lawrence S. Wittner, *One World or None: A History of the World Nuclear Disarmament Movement Through 1953*, vol. 1 of *The Struggle Against the Bomb* (Stanford: Stanford University Press, 1993).

4. "The Use of the Atomic Bomb," *Fellowship* 11, no. 9 (September 1945): 161.

5. "Use of the Atomic Bomb," 161.

6. Jonathan Schell has argued that, because nuclear warfare was unthinkable, Cold War military strategy relied heavily on its own kind of nonviolence, using threats, belligerent rhetoric, and symbolic displays of strength as psychological weapons. See Jonathan Schell, *The Unconquerable World: Power, Nonviolence, and the Will of the People* (New York: Metropolitan, 2003), 47–62.

7. A. J. Muste, *Not By Might: Christianity: The Way to Human Decency* (New York: Harper, 1947), 89. Paul Boyer calls *Not By Might* the "most powerful statement of the post-Hiroshima case for pacifism"; see Boyer, *By the Bomb's Early Light*, 219. See also Leilah Danielson, "Christianity, Dissent, and the Cold War: A. J. Muste's Challenge to Realism and U.S. Empire," *Diplomatic History* 30, no. 4 (September 2006): 645–69.

8. Muste, *Not By Might*, 54, 84–85.

9. Muste, *Not By Might*, 47; A. J. Muste, "Theology of Despair: An Open Letter to Reinhold Niebuhr," *Fellowship* 14, no. 8 (September 1948): 4–8.

10. Muste, *Not By Might*, 47. For a classic example of Christian existentialism in this period, see Paul Tillich, *The Courage to Be* (1952; repr., New Haven: Yale University Press, 2000). On the history of American existentialism, see George Cotkin, *Existential America* (Baltimore: Johns Hopkins University Press, 2003); and Doug Rossinow, *The Politics of Authenticity: Liberalism, Christianity, and the New Left in America* (New York: Columbia University Press, 1998).

11. Muste, *Not by Might*, 20–38. On the enthusiasm for "one world," see Wittner, *One World or None*.

12. Caleb Foote, "Politics and Freedom," *Fellowship* 14, no. 9 (October 1948): 13–16: Don Leiffer, letter to the editor, *Fellowship* 14, no. 11 (December 1948): 30. On the 1948 campaigns, see Mark Kleinman, *A World of Hope, a World of Fear: Henry A. Wallace, Reinhold Niebuhr, and American Liberalism* (Columbus: Ohio State University Press, 2000).

13. "Group Here Burns Many Draft Cards," *New York Times*, February 13, 1947, http://proquest.umi.com/; "Two Hundred Join Demonstrations Protesting Peacetime Draft," *Fellowship* 13, no. 4 (April 1947): 64; Robert Cooney and

Helen Michalowski, eds., *The Power of the People: Active Nonviolence in the United States* (Culver City, CA: Peace Press, 1977), 113; James Tracy, *Direct Action: Radical Pacifism from the Union Eight to the Chicago Seven* (Chicago: University of Chicago Press, 1996), 63–65; Lawrence S. Wittner, *Rebels Against War: The American Peace Movement, 1933–1983* (Philadelphia: Temple University Press, 1984), 162–64.

14. On Civil Defense, see Dee Garrison, *Bracing for Armageddon: Why Civil Defense Never Worked* (New York: Oxford University Press, 2006); and Guy Oakes, *The Imaginary War: Civil Defense and American Cold War Culture* (New York: Oxford University Press, 1994).

15. On the Civil Defense protests, see "Pacifists Demonstrate, Educate on CD Day," *Fellowship* 21, no. 7 (July 1955): 24–25; Scott H. Bennett, *Radical Pacifism: The War Resisters League and Gandhian Nonviolence in America, 1915–1963* (Syracuse: Syracuse University Press, 2003), 207–16; Garrison, *Bracing for Armageddon;* Dee Garrison, "'Our Skirts Gave Them Courage': The Civil Defense Protest Movement in New York City, 1955–1961," in Joanne Meyerowitz, ed., *Not June Cleaver: Women and Gender in Postwar America, 1945–1960* (Philadelphia: Temple University Press, 1994), 201–26; Maurice Isserman, *If I Had a Hammer: The Death of the Old Left and the Birth of the New Left* (New York: Basic Books, 1987), 144–47; Wittner, *Rebels Against War,* 264–66.

16. Anyway, Eisenhower said *something* like this; for the controversy, see Patrick Henry, "'And I Don't Care What It Is': The Tradition-History of a Civil Religion Proof-Text," *Journal of the American Academy of Religion* 49, no. 1 (March 1981): 35–49, http://www.jstor.org/.

17. James Hudnut-Beumler, *Looking for God in the Suburbs: The Religion of the American Dream and Its Critics, 1945–1965* (New Brunswick: Rutgers University Press, 1994), 50–51. See also Mark Silk, *Spiritual Politics: Religion and America Since World War II* (New York: Simon and Schuster, 1988).

18. Stephen J. Whitfield, *The Culture of the Cold War* (Baltimore: Johns Hopkins University Press, 1991), 107–13; Arthur Miller, *Timebends: A Life* (New York: Grove, 1987), 331–41. On the political history of American anticommunism, see Ellen Schrecker, *Many Are the Crimes: McCarthyism in America* (Boston: Little, Brown, 1998). On the peace movement's response to Communism, see Robbie Lieberman, *The Strangest Dream: Communism, Anticommunism, and the U.S. Peace Movement, 1945–1963* (Syracuse: Syracuse University Press, 2000).

19. Whittaker Chambers, *Witness* (New York: Random, 1952); Sam Tanenhaus, *Whittaker Chambers: A Biography* (New York: Random, 1997).

20. A. J. Muste, "Chambers, God, and the Communists," *Fellowship* 18, no. 7 (July 1952): 7–14; A. J. Muste, "Chambers, God, and the Communists—II," *Fellowship* 18, no. 8 (September 1952): 10–16.

21. Louis Fischer, *Gandhi and Stalin: Two Signs at the World's Crossroads* (New York: Harper, 1947), 52–53.

22. *Walk to Freedom;* Merritt S. Webster to "Friends," December 15, 1956, Box 19, Series E, Section II, Fellowship of Reconciliation Papers, Swarthmore College Peace Collection; Howard Thompson, "Newcomers in 16mm.," *New York Times,* October 21, 1956, http://proquest.umi.com/.

23. A. J. Muste to Henri Roser, October 20, 1952, Box 11, Series A, John Nevin Sayre Papers, Swarthmore College Peace Collection; A. J. Muste, "Prospect for Peace in 1953," *Fellowship* 19, no. 1 (January 1953): 4–9. On American anticolonialism in this period, see David L. Hostetter, *Movement Matters: American Apartheid Activism and the Rise of Multicultural Politics* (New York: Routledge, 2006); James H. Meriwether, *Proudly We Can Be Africans: Black Americans and Africa, 1935–1961* (Chapel Hill: University of North Carolina Press, 2002); Brenda Gayle Plummer, *Rising Wind: Black Americans and U.S. Foreign Affairs, 1935–1960* (Chapel Hill: University of North Carolina Press, 1996); Penny M. Von Eschen, *Race Against Empire: Black Americans and Anticolonialism, 1937–1957* (Ithaca: Cornell University Press, 1997).

24. Frantz Fanon, *The Wretched of the Earth*, trans. Constance Farrington (New York: Grove, 1963), 37; Robert J. C. Young, *Postcolonialism: An Historical Introduction* (Malden, MA: Blackwell, 2001). See also George M. Houser, *Nonviolent Revolution in South Africa* (New York: Fellowship Publications, 1953).

25. Hostetter, *Movement Matters*, 13–41; George Houser, *No One Can Stop the Rain: Glimpses of Africa's Liberation Struggle* (New York: Pilgrim, 1989).

26. Houser, *No One Can Stop the Rain*, 13; W. E. B. Du Bois to Florence H. Luscomb, October 22, 1956, Reel 18, *W. E. B. Du Bois Papers* (Sanford, NC: Microfilming Corporation of America, 1981), microfilm. For recent dismissals of American Committee on Africa leaders as tepid liberals, see Meriwether, *Proudly We Can Be Africans*, 171; Plummer, *Rising Wind*, 231–34; Von Eschen, *Race Against Empire*, 143–44. On Du Bois in this period, see David Levering Lewis, *W. E. B. Du Bois: The Fight for Equality and the American Century, 1919–1963* (New York: Holt, 2000), 554–71.

27. "The World in Focus," *Fellowship* 22, no. 11 (December 1956): 1–3.

28. On the importance of this period in the struggle for racial equality, see Jacquelyn Dowd Hall, "The Long Civil Rights Movement and the Political Uses of the Past," *Journal of American History* 91, no. 4 (March 2005): 1233–63.

29. George Houser, "A Personal Retrospective on the 1947 Journey of Reconciliation," [1992], Congress of Racial Equality Papers, Swarthmore College Peace Collection. The most detailed account of the Journey is in Raymond Arsenault, *Freedom Riders: 1961 and the Struggle for Racial Justice* (New York: Oxford University Press, 2006), 11–55, http://site.ebrary.com/.

30. Houser, "Personal Retrospective," 6; Conrad Lynn, *There Is a Fountain: The Autobiography of a Civil Rights Lawyer* (Westport, CT: Lawrence Hill, 1979), 109. For a close analysis of the Journey's gender politics, see Marian B. Mollin, "The Limits of Egalitarianism: Radical Pacifism, Civil Rights, and the Journey of Reconciliation," *Radical History Review* 88 (Winter 2004), 113–38.

31. Houser, "Personal Retrospective," 8; James Peck, *Freedom Ride* (New York: Simon and Schuster, 1962), 15–18. The sociodrama was invented by psychologist J. L. Moreno as a technique for resolving group conflicts by having disputants act out their grievances in a controlled setting; see J. L. Moreno, "The Concept of Sociodrama: A New Approach to the Problem of Inter-Cultural Relations," *Sociometry* 6, no. 4 (November 1943): 434–49. CORE apparently borrowed Moreno's term to describe its own somewhat different invention.

32. George Houser and Bayard Rustin, *We Challenged Jim Crow!* (n.p.: Fellowship of Reconciliation, 1947); Arsenault, *Freedom Riders*, 11–55.

33. Houser and Rustin, *We Challenged Jim Crow!*

34. Houser and Rustin, *We Challenged Jim Crow!*, 3, 11.

35. George Houser, interview by the author, April 21, 2007.

36. Arsenault, *Freedom Riders*, 40–41; Journey of Reconciliation radio script, CORE Papers, Swarthmore College; Houser and Rustin, *We Challenged Jim Crow!*

37. Houser and Rustin, *We Challenged Jim Crow!*, 6, 10.

38. Minutes of FOR Council, May 31, 1947, Box 3, Series A-2, Section II, FOR Papers, Swarthmore College.

39. On the early civil rights movement as a contest over public leisure spaces, see Lizabeth Cohen, *A Consumers' Republic: The Politics of Mass Consumption in Postwar America* (New York: Knopf, 2003).

40. George Houser, "Project: Brotherhood," *Fellowship* 16, no. 2 (February 1950): 13–18; Meier and Rudwick, *CORE*, 48–54.

41. Cohen, *Consumers' Republic*; Andrew Wiese, *Places of Their Own: African American Suburbanization in the Twentieth Century* (Chicago: University of Chicago Press, 2004).

42. Alfred Hassler, "Commuters' Community," *Fellowship* 19, no. 4 (April 1953): 5–11, 17–18. As of this writing, George and Jean Houser still live there.

43. Morris Milgram to A. Philip Randolph, December 7, 1955, Box 2, A. Philip Randolph Papers, Library of Congress; Alfred Hassler, "They Build Brotherhood," *Fellowship* 22, no. 2 (February 1956): 11–16; Morris Milgram, *Good Neighborhood: The Challenge of Open Housing* (New York: Norton, 1977), 54–59.

44. Constance Rumbough, *Crumbling Barriers* (New York: Fellowship Publications, [1948]), 9; Constance Rumbough, "Southern F.O.R. Conducts Camp," *Fellowship* 5, no. 8 (October 1939): 17; Constance Rumbough, "We Had a Work Camp," *Fellowship* 8, no. 11 (November 1942): 189; A. J. Muste, memorandum, February 13, 1947, Box 71, John Haynes Holmes Papers, Library of Congress; A. J. Muste, memorandum, March 25, 1947, Box 71, Holmes Papers; John Haynes Holmes to A. J. Muste, April 1, 1947, Box 219, Holmes Papers.

45. Detailed histories of the bus boycott include Taylor Branch, *Parting the Waters: America in the King Years, 1954–1963* (New York: Simon and Schuster, 1988), 143–205; Stewart Burns, ed., *Daybreak of Freedom: The Montgomery Bus Boycott* (Chapel Hill: University of North Carolina Press, 1997); David J. Garrow, *Bearing the Cross: Martin Luther King, Jr., and the Southern Christian Leadership Conference* (New York: Morrow, 1986), 11–82; Aldon D. Morris, *The Origins of the Civil Rights Movement: Black Communities Organizing for Change* (New York: Free Press, 1984), 40–63; J. Mills Thornton III, *Dividing Lines: Municipal Politics and the Struggle for Civil Rights in Montgomery, Birmingham, and Selma* (Tuscaloosa: University of Alabama Press, 2002), 20–140.

46. Martin Luther King Jr., "Pilgrimage to Nonviolence," in *Stride Toward Freedom* (New York: Harper, 1958), 90–107; Garrow, *Bearing the Cross*, 41; Branch, *Parting the Waters*, 74.

47. Coretta Scott King, *My Life with Martin Luther King, Jr.* (New York: Holt, Rinehart and Winston, 1969), 133; Branch, *Parting the Waters*, 179; *The Montgomery Bus Boycott and the Women Who Started It: The Memoir of Jo Ann Gibson Robinson*, ed. David J. Garrow (Knoxville: University of Tennessee Press, 1987), 110.

48. D'Emilio's *Lost Prophet* foregrounds the issue of Rustin's homosexuality; on the 1953 arrest, see pp. 184–205. D'Emilio, highly perceptive on antigay attitudes in American society as a whole, is less convincing in his assertion that strong homophobic tendencies in the FOR itself forced Rustin's dismissal. Rustin was, after all, a central figure in the organization for a decade, his homosexuality well known among the FOR staff during that time. Several of his colleagues, including David McReynolds and Igal Roodenko, were also gay, so one could in fact argue that radical pacifist culture was unusually *hospitable* to gay men. Further research may clarify these issues; see Ian Lekus, "Queer and Present Dangers: Homosexuality and American Antiwar Activism During the Vietnam Era" (PhD diss., Duke University, 2003).

49. Rustin quoted in Nat Hentoff, *Peace Agitator: The Story of A. J. Muste* (New York: Macmillan, 1963), 17.

50. On the indictments and Rustin's influence, see Branch, *Parting the Waters*, 168–80; D'Emilio, *Lost Prophet*, 223–48; Garrow, *Bearing the Cross*, 66–69; Lawrence D. Reddick, *Crusader Without Violence: A Biography of Martin Luther King, Jr.* (New York: Harper, 1959), 136–37. Nixon quoted in Garrow, *Bearing the Cross*, 23.

51. On the centrality of mass media images in the civil rights movement, see Mary L. Dudziak, *Cold War Civil Rights: Race and the Image of American Democracy* (Princeton: Princeton University Press, 2000); Steven Kasher, *The Civil Rights Movement: A Photographic History, 1954–1968* (New York: Abbeville, 2000); Sasha Torres, *Black, White, and in Color: Television and Black Civil Rights* (Princeton: Princeton University Press, 2003).

52. Reinhold Niebuhr, "The Way of Non-Violent Resistance," *Christianity and Society*, Spring 1956, 3. King uses the term *realistic pacifism* in King, *Stride Toward Freedom*, 99. For Niebuhr's prescient view of black nonviolence, see Reinhold Niebuhr, *Moral Man and Immoral Society* (1932; repr., New York: Scribner, 1960), 254. For his later caution regarding civil rights, see Mark Hulsether, *Building a Protestant Left: Christianity and Crisis Magazine, 1941–1993* (Knoxville: University of Tennessee Press, 1999), 49–55; and Carol Polsgrove, *Divided Minds: Intellectuals and the Civil Rights Movement* (New York: Norton, 2001). A significant Niebuhr-centric interpretation of King is Branch, *Parting the Waters*. For the contrary view that Niebuhr's influence has been overemphasized, see Keith D. Miller, *Voice of Deliverance: The Language of Martin Luther King, Jr., and Its Sources* (New York: Free Press, 1992). For a provocative attempt to harmonize Niebuhrian realist and radical pacifist contributions to civil rights under the auspices of "prophetic religion," see David L. Chappell, *A Stone of Hope: Prophetic Religion and the Death of Jim Crow* (Chapel Hill: University of North Carolina Press, 2004).

53. Margaret Cavin, "Glenn Smiley Was a Fool: The Use of the Comic as a Strategy of Nonviolence," *Peace and Change* 26, no. 2 (April 2001): 223–42; David L.

Chappell, *Inside Agitators: White Southerners in the Civil Rights Movement* (Baltimore: Johns Hopkins University Press, 1994), 58–61; "Conference on Creative Non-Violence as an Aid to Racial Understanding," program, Box 16, Series E, Section II, FOR Papers; John M. Swomley Jr., "Just Among Ourselves," *Fellowship* 15, no. 7 (July 1949): 35; "Southwest FOR Does Peace Education," *Fellowship* 16, no. 10 (November 1950): 30; Glenn Smiley and Helen Smiley, "Life in a Broken City," *Fellowship* 18, no. 9 (October 1952): 13–16.

54. Charles Lawrence to Martin Luther King Jr., February 24, 1956, *Papers of Martin Luther King, Jr.*, 3:136–38.

55. "Introduction," in *Papers of Martin Luther King, Jr.*, 3:19–20; Glenn Smiley to John Swomley and Alfred Hassler, February 29, 1956, Box 16, Series E, Section II, FOR Papers; Glenn Smiley to Matthew McCollum, [ca. January 10, 1956], Box 16, Series E, Section II, FOR Papers; William Robert Miller, *Nonviolence: A Christian Interpretation* (New York: Association Press, 1964), 306; Douglas Brinkley, *Rosa Parks* (New York: Penguin, 2000), 159.

56. Martin Luther King Jr., "Address to MIA Mass Meeting at Holt Street Baptist Church," November 14, 1956, in *Papers of Martin Luther King, Jr.*, 3:430; Richard Gregg, *The Power of Non-Violence*, rev. ed. (New York: Fellowship Publications, 1944), 53.

57. King, "Address to MIA Mass Meeting," 430.

58. King, *Stride Toward Freedom*, 163; see also Ralph David Abernathy, *And the Walls Came Tumbling Down: An Autobiography* (New York: Harper and Row, 1989), 156–59; Coretta Scott King, *My Life*, 144.

59. Erving Goffman, *The Presentation of Self in Everyday Life* (Edinburgh: University of Edinburgh, Social Sciences Research Centre, 1956). Goffman's book became highly influential when it was republished three years later; see Erving Goffman, *The Presentation of Self in Everyday Life* (Garden City, NY: Anchor, 1959).

60. For other examples of the civil rights movement's alternative media, see Leigh Raiford, "'Come Let Us Build a New World Together': SNCC and the Photography of the Civil Rights Movement," *American Quarterly* 59, no. 4 (December 2007): 1129–57.

61. On the filmstrip, see Alfred Hassler to John Haynes Holmes, June 28, 1948, Box 83, Holmes Papers; A. J. Muste to John Haynes Holmes, July 6, 1948, Box 83, Holmes Papers.

62. *Walk to Freedom;* Don O'Neal to Alfred Hassler, February 12, 1957, Box 19, Series E, Section II, FOR Papers.

63. "'Walk to Freedom' Lauded at Montgomery Premiere," *Fellowship* 22, no. 10 (November 1956): 24–25; William Robert Miller, *Martin Luther King, Jr.: His Life, Martyrdom, and Meaning for the World* (New York: Weybright and Talley, 1968), 52; Robert L. Cannon, "Comments on the Use of 'Walk to Freedom,'" [October 1956], Box 19, Series E, Section II, FOR Papers.

64. On comic books, see James Gilbert, *A Cycle of Outrage: America's Reaction to the Juvenile Delinquent in the 1950s* (New York: Oxford University Press, 1986); and Bradford W. Wright, *Comic Book Nation: The Transformation of Youth Culture*

in America (Baltimore: Johns Hopkins University Press, 2001). I am indebted to Jim Miller for telling me about the Scottsboro comics.

65. *Martin Luther King and the Montgomery Story* (n.p.: Fellowship of Reconciliation, [1957]); Martin Luther King Jr., "Walk for Freedom," *Fellowship* 22, no. 5 (May 1956): 5–7.

66. Alfred Hassler to Edward Reed, May 2, 1956, Box 19, Series E, Section II, FOR Papers; Alfred Hassler, "Suggestions for Aid in the Distribution of 'Martin Luther King and the Montgomery Story,'" Box 19, Series E, Section II, FOR Papers; John Lewis, *Walking with the Wind: A Memoir of the Movement,* with Michael D'Orso (San Diego: Harcourt Brace, 1998), 74–75; Brian P. Bunting to "Friends," July 27, 1959, Box 19, Series E, Section II, FOR Papers; Stephen Ellis and Tsepo Sechaba, *Comrades Against Apartheid: The ANC and the South African Communist Party in Exile* (Bloomington: Indiana University Press, 1992), 18; *Martin Luther King y la Historia de Montgomery* (n.p.: Fellowship Publications, [1957?]).

67. On white participation in the boycott, see Chappell, *Inside Agitators,* 53–83.

68. *Martin Luther King and the Montgomery Story.* On Graetz, see Robert S. Graetz, *A White Preacher's Memoir: The Montgomery Bus Boycott* (Montgomery: Black Belt Press, 1999).

69. Glenn Smiley to Helen Smiley, March 1, 1956, quoted in *Papers of Martin Luther King, Jr.,* 3:151; Chappell, *Inside Agitators,* 59–60, 240–41n24.

70. Lillian Eugenia Smith to Martin Luther King Jr., March 10, 1956; Homer Alexander Jack to Martin Luther King Jr., March 16, 1956; James Peck to Martin Luther King Jr., June 1, 1956—all in *Papers of Martin Luther King, Jr.,* 3:168–70, 178–79, 288–89.

71. King, *Stride Toward Freedom,* 173; Smiley quoted in Chappell, *Inside Agitators,* 60.

72. Chappell, *Inside Agitators,* 80; "Graetz Denies Bomb Hoax," *Montgomery Advertiser,* August 26, 1956, http://nl.newsbank.com/; interview with cab driver, by Anna Holden, in Burns, ed., *Daybreak of Freedom,* 145.

73. Rosa Parks and Jim Haskins, *Rosa Parks: My Story* (New York: Dial, 1992), 157–59.

74. *Fiftieth Anniversary Report of the Harvard Class of 1907* (Cambridge, 1957), 273; Mohandas Gandhi to Richard Gregg, November 11, 1947, *Collected Works of Mahatma Gandhi* (Ahmedabad: Publications Division, Ministry of Information and Broadcasting, Government of India, 1984), 90:3–4.

75. Richard Gregg, *Gandhiji's Satyagraha or Non-Violent Resistance* (Madras: Ganesan, 1930), 403; Richard Gregg, "Creative Group Fellowship," *Fellowship* 4, no. 8 (October 1938): 9–10.

76. *Fiftieth Anniversary Report,* 273. On Pfeiffer's agricultural program, see Ehrenfried Pfeiffer, *Bio-Dynamic Farming and Gardening,* 2nd ed. (New York: Anthroposophic Press, 1940). Helen Nearing and Scott Nearing, *Living the Good Life: How to Live Sanely and Simply in a Troubled World* (1954; repr., New York: Schocken, 1970); Helen Nearing and Scott Nearing, *Continuing the Good Life: Half a Century of Homesteading* (New York: Schocken, 1979).

77. Evelyn Speiden Gregg and Richard Gregg, form letter, April 1956, Richard B. Gregg Papers, Swarthmore College Peace Collection.

78. Martin Luther King Jr. to Richard Gregg, May 1, 1956, in *Papers of Martin Luther King, Jr.*, 3:244–45. The book list is in Martin Luther King Jr. to Lawrence M. Byrd, April 25, 1957, in Clayborne Carson, ed., *Papers of Martin Luther King, Jr.* (Berkeley: University of California Press, 2000), 4:183–84.

79. Martin Luther King Jr., foreword to *The Power of Nonviolence*, by Richard Gregg, 2nd rev. ed (Nyack, NY: Fellowship Publications, 1959); Richard Gregg to Martin Luther King Jr., April 2, 1956, in *Papers of Martin Luther King, Jr.*, 3:212; Martin Luther King Jr. to Richard Gregg, December 18, 1958, in *Papers of Martin Luther King, Jr.*, 4:548–49.

80. King, "Pilgrimage to Nonviolence," in *Stride Toward Freedom*, 102; Gregg, *Power of Non-Violence*, 93. On King's indebtedness to earlier interpreters of Gandhi, see Miller, *Voice of Deliverance*, 88–100. Miller discovered the matching passages shown above, though he mistakenly cites the 1959 edition of Gregg's text (published *after* "Pilgrimage to Nonviolence"), rather than the 1944 edition.

81. Richard B. Gregg, "The Structure of a Nonviolent Society," *Fellowship* 19, no. 5 (May 1953): 9–12.

82. Richard Gregg to Martin Luther King Jr., April 2, 1956, in *Papers of Martin Luther King, Jr.*, 3:211–12; Martin Luther King Jr., to Richard Gregg, December 18, 1958, in *Papers of Martin Luther King, Jr.*, 4:548; Richard B. Gregg, *A Philosophy of Indian Economic Development* (Ahmedabad: Navajivan, 1958).

Conclusion

1. On Lawson's career, see Taylor Branch, *Parting the Waters: America in the King Years, 1954–1963* (New York: Simon and Schuster, 1988); and David L. Chappell, *A Stone of Hope: Prophetic Religion and the Death of Jim Crow* (Chapel Hill: University of North Carolina Press, 2004). On the sit-ins, see Clayborne Carson, *In Struggle: SNCC and the Black Awakening of the 1960s* (Cambridge: Harvard University Press, 1995), 9–30; and John Lewis, *Walking with the Wind: A Memoir of the Movement*, with Michael D'Orso (San Diego: Harcourt Brace, 1998), 71–129. On radical religion in the sixties, see James J. Farrell, *The Spirit of the Sixties: Making Postwar Radicalism* (New York: Routledge, 1997).

2. *Student Voice* 1, no. 2 (August 1960), in Clayborne Carson, ed., *The Student Voice 1960–1965* (Westport, CT: Meckler, 1990), 12; King book list in *Christian Century*, May 23, 1962, 661; Branch, *Parting the Waters*, 259; Richard Gregg to John Nevin Sayre, February 14, 1961, Box 6, Series A, John Nevin Sayre Papers, Swarthmore College Peace Collection.

3. Martin Luther King Jr., *Why We Can't Wait* (New York: New American Library, 1964), 39. On television and the civil rights movement, see Sasha Torres, *Black, White, and in Color: Television and Black Civil Rights* (Princeton: Princeton University Press, 2003).

4. Lance Hill, *The Deacons for Defense: Armed Resistance and the Civil Rights Movement* (Chapel Hill: University of North Carolina Press, 2004); Charles M. Payne, *I've Got the Light of Freedom: The Organizing Tradition and the Mississippi Freedom Struggle* (Berkeley: University of California Press, 1995); Christopher B. Strain, *Pure Fire: Self-Defense as Activism in the Civil Rights Era* (Athens: University of Georgia Press, 2005); Timothy B. Tyson, *Radio Free Dixie: Robert F. Williams and the Roots of Black Power* (Chapel Hill: University of North Carolina Press, 1999); Jenny Walker, "A Media-Made Movement? Black Violence and Nonviolence in the Historiography of the Civil Rights Movement," in Brian Ward, ed., *Media, Culture, and the Modern African American Freedom Struggle* (Gainesville: University Press of Florida, 2001), 41–66; Simon Wendt, *The Spirit and the Shotgun: Armed Resistance and the Struggle for Civil Rights* (Gainesville: University Press of Florida, 2007).

5. Hill, *Deacons for Defense*, 8, 236.

6. On the importance of religion, see Chappell, *Stone of Hope*; Michael B. Friedland, *Lift Up Your Voice Like a Trumpet: White Clergy and the Civil Rights and Antiwar Movements, 1954–1973* (Chapel Hill: University of North Carolina Press, 1998); Paul Harvey, *Freedom's Coming: Religious Culture and the Shaping of the South from the Civil War through the Civil Rights Era* (Chapel Hill: University of North Carolina Press, 2005), 169–217; Charles Marsh, *God's Long Summer: Stories of Faith and Civil Rights* (Princeton: Princeton University Press, 1997).

7. Maurice Isserman, *If I Had a Hammer: The Death of the Old Left and the Birth of the New Left* (New York: Basic Books, 1987), 125–69; Marian Mollin, *Radical Pacifism in Modern America: Egalitarianism and Protest* (Philadelphia: University of Pennsylvania Press, 2006); Amy Swerdlow, *Women Strike for Peace: Traditional Motherhood and Radical Politics in the 1960s* (Chicago: University of Chicago Press, 1993); James Tracy, *Direct Action: Radical Pacifism from the Union Eight to the Chicago Seven* (Chicago: University of Chicago Press, 1996), 76–123; Lawrence S. Wittner, *Rebels Against War: The American Peace Movement, 1933–1983* (Philadelphia: Temple University Press, 1984), 240–75; Lawrence S. Wittner, *Resisting the Bomb: A History of the World Nuclear Disarmament Movement, 1954–1970*, vol. 2 of *The Struggle Against the Bomb* (Stanford: Stanford University Press, 1997).

8. On SDS and the New Left, see Todd Gitlin, *The Whole World Is Watching: Mass Media in the Making and Unmaking of the New Left* (Berkeley: University of California Press, 1980); Isserman, *If I Had a Hammer*, 125–69; Kevin Mattson, *Intellectuals in Action: The Origins of the New Left and Radical Liberalism, 1945–1970* (University Park: Pennsylvania State University Press, 2002); James Miller, *"Democracy Is in the Streets": From Port Huron to the Siege of Chicago* (Cambridge: Harvard University Press, 1994); Doug Rossinow, *The Politics of Authenticity: Liberalism, Christianity, and the New Left in America* (New York: Columbia University Press, 1998); Tracy, *Direct Action*.

9. On the Fellowship's influence in the antiwar movement, see Charles DeBenedetti, *An American Ordeal: The Antiwar Movement of the Vietnam Era*, with Charles Chatfield (Syracuse: Syracuse University Press, 1990); Mitchell K. Hall,

Because of Their Faith: CALCAV and Religious Opposition to the Vietnam War (New York: Columbia University Press, 1990); Mary Hershberger, *Traveling to Vietnam: American Peace Activists and the War* (Syracuse: Syracuse University Press, 1998); Charles Howlett, "Fellowship and Reconciliation: A Pacifist Organization Confronts the War in Southeast Asia," *Maryland Historian* 25, no. 1 (Spring/Summer 1994): 1–24; Tracy, *Direct Action*, 124–53.

10. Paul R. Dekar, *Creating the Beloved Community: A Journey with the Fellowship of Reconciliation* (Telford, PA: Cascadia, 2005), 223–34.

11. Pope John XXIII, *Pacem in Terris* (1963), par. 112, 126, http://www.vatican.va/.

12. Thomas Merton, *Blessed Are the Meek: The Christian Roots of Nonviolence* (Nyack, NY: Catholic Peace Fellowship, 1967). On the origins of the Catholic Peace Fellowship, see Thomas C. Cornell, "Catholic Peace Fellowship Ten Years Old," http://www.catholicpeacefellowship.org/; Thomas C. Cornell, "War and Conscience After Vatican II," http://www.catholicpeacefellowship.org/; Dekar, *Creating the Beloved Community*, 205–9; Patricia McNeal, *Harder Than War: Catholic Peacemaking in Twentieth-Century America* (New Brunswick: Rutgers University Press, 1992), 131–72; Penelope Adams Moon, "'Peace on Earth—Peace in Vietnam': The Catholic Peace Fellowship and Antiwar Witness, 1964–1976," *Journal of Social History* 36, no. 4 (Summer 2003): 1033–57, http://search.ebscohost.com/.

13. On Catholic radicalism in the sixties, see Francine du Plessix Gray, *Divine Disobedience: Profiles in Catholic Radicalism* (New York: Knopf, 1970); McNeal, *Harder than War*, 173–210; Murray Polner and Jim O'Grady, *Disarmed and Dangerous: The Radical Lives and Times of Daniel and Philip Berrigan* (New York: Basic Books, 1997).

14. Tracy, *Direct Action*, 127–28.

15. George Houser, *No One Can Stop the Rain: Glimpses of Africa's Liberation Struggle* (New York: Pilgrim, 1989), 91–92. For a provocative, if not wholly convincing, argument that American pacifists abandoned their opposition to violence in order to support Third World liberation movements, see Guenter Lewy, *Peace and Revolution: The Moral Crisis of American Pacifism* (Grand Rapids: Eerdmans, 1988).

16. DeBenedetti, *American Ordeal*; Howlett, "Fellowship and Reconciliation"; Tracy, *Direct Action*, 124–53.

17. Carson, *In Struggle*; Gitlin, *Whole World Is Watching*; Isserman, *If I Had a Hammer*, 125–69; William L. Van Deburg, *New Day in Babylon: The Black Power Movement and American Culture, 1965–1975* (Chicago: University of Chicago Press, 1992).

18. On *shock-a-buku*, compare Huey Newton, *Revolutionary Suicide* (New York: Harcourt Brace Jovanovich, 1973), 122, with Richard Gregg, *The Power of Nonviolence* (Nyack, NY: Fellowship Publications, 1959), 44. On the Black Panthers and the media, see Jane Rhodes, *Framing the Black Panthers: The Spectacular Rise of a Black Power Icon* (New York: New Press, 2007).

19. Daniel Boorstin, *The Image; or, What Happened to the American Dream* (New York: Atheneum, 1961). See also Marshall McLuhan, *Understanding Media: The Extensions of Man* (New York: McGraw-Hill, 1964).

20. Joan Daves to Martin Luther King Jr., October 18, 1957, in Clayborne Carson, ed., *Papers of Martin Luther King, Jr.* (Berkeley: University of California Press, 1997), 4:286–87; Robert S. Graetz, *A White Preacher's Memoir: The Montgomery Bus Boycott* (Montgomery: Black Belt Press, 1999), 114; Gitlin, *Whole World Is Watching.*

21. Dee Garrison, *Bracing for Armageddon: Why Civil Defense Never Worked* (New York: Oxford University Press, 2006), 93–101.

22. Branch, *Parting the Waters,* 601–32; Laurie Pritchett, interview by Howell Raines, in Howell Raines, ed., *My Soul Is Rested: Movement Days in the Deep South Remembered* (New York: Putnam, 1977), 361–66.

23. Gregg, *Power of Non-Violence,* 43.

24. DeBenedetti, *American Ordeal,* 107, 129–30; Polner and O'Grady, *Disarmed and Dangerous,* 122–29; Jo Ann Ooiman Robinson, *Abraham Went Out: A Biography of A. J. Muste* (Philadelphia: Temple University Press, 1981), 202.

25. Bayard Rustin, "From Protest to Politics: The Future of the Civil Rights Movement," *Commentary* 39, no. 2 (February 1965): 25–31. On this period in Rustin's career, see John D'Emilio, *Lost Prophet: The Life and Times of Bayard Rustin* (New York: Free Press, 2003), 393–439; Daniel Levine, *Bayard Rustin and the Civil Rights Movement* (New Brunswick: Rutgers University Press, 2000), 151–252. On the tensions between the civil rights movement and the peace movement, see Simon Hall, *Peace and Freedom: The Civil Rights and Antiwar Movements in the 1960s* (Philadelphia: University of Pennsylvania Press, 2005).

26. Robert T. Handy, *A History of Union Theological Seminary in New York* (New York: Columbia University Press, 1987), 259–314; DeBenedetti, *American Ordeal,* 320.

27. Barbara Epstein, *Political Protest and Cultural Revolution: Nonviolent Direct Action in the 1970s and 1980s* (Berkeley: University of California Press, 1991); Christian Smith, *Resisting Reagan: The U.S. Central America Peace Movement* (Chicago: University of Chicago Press, 1996); Lawrence S. Wittner, *Toward Nuclear Abolition: A History of the World Nuclear Disarmament Movement, 1971 to the Present,* vol. 3 of *The Struggle Against the Bomb* (Stanford: Stanford University Press, 2003); Kenneth Cmiel, "The Emergence of Human Rights Politics in the United States," *Journal of American History* 86, no. 3 (December 1999): 1231–50, http://www.jstor.org/; Rex Weyler, *Greenpeace: How a Group of Journalists, Ecologists, and Visionaries Changed the World* (Vancouver: Raincoast, 2004).

28. Polner and O'Grady, *Disarmed and Dangerous,* 344. On Christian nonviolence in the antiabortion movement, see James Risen and Judy L. Thomas, *Wrath of Angels: The American Abortion War* (New York: Basic Books, 1998).

29. On global nonviolence, see Taylor Branch, "Globalizing King's Legacy," *New York Times,* January 16, 2006, http://www.nytimes.com/; and Jonathan Schell, *The Unconquerable World: Power, Nonviolence, and the Will of the People* (New

York: Metropolitan, 2003). For Havel's politics of conscience, see Jan Vladislav, ed., *Václav Havel: Living in Truth* (Boston: Faber and Faber, 1989). On Christianity's non-Western future, see Philip Jenkins, *The Next Christendom: The Coming of Global Christianity*, rev. ed. (New York: Oxford University Press, 2007). On the Fellowship of Reconciliation today, see http://www.forusa.org/.

30. Reinhold Niebuhr, "Christian Revolutionary," review of *The Essays of A. J. Muste*, ed. Nat Hentoff, *New York Times*, April 16, 1967, http://proquest .umi.com/.

Bibliography

Manuscript Sources

Allen, Devere. Papers. Swarthmore College Peace Collection.

Brookwood Labor College. Papers. Tamiment Library. New York University.

Chaffee, Edmund B. Papers. Special Collections Research Center. Syracuse University Library.

Committee on Militarism in Education. Papers. Swarthmore College Peace Collection.

Congress of Racial Equality. Papers. Swarthmore College Peace Collection.

Eddy, Sherwood. Papers. Divinity Library. Yale University.

Evans, Edward W. Papers. Swarthmore College Peace Collection.

Fellowship of Reconciliation. Papers. Swarthmore College Peace Collection.

Gregg, Richard B. Papers. Harvard University Archives.

Gregg, Richard B. Papers. Swarthmore College Peace Collection.

Holmes, John Haynes. Papers. Library of Congress.

Hughes, Langston. Papers. Beinecke Rare Book and Manuscript Library. Yale University.

Mott, John R. Papers. Divinity Library. Yale University.

Niebuhr, Reinhold. Papers. Library of Congress.

Page, Kirby. Papers. Special Collections. Claremont School of Theology Library.

Pendle Hill School. Papers. Friends Historical Library.

Randolph, A. Philip. Papers. Library of Congress.

Sayre, John Nevin. Papers. Swarthmore College Peace Collection.

Published Manuscript Collections

The Letters of Maxwell Chaplin. Edited by George Stewart. New York: Association Press, 1928.

W. E. B. Du Bois Papers. Sanford, NC: Microfilming Corporation of America, 1981.

Collected Works of Mahatma Gandhi. Ahmedabad: Publications Division, Ministry of Information and Broadcasting, Government of India, 1966–1984.

Gray, Harold. *Character "Bad": The Story of a Conscientious Objector*. Edited by Kenneth Irving Brown. New York: Harper, 1934.

Howard A. Kester Papers. Glen Rock, NJ: Microfilming Corporation of America, 1973.

Papers of Martin Luther King, Jr. 5 vols. Edited by Clayborne Carson. Berkeley: University of California Press, 1992–.

Lenin, Vladimir. *Collected Works*. Moscow: Progress Publishers, 1976. http://www.marxists.org/.

The Papers of A. J. Muste, 1920–1967. Swarthmore College Peace Collection, Swarthmore, PA. Wilmington, DE: Scholarly Resources, 1991.

Bayard Rustin Papers, 1942–1987. Library of Congress. Frederick, MD: University Publications of America, 1988.

The Radical "No": The Correspondence and Writings of Evan Thomas on War. Edited by Charles Chatfield. New York: Garland, 1974.

The Norman Thomas Papers. New York Public Library. Alexandria, VA: Chadwyck-Healey, 1983.

Books, Articles, Dissertations, and Films

"45 Years Later, An Apology from the U.S. Government." *Newsletter of the University of Washington College of Arts and Sciences*, Winter 2000. http://www.artsci.washington.edu/.

Abell, Aaron. *The Urban Impact on American Protestantism, 1865–1900*. Cambridge: Harvard University Press, 1943.

Abernathy, Ralph David. *And the Walls Came Tumbling Down: An Autobiography*. New York: Harper and Row, 1989.

Adamic, Louis. *Dynamite: The Story of Class Violence in America*. Rev. ed. New York: Viking, 1934.

Adams, J. Donald. "Mr. Wilder's Comedy of Virtue." Review of *Heaven's My Destination*, by Thornton Wilder. *New York Times*, January 6, 1935. http://proquest.umi.com/.

Adams, Michael C. C. *The Best War Ever: America and World War II*. Baltimore: Johns Hopkins University Press, 1994.

Addams, Jane. *Peace and Bread in Time of War*. New York: Macmillan, 1922.

Allen, Devere. *The Fight for Peace*. New York: Macmillan, 1930.

———. "War Resistance as War Prevention." In Devere Allen, ed., *Pacifism in the Modern World*, 171–83. Garden City, NY: Doubleday, Doran, 1929.

————. "Would Jesus Be a Sectarian Today?" *World Tomorrow* 11, no. 11 (November 1928): 458–61.

Allen, Devere, ed. *Pacifism in the Modern World*. Garden City, NY: Doubleday, Doran, 1929.

Allinson, Brent Dow. "'Quo Vadis,' Quaker?" *World Tomorrow* 6, no. 8 (August 1923): 245–48.

Alonso, Harriet Hyman. *Peace as a Women's Issue: A History of the U.S. Movement for World Peace and Women's Rights*. Syracuse: Syracuse University Press, 1993.

Alpers, Benjamin L. *Dictators, Democracy, and American Public Culture: Envisioning the Totalitarian Enemy, 1920s–1950s*. Chapel Hill: University of North Carolina Press, 2003.

Altenbaugh, Richard J. *Education for Struggle: The American Labor Colleges of the 1920s and 1930s*. Philadelphia: Temple University Press, 1990.

Alter, Joseph S. *Gandhi's Body: Sex, Diet, and the Politics of Nationalism*. Philadelphia: University of Pennsylvania Press, 2000.

Anderson, Jervis. *Bayard Rustin: Troubles I've Seen*. New York: HarperCollins, 1997.

Andrew, Edward G. *Conscience and Its Critics: Protestant Conscience, Enlightenment Reason, and Modern Subjectivity*. Buffalo: University of Toronto Press, 2001.

Andrews, C.F. *Mahatma Gandhi's Ideas: Including Selections from His Writings*. New York: Macmillan, 1930.

Anthony, David H., III. *Max Yergan: Race Man, Internationalist, Cold Warrior*. New York: New York University Press, 2006.

Appelbaum, Patricia Faith. "The Legions of Good Will: The Religious Culture of Protestant Pacifism, 1918–1963." PhD diss., Boston University, 2001.

Armstrong, James S. "The Labor Temple, 1910–1957: A Social Gospel Action in the Presbyterian Church." PhD diss., University of Wisconsin, 1974.

Arnold, Thurman. *The Folklore of Capitalism*. New Haven: Yale University Press, 1937.

————. *The Symbols of Government*. New Haven: Yale University Press, 1935.

Arsenault, Raymond. *Freedom Riders: 1961 and the Struggle for Racial Justice*. New York: Oxford University Press, 2006. http://site.ebrary.com/.

Bancroft, Frank C. "A Textbook of Revolution." Review of *The Power of Non-Violence*, by Richard B. Gregg. *Christian Century*, November 7, 1934, 1414–15.

Barber, Lucy. *Marching on Washington: The Forging of an American Political Tradition*. Berkeley: University of California Press, 2002.

Barnes, Harry Elmer. *The Twilight of Christianity*. New York: Vanguard, 1929.

Bederman, Gail. "'The Women Have Had Charge of the Church Work Long Enough': The Men and Religion Forward Movement of 1911–1912 and the Masculinization of Middle-Class Protestantism." *American Quarterly* 41, no. 3 (September 1989): 432–65.

Beinart, Peter. *The Good Fight: Why Liberals—and Only Liberals—Can Win the War on Terror and Make America Great Again*. New York: HarperCollins, 2006.

Bennett, Scott H. *Radical Pacifism: The War Resisters League and Gandhian Nonviolence in America, 1915–1963*. Syracuse: Syracuse University Press, 2003.

Berlin, Ira. *Many Thousands Gone: The First Two Centuries of Slavery in North America*. Cambridge: Harvard University Press, 1998.

Bernstein, Irving. *The Lean Years: A History of the American Worker, 1920–1933*. Boston: Houghton Mifflin, 1960.

Bondurant, Joan. *Conquest of Violence: The Gandhian Philosophy of Conflict*. Princeton: Princeton University Press, 1988.

Boorstin, Daniel. *The Image; or, What Happened to the American Dream*. New York: Atheneum, 1961.

Boyer, Paul. *By the Bomb's Early Light: American Thought and Culture at the Dawn of the Atomic Age*. Chapel Hill: University of North Carolina Press, 1994.

———. *Urban Masses and Moral Order in America, 1820–1920*. Cambridge: Harvard University Press, 1978.

Branch, Taylor. "Globalizing King's Legacy." *New York Times*, January 16, 2006. http://www.nytimes.com/.

———. *Parting the Waters: America in the King Years, 1954–1963*. New York: Simon and Schuster, 1988.

Brinkley, Alan. *The End of Reform: New Deal Liberalism in Recession and War*. New York: Knopf, 1995.

Brinkley, Douglas. *Rosa Parks*. New York: Penguin, 2000.

Brinton, Howard H. "Pacifist Not Isolationist." *Fellowship* 6, no. 6 (June 1940): 91.

Brittain, Vera. "Massacre by Bombing." *Fellowship* 10, no. 3/2 (March 1944).

———. *The Rebel Passion: A Short History of Some Pioneer Peacemakers*. London: Allen and Unwin, 1964.

———. *Seed of Chaos: What Mass Bombing Really Means*. London: New Vision, 1944.

Brock, Peter. *Freedom from Violence: Sectarian Nonresistance from the Middle Ages to the Great War*. Buffalo: University of Toronto Press, 1991.

———. *Twentieth-Century Pacifism*. New York: Van Nostrand Reinhold, 1970.

Brock, Peter, and Thomas P. Socknat, eds. *Challenge to Mars: Essays on Pacifism from 1918 to 1945*. Buffalo: University of Toronto Press, 1999.

Brown, Ethelred. "A Liberal Church for Negroes." *World Tomorrow* 12, no. 8 (August 1929): 379.

Brown, Judith M. *Gandhi and Civil Disobedience: The Mahatma in Indian Politics, 1928–1934*. New York: Cambridge University Press, 1977.

———. *Gandhi: Prisoner of Hope*. New Haven: Yale University Press, 1989.

Brown, William Adams. *Is Christianity Practicable?* New York: Scribner, 1916.

Buhle, Paul. *Marxism in the United States: Remapping the History of the American Left*. Rev. ed. New York: Verso, 1991.

Burbank, Rex. *Thornton Wilder*. 2nd ed. Boston: Twayne, 1978.

Burns, Stewart, ed. *Daybreak of Freedom: The Montgomery Bus Boycott*. Chapel Hill: University of North Carolina Press, 1997.

Bush, Perry. *Two Kingdoms, Two Loyalties: Mennonite Pacifism in Modern America*. Baltimore: Johns Hopkins University Press, 1998.

Butler, Judith. *Excitable Speech: A Politics of the Performative*. New York: Routledge, 1997.

————. *Gender Trouble: Feminism and the Subversion of Identity.* New York: Routledge, 1990.

Calvino, Italo. "The Duce's Portraits." In Martin McLaughlin, trans., *Hermit in Paris: Autobiographical Writings,* 207–20. New York: Pantheon, 2003.

Camus, Albert. "Neither Victims Nor Executioners." Translated by Dwight Macdonald. *politics,* July–August 1947, 141–47.

Cannon, James P. *The History of American Trotskyism: Report of a Participant.* New York: Pioneer, 1944.

Capozzola, Christopher. "The Only Badge Needed Is Your Patriotic Fervor: Vigilance, Coercion, and the Law in World War I America." *Journal of American History* 88, no. 4 (March 2002): 1354–82. http://www.historycooperative.org/.

Carson, Clayborne. *In Struggle: SNCC and the Black Awakening of the 1960s.* Cambridge: Harvard University Press, 1995.

Carter, Paul A. *The Decline and Revival of the Social Gospel: Social and Political Liberalism in American Protestant Churches, 1920–1940.* Ithaca: Cornell University Press, 1954.

"The Case Against Roosevelt." *World Tomorrow* 15, no. 12 (October 5, 1932): 320.

Case, Clarence Marsh. *Non-Violent Coercion: A Study in Methods of Social Pressure.* New York: Century, 1923.

Casey, Michael W. "From Religious Outsiders to Insiders: The Rise and Fall of Pacifism in the Churches of Christ." *Journal of Church and State* 44, no. 3 (Summer 2002): 455–75, http://web.ebscohost.com/.

Cavin, Margaret. "Glenn Smiley Was a Fool: The Use of the Comic as a Strategy of Nonviolence." *Peace and Change* 26, no. 2 (April 2001): 223–42.

Ceadel, Martin. *Pacifism in Britain, 1914–1945: The Defining of a Faith.* New York: Oxford University Press, 1980.

Chaffee, Edmund B. "Do You Believe in Free Speech?" *Outlook and Independent,* May 15, 1929, 99.

————. *The Protestant Churches and the Industrial Crisis.* New York: Macmillan, 1933.

Chambers, John Whiteclay, II. *To Raise an Army: The Draft Comes to Modern America.* New York: Free Press, 1987.

Chambers, Whittaker. *Witness.* New York: Random, 1952.

Chappell, David L. *Inside Agitators: White Southerners in the Civil Rights Movement.* Baltimore: Johns Hopkins University Press, 1994.

————. *A Stone of Hope: Prophetic Religion and the Death of Jim Crow.* Chapel Hill: University of North Carolina Press, 2004.

Chase, Stuart, and Marian Tyler. *Mexico: A Study of Two Americas.* New York: Macmillan, 1931.

Chatfield, Charles. *For Peace and Justice: Pacifism in America, 1914–1941.* Knoxville: University of Tennessee Press, 1971.

Chatfield, Charles, ed. *The Americanization of Gandhi: Images of the Mahatma.* New York: Garland, 1976.

Churchill, Ward. *Pacifism as Pathology: Reflections on the Role of Armed Struggle in North America.* With Mike Ryan. Winnipeg: Arbeiter Ring, 1998.

Cleghorn, Sarah N. *Threescore: The Autobiography of Sarah N. Cleghorn*. New York: Smith and Haas, 1936.

Cmiel, Kenneth. "The Emergence of Human Rights Politics in the United States." *Journal of American History* 86, no. 3 (December 1999): 1231–50, http://www.jstor.org/.

Cohen, Lizabeth. *A Consumers' Republic: The Politics of Mass Consumption in Postwar America*. New York: Knopf, 2003.

Cohen, Robert. *When the Old Left Was Young: Student Radicals and America's First Mass Student Movement, 1929–1941*. New York: Oxford University Press, 1993.

Collins, George L. "Pacifism and Social Injustice." In Devere Allen, ed., *Pacifism in the Modern World*, 103–14. Garden City, NY: Doubleday, Doran, 1929.

Conner, Valerie Jean. *The National War Labor Board: Stability, Social Justice, and the Voluntary State in World War I*. Chapel Hill: University of North Carolina Press, 1983.

"The Conviction of the Christian Pacifists." *New World* 1, no. 1 (January 1918): 16.

Cooney, Robert, and Helen Michalowski, eds. *The Power of the People: Active Nonviolence in the United States*. Culver City, CA: Peace Press, 1977.

Cornell, Thomas C. "Catholic Peace Fellowship Ten Years Old." http://www.catholicpeacefellowship.org/.

———. "War and Conscience After Vatican II." http://www.catholicpeacefellowship.org/.

Cotkin, George. *Existential America*. Baltimore: Johns Hopkins University Press, 2003.

Cotrell, Robert C. *Roger Nash Baldwin and the American Civil Liberties Union*. New York: Columbia University Press, 2000.

Craig, Robert H. *Religion and Radical Politics: An Alternative Christian Tradition in the United States*. Philadelphia: Temple University Press, 1992.

Crane, Conrad C. *Bombs, Cities, and Civilians: American Airpower Strategy in World War II*. Lawrence: University Press of Kansas, 1993.

Creel, George. *How We Advertised America*. 1920. Reprint, New York: Arno, 1972.

Crist, Miriam J. "'Everybody on the Left Knew Her': Winifred L. Chappell." MDiv thesis, Union Theological Seminary, 1979.

Curran, Thomas F. *Soldiers of Peace: Civil War Pacifism and the Postwar Radical Peace Movement*. New York: Fordham University Press, 2003.

Curtis, Susan. *A Consuming Faith: The Social Gospel and Modern American Culture*. Baltimore: Johns Hopkins University Press, 1991.

Daniels, Roger. *Concentration Camps USA: Japanese Americans and World War II*. New York: Holt, Rinehart and Winston, 1971.

Danielson, Leilah. "Christianity, Dissent, and the Cold War: A.J. Muste's Challenge to Realism and U.S. Empire." *Diplomatic History* 30, no. 4 (September 2006): 645–69.

———. "'In My Extremity I Turned to Gandhi': American Pacifists, Christianity, and Gandhian Nonviolence, 1915–1941." *Church History* 72, no. 2 (June 2003): 361–88.

———. "The 'Two-Ness' of the Movement: James Farmer, Nonviolence, and Black Nationalism." *Peace and Change* 29, no. 3–4 (July 2004): 431–52.

Dasgupta, Subrata. *Jagadis Chandra Bose and the Indian Response to Western Science.* New York: Oxford University Press, 1999.

Davis, Colin J. *Power at Odds: The 1922 National Railroad Shopmen's Strike.* Urbana: University of Illinois Press, 1997.

Davis, Jerome. *A Life Adventure for Peace.* New York: Citadel, 1967.

Davis, Rebecca L. "'Not Marriage at All, but Simple Harlotry': The Companionate Marriage Controversy." *Journal of American History* 94, no. 4 (March 2008): 1137–63, http://web.ebscohost.com/.

Dawes, James. *The Language of War: Literature and Culture in the U.S. from the Civil War Through World War II.* Cambridge: Harvard University Press, 2002.

Dawley, Alan. *Changing the World: American Progressives in War and Revolution.* Princeton: Princeton University Press, 2003.

DeBenedetti, Charles. *An American Ordeal: The Antiwar Movement of the Vietnam Era.* With Charles Chatfield. Syracuse: Syracuse University Press, 1990.

———. *Origins of the Modern American Peace Movement, 1915–1929.* Millwood, NY: KTO, 1978.

———. *The Peace Reform in American History.* Bloomington: Indiana University Press, 1980.

De Caux, Len. *Labor Radical: From the Wobblies to the CIO.* Boston: Beacon, 1970.

Dekar, Paul R. *Creating the Beloved Community: A Journey with the Fellowship of Reconciliation.* Telford, PA: Cascadia, 2005.

Dellinger, David. *From Yale to Jail: The Life Story of a Moral Dissenter.* New York: Pantheon, 1993.

D'Emilio, John. *Lost Prophet: The Life and Times of Bayard Rustin.* New York: Free Press, 2003.

De Nevers, Klancy Clark. *The Colonel and the Pacifist: Karl Bendetsen, Perry Saito, and the Incarceration of Japanese Americans During World War II.* Salt Lake City: University of Utah Press, 2004.

Denning, Michael. *The Cultural Front: The Laboring of American Culture in the Twentieth Century.* New York: Verso, 1997.

Dewey, John. "Conscience and Compulsion." *New Republic,* July 14, 1917. In Jo Anne Boydston, ed., *The Middle Works, 1899–1924,* 10:260–64. Carbondale: Southern Illinois University Press, 1980.

———. "The Discrediting of Idealism." *New Republic,* October 8, 1919. In Jo Anne Boydston, ed., *The Middle Works, 1899–1924,* 10:180–85. Carbondale: Southern Illinois University Press, 1980.

———. "Fiat Justitia, Ruat Coelum." *New Republic,* September 29, 1917. In Jo Anne Boydston, ed., *The Middle Works, 1899–1924,* 10:281–84. Carbondale: Southern Illinois University Press, 1980.

———. "In Explanation of Our Lapse." *New Republic,* November 3, 1917. In Jo Anne Boydston, ed., *The Middle Works, 1899–1924,* 10:292–95. Carbondale: Southern Illinois University Press, 1980.

———. *Individualism Old and New.* New York: Minton, Balch, 1930.

Dilling, Elizabeth. *The Red Network*. Chicago: Published by Author, 1934.

Dorrien, Gary. *The Making of American Liberal Theology*, vol. 2: *Idealism, Realism, and Modernity, 1900–1950*. Louisville: Westminster John Knox, 2003.

Dower, John W. *War Without Mercy: Race and Power in the Pacific War*. New York: Pantheon, 1986.

Dubofsky, Melvin. *We Shall Be All: A History of the Industrial Workers of the World*. Chicago: Quadrangle, 1969.

Dudziak, Mary. *Cold War Civil Rights: Race and the Image of American Democracy*. Princeton: Princeton University Press, 2000.

Duke, David Nelson. *In the Trenches with Jesus and Marx: Harry F. Ward and the Struggle for Social Justice*. Tuscaloosa: University of Alabama Press, 2003.

Dunbar, Anthony P. *Against the Grain: Southern Radicals and Prophets, 1929–1959*. Charlottesville: University Press of Virginia, 1981.

Eddy, Sherwood. *The Challenge of Russia*. New York: Farrar and Rinehart, 1931.

———. *Eighty Adventurous Years*. New York: Harper, 1955.

———. *A Pilgrimage of Ideas; or, The Re-Education of Sherwood Eddy*. New York: Farrar and Rinehart, 1934.

———. *The Right to Fight: The Moral Grounds of War*. New York: Association Press, 1918.

———. *Russia Today: What Can We Learn from It?* New York: Farrar and Rinehart, 1934.

———. *With Our Soldiers in France*. New York: Association Press, 1917.

Eddy, Sherwood, and Kirby Page. *The Abolition of War*. New York: Doran, 1924.

———. *Makers of Freedom: Biographical Sketches in Social Progress*. New York: Doran, 1926.

Egerton, John. *Speak Now Against the Day: The Generation Before the Civil Rights Movement in the South*. Chapel Hill: University of North Carolina Press, 1994.

Eksteins, Modris. *Rites of Spring: The Great War and the Birth of the Modern Age*. New York: Anchor, 1989.

Eller, Cynthia. *Conscientious Objectors and the Second World War: Moral and Religious Arguments in Support of Pacifism*. New York: Praeger, 1991.

Ellis, Stephen, and Tsepo Sechaba. *Comrades Against Apartheid: The ANC and the South African Communist Party in Exile*. Bloomington: Indiana University Press, 1992.

Emerson, Ralph Waldo. *English Traits*. 1856. In Joseph Slater, ed., *The Collected Works of Ralph Waldo Emerson*, vol. 5. Cambridge: Harvard University Press, 1994.

Emmett, William. "Mania in Los Angeles." *Nation*, January 17, 1918, 58–59.

Epstein, Barbara. *Political Protest and Cultural Revolution: Nonviolent Direct Action in the 1970s and 1980s*. Berkeley: University of California Press, 1991.

Erickson, Christine K. "'I Have Not Had One Fact Disproven': Elizabeth Dilling's Crusade Against Communism in the 1930s." *Journal of American Studies* 36, no. 3 (December 2002): 473–89.

Erikson, Erik H. *Gandhi's Truth: On the Origins of Militant Nonviolence*. New York: Norton, 1969.

Estes, Steve. *I Am a Man! Race, Manhood, and the Civil Rights Movement*. Chapel Hill: University of North Carolina Press, 2005.

"Extension of Draft." *Fellowship* 8, no. 2 (February 1942): 28.

Fanon, Frantz. *The Wretched of the Earth*. Translated by Constance Farrington. New York: Grove, 1963.

Farmer, James. *Lay Bare the Heart: An Autobiography of the Civil Rights Movement*. New York: Arbor, 1985.

———. "The Race Logic of Pacifism." *Fellowship* 8, no. 2 (February 1942): 24–25.

Farrell, James J. *The Spirit of the Sixties: Making Postwar Radicalism*. New York: Routledge, 1997.

Fass, Paula. *The Damned and the Beautiful: American Youth in the 1920's*. New York: Oxford University Press, 1977.

"Fellowship Made Dynamic." *Inquiry*, September 1925, 43–44.

"Fellowship Members and Exemption." *News Sheet* 3 (July 1917): 6.

[Fellowship of Reconciliation]. "Statement on Far Eastern Situation by the 1938 Conference of the Fellowship of Reconciliation." *Fellowship* 4, no. 8 (October 1938): 2.

[Fellowship of Reconciliation Council]. "A Statement by the Council of the Fellowship of Reconciliation: Foreign Policy and Neutrality Legislation." *Fellowship* 5, no. 3 (March 1939): 14–15.

[Fellowship of Reconciliation Executive Committee]. "The Course Before Us: Statement of F.O.R. Executive Committee, December 10, 1941." *Fellowship* 8, no. 1 (January 1942): 2.

[———]. "We Will Not Fight in Spain: Statement of Executive Committee Fellowship of Reconciliation on Socialist Party Recruiting for Spanish War." *Fellowship* 3, no. 1 (January 1937): 10.

"Fellowship of Reconciliation in Conference." *Christian Century*, September 27, 1923, 1238.

Ferguson, Niall. *The War of the World: Twentieth-Century Conflict and the Descent of the West*. New York: Penguin, 2006.

Fey, Harold. "Again the Merchant of Death." *Fellowship* 6, no. 3 (March 1940): 44.

Fink, Leon. *Progressive Intellectuals and the Dilemmas of Democratic Commitment*. Cambridge: Harvard University Press, 1997.

Fischer, Louis. *Gandhi and Stalin: Two Signs at the World's Crossroads*. New York: Harper, 1947.

———. *The Life of Mahatma Gandhi*. New York: Harper, 1950.

Fisher, James Terence. *The Catholic Counterculture in America, 1933–1962*. Chapel Hill: University of North Carolina Press, 1989.

Fleischman, Harry. *Norman Thomas: A Biography*. New York: Norton, 1969.

"Following Up the Peace Pact: A Symposium." *Inquiry*, February 1929, 26–31.

Foote, Caleb. *Outcasts! The Story of America's Treatment of Her Japanese-American Minority*. New York: Fellowship of Reconciliation, [1943?].

———. "Politics and Freedom." *Fellowship* 14, no. 9 (October 1948): 13–16.

"FOR Changes Its Relationship to NSBRO." *Fellowship* 11, no. 1 (January 1945): 11.

Ford, Henry. *Today and Tomorrow.* Garden City, NY: Doubleday, Page, 1926.

Forty Years for Peace: A History of the Fellowship of Reconciliation, 1914–1954. New York: Fellowship of Reconciliation, 1954.

Foster, Carrie A. *The Women and the Warriors: The U.S. Section of the Women's International League for Peace and Freedom.* Syracuse: Syracuse University Press, 1995.

Foster, William Z. *Toward Soviet America.* New York: Coward-McCann, 1932.

Foucault, Michel. *Discipline and Punish: The Birth of the Prison.* New York: Vintage, 1995.

Fox, Richard Wightman. *Reinhold Niebuhr: A Biography.* San Francisco: Harper and Row, 1987.

Frederick, Peter J. *Knights of the Golden Rule: The Intellectual as Christian Social Reformer in the 1890s.* Lexington: University Press of Kentucky, 1976.

Friedland, Michael B. *Lift Up Your Voice Like a Trumpet: White Clergy and the Civil Rights and Antiwar Movements, 1954–1973.* Chapel Hill: University of North Carolina Press, 1998.

"Free the Philippines Now!" *World Tomorrow* 15, no. 3 (March 1932): 69–70.

Fussell, Paul. *The Great War and Modern Memory.* New York: Oxford University Press, 2000.

Gandhi, Mohandas. *An Autobiography: The Story of My Experiments with Truth.* Translated by Mahadev Desai. Washington, DC: Public Affairs Press, 1960.

———. *Hind Swaraj and Other Writings.* Edited by Anthony J. Parel. New York: Cambridge University Press, 1997.

———. "The Jews." *Harijan* 6, no. 42 (November 26, 1938): 352–53.

———. "Jews in a World of Violence: A Symposium, I: 'Death Has No Terror,'" *Jewish Frontier,* March 1939, 9–11.

———. "The Law of Suffering." *World Tomorrow* 3, no. 9 (September 1920): 266–67.

———. *Mahatma Gandhi: His Own Story.* Edited by C. F. Andrews. New York: Macmillan, 1930.

———. *Mahatma Gandhi at Work: His Own Story Continued.* Edited by C. F. Andrews. New York: Macmillan, 1931.

Garrison, Dee. *Bracing for Armageddon: Why Civil Defense Never Worked.* New York: Oxford University Press, 2006.

———. "'Our Skirts Gave Them Courage': The Civil Defense Protest Movement in New York City, 1955–1961." In Joanne Meyerowitz, ed., *Not June Cleaver: Women and Gender in Postwar America, 1945–1960,* 201–26. Philadelphia: Temple University Press, 1994.

Garrison, William Lloyd. "Declaration of Sentiments, 1838." In Staughton Lynd and Alice Lynd, eds., *Nonviolence in America: A Documentary History,* 13–17. Rev. ed. Maryknoll, NY: Orbis, 1995.

Garrow, David. *Bearing the Cross: Martin Luther King, Jr., and the Southern Christian Leadership Conference.* New York: Morrow, 1986.

Gary, Brett. *The Nervous Liberals: Propaganda Anxieties from World War I to the Cold War.* New York: Columbia University Press, 1999.

Geertz, Clifford. "Religion as a Cultural System." In *The Interpretation of Cultures: Selected Essays*, 87–125. New York: Basic Books, 1973.

Genovese, Eugene. *Roll, Jordan, Roll: The World the Slaves Made*. New York: Vintage, 1976.

"Gifts to Nisei Children Arouse Town's Ire." *Fellowship* 9, no. 2 (February 1943): 36.

Gilbert, James. *A Cycle of Outrage: America's Reaction to the Juvenile Delinquent in the 1950s*. New York: Oxford University Press, 1986.

Gitlin, Todd. *The Whole World Is Watching: Mass Media in the Making and Unmaking of the New Left*. Berkeley: University of California Press, 1980.

Gobat, Michel. *Confronting the American Dream: Nicaragua Under U.S. Imperial Rule*. Durham: Duke University Press, 2005.

Goffman, Erving. *The Presentation of Self in Everyday Life*. Edinburgh: University of Edinburgh, Social Sciences Research Centre, 1956.

———. *The Presentation of Self in Everyday Life*. Garden City, NY: Anchor, 1959.

Gold, Michael. "Wilder: Prophet of the Genteel Christ." *New Republic*, October 22, 1930, 266–67.

Goldberg, David J. *A Tale of Three Cities: Labor Organization and Protest in Paterson, Passaic, and Lawrence, 1916–1921*. New Brunswick: Rutgers University Press, 1989.

Goldstein, Robert Justin. *Political Repression in Modern America: From 1870 to 1976*. Urbana: University of Illinois Press, 2001.

Goodman, James E. *Stories of Scottsboro*. New York: Pantheon, 1994.

Goossen, Rachel Waltner. *Women Against the Good War: Conscientious Objection and Gender on the American Home Front, 1941–1947*. Chapel Hill: University of North Carolina Press, 1997.

Graetz, Robert S. *A White Preacher's Memoir: The Montgomery Bus Boycott*. Montgomery: Black Belt Press, 1999.

Gray, Francine du Plessix. *Divine Disobedience: Profiles in Catholic Radicalism*. New York: Knopf, 1970.

Grayling, A. C. *Among the Dead Cities: The History and Moral Legacy of the WWII Bombing of Civilians in Germany and Japan*. New York: Walker, 2006.

Green, Martin. *New York 1913: The Armory Show and the Paterson Strike Pageant*. New York: Scribner, 1988.

Greenberg, Hayim. "Jews in a World of Violence: A Symposium, II: We Are Treated As Subhumans—We Are Asked to Be Superhuman." *Jewish Frontier*, March 1939, 11–15.

Gregg, Richard B. "Aspects of Spiritual and Moral Beauty in Charkha and Khaddar." *Modern Review*, November 1925, 560–66.

———. *Economics of Khaddar*. Madras: Ganesan, 1928.

———. *Gandhiism Versus Socialism*. New York: John Day, 1932.

———. *Gandhiji's Satyagraha or Non-Violent Resistance*. Madras, 1930.

———. *Gandhism and Socialism: A Study and Comparison*. Madras: Ganesan, 1931.

———. "India Confronts Britain." *Nation*, June 18, 1930, 696–99.

———. "The Morals of Machinery." *Current Thought*, February 1926, 172–79.

———. "The National War Labor Board." *Harvard Law Review* 33, no. 1 (November 1919): 39–63.

———. "The Next Two Years." *Fellowship* 5, no. 5 (May 1939): 4–5.

———. *A Philosophy of Indian Economic Development*. Ahmedabad: Navajivan, 1958.

———. *The Power of Non-Violence*. Philadelphia: Lippincott, 1934.

———. *The Power of Non-Violence*. Philadelphia: Lippincott, 1935.

———. *The Power of Non-Violence*. Rev. ed. New York: Fellowship Publications, 1944.

———. *The Power of Nonviolence*. 2nd rev. ed. Nyack, NY: Fellowship Publications, 1959.

———. *A Preparation for Science*. Ahmedabad: Narahari Dwarkadas Parikh, [1928].

———. *The Psychology and Strategy of Gandhi's Non-Violent Resistance*. Madras: Ganesan, 1929. Reprint, New York: Garland, 1972.

———. "The Structure of a Nonviolent Society." *Fellowship* 19, no. 5 (May 1953): 9–12.

———. *Training for Peace: A Program for Peace Workers*. Philadelphia: Lippincott, 1937.

———. "Will Gandhi Win?" *Nation*, June 4, 1930, 661–63.

Gupta, S. P. K. *Apostle John and Gandhi*. Ahmedabad: Navajivan, 1988.

Hall, Jacquelyn Dowd. "The Long Civil Rights Movement and the Political Uses of the Past." *Journal of American History* 91, no. 4 (March 2005): 1233–63.

Hall, Mitchell. *Because of Their Faith: CALCAV and Religious Opposition to the Vietnam War*. New York: Columbia University Press, 1990.

Hall, Simon. *Peace and Freedom: The Civil Rights and Antiwar Movements in the 1960s*. Philadelphia: University of Pennsylvania Press, 2005.

Hamalian, Linda. *A Life of Kenneth Rexroth*. New York: Norton, 1991.

Handy, Robert T. *A History of Union Theological Seminary in New York*. New York: Columbia University Press, 1987.

Hankins, Barry. *God's Rascal: J. Frank Norris and the Beginnings of Southern Fundamentalism*. Lexington: University Press of Kentucky, 1996.

Hardiman, David. *Gandhi in His Time and Ours: The Global Legacy of His Ideas*. New York: Columbia University Press, 2003.

Harrison, Gilbert A. *The Enthusiast: A Life of Thornton Wilder*. New Haven: Ticknor and Fields, 1983.

Harvey, Paul. *Freedom's Coming: Religious Culture and the Shaping of the South from the Civil War through the Civil Rights Era*. Chapel Hill: University of North Carolina Press, 2005.

"Has Not Renounced Satyagraha." *Fellowship* 8, no. 1 (January 1942): 15.

Hassler, Alfred. "Commuters' Community." *Fellowship* 19, no. 4 (April 1953): 5–11, 17–18.

———. "Slaughter of the Innocent." *Fellowship* 10, no. 2 (February 1944): 19–21.

———. "They Build Brotherhood." *Fellowship* 22, no. 2 (February 1956): 11–16.

Hedstrom, Matthew Sigurd. "Seeking a Spiritual Center: Mass-Market Books and Liberal Religion in America, 1921–1948." PhD diss., University of Texas at Austin, 2006.

Henry, Patrick. "'And I Don't Care What It Is': The Tradition-History of a Civil Religion Proof-Text." *Journal of the American Academy of Religion* 49, no. 1 (March 1981): 35–49. http://www.jstor.org/.

Hentoff, Nat. *Peace Agitator: The Story of A. J. Muste.* New York: Macmillan, 1963.

Hershberger, Guy. *War, Peace, and Nonresistance.* Scottdale, PA: Herald, 1944.

Hershberger, Mary. *Traveling to Vietnam: American Peace Activists and the War.* Syracuse: Syracuse University Press, 1998.

Hill, Lance. *The Deacons for Defense: Armed Resistance and the Civil Rights Movement.* Chapel Hill: University of North Carolina Press, 2004.

Holmes, John Haynes. "America and Russia: When Shall They Be Friends?" *Community Pulpit*, Series 1927–1928, no. 7.

———. "Christ at the Peace-Table." *Messiah Pulpit*, Series 1918–1919, no. 5.

———. "Damaged Souls." *Community Pulpit*, Series 1923–1924, no. 5.

———. "The Ethics of Chastity." *Messiah Pulpit*, April 1917.

———. "From My Standpoint." *Fellowship* 8, no. 8 (August 1942): 126.

———. "Gandhi Before Pilate: A Sermon on the Indian Revolution." *Community Pulpit*, Series 1929–1930, no. 17.

———. *I Speak for Myself: The Autobiography of John Haynes Holmes.* New York: Harper, 1959.

———. "Is America a Civilized Country?" *Community Pulpit*, Series 1922–1923, no. 14.

———. *Is Violence the Way out of Our Industrial Disputes?* New York: Dodd, Mead, 1920.

———. "Lenin and Gandhi—Apostles of Utopia." *Community Pulpit*, Series 1927–1928, no. 5.

———. "Leo Tolstoy." *Messiah Pulpit*, January 1911.

———. *My Gandhi.* New York: Harper, 1953.

———. *New Wars for Old.* New York: Dodd, Mead, 1916.

———. "O Beautiful, My Country." *Messiah Pulpit*, July 1917.

———. *Out of Darkness.* New York: Harper, 1942.

———. "Outlawry of War—A Policy of Abolition." *World Tomorrow* 9, no. 6 (November 1926): 204–7.

———. "Pacifism in Personal Relations." In Devere Allen, ed., *Pacifism in the Modern World*, 239–53. Garden City, NY: Doubleday, Doran, 1929.

———. "Religion's New War with Science." *Christian Century*, October 27, 1937, 1322–24.

———. "Religious Defeatism." Review of *Moral Man and Immoral Society*, by Reinhold Niebuhr. *New York Herald Tribune*, January 8, 1933.

———. *The Revolutionary Function of the Modern Church.* New York: Putnam, 1912.

———. "Should Jews Be Pacifists?" *Opinion*, September 1940, 6–8.

———. "A Statement to My People on the Eve of War." *Messiah Pulpit*, May 1917.

———. "This Enormous Year (1917): Its Terrors, Tragedies, and Triumphs." *Messiah Pulpit*, February 1918.

———. "The Treaty a Flat Betrayal, Says Dr. Holmes." *World Tomorrow* 2, no. 6 (June 1919): 169.

————. "What Anyone Can Do." *World Tomorrow* 7, no. 2 (February 1924): 56–57.

————. "What Is a Religious Life?" *Community Pulpit*, Series 1926–1927, no. 3.

————. "What the World Owes the Bolsheviki!" *Community Pulpit*, Series 1927–1928, no. 3.

————. "Who Is the Greatest Man in the World Today?" *Community Pulpit*, Series 1920–1921, no. 19.

————. "The World Significance of Mahatma Gandhi." *Community Pulpit*, Series 1921–1922, no. 15.

Holmes, John Haynes, and Reginald Lawrence. *If This Be Treason*. New York: Macmillan, 1935.

Homan, Gerlof D. *American Mennonites and the Great War, 1914–1918*. Scottdale, PA: Herald, 1994.

Hook, Sidney. *Out of Step: An Unquiet Life in the Twentieth Century*. New York: Harper and Row, 1987.

————. "Violence." In E. R. A. Seligman, ed., *Encyclopaedia of the Social Sciences*, 15:264–67. New York: Macmillan, 1934.

Hopkins, C. Howard. *History of the Y.M.C.A. in North America*. New York: Association Press, 1951.

————. *John R. Mott, 1865–1955*. Grand Rapids: Eerdmans, 1979.

————. *The Rise of the Social Gospel in American Protestantism*. New Haven: Yale University Press, 1940.

Hostetter, David L. *Movement Matters: American Apartheid Activism and the Rise of Multicultural Politics*. New York: Routledge, 2006.

Houser, George. "'Interim Period' in South Africa." *Fellowship* 21, no. 1 (January 1955): 17–21.

————. *No One Can Stop the Rain: Glimpses of Africa's Liberation Struggle*. New York: Pilgrim, 1989.

————. *Nonviolent Revolution in South Africa*. New York: Fellowship Publications, 1953.

————. "Project: Brotherhood." *Fellowship* 16, no. 2 (February 1950): 13–18.

————. "Reflections of a Religious War Objector (Half a Century Later)." In Larry Gara and Lenna Mae Gara, eds., *A Few Small Candles: War Resisters of World War II Tell Their Stories*, 130–51. Kent: Kent State University Press, 1999.

Houser, George, and Bayard Rustin. *We Challenged Jim Crow!* N.p.: Fellowship of Reconciliation, 1947.

Howlett, Charles F. *Brookwood Labor College and the Struggle for Peace and Social Justice in America*. Lewiston, NY: Mellen, 1993.

————. "Fellowship and Reconciliation: A Pacifist Organization Confronts the War in Southeast Asia." *Maryland Historian* 25, no. 1 (Spring/Summer 1994): 1–24.

————. "Neighborly Concern: John Nevin Sayre and the Mission of Peace and Goodwill to Nicaragua, 1927–28." *Americas* 45 (July 1988): 19–46.

Hughes, Richard T. *Reviving the Ancient Faith: The Story of Churches of Christ in America*. Grand Rapids: Eerdmans, 1996.

Hulsether, Mark. *Building a Protestant Left:* Christianity and Crisis *Magazine, 1941–1993*. Knoxville: University of Tennessee Press, 1999.

Hunt, Andrew E. *David Dellinger: The Life and Times of a Nonviolent Revolutionary.* New York: New York University Press, 2006.

Hunt, Lynn. *Inventing Human Rights: A History.* New York: Norton, 2007.

Hutchins, Grace. "Our Inferiority Complex." *World Tomorrow* 6, no. 12 (December 1923): 362–63.

Hutchins, Grace, and Anna Rochester. *Jesus Christ and the World Today.* New York: Doran, 1922.

Hutchison, William R. *Errand to the World: American Protestant Thought and Foreign Missions.* Chicago: University of Chicago Press, 1987.

———. *The Modernist Impulse in American Protestantism.* Cambridge: Harvard University Press, 1976.

Illy, József, ed. *Albert Meets America: How Journalists Treated Genius During Einstein's 1921 Travels.* Baltimore: Johns Hopkins University Press, 2006.

Immerwahr, Daniel. "Caste or Colony? Indianizing Race in the United States." *Modern Intellectual History* 4, no. 2 (August 2007): 275–301.

Ingram, Norman. *The Politics of Dissent: Pacifism in France, 1919–1939.* New York: Oxford University Press, 1991.

"Interracial Group Marches to Washington." *Fellowship* 8, no. 11 (November 1942): 192.

Irons, Peter. *Justice at War: The Story of the Japanese American Internment Cases.* Berkeley: University of California Press, 1983.

Isserman, Maurice. *If I Had a Hammer: The Death of the Old Left and the Birth of the New Left.* New York: Basic Books, 1987.

———. *Which Side Were You On? The American Communist Party During the Second World War.* Urbana: University of Illinois Press, 1993.

James, William. "The Moral Equivalent of War." In Bruce W. Wilshire, ed., *William James: The Essential Writings*, 349–61. Albany: State University of New York Press, 1984.

Jameson, Elizabeth. *All That Glitters: Class, Conflict, and Community in Cripple Creek.* Urbana: University of Illinois Press, 1998.

Jarvis, Christina. *The Male Body at War: American Masculinity During World War II.* DeKalb: Northern Illinois University Press, 2004.

Jenkins, Philip. *The Next Christendom: The Coming of Global Christianity.* Rev. ed. New York: Oxford University Press, 2007.

Jha, Manoranhan. *Civil Disobedience and After: The American Reaction to Political Developments in India During 1930–1935.* Meerut: Meenakshi Prakashan, 1973.

John XXIII, Pope. *Pacem in Terris* (1963). http://www.vatican.va/.

Johnpoll, Bernard K. *Pacifist's Progress: Norman Thomas and the Decline of American Socialism.* Chicago: Quadrangle, 1970.

Johnson, Alan Campbell. *Peace Offering.* London: Methuen, 1936.

Johnson, Robert David. *The Peace Progressives and American Foreign Relations.* Cambridge: Harvard University Press, 1995.

Jones, E. Stanley. "I Join the Fellowship." *Fellowship* 6, no. 10 (December 1940): 150.

———. "The Soul of Mahatma Gandhi." *World Tomorrow* 7, no. 12 (December 1924): 367.

Jones, Paul. "Editing Creatively." *World Tomorrow* 15, no. 6 (June 1932): 187.

Juergensmeyer, Mark. *Terror in the Mind of God: The Global Rise of Religious Violence.* 3rd ed. Berkeley: University of California Press, 2003.

Kapur, Sudarshan. *Raising Up a Prophet: The African-American Encounter with Gandhi.* Boston: Beacon, 1992.

Kasher, Steven. *The Civil Rights Movement: A Photographic History, 1954–1968.* New York: Abbeville, 2000.

Kates, Susan. *Activist Rhetorics and American Higher Education.* Carbondale: Southern Illinois University Press, 2001.

Keith, Jeanette. *Rich Man's War, Poor Man's Fight: Race, Class, and Power in the Rural South During the First World War.* Chapel Hill: University of North Carolina Press, 2003.

Kelley, Robin D. G. *Hammer and Hoe: Alabama Communists During the Great Depression.* Chapel Hill: University of North Carolina Press, 1990.

———. *Race Rebels: Culture, Politics, and the Black Working Class.* New York: Free Press, 1996.

Kempton, Murray. "O'er Moor and Fen: J. B. Matthews and the Multiple Revelation." In *Part of Our Time: Some Ruins and Monuments of the Thirties,* 155–79. New York: Simon and Schuster, 1955.

Kennedy, David M. *Freedom from Fear: The American People in Depression and War, 1929–1945.* New York: Oxford University Press, 1999.

———. *Over Here: The First World War and American Society.* New York: Oxford University Press, 1980.

King, Coretta Scott. *My Life with Martin Luther King, Jr.* New York: Holt, Rinehart and Winston, 1969.

King, Martin Luther, Jr. *Stride Toward Freedom.* New York: Harper, 1958.

———. "Walk for Freedom." *Fellowship* 22, no. 5 (May 1956): 5–7.

———. *Why We Can't Wait.* New York: New American Library, 1964.

Klehr, Harvey. *The Heyday of American Communism: The Depression Decade.* New York: Basic Books, 1984.

Kleinman, Mark. *A World of Hope, a World of Fear: Henry A. Wallace, Reinhold Niebuhr, and American Liberalism.* Columbus: Ohio State University Press, 2000.

Kloppenberg, James. *Uncertain Victory: Social Democracy and Progressivism in European and American Thought, 1870–1920.* New York: Oxford University Press, 1986.

Knock, Thomas J. *To End All Wars: Woodrow Wilson and the Quest for a New World Order.* New York: Oxford University Press, 1992.

Kutulas, Judy. *The Long War: The Intellectual People's Front and Anti-Stalinism, 1930–1940.* Durham: Duke University Press, 1995.

Laqueur, Walter. *Guerrilla Warfare: A Historical and Critical Study.* New Brunswick, NJ: Transaction, 1998.

Lasch, Christopher. *American Liberals and the Russian Revolution.* New York: Columbia University Press, 1962.

————. "Religious Contributions to Social Movements: Walter Rauschenbusch, the Social Gospel, and Its Critics." *Journal of Religious Ethics* 18, no. 1 (Spring 1990): 7–25.

Lawson, R. Alan. *The Failure of Independent Liberalism, 1930–1941.* New York: Putnam, 1971.

Lee, Janet. *Comrades and Partners: The Shared Lives of Grace Hutchins and Anna Rochester.* Lanham, MD: Rowman and Littlefield, 2000.

Lekus, Ian. "Queer and Present Dangers: Homosexuality and American Antiwar Activism During the Vietnam Era." PhD diss., Duke University, 2003.

Lemke-Santangelo, Gretchen. "The Radical Conscientious Objectors of World War II: Wartime Experience and Postwar Activism." *Radical History Review* 45 (Fall 1989): 5–29.

Lepore, Jill. *The Name of War: King Philip's War and the Origins of American Identity.* New York: Knopf, 1998.

Lerner, Michael. *The Left Hand of God: Taking Back Our Country from the Religious Right.* San Francisco: Harper, 2006.

Levine, Daniel. *Bayard Rustin and the Civil Rights Movement.* New Brunswick: Rutgers University Press, 2000.

Lewis, David Levering. *W. E. B. Du Bois: The Fight for Equality and the American Century, 1919–1963.* New York: Holt, 2000.

Lewis, John. *Walking with the Wind: A Memoir of the Movement.* With Michael D'Orso. San Diego: Harcourt Brace, 1998.

Lewy, Guenter. *Peace and Revolution: The Moral Crisis of American Pacifism.* Grand Rapids: Eerdmans, 1988.

Lieberman, Robbie. *The Strangest Dream: Communism, Anticommunism, and the U.S. Peace Movement, 1945–1963.* Syracuse: Syracuse University Press, 2000.

Link, Eugene P. *Labor-Religion Prophet: The Times and Life of Harry F. Ward.* Boulder, CO: Westview, 1984.

Lippmann, Walter. *Public Opinion.* 1922. Reprint, New York: Free Press, 1949.

————. "The War in the Air." *New York Herald Tribune,* March 11, 1944.

Long, Cedric. "Can Capital and Labor Get Together?" *World Tomorrow* 12, no. 9 (September 1929): 358–61.

————. "The Consumer as Revolutionist." *World Tomorrow* 4, no. 11 (November 1921): 334–36.

Longfield, Bradley J. "From Evangelicalism to Liberalism: Public Midwestern Universities in Nineteenth-Century America." In George M. Marsden and Bradley J. Longfield, eds., *The Secularization of the Academy,* 46–73. New York: Oxford University Press, 1992.

Luker, Ralph E. *The Social Gospel in Black and White: American Racial Reform, 1885–1912.* Chapel Hill: University of North Carolina Press, 1991.

Lynn, Conrad. *There Is a Fountain: The Autobiography of a Civil Rights Lawyer.* Westport, CT: Lawrence Hill, 1979.

Macaulay, Neill. *The Sandino Affair.* Chicago: Quadrangle, 1967.

Macdonald, Dwight. *The Root Is Man.* 1946. Reprint, New York: Autonomedia, 1995.

Manela, Erez. *The Wilsonian Moment: Self Determination and the International Origins of Anticolonial Nationalism*. New York: Oxford University Press, 2007.

Marchand, C. Roland. *The American Peace Movement and Social Reform, 1898–1918*. Princeton: Princeton University Press, 1972.

Marsden, George M. *Fundamentalism and American Culture*. 2nd ed. New York: Oxford University Press, 2006.

———. "The Soul of the American University: An Historical Overview." In George M. Marsden and Bradley J. Longfield, eds., *The Secularization of the Academy*, 9–45. New York: Oxford University Press, 1992.

Marsh, Charles. *God's Long Summer: Stories of Faith and Civil Rights*. Princeton: Princeton University Press, 1997.

Martin Luther King and the Montgomery Story. N.p.: Fellowship of Reconciliation, [1957].

Martin Luther King y la Historia de Montgomery. N.p.: Fellowship Publications, [1957?].

Martin, Robert F. *Howard Kester and the Struggle for Social Justice in the South, 1904–1977*. Charlottesville: University Press of Virginia, 1991.

Matthews, J. B. *Christianity the Way*. Garden City, NY: Doubleday, Doran, 1929.

———. *Odyssey of a Fellow Traveler*. New York: Mount Vernon, 1938.

Mattson, Kevin. *Intellectuals in Action: The Origins of the New Left and Radical Liberalism, 1945–1970*. University Park: Pennsylvania State University Press, 2002.

———. *When America Was Great: The Fighting Faith of Postwar Liberalism*. New York: Routledge, 2006.

May, Henry. *Protestant Churches and Industrial America*. New York: Harper, 1949.

Mayer, Milton. "The Christer." *Fellowship* 18, no. 1 (January 1952): 1–10.

McCarraher, Eugene. *Christian Critics: Religion and the Impasse in Modern American Social Thought*. Ithaca: Cornell University Press, 2000.

McCartin, Joseph A. *Labor's Great War: The Struggle for Industrial Democracy and the Origins of Modern American Labor Relations, 1912–1921*. Chapel Hill: University of North Carolina Press, 1997.

McLuhan, Marshall. *Understanding Media: The Extensions of Man*. New York: McGraw-Hill, 1964.

McNeal, Patricia. *Harder Than War: Catholic Peacemaking in Twentieth-Century America*. New Brunswick: Rutgers University Press, 1992.

Mead, Margaret. *Coming of Age in Samoa*. New York: Morrow, 1928.

Mehta, Ved. "Gandhiism Is Not Easily Copied." *New York Times*, July 9, 1961. http://proquest.umi.com/.

Meier, August, and Elliott Rudwick. *CORE: A Study in the Civil Rights Movement, 1942–1968*. New York: Oxford University Press, 1973.

Meigs, Mark. *Optimism at Armageddon: Voices of American Participants in the First World War*. New York: New York University Press, 1997.

Melish, John Howard. *Paul Jones: Minister of Reconciliation*. New York: Fellowship of Reconciliation, 1942.

Menand, Louis. *The Metaphysical Club*. New York: Farrar, Straus and Giroux, 2001.

Meriwether, James H. *Proudly We Can Be Africans: Black Americans and Africa, 1935–1961.* Chapel Hill: University of North Carolina Press, 2002.

Merton, Thomas. *Blessed Are the Meek: The Christian Roots of Nonviolence.* Nyack, NY: Catholic Peace Fellowship, 1967.

Meyer, Donald B. *The Protestant Search for Political Realism, 1919–1941.* 2nd ed. Middletown, CT: Wesleyan University Press, 1988.

Meyer, Frank S. "The Violence of Nonviolence." *National Review,* April 20, 1965, 327.

Milgram, Morris. *Good Neighborhood: The Challenge of Open Housing.* New York: Norton, 1977.

Miller, Arthur. *Timebends: A Life.* New York: Grove, 1987.

Miller, James. *"Democracy Is in the Streets": From Port Huron to the Siege of Chicago.* Cambridge: Harvard University Press, 1994.

Miller, Keith D. *Voice of Deliverance: The Language of Martin Luther King, Jr., and Its Sources.* New York: Free Press, 1992.

Miller, Robert Moats. *American Protestantism and Social Issues, 1919–1939.* Chapel Hill: University of North Carolina Press, 1958.

Miller, William Robert. *Martin Luther King, Jr.: His Life, Martyrdom, and Meaning for the World.* New York: Weybright and Talley, 1968.

———. *Nonviolence: A Christian Interpretation.* New York: Association Press, 1964.

"A Minister and His Church in War." *Survey,* June 2, 1917, 228–29.

Moeller, Susan D. *Compassion Fatigue: How the Media Sell Disease, Famine, War, and Death.* New York: Routledge, 1999.

Mollin, Marian B. "The Limits of Egalitarianism: Radical Pacifism, Civil Rights, and the Journey of Reconciliation." *Radical History Review* 88 (Winter 2004): 113–38.

———. *Radical Pacifism in Modern America: Egalitarianism and Protest.* Philadelphia: University of Pennsylvania Press, 2006.

Montgomery, David. *The Fall of the House of Labor: The Workplace, the State, and American Labor Activism, 1865–1925.* New York: Cambridge University Press, 1987.

Moon, Penelope Adams. "'Peace on Earth—Peace in Vietnam': The Catholic Peace Fellowship and Antiwar Witness, 1964–1976." *Journal of Social History* 36, no. 4 (Summer 2003): 1033–57. http://search.ebscohost.com/.

Moreno, J. L. "The Concept of Sociodrama: A New Approach to the Problem of Inter-Cultural Relations." *Sociometry* 6, no. 4 (November 1943): 434–49.

Morris, Aldon D. *The Origins of the Civil Rights Movement: Black Communities Organizing for Change.* New York: Free Press, 1984.

Morrison-Reed, Mark D. *Black Pioneers in a White Denomination.* Boston: Beacon, 1984.

Mott, John R. *The Evangelization of the World in This Generation.* New York: Student Volunteer Movement for Foreign Missions, 1900.

Muller, Eric L. *Free to Die for Their Country: The Story of the Japanese American Draft Resisters in World War II.* Chicago: University of Chicago Press, 2001.

Mumford, Lewis. *Values for Survival.* New York: Harcourt, Brace, 1946.

Murphy, Paul L. *World War I and the Origins of Civil Liberties in the United States.* New York: Norton, 1979.

Muste, Abraham J. "Can We Have Unity?" *World Tomorrow* 8, no. 1 (January 1925): 14–16.

———. "Catholic Workers Unite." *Fellowship* 3, no. 6 (June 1937): 5–6.

———. "Chambers, God, and the Communists." *Fellowship* 18, no. 7 (July 1952): 7–14.

———. "Chambers, God, and the Communists—II." *Fellowship* 18, no. 8 (September 1952): 10–16.

———. "Fellowship in Discovering Truth." *Fellowship* 10, no. 9 (November 1944): 188–89.

———. "The First and Fourth of July." *Fellowship* 7, no. 6 (July 1941): 115–16.

———. *Non-Violence in an Aggressive World.* New York: Harper, 1940.

———. *Not By Might: Christianity: The Way to Human Decency.* New York: Harper, 1947.

———. "Prospect for Peace in 1953." *Fellowship* 19, no. 1 (January 1953): 4–9.

———. "Return to Pacifism." *Christian Century*, December 2, 1936, 1603–6.

———. Review of *My India, My America,* by Krishnalal Shridharani. *Fellowship* 7, no. 12 (December 1941): 194.

———. "Revolutionary Movements: What They Have In Common." *World Tomorrow* 5, no. 4 (April 1922): 116–17.

———. "Sketches for an Autobiography." In Nat Hentoff, ed., *The Essays of A. J. Muste*, 1–174. New York: Simon and Schuster, 1967.

———. "Theology of Despair: An Open Letter to Reinhold Niebuhr." *Fellowship* 14, no. 8 (September 1948): 4–8.

———. "The Two Tests." *World Tomorrow* 3, no. 7 (July 1920): 214.

———. "U.S.A.—Arsenal." *Fellowship* 7, no. 4 (April 1941): 59–60.

———. "What Is Left to Do?" *Fellowship* 17, no. 7 (July 1951): 11–16.

Muzumdar, Haridas T. *America's Contributions to India's Freedom.* Allahabad: Central Book Depot, 1962.

———. *Gandhi the Apostle.* Chicago: Universal, 1923.

Nandy, Ashis. *Alternative Sciences: Creativity and Authenticity in Two Indian Scientists.* Bombay: Allied Publishers, 1980.

Nearing, Helen, and Scott Nearing. *Continuing the Good Life: Half a Century of Homesteading.* New York: Schocken, 1979.

———. *Living the Good Life: How to Live Sanely and Simply in a Troubled World.* 1954. Reprint, New York: Schocken, 1970.

Neiberg, Michael S. *Making Citizen-Soldiers: ROTC and the Ideology of Military Service.* Cambridge: Harvard University Press, 2000.

Newton, Huey. *Revolutionary Suicide.* New York: Harcourt Brace Jovanovich, 1973.

Niebuhr, Reinhold. "Building Tomorrow's World: Missions and World Peace." *World Tomorrow* 10, no. 4 (April 1927): 170–71.

———. "Christian Revolutionary." Review of *The Essays of A. J. Muste,* ed. Nat Hentoff. *New York Times*, April 16, 1967. http://proquest.umi.com/.

———. *Christianity and Power Politics.* 1940. Reprint, n.p.: Archon, 1969.

———. *Does Civilization Need Religion? A Study in the Social Resources and Limitations of Religion in Modern Life.* New York: Macmillan, 1927.

[———]. "Gandhiism Versus Socialism." *World Tomorrow* 15, no. 24 (December 1932): 607.

———. *An Interpretation of Christian Ethics.* New York: Harper, 1935.

———. "Is the Bombing Necessary?" *Christianity and Crisis,* April 3, 1944, 1–2.

———. *Leaves from the Notebook of a Tamed Cynic.* New York: Willett, Clark and Colby, 1929.

———. "Militant Pacifism." Review of *The Power of Non-Violence,* by Richard B. Gregg. *Nation,* December 19, 1934, 718.

———. *Moral Man and Immoral Society.* 1932. Reprint, New York: Scribner, 1960.

———. *The Nature and Destiny of Man.* New York: Scribner, 1941.

———. "A Reorientation of Radicalism." *World Tomorrow* 16, no. 19 (July 1933): 443–44.

———. "The Threat of the R.O.T.C." *World Tomorrow* 9, no. 5 (October 1926): 154–56.

———. "The Way of Non-Violent Resistance." *Christianity and Society,* Spring 1956, 3.

———. "Would Jesus Be a Modernist Today?" *World Tomorrow* 12, no. 3 (March 1929): 122–24.

Nietzsche, Friedrich. *On the Genealogy of Morals.* In Walter Kaufmann, trans. and ed., *Basic Writings of Nietzsche,* 437–600. New York: Modern Library, 2000.

Norton, Helen G. "Considering the Negro: Significant Symposium at Brookwood." *Labor Age* 16, no. 8 (August 1927): 11.

Nutt, Rick L. *The Whole Gospel for the Whole World: Sherwood Eddy and the American Protestant Mission.* Macon, GA: Mercer University Press, 1997.

Oakes, Guy. *The Imaginary War: Civil Defense and American Cold War Culture.* New York: Oxford University Press, 1994.

Oberdeck, Kathryn J. *The Evangelist and the Impresario: Religion, Entertainment, and Cultural Politics in America, 1884–1914.* Baltimore: Johns Hopkins University Press, 1999.

"The One Course for Us Is Penitence." *New World* 1, no. 5 (May 1918): 99–101.

"An Open Letter to John Haynes Holmes." *Fellowship* 9, no. 9 (September 1943): 167.

Orsi, Robert. *The Madonna of 115th Street: Faith and Community in Italian Harlem, 1880–1950.* New Haven: Yale University Press, 1985.

"Pacifists Demonstrate, Educate on CD Day." *Fellowship* 21, no. 7 (July 1955): 24–25.

Page, Kirby. "Building Tomorrow's World." *World Tomorrow* 9, no. 5 (October 1926): 168.

———. *Christianity and Economic Problems.* New York: Association Press, 1922.

———. "Class War and Religion." *World Tomorrow* 16, no. 10 (March 8, 1933): 225–28.

———. "The Danger of Drifting." *World Tomorrow* 10, no. 2 (February 1927): 57–58.

————. "Empty the Relocation Centers!" *Christian Century*, June 16, 1943, 715–16.

————. *Individualism and Socialism: An Ethical Survey of Economic and Political Forces*. New York: Farrar and Rinehart, 1933.

————. "Is Coercion Ever Justifiable?" *World Tomorrow* 15, no. 6 (June 1932): 173–75.

————. *Is Mahatma Gandhi the Greatest Man of the Age?* New York: K. Page, 1930.

————. *Jesus or Christianity: A Study in Contrasts*. Garden City, NY: Doubleday, Doran, 1929.

————. *Kirby Page, Social Evangelist: The Autobiography of a 20th Century Prophet for Peace*. Edited by Harold E. Fey. Nyack, NY: Fellowship Press, 1975.

————. *National Defense*. New York: Farrar and Rinehart, 1931.

[————]. "The Point of View." *World Tomorrow* 10, no. 11 (November 1927): 434.

————. "The Price of Philippine Independence." *World Tomorrow* 13, no. 4 (April 1930): 156–58.

————. *The Sword or the Cross: Which Should Be the Weapon of the Christian Militant?* Chicago: Christian Century Press, 1921.

————. "The United Front." *Fellowship* 1, no. 1 (March 1935): 6–7.

————. "United States Steel Corporation." *Atlantic Monthly*, May 1922, 585–93.

————. *War: Its Causes, Consequences, and Cure*. New York: Doran, 1923.

————. "Will India Become a Lost Dominion?" *World Tomorrow* 13, no. 3 (March 1930): 104–7.

Parker, Michael. *The Kingdom of Character: The Student Volunteer Movement for Foreign Missions, 1886–1926*. New York: University Press of America, 1998.

Parks, Rosa, and Jim Haskins. *Rosa Parks: My Story*. New York: Dial, 1992.

Payne, Charles M. *I've Got the Light of Freedom: The Organizing Tradition and the Mississippi Freedom Struggle*. Berkeley: University of California Press, 1995.

"Peace and Honor Yet to Be Won." *World Tomorrow* 2, no. 6 (June 1919): 145–48.

"Peace and the Financiers." *World Tomorrow* 2, no. 12 (December 1919): 327.

Peck, James. *Freedom Ride*. New York: Simon and Schuster, 1962.

Pells, Richard H. *Radical Visions and American Dreams: Culture and Social Thought in the Depression Years*. Urbana: University of Illinois Press, 1998.

Perry, Lewis. *Radical Abolitionism: Anarchy and the Government of God in Antislavery Thought*. Knoxville: University of Tennessee Press, 1995.

Peterson, H. C., and Gilbert Fite. *Opponents of War, 1917–1918*. Madison: University of Wisconsin Press, 1957.

Pfeffer, Paula F. *A. Philip Randolph: Pioneer of the Civil Rights Movement*. Baton Rouge: Louisiana State University Press, 1990.

Pfeiffer, Ehrenfried. *Bio-Dynamic Farming and Gardening*. 2nd ed. New York: Anthroposophic Press, 1940.

Piehl, Mel. *Breaking Bread: The Catholic Worker and the Origin of Catholic Radicalism in America*. Philadelphia: Temple University Press, 1982.

Piper, John F., Jr. *The American Churches in World War I.* Athens: Ohio University Press, 1985.

Plummer, Brenda Gayle. *Rising Wind: Black Americans and U.S. Foreign Affairs, 1935–1960.* Chapel Hill: University of North Carolina Press, 1996.

Polner, Murray, and Jim O'Grady. *Disarmed and Dangerous: The Radical Lives and Times of Daniel and Philip Berrigan.* New York: Basic Books, 1997.

Polsgrove, Carol. *Divided Minds: Intellectuals and the Civil Rights Movement.* New York: Norton, 2001.

"Preacher Without Authority: The Story of John Haynes Holmes." *World Tomorrow* 13, no. 3 (March 1930): 119–22.

Purcell, Edward A., Jr. *The Crisis of Democratic Theory: Scientific Naturalism and the Problem of Value.* Lexington: University Press of Kentucky, 1973.

Putney, Clifford. *Muscular Christianity: Manhood and Sports in Protestant America, 1880–1920.* Cambridge: Harvard University Press, 2001.

Rabban, David M. *Free Speech in Its Forgotten Years.* New York: Cambridge University Press, 1997.

Raiford, Leigh. "'Come Let Us Build a New World Together': SNCC and the Photography of the Civil Rights Movement." *American Quarterly* 59, no. 4 (December 2007): 1129–57.

Raines, Howell, ed. *My Soul Is Rested: Movement Days in the Deep South Remembered.* New York: Putnam, 1977.

Raucher, Alan. "American Anti-Imperialists and the Pro-India Movement, 1900–1932." *Pacific Historical Review* 43, no. 1 (February 1974): 83–110.

Reddick, Lawrence D. *Crusader Without Violence: A Biography of Martin Luther King, Jr.* New York: Harper, 1959.

Rhodes, Jane. *Framing the Black Panthers: The Spectacular Rise of a Black Power Icon.* New York: New Press, 2007.

Ribuffo, Leo. *The Old Christian Right: The Protestant Far Right from the Great Depression to the Cold War.* Philadelphia: Temple University Press, 1983.

Risen, James, and Judy L. Thomas. *Wrath of Angels: The American Abortion War.* New York: Basic Books, 1998.

Roberts, Nancy L. *Dorothy Day and the* Catholic Worker. Albany: State University of New York Press, 1984.

Robinson, Greg. *By Order of the President: FDR and the Internment of Japanese Americans.* Cambridge: Harvard University Press, 2001.

Robinson, Jo Ann Gibson. *The Montgomery Bus Boycott and the Women Who Started It: The Memoir of Jo Ann Gibson Robinson.* Edited by David Garrow. Knoxville: University of Tennessee Press, 1987.

Robinson, Jo Ann Ooiman. *Abraham Went Out: A Biography of A. J. Muste.* Philadelphia: Temple University Press, 1981.

———. "The Pharos of the East Side, 1937–1940: Labor Temple Under the Direction of A. J. Muste." *Journal of Presbyterian History* 48, no. 1 (1970): 18–37.

Rochester, Stuart I. *American Liberal Disillusionment in the Wake of World War I.* University Park: Pennsylvania State University Press, 1977.

Roosevelt, Franklin D. "An Appeal to Great Britain, France, Italy, Germany, and Poland to Refrain from Air Bombing of Civilians." September 1, 1939. In John T.
Woolley and Gerhard Peters, *The American Presidency Project*. Santa Barbara:
University of California (hosted), Gerhard Peters (database). http://www
.presidency.ucsb.edu/ws/?pid = 15797.

——. "Radio Address Before the Eighth Pan American Scientific Congress,
Washington, DC." May 10, 1940. In John T. Woolley and Gerhard Peters, *The
American Presidency Project*. Santa Barbara: University of California (hosted),
Gerhard Peters (database). http://www.presidency.ucsb.edu/ws/?pid = 15948.

Rorty, Richard. "Religion as Conversation-Stopper." In *Philosophy and Social Hope*,
168–74. New York: Penguin, 2000.

Rossinow, Doug. *The Politics of Authenticity: Liberalism, Christianity, and the New
Left in America*. New York: Columbia University Press, 1998.

——. "The Radicalization of the Social Gospel: Harry F. Ward and the Search
for a New Social Order, 1898–1936." *Religion and American Culture* 15, no. 1
(Winter 2005): 63–106.

Rotzel, Harold. "Pacifism in the Labor Field." *World Tomorrow* 9, no. 3 (March
1926): 81–83.

Rozario, Kevin. "'Delicious Horrors': Mass Culture, the Red Cross, and the Appeal of Modern American Humanitarianism." *American Quarterly* 55, no. 3
(September 2003): 417–55.

Rubin, Joan Shelley. *The Making of Middlebrow Culture*. Chapel Hill: University of
North Carolina Press, 1992.

Rumbough, Constance. *Crumbling Barriers*. New York: Fellowship Publications,
1948.

——. "Southern F.O.R. Conducts Camp." *Fellowship* 5, no. 8 (October 1939): 17.

——. "We Had a Work Camp." *Fellowship* 8, no. 11 (November 1942): 189.

Russell, Elbert. *Elbert Russell, Quaker: An Autobiography*. Jackson, TN: Friendly
Press, 1956.

Rustin, Bayard. "From Protest to Politics: The Future of the Civil Rights Movement." *Commentary* 39, no. 2 (February 1965): 25–31.

——. "The Negro and Non-Violence." *Fellowship* 8, no. 10 (October 1942): 166–67.

Sayre, John Nevin. "American Postscript." *Fellowship* 10, no. 3/2 (March 1944):
63–64.

——. "Disarmament and Defense." *World Tomorrow* 5, no. 1 (January 1922): 3–7.

——. "The Power of Opinion." *World Tomorrow* 8, no. 4 (April 1925): 105–7.

——. "Recognize Russia Now." *World Tomorrow* 13, no. 1 (January 1930): 8–9.

——. "Some I Can Save." *Fellowship* 4, no. 9 (November 1938): 4–5.

——. "A Try at Peace and Justice with Sandino." *World Tomorrow* 11, no. 3
(March 1928): 113–17.

——. "Why We Are Squeamish." *World Tomorrow* 15, no. 7 (July 1932): 214.

Scarry, Elaine. *The Body in Pain: The Making and Unmaking of the World*. New
York: Oxford University Press, 1985.

Schaffer, Ronald. *Wings of Judgment: American Bombing in World War II*. New
York: Oxford University Press, 1985.

Schell, Jonathan. *The Unconquerable World: Power, Nonviolence, and the Will of the People*. New York: Metropolitan, 2003.

Schott, Linda K. *Reconstructing Women's Thoughts: The Women's International League for Peace and Freedom Before World War II*. Stanford: Stanford University Press, 1997.

Schrecker, Ellen. *Many Are the Crimes: McCarthyism in America*. Boston: Little, Brown, 1998.

Scott, James C. *Domination and the Arts of Resistance: Hidden Transcripts*. New Haven: Yale University Press, 1990.

————. *Weapons of the Weak: Everyday Forms of Peasant Resistance*. New Haven: Yale University Press, 1985.

Seidler, Murray B. *Norman Thomas: Respectable Rebel*. Syracuse: Syracuse University Press, 1967.

Selekman, Benjamin M. *Sharing Management with the Workers: A Study of the Partnership Plan of the Dutchess Bleachery, Wappinger Falls, New York*. New York: Russell Sage Foundation, 1924.

Seshachari, C. *Gandhi and the American Scene: An Intellectual History and Inquiry*. Bombay: Nachiketa, 1969.

Setran, David P. *The College "Y": Student Religion in the Era of Secularization*. New York: Palgrave Macmillan, 2007.

Shaffer, Robert. "Cracks in the Consensus: Defending the Rights of Japanese Americans During World War II." *Radical History Review* 72 (Fall 1998): 84–120.

Shapiro, Edward S. "Decentralist Intellectuals and the New Deal." *Journal of American History* 58, no. 4 (March 1972): 938–57.

Sharp, Gene. *The Politics of Nonviolent Action*. Boston: Sargent, 1973.

Showalter, Nathan D. *The End of a Crusade: The Student Volunteer Movement for Foreign Missions and the Great War*. Lanham, MD: Scarecrow, 1998.

Shridharani, Krishnalal. *My India, My America*. New York: Duell, Sloan and Pearce, 1941.

————. *War Without Violence: A Study of Gandhi's Method and Its Accomplishments*. New York: Harcourt, Brace, 1939.

Sibley, Mulford Q., and Philip E. Jacob. *Conscription of Conscience: The American State and the Conscientious Objector, 1940–1947*. Ithaca: Cornell University Press, 1952.

Silk, Mark. *Spiritual Politics: Religion and America Since World War II*. New York: Simon and Schuster, 1988.

Sillito, John R., and Timothy S. Hearn. "A Question of Conscience: The Resignation of Bishop Paul Jones." *Utah Historical Quarterly* 50, no. 3 (Summer 1982): 208–23.

Sittser, Gerald L. *A Cautious Patriotism: The American Churches and the Second World War*. Chapel Hill: University of North Carolina Press, 1997.

Sklaroff, Lauren Rebecca. "Constructing G.I. Joe Louis: Cultural Solutions to the 'Negro Problem' During World War II." *Journal of American History* 89, no. 3 (December 2002): 958–83.

Smiley, Glenn, and Helen Smiley. "Life in a Broken City." *Fellowship* 18, no. 9 (October 1952): 13–16.

Smith, Adam. *The Theory of Moral Sentiments.* 1759. Reprint, Amherst, NY: Prometheus, 2000.

Smith, Christian. *Resisting Reagan: The U.S. Central America Peace Movement.* Chicago: University of Chicago Press, 1996.

Smith, J. Holmes. "A Missionary Leaves India." *Christian Century,* April 10, 1940, 485.

———. "Non-Violent Direct Action." *Fellowship* 7, no. 12 (December 1941): 207.

———. "Our New York Ashram." *Fellowship* 7, no. 1 (January 1941): 2.

———. "Why J. Holmes Smith Registered." *Conscientious Objector,* March 1942, 3.

Smith, Rupert. *The Utility of Force: The Art of War in the Modern World.* New York: Knopf, 2007.

"Social Equality: Three Views by Southern Whites." *World Tomorrow* 9, no. 4 (April 1926): 117.

"Some Questions for Liberals." *World Tomorrow* 1, no. 12 (December 1918): 295.

Sontag, Susan. *Regarding the Pain of Others.* New York: Farrar, Straus and Giroux, 2003.

"Southwest FOR Does Peace Education." *Fellowship* 16, no. 10 (November 1950): 30.

Stansell, Christine. *American Moderns: Bohemian New York and the Creation of a New Century.* New York: Metropolitan, 2000.

Stauffer, Jon. *The Black Hearts of Men: Radical Abolitionism and the Transformation of Race.* Cambridge: Harvard University Press, 2002.

Stelzle, Charles. *A Son of the Bowery.* New York: Doran, 1926.

Stevenson, Lilian. *Towards a Christian International: The Story of the International Fellowship of Reconciliation.* New York: Fellowship of Reconciliation, 1936.

Strain, Christopher B. *Pure Fire: Self-Defense as Activism in the Civil Rights Era.* Athens: University of Georgia Press, 2005.

Stubblefield, Harold W., and Patrick Keane. *Adult Education in the American Experience: From the Colonial Period to the Present.* San Francisco: Jossey-Bass, 1994.

Studdert-Kennedy, Gerald. *British Christians, Indian Nationalists, and the Raj.* New York: Oxford University Press, 1991.

Susman, Warren. "The Culture of the Thirties." In *Culture as History: The Transformation of American Society in the Twentieth Century,* 150–83. New York: Pantheon, 1984.

Swanberg, W. A. *Norman Thomas: The Last Idealist.* New York: Scribner, 1976.

Swerdlow, Amy. *Women Strike for Peace: Traditional Motherhood and Radical Politics in the 1960s.* Chicago: University of Chicago Press, 1993.

Swomley, John M., Jr. *Confronting Systems of Violence: Memoirs of a Peace Activist.* Nyack, NY: Fellowship Publications, 1998.

———. "Just Among Ourselves." *Fellowship* 15, no. 7 (July 1949): 35.

———. "Richard Gregg." *Fellowship* 40, no. 4 (April 1974): 23.

———. "Youth News and Plans." *Fellowship* 7, no. 4 (April 1941): 63.

Takaki, Ronald. *Double Victory: A Multicultural History of America in World War II*. Boston: Little, Brown, 2000.

Tanenhaus, Sam. *Whittaker Chambers: A Biography*. New York: Random, 1997.

Taylor, Cynthia. *A. Philip Randolph: The Religious Journey of an African American Labor Leader*. New York: New York University Press, 2006.

Tendulkar, D. G. *Mahatma: Life of Mohandas Karamchand Gandhi*, vol. 3. Delhi: Ministry of Information and Broadcasting, Government of India, 1961.

Thomas, Evan. "CPS and the Second Mile." *Fellowship* 10, no. 2 (February 1944): 28.

———. "The Strike a Necessary Compromise in a Practical World." *World Tomorrow* 3, no. 6 (June 1920): 177.

Thomas, Norman. "Afterthoughts on the Suffrage Victory." *World Tomorrow* 4, no. 1 (January 1921): 20–21.

———. *As I See It*. New York: Macmillan, 1932.

———. *The Case of the Christian Pacifists at Los Angeles, Cal*. New York: National Civil Liberties Bureau, 1918.

———. *The Christian Patriot*. Philadelphia: Jenkins, 1917.

———. "The Conscientious Objector: II—Conscience and the Church." *Nation*, August 23, 1917, 198–99.

———. *The Conscientious Objector in America*. New York: Huebsch, 1923.

———. "Moral Man and Immoral Society." Review of *Moral Man and Immoral Society*, by Reinhold Niebuhr. *World Tomorrow* 15, no. 22 (December 14, 1932): 565.

———. "Norman Thomas Replies: Socialist Party Head Answers F.O.R. Indictment of Debs Column." *Fellowship* 3, no. 2 (February 1937): 13.

———. "The Strike: II. The Strike a Justifiable Form of Passive Resistance." *World Tomorrow* 3, no. 5 (May 1920): 133–35.

Thoreau, Henry David. "Resistance to Civil Government." 1849. In David A. Hollinger and Charles Capper, eds., *The American Intellectual Tradition*, 1:401–14. 5th ed. New York: Oxford University Press, 2006.

Thornton, J. Mills, III. *Dividing Lines: Municipal Politics and the Struggle for Civil Rights in Montgomery, Birmingham, and Selma*. Tuscaloosa: University of Alabama Press, 2002.

Thurman, Howard. *With Head and Heart: The Autobiography of Howard Thurman*. New York: Harcourt Brace Jovanovich, 1979.

Tillich, Paul. *The Courage to Be*. 1952. New Haven: Yale University Press, 2000.

Tolstoy, Leo. *The Kingdom of God Is Within You*. Translated by Aline Delano. 1894. Reprint, New York: Scribner, 1911.

Torres, Sasha. *Black, White, and in Color: Television and Black Civil Rights*. Princeton: Princeton University Press, 2003.

Tracy, James. *Direct Action: Radical Pacifism from the Union Eight to the Chicago Seven*. Chicago: University of Chicago Press, 1996.

"Two Hundred Join Demonstrations Protesting Peacetime Draft." *Fellowship* 13, no. 4 (April 1947): 64.

Tyson, Timothy. *Radio Free Dixie: Robert F. Williams and the Roots of Black Power*. Chapel Hill: University of North Carolina Press, 1999.

Uphaus, Willard. *Commitment*. New York: McGraw Hill, 1963.

"The Use of the Atomic Bomb." *Fellowship* 11, no. 9 (September 1945): 161.

Van Deburg, William L. *New Day in Babylon: The Black Power Movement and American Culture, 1965–1975*. Chicago: University of Chicago Press, 1992.

Van Dusen, Lewis H., Jr. "Civil Disobedience: Destroyer of Democracy." *American Bar Association Journal* 55 (February 1969): 123–26.

Van Notten, Eleonore. *Wallace Thurman's Harlem Renaissance*. Costerus New Series 93. Atlanta: Rodopi, 1994.

Vaughn, Stephen. *Holding Fast the Inner Lines: Democracy, Nationalism, and the Committee on Public Information*. Chapel Hill: University of North Carolina Press, 1980.

Vladislav, Jan, ed. *Václav Havel: Living in Truth*. Boston: Faber and Faber, 1989.

Von Eschen, Penny. *Race Against Empire: Black Americans and Anticolonialism, 1937–1957*. Ithaca: Cornell University Press, 1997.

Voss, Carl Hermann. *Rabbi and Minister: The Friendship of Stephen S. Wise and John Haynes Holmes*. Cleveland: World, 1964.

Wacker, Grant. "A Plural World: The Protestant Awakening to World Religions." In William R. Hutchison, ed., *Between the Times: The Travail of the Protestant Establishment in America, 1900–1960*, 253–77. New York: Cambridge University Press, 1989.

Wald, Alan. *The New York Intellectuals: The Rise and Decline of the Anti-Stalinist Left from the 1930s to the 1980s*. Chapel Hill: University of North Carolina Press, 1987.

Walk to Freedom. Fellowship of Reconciliation, 1956. Colorlab, 2002. Videocassette.

"'Walk to Freedom' Lauded at Montgomery Premiere." *Fellowship* 22, no. 10 (November 1956): 24–25.

Walker, Jenny. "A Media-Made Movement? Black Violence and Nonviolence in the Historiography of the Civil Rights Movement." In Brian Ward, ed., *Media, Culture, and the Modern African American Freedom Struggle*, 41–66. Gainesville: University Press of Florida, 2001.

Wallis, Jill. *Valiant for Peace: A History of the Fellowship of Reconciliation, 1914–1989*. London: Fellowship of Reconciliation, 1991.

Wallis, Jim. *God's Politics: Why the Right Gets It Wrong and the Left Doesn't Get It*. San Francisco: HarperSanFrancisco, 2005.

Walzer, Michael. *Just and Unjust Wars: A Moral Argument with Historical Illustrations*. 4th ed. New York: Basic Books, 2006.

Warren, Frank. *An Alternative Vision: The Socialist Party in the 1930's*. Bloomington: Indiana University Press, 1974.

———. *Liberals and Communism: The "Red Decade" Revisited*. Bloomington: Indiana University Press, 1966.

———. *Noble Abstractions: American Liberal Intellectuals and World War II*. Columbus: Ohio State University Press, 1999.

Warren, Heather A. *Theologians of a New World Order: Reinhold Niebuhr and the Christian Realists, 1920–1948*. New York: Oxford University Press, 1997.

Weddle, Meredith Baldwin. *Walking in the Way of Peace: Quaker Pacifism in the Seventeenth Century.* New York: Oxford University Press, 2001.

"A Welcome Telegram from Los Angeles." *World Tomorrow* 1, no. 11 (November 1918): 285.

Wendt, Simon. *The Spirit and the Shotgun: Armed Resistance and the Struggle for Civil Rights.* Gainesville: University Press of Florida, 2007.

Westbrook, Robert B. *John Dewey and American Democracy.* Ithaca: Cornell University Press, 1991.

Weyler, Rex. *Greenpeace: How a Group of Journalists, Ecologists, and Visionaries Changed the World.* Vancouver: Raincoast, 2004.

"What, Then, Shall We Do?" *World Tomorrow* 2, no. 10 (October 1919): 263–66.

Whitaker, Robert. "The Anti-Japanese Agitation in California." *World Tomorrow* 3, no. 11 (November 1920): 329–30.

———. "The Strike a Release from Industrial Warfare." *World Tomorrow* 3, no. 6 (June 1920): 186.

White, Ronald C., Jr. *Liberty and Justice for All: Racial Reform and the Social Gospel, 1877–1925.* San Francisco: Harper and Row, 1990.

"The White Terror in America." *World Tomorrow* 2, no. 11 (November 1919): 306–7.

Whitfield, Stephen J. *The Culture of the Cold War.* Baltimore: Johns Hopkins University Press, 1991.

Wiese, Andrew. *Places of Their Own: African American Suburbanization in the Twentieth Century.* Chicago: University of Chicago Press, 2004.

Wilder, Thornton. *Heaven's My Destination.* 1934. Reprint, New York: HarperCollins, 2003.

Wilson, Edmund. "Thornton Wilder in the Middle West." In *The Shores of Light: A Literary Chronicle of the 1920s and 1930s,* 587–92. Boston: Northeastern University Press, 1985.

Wilson, Woodrow. "An Address at the University of Paris." December 21, 1918. In Arthur S. Link, ed., *Papers of Woodrow Wilson,* 53:461–63. Princeton: Princeton University Press, 1993.

———. "An Address to a Joint Session of Congress." April 2, 1917. In Arthur S. Link, ed., *Papers of Woodrow Wilson,* 41:519–27. Princeton: Princeton University Press, 1993.

Wittner, Lawrence S. *One World or None: A History of the World Nuclear Disarmament Movement Through 1953.* Vol. 1 of *The Struggle Against the Bomb.* Stanford: Stanford University Press, 1993.

———. *Rebels Against War: The American Peace Movement, 1933–1983.* Philadelphia: Temple University Press, 1984.

———. *Resisting the Bomb: A History of the World Nuclear Disarmament Movement, 1954–1970.* Vol. 2 of *The Struggle Against the Bomb.* Stanford: Stanford University Press, 1997.

———. *Toward Nuclear Abolition: A History of the World Nuclear Disarmament Movement, 1971 to the Present.* Vol. 3 of *The Struggle Against the Bomb.* Stanford: Stanford University Press, 2003.

Wolpert, Stanley. *Gandhi's Passion: The Life and Legacy of Mahatma Gandhi*. New York: Oxford University Press, 2001.

Woodcock, George. *Anarchism: A History of Libertarian Ideas and Movements*. New York: Meridian, 1962.

"The World in Focus." *Fellowship* 22, no. 11 (December 1956): 1–3.

Wright, Bradford W. *Comic Book Nation: The Transformation of Youth Culture in America*. Baltimore: Johns Hopkins University Press, 2001.

Young, Mildred B. "Richard B. Gregg, In Memoriam." *Friends Journal*, May 15, 1974, 303.

Young, Robert J. C. *Postcolonialism: An Historical Introduction*. Malden, MA: Blackwell, 2001.

Ziegler, Valarie H. *The Advocates of Peace in Antebellum America*. Bloomington: Indiana University Press, 1992.

Index

Page numbers in *italics* indicate illustrations.

Boorstin, Daniel, 238
Borah, William, 78
Borsodi, Ralph, 95
Boston Tea Party, 86
Boston University, 212
brahmacharya, 105
Brandeis, Louis, 30
Brethren, 11, 164, 286n41
Bridge of San Luis Rey, The (Wilder),
    112
Brinton, Howard, 154
Brittain, Vera, 158; "Massacre by Bomb-
    ing," 158
Brookwood Labor College, 61–62,
    70–73, 81, 86–87, 147. *See also*
    Muste, A. J. (Abraham Johannes)
Browder, Earl, 115
Brown, Egbert Ethelred, 67–68, 117
Brown, John, 162
Brown, William Adams, 28, 31–33, 139;
    Is Christianity Practicable?, 31–32
Brush, George Marvin, 112–14
Bryan, William Jennings, 30
Buddhism, Buddhists, 234, 237–38,
    244
Buddhist Peace Fellowship, 234
Burleson, Albert, 36, 259n58

Calverton, V. F., 55, 179
Calvin, John, 11, 100
Cambridge University, 26
Canby, Henry Seidel, 127
Cannon, James P., 122, 148
Cannon, Robert, 192, 218
capitalism: FOR leaders' views of,
    43–45, 69–73, 94–96, 124–28,
    135–36; in 1920s, 69; and violence,
    43–45, 142; and World War I, 43. *See
    also* Communism, Communists;
    labor movement; socialism
Capra, Frank, 80
Capraro, Anthony, 46
Carnegie Endowment for International
    Peace, 12, 104

Carver, George Washington, 129
Case, Clarence Marsh, 49; *Non-Violent
    Coercion*, 49–50
Catholicism, Catholics, 11, 71, 84, 116,
    118, 147, 194; FOR leaders' views
    of, 84, 121, 162, 234–36. *See also*
    Catholic Peace Fellowship; Catholic
    Worker
Catholic Peace Fellowship, 234–36
Catholic Worker, 4, 104, 198, 241; and
    Catholic Peace Fellowship, 235;
    cooperates with FOR and CORE,
    104, 162, 187–88, 234–35. *See also*
    Dorothy Day
Catonsville Nine, 235
Chaffee, Edmund, 54, 59–60, 65, 70,
    77, 127, 139; and Communism,
    121–22; death of, 148; early career of,
    53; "Ethics and Propaganda," 56–57;
    and 1933–34 FOR split, 143–44;
    and Mohandas Gandhi, 82, 95, 124;
    "Gandhi or Dynamite?," 124; as La-
    bor Temple director, 53–56, 60–61,
    67, 121–22; nonviolence theorized
    by, 56–57, 134; and Socialist Party,
    127; and World War I, 35, 53. *See also*
    Labor Temple
Chaffee, Florence, 77
Challenge of Russia, The (Eddy), 121
Chalmers, Allan Knight, 212
Chambers, Whittaker, 199–200; *Wit-
    ness*, 199–200
Chapel Hill, NC, 205–6, 208
Chaplin, Charles, 104
Chappell, Winifred, 119–20
Chase, Stuart, 95
Cheney, Richard, 5
Chicago, 32, 43, 91–92; CORE starts in,
    186–89
China, 6, 10–11, 97–98, 200, 244; mis-
    sionary work in, 19, 76–77, 119
Christian Ashram, 186
Christian Century, 110, 229
Christianity and Crisis, 153

219; Martin Luther King y la Historia de Montgomery, 220; membership statistics for, 50, 146; and Montgomery bus boycott, 211–27; Nicaragua peace mission of, 77–81; 1933–34 split in, 140–145; and peace churches, 12; print culture of, 60–63; and race, 67–68, 76, 129–30, 177–90; religion of, 7–9, 147, 162, 264n39; supports Socialist Party, 126–28; in the South, 129–30, 142–43, 204, 206–7, 211; and Spanish Civil War, 153–54; *Walk to Freedom*, 191–92, 200–201, 217–18; and War Resisters League, 264n39; sponsors Washington Interracial Workshops, 208–10; in the West, 34–35, 171; women in, 65–67; and *World Tomorrow*, 36; in World War I, 26–27, 33–36, 38, 41–43; in World War II, 146–90, 194
Fellowship of Socialist Christians, 145
Fincke, Helen, 70
Fincke, William, 35, 53, 70
Fire!!, 68
First World War. *See* World War I
Fischer, Louis, 85, 224; *Gandhi and Stalin*, 200
Flight, 80
Flynn, Elizabeth Gurley, 44
Folklore of Capitalism, The (Arnold), 124–25
Fonda, Jane, 234
Foote, Caleb, 147, 162, 165, 171–72, 175–77, 196–97; *Outcasts!*, 172
FOR. *See* Fellowship of Reconciliation
Ford, Henry, 96
Ford Motor Company, 21, 96
Forest, James, 235
Fort Riley, KS, 38–39, 39
Fosdick, Harry Emerson, 33; *The Manhood of the Master*, 24
Foster, William Z., 115, 121
France, 200, 252n9; and war in Algeria, 237; FOR in, 201; A. J. Muste visits,

147–48; peace movement in, 142; and World War I, 19–20, 42, 155; and World War II, 6, 152; YMCA work in, 19–20
Frazier, E. Franklin, 71
Freedom Rides, 204, 207, 229, 238
free speech, 50–64; and Communism, 121–22
Friends of the World, 173
"From Protest to Politics" (Rustin), 241–42
Front de Liberation Nationale, 237
"fulfilment theology," 82–83
fundamentalism, 18–19, 32, 116–17
Fundamentalist, 116–17
Fugitive Slave Law, 13
Furuseth, Andrew, 107

Gandhi, Mohandas: and Charles Andrews, 87; anticolonialism of, 81–82; ashrams of, 93, 186; and Edmund Chaffee, 95; and Communism, 113–15, 123–26, 200; death of, 223; early career of, 92–93; economic ideas of, 94–95, 124–26; and Sherwood Eddy, 86–88; and Frantz Fanon, 81, 202; FOR leaders discover, 81–84; and Richard Gregg, 92–111, 123–26, 223–27; and John Haynes Holmes, 82–84, 86–88, 98; and Grace Hutchins, 119; and Martin Luther King Jr., 212, 216, 218, 220, 224; March to the Sea by, 85–86; and mass media, 85–88, 181; and Montgomery bus boycott, 211–26; and Reinhold Niebuhr, 95, 136–37; noncooperation campaign by, 81, 92–93; nonviolence of, 10, 84, 96–111, 112–113, 123–26, 136–37, 142–43, 152, 179–81; and Kirby Page, 60, 82, 86–88, 98; listed in *The Red Network*, 115; and religion, 7–8, 81–84, 86–87, 179–81; and Anna Rochester 119; and Krishnalal Shridharani, 179–81; Jay Holmes

New York Times, 28, 32, 81, 88, 159, 165, 201, 245

Nicaragua, 3, 6; U.S. occupation of, 77–78; peace mission to, 78–81, 79, 234

Nicaraguan Federation of Labor, 78

Nicaraguan National Guard, 77

Niebuhr, Reinhold, 2, 14, *133*, 144, 227, 230, 280n53; antiwar views of, 74–75, 134–35; analyzes class conflict, 135–36, 142; *Does Civilization Need Religion?*, 131–32; early career of, 131–32; and Sherwood Eddy, 153; the family extolled by, 65, 136; and Mohandas Gandhi, 95, 136–37; and Richard Gregg, 110–11, 124, 133–38, 151–52; and John Haynes Holmes, 98, 134, 139; and Martin Luther King Jr., 137, 214–15, 295n52; and 1933–34 FOR split, 141; and Manchurian crisis, 152; and Marxism, 135–36; criticizes foreign missions, 77; *Moral Man and Immoral Society*, 62, 131, 132–39, 142, 151, 158, 215; and Montgomery bus boycott, 214–15; and A. J. Muste, 9–10, 195, 245; criticizes pacifism, 110–11, 137–38, 151–52, 155–56; advocates racial equality, 137; "realist" liberalism of, 4–5; religious views of, 131–32, 138; as Socialist, 126; and World War I, 131; and World War II, 151–52, 155–61, 171, 172, 193–94

Nietzsche, Friedrich, 8

Nisei. *See* Japanese Americans

Nixon, Edgar D., 214

Nkrumah, Kwame, 202, 237

Nonconformists, English, 11. *See also* specific groups

noncooperation campaign in India (1920–22), 81–82, 85, 93

Non-Violent Coercion (Case), 49–50

Norris, J. Frank, 116–17

Not by Might (Muste), 195–98, 200, 203

Nuremberg trials, 159

NWLB. *See* National War Labor Board

Ochs, Adolph S., 88

Okuda, Kenji, 172

On the Waterfront, 199

Orchard, William, 24

Our Town (Wilder), 112

Outcasts! (Foote), 172

outlawry movement, 73–74, 78

Pacem in Terris (John XXIII), 234

Page, Kirby, 51–52, 60, 69, 70, 132, 152, 160, 171, 232, 239; and anticolonialism, 75; *Christianity and Economic Problems*, 61; and Communism, 115–21, 150; early career of, 20–21, 57–58; and Sherwood Eddy, 20–26, 57–64, 75, 152–53, 283n15; the family extolled by, 65; and 1933–34 FOR split, 141, 143; and Mohandas Gandhi, 60, 82, 86–88, 98, 105; and Harold Gray, 20–26; *Individualism and Socialism*, 127; *Is Mahatma Gandhi the Greatest Man of the Age?*, 98; and mass communication, 57–64, 87; *National Defense*, 62; and Reinhold Niebuhr, 62, 133–35, 141; peace plans supported by, 73–74, 104; and racial equality, 13, 21, 75–76, 117; on the radio, 59–60; religion of, 7–8, 20–26, 64, 74; and Socialist Party, 126–28; "The Sword or the Cross," 24; *The Sword or the Cross*, 61, 120; and Wallace Thurman, 68; and Harry Ward, 120; *War: Its Causes, Consequences, and Cure*, 61–62, 70; as *World Tomorrow* editor, 68, 119; and World War I, 20–26; and World War II, 152–53, 158, 194; and Max Yergan, 21; in YMCA, 20–26

Palestine, 53

Parker, Theodore, 12–13, 28, 29, 32, 76

Parks, Rosa, 192, 211–12, 223